3-11-57

CHRISTIANITY AND WORLD ISSUES

THE MACMILLAN COMPANY
NEW YORK · CHICAGO
DALLAS · ATLANTA · SAN FRANCISCO
LONDON · MANILA

BRETT-MACMILLAN LTD.
TORONTO

Christianity
and
World Issues

by

T. B. MASTON

New York—1957
THE MACMILLAN COMPANY

First Printing

Printed in the United States of America

Library of Congress catalog card number: 57–5221

TO
ESSIE MAE
companion of the years

966626

PREFACE

THERE ARE many books that discuss from various viewpoints the major issues or problems of the contemporary world. Most of these books, however, consider only one issue. The present volume attempts to combine into one book the discussion of various but related world issues. It also represents an effort to utilize various disciplines or approaches to these problems. Particular attention is given to the biblical, the historical, the theological, and the sociological. The relative emphasis on these different approaches varies from chapter to chapter. The major emphasis throughout, however, is on the Christian social ethic and its application to the various areas that are discussed.

It is admitted that some important issues or problems are not considered at all, while others are discussed rather inadequately. Some selection was necessary. An effort was made to choose issues that are contemporary and at the same time those that have been continuously challenging to the Christian movement. Those finally selected for study were the ones to which the Christian ethical approach could be most logically applied. It is also true that the various chapters are related, to a greater or a lesser degree, to the contemporary world crisis, which is the most serious the world has known since the days of the Renaissance and the Reformation. This gives to the book some degree of unity.

This volume represents an attempt to provide an introduction to the field of Christian social ethics or applied Christianity. An acquaintance with the social and ethical teachings of the Bible and with basic Christian principles has been assumed. It is hoped that the book will be acceptable as a text by seminary teachers and by teachers in church-related colleges who are looking for a book with a definitely Christian orientation. While it has been written primarily for textbook purposes, it should have some appeal to ministers and to Christian laymen who are concerned about the pressing world issues of the contemporary period.

A definite organizational pattern has been followed in the writing of the book. Chapter I, on the general relation of the church to the world, is introductory in a sense, although it deals with a major problem which has constantly faced Christianity. Following this chapter is one on Christianity and the individual. The individual and his worth and dignity are involved, in some way and to some degree, in every major world issue. That makes Chapter II foundational for the succeeding chapters, which are, in a sense, on a constantly expanding basis. Chapter III considers the family, which is the basic social unit. It is succeeded by chapters on such world issues as race relations, economic life, communism, war, and the relation of church and state. Chapter XI is on the world crisis, followed by a concluding chapter on Christianity and the transformation of the world.

Some teaching aids are provided at the close of the book. There are brief annotated reference lists of ten to twelve books for each of the chapters. In all cases these references are to entire books. They are provided primarily for the teacher rather than for use by the students. It has been assumed that the teacher can and would prefer to work out reading lists for his own students from the sources available in his college, university, or seminary library. Some topics for thought and discussion are also provided. These have been devised to get the student to think through and to state clearly his position regarding some of the current social and world problems. These topics are made available because of a conviction that many students complete their education without ever reaching intelligent personal Christian conclusions concerning some of the most common problems of life.

Any book is, in some ways, a joint production. That is certainly true of this one. I have sought in the footnotes to acknowledge my indebtedness to various authors. I also express my appreciation to many other people, who have been helpful in many different ways.

Preface

I am grateful to a group of busy educators—teachers and administrators—who responded to a questionnaire I sent to them before I wrote the final draft of the manuscript. Their replies helped me to make a number of rather important decisions concerning the problems to discuss, the teaching aids to include, and the general structure of the book. Among those responding were: E. W. Bailey, J. A. Barry, Nat C. Bettis, George T. Blackmon, Hugh Brimm, J. A. Bryan, W. A. Carleton, James H. Chapman, John W. Cobb, H. I. Hester, Charles H. Hopkins, George C. Humphrey, Charles D. Johnson, Russell Bradley Jones, Charles W. Koller, Perry F. Langston, Leon Marsh, Herbert J. Miles, Ralph A. Phelps, Jr., Culbert G. Rutenber, Howard E. Spell, D. D. Tidwell, James S. Timberlake, H. Clayton Waddell, Marguerite Woodruff.

I am heavily indebted to those who read portions or all of the manuscript and who made valuable criticisms and suggestions: Robert A. Baker, Henlee H. Barnette, O. T. Binkley, W. Boyd Hunt, Dale Moody, John P. Newport, Wayne E. Oates, and J. B. Weatherspoon. I owe a great deal to my colleague C. W. Scudder, who used this material on an experimental basis in the classroom, and who gave many constructive suggestions concerning it.

I am grateful to the secretaries who assisted me at various stages of the work, but particularly to Ray Childers and Mrs. Cecil L. Thompson. Both of them were efficient and patient. In addition to their typing, which was unusually accurate, they helped in many other ways.

I am indebted in many tangible and intangible ways to my wife and to our son Gene, who read portions of the manuscript and made constructive recommendations concerning it.

T. B. MASTON

CONTENTS

ix

I

THE CHURCH
AND THE WORLD

WHAT SHOULD be the relation of the church to the world?
What contributions can and should organized Christianity make to
the solution of the problems of the world? These and similar questions are persistently and continuously asked of the church and by
the church. There is a sense in which the relation of the church to the
world has been and is a major world issue itself. In turn, answers to
questions concerning this relationship are important for every other
major world issue. The church cannot make a significant contribution to the family, to race relations, to economic and political life,
unless it first settles its relation to the world in general.

An understanding of the nature of the church may be a beginning
point for an interpretation of the proper relation of the church and
the world. Whether we think of "the church" as a local congregation
or as the body of Christ inclusive of all who know him, it is a divine-
human institution. Just as Jesus was both human and divine and the
Bible a blending of human and divine elements, so the church
founded by Christ is both human and divine. Its history is a record
of a "divine-human process." [1] It has both a this-worldly and an other-
worldly aspect. It was and is divine in its origin and in its mission,
but it cannot escape its human and worldly environment. It is the

[1] Nicolas Berdyaev, *The Fate of Man in the Modern World*, trans. Donald A.
Lowrie (Milwaukee, Morehouse Publishing Co., 1935), p. 108.

body of Christ, but that body is composed of men and women with all the ordinary human frailties and sins.

The proper blending and balancing of the human and divine elements of the church create for it some of its most difficult problems, and yet give to it its greatest influence and power. When the church emphasizes too exclusively either its human or its divine nature, it reduces to some degree its power to serve effectively. When the emphasis is placed too exclusively upon its divine origin and purpose, the church tends to draw its righteous robes around it and to separate itself from the world. Nothing can be more self-defeating to the church and more tragic for the world than such a holier-than-thou self-righteousness unless it is the crass worldliness of the church when it goes too far, as a human institution, in accommodating itself to its worldly environment.

Such a worldly church has no power to lift the world toward the Christian ideal because, to a large degree, it identifies the real world with all its limitations and faults with the Christian ideal for the world. The vision of the ideal, which is an ideal of perfection, is lost. There is little or no tension between what such a church preaches, teaches, and stands for and what the world practices. Without such tension there can be no progress toward the ideal. A worldly church cannot make any effective and constructive contribution to the reconstruction of society, to the resolving of the issues and problems that face and sometimes plague the world.

The Historic Church and the World

Some insight into the historic relation of the church to the world may give us a better understanding of what that relation should be and what contribution the church can and should make to the world. There is little attempt in this section to trace the effects of the church upon the world or the world upon the church. This has been done thoroughly and scholarly from differing viewpoints.[2]

[2] See particularly Ernst Troeltsch, *The Social Teaching of the Christian Churches*, trans. Olive Wyon (2 vols.; New York, Macmillan, 1931), and C. J. Cadoux, *The Early Church and the World* (Edinburgh, T. and T. Clark, 1925). Kenneth Scott Latourette in his *A History of the Expansion of Christianity* (New York, Harper, 1937–1945) has a chapter in each of the first four volumes, which cover the Christian era through 1914, on the effects of Christianity on its en-

1. *The church separated from the world.* The early church, to an unusual degree, separated itself from the world. Its attitude was one of "renunciation of the world, and not world reform." [3] Its message was one of judgment against the world rather than of redemption for the world.[4]

Why did the early church so largely withdraw from the world and from participation in the affairs of the world? The unfriendly attitude of the world toward the Christian movement with the attendant severe persecution was certainly one explanation for the church's attitude. Jesus had warned the disciples that they would be hated and persecuted.[5] Peter and John were the first to feel such persecution.[6] Then followed in rather rapid succession the imprisonment of "the apostles," [7] the stoning of Stephen,[8] "a great persecution" of the church at Jerusalem led by Saul who "laid waste the church," [9] the killing of James, and the imprisonment of Peter by Herod.[10] The book of Acts reveals many more incidents of severe persecution both by the Jews and by the government.[11]

This extremely unfriendly attitude by the world, and particularly of the Roman government, continued at least spasmodically through the first three Christian centuries. The periods of most severe persecution were those initiated by Nero in 64 A.D., by Domitian in 95 A.D., by Decius in 249 A.D., and continuing until the ascension to the throne of Gallienus in 260 A.D., and "the last and most terrible persecution inflicted on the early church," which began under Diocletian in 303 A.D., but which was largely inspired by Galerius. This last period of persecution continued through 311 A.D., six years after the abdication of Diocletian.[12] The belligerent persecuting attitude of the world toward the church helps to explain the unfriendly attitude of the early

---

vironment and another chapter in each of these volumes on the effects of the environment on the Christian movement.

[3] Troeltsch, *op. cit.,* I, 132.

[4] Ernst Luthardt, *History of Christian Ethics,* trans. W. Hastie (Edinburgh, T. and T. Clark, 1889), I, 185.

[5] Matt. 10:16–23; John 15:18–21; cf. John 17:14.   [6] Acts 4:3.

[7] *Ibid.,* 5:18.   [8] *Ibid.,* 7:58.

[9] *Ibid.,* 8:1–3.   [10] *Ibid.,* 12:1–3.

[11] See *ibid.,* 13:50; 14:19; 16:19–24. For Paul's summary of his sufferings for the gospel see 2 Cor. 11:23–27.

[12] W. E. H. Lecky, *History of European Morals* (3rd ed.; New York, D. Appleton, 1880), I, 428–63.

church toward the world and its tendency to withdraw from the world.

Another factor contributing to the separation of the church from the world was the church's interpretation of the moral conditions in the world. The early church's view that the world was morally evil was based, to some degree, upon a conception of the world that is found in the New Testament. Hobhouse suggests that while the word "cosmos" in the New Testament does not always carry a moral connotation, nevertheless it frequently does and that when it does it implies alienation from God. This conception of the world as morally evil is found in some of Paul's epistles, but it is particularly prevalent in the Johannine writings, with probably as many as twenty-seven references with moral implications in John 14–18 and sixteen references in 1 John.[13] This New Testament idea of the world as morally evil rather accurately portrayed the conditions in the world into which the church was born and spent its infancy. The immoral conditions of those days may be overdrawn by some, but certainly that world was an evil world. One author estimates that there were 60,-000,000 slaves in the Roman Empire, with 20,000,000 in Italy alone and 650,000 in Rome.[14] The position of women and children was decidedly inferior to their position among the Jews and particularly within Christian circles. Abortion, infanticide, and exposure were common practices. Homosexuality was rampant and was participated in and defended by philosophers and leaders of the government.[15] Some of the amusements were the cruelest and most debauching the world has known. It was a decadent world, "a culture already suffering from senescence." [16] While the wickedness of the world may have been part of its preparation for the coming of Christ, yet that wickedness also helps to explain the strong tendency of the early church to separate itself from the world.

There were yet other factors which contributed to the separation

[13] Walter Hobhouse, *The Church and the World in Idea and in History* (London, Macmillan, 1910), pp. 352–53. Hobhouse says "cosmos" is found 177 times in the New Testament, 102 of these in the Johannine writings, and 46 times in Paul's letters, with more than half of these being in the two Corinthian letters.

[14] S. Angus, *The Environment of Early Christianity* (New York, Scribner's, 1914), p. 38.

[15] *Ibid.*, p. 50; cf. Rom. 1:26–27.

[16] Latourette, *op. cit.*, I, 243. For some of the better side of the picture, see Angus, *op. cit.*, pp. 51–67.

of the church from the world. One was the conviction that Christ would soon return and bring an end to the world and worldly powers. If that was to be true, why should one be concerned about the world? Another was the fact that the Christian movement first made its most rapid progress among the lower social and economic classes. They were the disinherited of society. They had little stake in the existing world order and little hope of basically changing the *status quo*.

There is some evidence that certain phases of Greek philosophy also made a considerable contribution to the spirit of withdrawal from the world, so prevalent in the early church. At least, Greek philosophy was used to strengthen and to support the trend toward sectarianism and separation. This Greek influence, which has continued throughout the history of Christianity, first came into the stream of the Christian movement through Hellenism, whose influence is evident in the New Testament. Hellenism considered all evil as "due to the condition of earthly existence." [17] Various schools of Greek thought contributed to the tendency on the part of many Christians to withdraw from a world that was considered evil or unreal. Gnosticism, which contained "an underlying dualistic view of the universe," [18] was one of those schools or movements. Others were Platonism, which distinguished between the phenomenal and the real world, the so-called "Christian Platonists," [19] and particularly Neoplatonism. The last of these maintained a hierarchy of existence with an emphasis on mystical union as a way of escape from the evil or the material world.[20]

This conception of the physical and the material as evil helps to

---

[17] Ernest F. Scott, *The Gospel and Its Tributaries* (New York, Scribner's, 1929), p. 118.

[18] G. H. C. Macgregor and A. C. Purdy, *Jew and Greek, Tutors Unto Christ* (New York, Scribner's, 1936), p. 312.

[19] See Charles Bigg, *The Christian Platonists of Alexandria* (New York, Macmillan, 1886). This book is a discussion of Philo and the Gnostics to some degree but particularly of Clement and Origen. See also Vernon J. Bourke's *Augustine's Quest of Wisdom* (Milwaukee, Bruce Publishing Co., 1945). Chap. IV is entitled "Birth of a Christian Platonist."

[20] See Arthur K. Rogers, *A Student's History of Philosophy* (3rd ed.; New York, Macmillan, 1932), pp. 167–75. There were some schools of Greek philosophy that were not dualistic and did not consider the material world inherently evil. This was true of Epicureanism, which was naturalistic, and of Stoicism, which influenced early Christianity a great deal and whose basic philosophy was materialistic pantheism.

explain the movement in the early church toward asceticism, the exaltation of celibacy, and other world-renouncing trends. Frequently coupled with the ascetic trend, although not a necessary part of it, was an extreme type of mysticism. At least, the ascetic tendency and mysticism stemmed, to a considerable degree, from the same source: from certain schools of Greek philosophy as they in turn had been influenced by Oriental religious and mystery cults.

It should not be inferred from what has been said above that the church, because it so largely withdrew from the world, did not appreciably influence that world. Cadoux says that we have

in the work of the pre-Constantinian Church . . . a moral reformative movement on a scale and with a potency unparalleled at any other epoch before or since . . . the achievements of the early Church can defy comparison with those of any other moral or religious movement known to history.[21]

Paradoxically, though the church separated itself from the world, it became the most dynamic power in that world.

2. *The world accepted by the church.* The conflict between the church and the world continued with varying but generally decreasing intensity for the first three Christian centuries. The general trend was for the church to accept the world and to make its peace with the world. With the accession to the throne of Constantine this peace became relatively complete. The power of the state was used to protect the church and to promote its program. In turn the church supported the state and placed ecclesiastical approval upon the world in general.

There were many factors that contributed to this new attitude of the church. The church was increasingly accepted by the world. Persecution decreased, although it was spasmodically rather severe. More and more the persecution was directed exclusively to minority Christian groups, and was instigated, at times, by the church itself, which represented the main stream of the Christian movement.

Other factors that had contributed to the separation of the early church from the world declined in their significance for the church. For example, the church lost, to a marked degree, the expectation

[21] Cadoux, *op. cit.,* p. 611.

of the early return of the Lord, and changed its view concerning the kingdom of God. There was a deepening conviction that the end of the world was not immediate and that the church would be in the world for some time. It was felt that a more suitable strategy should be worked out. As the church lost its eschatological hope it tended to become more of a socialized movement with a long-range program. This did not necessarily and immediately mean a movement toward social reform. It was more of a movement of social adjustment.

Another factor in the change was the tendency for the Christian movement to move upward. More and more people who were prominent in social, economic, and political circles were converted. Such a movement to the so-called upper classes almost inevitably meant and means a toning down of previous sharp distinctions between the Christian and the non-Christian, the church and the world. Such a tendency is seen on the mission fields and in new religious movements even in the contemporary period.

Still another factor in the church's acceptance of the world was the influence of second- and third-generation Christians. They frequently lack the fervor and the spirit of sacrifice so characteristic, in most cases, of first-generation Christians. This tendency is evident, even today, on the mission fields.

Regardless of the basis for the church's acceptance of the world, the peace was not agreeable to all. Many of the early Christians and those of succeeding generations refused to accept the peace. Some of these recalcitrant church members were kept within the main stream of the Christian movement by the church's providing monasteries where they could withdraw from the world and practice what they interpreted to be the true Christian way of life. The church, as represented by the majority of church members, developed a dualistic ethic: one moral standard for the clergy and particularly for those living apart from the world, and another and lower standard of morality for the ordinary Christian who must continue to live in the world.

However, some of those who refused to accept the church's peace with the world were not provided for by the church. They became the sectarians who in many cases were persecuted by the church and sometimes also by the world. This separatist tendency has continued until today. The Quakers and more particularly the Mennonites have consistently maintained from their beginnings this sectarian em-

7

phasis. To varying degrees, they deny the world and separate themselves from the world. The modern "holiness groups" also have a strong sectarian tinge; and the same trend is evident, to a less degree, in some of the major denominations such as the Baptists. The sectarians have claimed, over and over again, that they go back to the genius and spirit of original Christianity.

3. *The church became a worldly power.* When Christianity made its peace with the world it was recognized by the state first as *an* official religion and later as *the* official religion. With the making of the peace there were surprises both for the church and for the world. The effects on both sides were neither entirely good nor bad, although for the church the bad outweighed the good. The church found itself practically identified with the state. At first the church was largely controlled by the state, but there was a mounting struggle between the church and the state to determine which would be the dominant power in the world.

With the making of her peace with the world, the church abandoned "the intensive policy" and "embarked upon a policy of extension." Her aim was "to become co-extensive with the World." This was her aim not merely for some far distant future; it was also an immediate objective. She set as her program the conquest and control of the state and the world.

To accomplish this purpose the church adopted worldly methods. She enlisted the aid of the civil power, and through this power she made Christian discipleship a matter of civil obligation.[22] There were wholesale "conversions" and a "promiscuous baptism of hundreds of thousands." [23] These wholesale "conversions," however, created some problems for the church. Because she found herself swamped with the pagan world, she deliberately made compromises with pagan rites, ceremonies, and customs.[24] Some of these rites, although "baptized and purged," [25] helped to paganize the church, and fixed on the church patterns of worship and conduct that have continued through the centuries. This influence is particularly seen in the worship of the Virgin Mary, of martyrs, and of the relics of the saints by Roman Catholics.

[22] Hobhouse, *op. cit.,* p. 171.
[24] *Ibid.,* p. 116.
[23] *Ibid.,* p. 112.
[25] Latourette, *op. cit.,* I, 326.

In seeking to become a worldly power, the church more and more patterned her organization after the Roman Empire. The church's view was that her boundaries should be conterminous with the Empire. To achieve this end the church had to be unified. There were several forces within the church that contributed to this unification. The church councils made a considerable contribution toward a unified church. However, the rise of the papacy did more than any other one factor to bind, at least the Western world, into one ecclesiastical unit.

There were various reasons for the increasing prestige and power of the bishop of Rome, which culminated in his recognition as the pope. Rome was the seat of the government for the Empire, which naturally gave the bishop at Rome a certain degree of prestige. It is also true that the decline of Rome as the center of political power and the rise of Constantinople under Constantine and his successors enhanced the position of the bishop of Rome. The power that the emperor lost the bishop gained. Hobhouse describes the papacy as the ghost of the old Roman Empire "sitting enthroned on the grave thereof." [26]

Once the trend within the church toward worldly power and the use of worldly methods crystallized, certain results inevitably followed. The line of demarcation between the church and the world was largely erased. "The Church made alliance with a World which became Christian in name, but only in name." [27] The world got into the church, and the church through the centuries has never been able to get it out. In becoming a worldly power, the church lost to a large degree her spiritual power.

4. *Need for periodic revival and renewal.* A church that thinks it can overcome the world by adopting the methods of the world finds itself, as suggested above, overcome by the world. But the inner heart or nucleus which comes from original Christianity is never lost. It is this inner core, which has lived through the centuries, that gives to the Christian movement its remarkable power of survival and renewal. Civilizations may rise and fall, and organized forms of Christianity with them, but the Christian movement as such lives on, and many times with new power and vigor.

[26] Hobhouse, *op. cit.*, p. 212.   [27] *Ibid.*, p. 124.

The periods of renewal within the Christian movement have usually represented a return to the first principles of Christianity. Many of the accretions of the years are thrown off. This was what happened during the Protestant Reformation, which was accompanied by the Counter Reformation in the Roman Catholic Church. This was also true of the Wesleyan Revival in England, the Great Awakening in America, and many other revivals of lesser breadth and prominence. But these periods of renewal do not throw off all the accumulations of the years. Whether this latter is good or bad, it is understandable. The church is a divine-human institution, and it can never escape entirely its environment—present or past.

The new forms of religion that arise out of the periods of renewal rather readily adapt themselves to the new environment which arises with them and which, to at least a limited degree, gave them birth. For example, Calvinism adapted itself, or at least it was adapted, to the new economic system that was arising—capitalism, and to the nation-state concept in the political order.

This means that organized Christianity tends to go through a regular cycle in its relation to the world. There is a period of withdrawal for revival and renewal, followed by a gradual adaptation to the world, which means an infiltration by the world. The world so completely permeates and dominates the church that another period of withdrawal from the world for renewal is necessary.[28]

Another way of saying somewhat the same thing is to suggest that the church "actualized and incarnate" cannot escape its environment. Its adaptation, to some degree, to its age is necessary if it is to minister effectively to that age. On the other hand, it must never forget nor neglect its divine nature if it is to lift the world toward the high ideals its unique message contains. As a divine institution "its infinity lies beyond its boundaries"[29] and must do so. For the church and the Christian individual there must be a more or less constant movement from God to man and the world and from man and the world back to God.

[28] See H. Richard Niebuhr, Wilhelm Pauck, and Francis P. Miller, *The Church Against the World* (Chicago, Willett, Clark, 1935), p. 123.

[29] Nicolas Berdyaev, *Freedom and the Spirit*, trans. Oliver Fielding Clarke (3rd ed.; London, Geoffrey Bles: Centenary Press, 1944), p. 335.

The Contemporary Church and the World

If the church tends to move in a cycle where is the contemporary church in that cycle? What is the direction of its movement? Those questions are not easy to answer. The answer depends largely on one's viewpoint or perspective. The contemporary church has within it many conflicting trends and tendencies. There is a possibility of movement in more than one direction at the same time.

1. *A divided church.* One of the most serious handicaps of the contemporary church in its effort to move into the world with a constructive contribution to the solution of the problems of the world is the fact that the church is seriously divided within itself. The major divisions within organized Christianity are threefold. First, there is the organizational division. The three major divisions with many minor divisions are Roman Catholic, Orthodox, and Protestant. Second, there is a theological division. The three major theological schools or camps are the liberal, the neo-orthodox, and the traditional orthodox. The third of these three divisions is the separation of churches by classes and castes. There are churches of the disinherited, of the middle class, of the upper class, and of racial and other minority groups.[30] There is a complex overlapping or intermingling of all of these divisions.

Through the ecumenical movement there is a definite attempt by some Christian leaders and groups to heal the organizational breach. Without making an attempt to evaluate this movement, it should be said that it will be unfortunate if Christian leaders depend too exclusively upon an organizational union or even closer cooperation to give added prestige and particularly power to organized Christianity. Such dependence would be a false hope and might be an evidence of the spiritual impotence and decay of contemporary Christianity. The outstanding weakness of modern-day Christianity is not organizational but moral and spiritual. There is a danger in the ecumenical movement and in Christian groups in general, including local churches, that organizational strength will be considered a substitute for spiritual power. The church may need greater unification, but

[30] See Liston Pope, *Millhands and Preachers* (New Haven, Yale University Press, 1942), and H. Richard Niebuhr, *The Social Sources of Denominationalism* (New York, Henry Holt, 1929).

what she needs far more is a deepened sense of a divine mission, a clearer insight into the distinction between the church and the world, and a more deeply spiritual approach to the problems of the world.

Possibly the most immediately serious division within contemporary Christianity, from the viewpoint of this study, is the conflicting viewpoints concerning the nature of the Christian message and the church's relation to the world. Some Christians and Christian groups believe that the Christian message is exclusively one of personal salvation, while others place primary emphasis on the reformation of society. Some are concerned primarily with the next life, while others emphasize almost exclusively this life. Some contend that the Christian gospel is concerned only with getting men right in their relations with God and that if this is done they will inevitably be right in their relations with their fellow man. Others just as strongly suggest that the only way to judge one's relation to God is by his relation to his fellow man.[31] Some suggest that the Christian and even the church should withdraw as far as possible from the world, while others just as vigorously contend that Christians and Christian groups should make the world "into the beloved community." Some believe that Satan is the prince of this world, while others believe that God controls the world and ultimately will work out his will and purpose in and with the world.

But must we accept one or the other of the preceding propositions or positions? No, in most cases the choice should not be an "either . . . or" but a "both . . . and." This will give us a balanced viewpoint concerning the nature of the Christian religion and of the church's relation to the world. Such a sane, balanced position will enable the church and the individual Christian to make a maximum contribution to lifting the world toward the Christian ideal.

2. *A church challenged by the world.* The church has been and is constantly challenged by the world. At times this challenge comes from without; at other times it is a more indirect attack from within.

---

[31] John C. Bennett, *Social Salvation: A Religious Approach to the Problems of Social Change* (New York, Scribner's, 1935), pp. 45 ff., recognizes three half-truths concerning the relation of individual and social salvation. They are as follows: (1) that individuals can rise above any combination of social circumstances, (2) that since individuals control institutions and systems it is enough to change individuals, and (3) that you can change society without changing individuals.

There are periods when the challenge is pressed vigorously both from without and from within; this seems to be typical of the present era.

The chief modern challengers of the Christian movement are insidious secularism, grasping materialism, narrow nationalism, and atheistic communism. The last represents a direct frontal attack on the Christian religion. The other three are more insidious in their approach, and hence in some ways are more dangerous. They are closely related to and to some extent have been created by capitalism and democracy. The latter movements, in turn, have been rather closely related to the Christian movement.[32] However, it would be a mistake to identify Christianity with these or any other political or economic movements or programs.

In the early days of capitalism and democracy their indebtedness to Christianity was frankly admitted. Religion was recognized as basic. But what happened? There was largely lost the sense of relatedness to and dependence upon fundamental moral and spiritual values. Increasingly economic or political values became the supreme values, and things spiritual, if they had any place at all, were consigned to a decidedly secondary position.

This trend has gone so far that these and other areas of life, that once recognized spiritual values and principles as foundational for all of life, are now asserting their independence of any source of authority outside themselves. The result has been "an unprecedented dualism between the Church and the world, between the sacred and the profane, between religion and life . . . religion being relegated to a mere corner of existence." [33] This relegation of religion has become of such serious proportions that Richard Niebuhr speaks of "The Captive Church." [34]

[32] For the contribution of Protestantism and more particularly Calvinism to the rise and spread of capitalism, see R. H. Tawney, *Religion and the Rise of Capitalism* (New York, Harcourt, Brace, 1926), and Max Weber, *The Protestant Ethic and the Spirit of Capitalism,* trans. Talcott Parsons (London, George Allen and Unwin, 1930). For the Christian influence on democracy, see Arthur E. Holt, *Christian Roots of Democracy in America* (New York, Friendship Press, 1941), and James Hastings Nichols, *Democracy and the Churches* (Philadelphia, Westminster Press, 1951).

[33] Berdyaev, *Freedom and the Spirit,* p. 343.

[34] Niebuhr, Pauck, and Miller, *op. cit.,* pp. 128 ff. For the bondage to capitalism, see Jerome Davis, *Capitalism and Its Culture* (New York, Farrar and Rinehart, 1935), Chap. XIX.

The Christian religion cannot remain in the fullest sense Christian and be pushed to the circumference of the life of the individual and the world. It demands centrality. It demands that it be the supreme value around which all lesser values are integrated. The church, which is the organized expression of the Christian religion, must meet the challenge of the contemporary world. If it does not, it will no longer merit the name "church" and will lose its opportunity to minister to the world. It must challenge the world to make the Christian religion the total, with every other phase of life made subservient to that total. All of life must be unified around supreme devotion to God and to his purposes in the world.

Time alone will reveal whether or not the contemporary forms of organized Christianity can win their freedom from the world and become truly Christian or whether or not Christianity will have to have another great period of renewal when it will emerge again in new and more vital forms.

3. *An awakening church.* There are indications that the contemporary church is awakening to the challenge of the world and to the challenge of the message it proclaims to the world. There are at least strivings within the church; it is disturbed by an uneasy conscience. There seems to be increasing tension both within the church itself and between the church and the world. Latourette in the third volume of the Interseminary Series sums up the present situation as follows: "A feature of the current scene which conditions all the rest is the mounting antagonism between Christianity and the world about it." He suggests that this antagonism has grown out of the secular atmosphere of our age, the rise of "aggressive ideologies which seek to control or displace the Church," and the awakening from within the church which have resulted, to a degree, from the challenges of our age.[35]

As is true of any great movement within or outside the church, the historic roots of the present awakening within the contemporary church go back many years. It stems, to some degree, from the work of Walter Rauschenbusch and his contemporaries who helped to formulate but who did not create the social gospel movement.[36] This

[35] Kenneth Scott Latourette (ed.), *The Gospel, the Church and the World* (New York, Harper, 1946), p. 109.
[36] See Charles Howard Hopkins, *The Rise of the Social Gospel in American*

movement, which has contributed so much to the awakening of a social conscience among both conservative and liberal Christians, goes back at least to the days immediately following the Civil War.[37]

Some of Rauschenbusch's followers and successors went to the extreme in emphasizing the social gospel in contrast to the individual gospel. They were also unrealistic concerning man and his ability in his own strength to solve his problems and the problems of the world. Neo-Protestantism, in one sense, represents a reaction to this extreme humanistic, optimistic emphasis. Actually, some of the men who belong within the Neo-Protestant tradition, such as Reinhold Niebuhr, must be counted among the leading contributors to whatever moral and social awakening there is within the contemporary church. Many of those identified with this new theological movement retain a strong social passion and program. This modern theological movement stresses vigorously the seriousness of sin in human life and in society. There is a companion emphasis on the necessity for God's intervention in the human process if Christian goals for society are to be achieved.

As the church seeks to assert its independence of the world and to be victorious over and in the world, it should guard against certain dangers. There is considerable possibility that those who would attempt to reconstruct the world may become so anxious for immediate and tangible results that they will form unwise alliances with secular movements of reform. A recognition that some of those movements have real contributions to make, and a limited cooperation of the church with such movements, will not necessarily do any damage to the church or to its program for and in the world. It will be most unfortunate, however, if the church identifies any secular program with the ultimate will of God, with the kingdom of God among men. Such an identification of God's program and will with a program of change would be just as unfortunate as to give the stamp of divine approval to the *status quo*. No human program can be completely identified with the will of God; the kingdom of God cannot be equated with any earthly institution or system.

By way of contrast, it is possible that other Christians, because they see the evil in the existing world order and also in the programs of

Protestantism, 1865–1915 (New Haven, Yale University Press, 1940), Chap. XIII.

[37] *Ibid.*, pp. 3 ff.

change, will be gripped with a deep sense of frustration and futility. This is particularly a problem for the perfectionists who want the kingdom in its entirety right now or none at all. They will not accept it on the installment plan. They cannot understand, or, if they understand, they will not agree to, Reinhold Niebuhr's principle "that there are no ultimate solutions in history, that our life must move from one proximate solution to another." [38]

Those who become disillusioned and disappointed in both what is and what is proposed tend to withdraw from the world and to deny that they have any responsibility for society and its problems. They tend to lose all hope for the realization of Christian ideals in the world. It may be that they have, in the past, identified prohibition, disarmament, or United Nations with the Christian goal for the world and have been disappointed in the results. Now their reaction is: "Why try to do anything? The world is hopeless. I shall live my life alone with the Lord." This reaction may not be unfortunate if it will merely mean a temporary withdrawal for renewal, for new insights and strength; but its results will be tragic for the Christians involved and for the world, if it becomes prevalent enough to lead to a permanent revival of a strictly individualistic, other-worldly conception of the Christian religion.

The Church's Strategies in Relation to the World

It will be well for the awakening church to consider the strategies the historic church has used in its relation to the world. Church history could be written in terms of those strategies. This does not necessarily mean that the church's historic strategies have followed a chronological pattern, although that has been true to a limited degree. Most of the strategies have been prevalent, to some degree, in every period of church history, and all of them are followed by some Christians or Christian groups in the contemporary period.

1. *The rejection or withdrawal strategy.* The natural tendency to withdraw from the evil world, mentioned previously, has been crystalized by some Christians into a conscious strategy to deal with the world. Throughout the Christian centuries there have been many

[38] Latourette (ed.), *The Gospel, the Church and the World,* p. 136.

Christians and some Christian groups that have looked upon the world as the kingdom of darkness, a kingdom controlled by Satan. They have contended that Christians should withdraw from the world as far as possible. This withdrawal has to be a matter of degree because they cannot avoid some contact with the world while they live in the world. However, a Christian while he is in the world should not be of the world. He should come out from among them (the people of the world) and be separate.

This position represents what H. Richard Niebuhr calls "Christ Against Culture." [39] Those who hold to the withdrawal strategy reject culture as far as possible and tend to separate themselves from the world and from activities in the world. This attitude was quite prevalent in the early church period. It was particularly strong in Tertullian, who was "one of the foremost illustrations of the anticultural movement to be found in the history of the church." [40]

Leo Tolstoi was another representative of this position. He "in his own way and under circumstances of his own time and place stated the radical position as vehemently and consistently as Tertullian." [41] For him "every phase of culture falls under indictment. Though state, church, and property system are the citadels of evil, philosophy and sciences and arts also come under condemnation." [42]

There have been groups as well as individuals who have followed the withdrawal strategy. This has been generally true of the smaller sectarian groups such as the Anabaptists, the Mennonites, and the Friends, or Quakers. There have been at least some phases of the culture of the world that they have rejected. It might be war or politics or amusement or certain forms of economic pursuits.

The Quakers have deserted, to a large degree, the withdrawal strategy except in regard to war. The contemporary groups that follow most consistently this strategy are some branches of the Mennonites. This has been particularly true of the Hutterian Brethren, who had a common source with the Mennonites and who are sometimes called "Hutterian Mennonites." Scattered in different parts of the world but found particularly in Canada, the United States, and

[39] *Christ and Culture* (New York, Harper, 1951), Chap. 2. The other positions discussed by Niebuhr are "The Christ of Culture," "Christ Above Culture," "Christ and Culture in Paradox," and "Christ the Transformer of Culture." His chapters are closely related to the historic Christian strategies.
[40] *Ibid.*, p. 55.   [41] *Ibid.*, p. 57.   [42] *Ibid.*, p. 60.

South America, they live in distinct communities and practice community of property.[43]

The withdrawal strategy is not entirely negative in its emphasis. There are some who contend that only by means of such a withdrawal can a Christian group demonstrate to an evil world the true Christian ideal for the world. Thus they would seek to develop what John Bennett calls, "Islands of Christian holiness in a sea that will always be the scene of violence and injustice." [44]

In appraising the rejection or withdrawal strategy we should remember that there is a very valid place for a type of limited withdrawal in the Christian's life. There should be a withdrawal by every Christian from the evils and sin of the world. In addition, if one is to minister most effectively to the world, he must have his periods of withdrawal from the world for renewed and deepened fellowship with God. Through that fellowship he is inspired to go back to the world with a clearer insight into God's will for the world and a strengthened purpose to carry the spirit of Christ into the life of the world.

It is also true that

In history these Christian withdrawals from and rejections of the institutions of society have been of very great importance to both church and culture. They have maintained the distinction between Christ and Caesar, between revelation and reason, between God's will and man's. They have led to reformations in both church and world, though this was never their intention. Hence men and movements of this sort are often celebrated for their heroic roles in the history of a culture which they rejected.[45]

While those heroic groups and individuals who have consistently separated themselves from the world should be respected, nevertheless, their attitude is not compatible with the spirit of original Christianity:

There can be no retreat from the world, for the divine election calls for a positive, rather than a negative relation to all outside the [Christian] com-

[43] See John Horsch, *The Hutterian Brethren, 1528–1931* (Goshen, Ind., Mennonite Historical Society, 1931).

[44] John C. Bennett, *Christian Ethics and Social Policy* (New York, Scribner's, 1946), p. 45.

[45] Niebuhr, *Christ and Culture,* p. 66. Reprinted by permission.

munity. God is Lord of the world and is engaged in the struggle to extend his sovereignty over it. The positive relationship which he requires of his people involves both acceptance and rejection of earthly cultures and earthly masters.[46]

Christians are to be the salt of the earth. Salt does not perform its purposes by remaining in a saltcellar but by being applied. Christians are the light of the world, but light cannot perform its functions for the world if it is placed under a bushel.

Jesus did not pray that his disciples be taken out of the world but that they be kept from the evil one or from the evil of the world. What is needed is not a physical separation but a spiritual separation from the world. The child of God should keep himself separated from the evils of the world, while at the same time he should seek to apply the Christian spirit and Christian principles to every area of the life of the world. Christianity cannot permeate the world by separating itself from the world. The individual Christian cannot overcome the world by withdrawing from the world.

2. *The identification strategy.* From the days of the early Christian Gnostics there have been Christian leaders and groups who have made of Jesus "The Christ of Culture." [47] They have sought to reconcile the gospel with the science, the philosophy, and the general cultural environment of the day. Ritschl is generally considered the best modern example of the Christ-of-culture type. Theological liberalism, or what Barth calls "Culture-Protestantism," belongs within this tradition.

There is some trend toward identification in all the major branches of Christendom. The Eastern Orthodox churches tend toward "a mystical identity of church and world" and toward a deification of the world.[48] While the reformers condemned the worldliness of the Roman Church, they followed the Roman Church in retaining "the ideal of a church that should embrace the whole community." [49] Such an

[46] G. Ernest Wright, *The Biblical Doctrine of Man in Society* (London, S.C.M. Press, 1954), p. 162. Alec R. Allenson, Inc., of Naperville, Ill., distributor in the United States.

[47] Niebuhr, *Christ and Culture,* pp. 83 ff.

[48] W. A. Visser 't Hooft and J. H. Oldham, *The Church and Its Function in Society* (Chicago, Willett, Clark, 1937), p. 119.

[49] John Baillie, *What Is Christian Civilization?* (New York, Scribner's, 1945), p. 18.

ideal does not necessarily mean an identification of the church with the community, although the tendency is always present.

There may be an inclination to identify the Christian movement with a particular phase of the culture rather than with the entire culture. This may involve an identification of the Christian ideal with some phase of the *status quo* or, on the other hand, with a particular program of reconstruction or change. For example, some people would identify the Christian movement with a particular economic order or a certain political system. This is a dangerous procedure. What T. S. Eliot says concerning the political could be just as truly said regarding the economic order. His statement is as follows:

To identify any particular form of government with Christianity is a dangerous error: for it confounds the permanent with the transitory, the absolute with the contingent. Forms of government, and of social organisation, are in constant process of change.[50]

The same danger is inherent in the tendency, on the part of some people, to identify Christianity with a program of change or reconstruction such as the cooperative movement, socialism, or communism. These movements are temporal and transitory. They also involve policies and techniques, an area in which Christianity should not attempt to speak authoritatively:

It is of crucial importance that the church acting corporately should not commit itself to any particular policy. A policy always depends on technical decisions concerning the actual relations of cause and effect in the political and economic world; about these, a Christian as such has no more reliable judgment than an atheist, except so far as he should be more immune to the temptations of self-interest.[51]

Identification of the church with its environment to a limited degree seems to be more or less inevitable and necessary. The church at any particular point in history is at least dependent on its cultural environment for words and thought patterns for the communication of its message. However, as a major Christian strategy identification tends to be self-defeating. When it is followed, the Christian mes-

[50] T. S. Eliot, *The Idea of a Christian Society* (London, Faber & Faber, 1939), p. 57.
[51] William Temple, *Christianity and Social Order* (3rd ed.; London, S.C.M. Press, 1942), p. 24.

sage tends to become so diluted that it loses its power to challenge and to lift the world toward the Christian ideal. Being so largely overcome by the world the Christian movement loses its power to overcome the world.

3. *Accommodation strategies.* Still another strategy or group of Christian social strategies is what might be termed accommodation, adjustment, or compromise strategies. There are several of these, some rather closely related.

One is the strategy generally followed by the Roman Catholic Church. For the Roman Church the natural or the this-worldly is closely related to the supernatural or other-worldly. The natural provides the foundation on which the church builds a supernatural superstructure.

As an illustration, Thomas Aquinas accepted the ethics of Aristotle almost *in toto* and built upon this natural foundation a Christian superstructure. The moral and intellectual virtues of Aristotle were incorporated into Aquinas' system. He then added the theological virtues—faith, hope, and love. These theological virtues represented the supernatural superstructure. Aristotle was brought into full fellowship with Augustine and became, for Roman Catholics, little less a saint than the latter. Aquinas "combined into one system of divine demands and promises the requirements cultural reason discerned and those which Jesus uttered." [52] This general position is what Niebuhr describes as "Christ Above Culture," which is one of the three median positions. The two extreme positions are "Christ Against Culture" (withdrawal strategy) and "The Christ of Culture" (identification strategy) discussed previously.

Roman Catholicism also contains the idea of two levels of the Christian life, a dualistic approach to the problems of the world. There are two levels of morality: one maintained by the average Christian citizen in contact with the ordinary affairs of life, and the higher level maintained by the clergy, particularly by those who have separated themselves from the world and live the monastic life.

In a sense this ethical dualism holds within one strategy two rather distinct strategies—the withdrawal strategy as represented by those maintaining the monastic ideal; and the accommodation strategy,

[52] Niebuhr, *Christ and Culture,* pp. 130–31.

with a tendency toward identification, used by those living on the secondary level of morality. Theoretically those who have withdrawn from the world are to live in accordance with the perfect Christian ideal; those who carry on the workaday tasks have to accommodate that ideal to the realities of life and in a way identify themselves with the world. The two working together, so some contend, will contribute to the Christianization of society. One will be a demonstration of what a perfect Christian society would be. The other will demonstrate the next steps in the progress toward that ideal.

Still another type of accommodation strategy is the one that would make a rather sharp distinction between personal and public morality. Reinhold Niebuhr is a representative of this type of thinking. It is a part of his general perspective. It is stated quite clearly in one of his earlier and more basic books.[53] The thesis of this volume is that human collectives of all types are less moral than the individuals who compose those collectives. Hence "group relations can never be as ethical as those which characterise individual relations." [54] John Bennett describes this strategy as follows:

It is based upon the assumption that Christian ethics are so distant from social policy that they are irrelevant to the problems of public life and that there must be two independent moral standards, one for personal relationships, for the Church or for the Kingdom of God understood in either an other-worldly or in a futuristic sense, the other for the state and the world of nations.[55]

According to those who maintain the rather sharp distinction between private and public morality, the very best the Christian can do in the area of public policy is to seek for what has been popularly classified in recent years as "middle axioms." These middle axioms are an attempt "to define the directions in which, in a particular state of society, Christian faith must express itself. They are not binding for all time, but are provisional definitions of the type of behavior required of Christians at a given period and in given

[53] *Moral Man and Immoral Society* (New York, Scribner's, 1932).
[54] *Ibid.*, p. 83.
[55] Bennett, *Christian Ethics and Social Policy*, pp. 51–52. In fairness it should be said that Bennett does not identify Niebuhr with the preceding strategy. He suggests that Niebuhr represents a strategy that holds in balance the relevance and on the other hand the transcendence of the Christian ethic. This strategy will be considered later.

circumstances." [56] Bennett suggests that "a middle axiom is more concrete than a universal ethical principle and less specific than a program that includes legislation and political strategy." [57]

Another position which involves a distinctive strategy is the conviction that the Christian is a citizen of two worlds. This likewise represents a dualistic approach to the problems of Christian conduct. It is a viewpoint that is quite prevalent among the rank and file of Christians. Those who hold the position divide life into the secular and the sacred, the temporal and the eternal, the kingdom of this world and the kingdom of God. As long as the Christian lives in the world he is a citizen of two worlds.

This idea of a twofold citizenship is applied particularly to one's relation to the church and to the state. In the secular and the temporal area the state's word is final, while the church or the voice of God is authoritative in the sacred or eternal area. Some contend that what one does in one area does not necessarily affect what he does in the other. This position is closely related to the distinction between private and public morality.

Luther is generally considered the outstanding historic example of the preceding type of dualism. For him "there are two kingdoms, one the kingdom of God, the other the kingdom of the world. . . . God's kingdom is a kingdom of grace and mercy. . . . But the kingdom of the world is a kingdom of wrath and severity." He adds: "Now he who would confuse these two kingdoms—as our false fanatics do—would put wrath into God's kingdom and mercy into the world's kingdom; and that is the same as putting the devil in heaven and God in hell." [58]

Richard Niebuhr sums up Luther's position as follows:

He seems to have a double attitude toward reason and philosophy, toward business and trade, toward religious organizations and rites, as well as toward state and politics. These antinomies and paradoxes have often led to the suggestion that Luther divided life into compartments, or taught that the Christian right hand should not know what a man's worldly left hand was doing. [59]

[56] Visser 't Hooft and Oldham, *op. cit.*, p. 194.
[57] *Christian Ethics and Social Policy*, p. 77.
[58] Martin Luther, *Works of Martin Luther* (Philadelphia, Board of Publication, United Lutheran Church in America, 1931), IV, 265–66.
[59] *Christ and Culture*, p. 171.

Another viewpoint, expressed by several prominent theologians, is the maintenance of both the relevance and the transcendence of the Christian ethic. This position or strategy has become very prevalent in the contemporary period. It involves accommodation, to a degree, although there is some question whether or not it should be labeled an accommodation strategy.[60]

Bennett lists William Temple, Reinhold Niebuhr, and Emil Brunner as representatives of this strategy, each with a distinctive emphasis. Of Niebuhr he says:

> His thought represents an extraordinarily delicate balance between the relevance of Christian ethics to action and emphasis upon the transcendence of Christianity and upon the sin of man. It is a dialectical balance according to which the opposing emphases actually support each other. The doctrine of sin becomes a reason for supporting social policies based upon radical criticism of the *status quo,* and the transcendence of Christianity provides a perspective from which these policies are kept under criticism.[61]

An adjustment, at least to a limited degree, of the Christian ideal is involved in such a strategy. The Christian may and should support some social policies, although he recognizes that evil is involved in them. He needs to understand that he is in an evil world, and that sin is involved in the *status quo* and in every program of change. If he is going to do anything about the conditions of the world his choices will frequently be between relative evils. The only other alternative is for him to withdraw as far as possible from the world. But to withdraw from the world would really involve one in the evil of the world. His withdrawal would be used to help to maintain the *status quo* with its evil. One cannot escape involvement in the evil of the world. He should always seek to be identified with individuals and movements that are associated with the lesser rather than the greater evil.

The strategy of Brunner, Niebuhr, Temple, and others has a great deal to recommend it. The one great danger is that the Christian will not maintain in proper balance the relevance and the transcendence of the Christian ethic. The greatest danger seems to be that the sense of transcendence will be lost. There will be a tend-

[60] See Bennett, *Christian Ethics and Social Policy,* pp. 58 ff.
[61] *Ibid.,* p. 60.

ency to identify the relative with the absolute, to defend as ideal that which may be necessary at the present level of living. The "middle axioms" may become confused with the absolutes of life. If this happens then Christian morality will sink to the level of the customary.

4. *Transformation.* Most and possibly all of the preceding strategies might be used in a way and to different degrees as methods to transform the world into a Christian order. This might imply that transformation does not represent so much a distinct strategy as a goal. This, in a sense, is correct. But as a matter of emphasis, transformation represents a strategy just as definitely as the withdrawal or the identification strategies. This strategy would not reject the world nor identify the Christian ethic with the ethic of the world but would transform the world into the likeness of the Christian ideal.

Those who take this position "claim for Christ the whole of man's life. . . . no part of life is outside the sovereignty of God."[62] The world is to be made into the beloved community. The definition of "the beloved community" may vary; the important thing, however, is a conviction that Christians are to transform the world, every phase of the world's life. A Christian society might be, as Baillie suggests,

both more and less than a society of Christians. It would be more, because it would be Christian in the impersonal configuration of its life and not merely in the individual dispositions of its members. It would be less, because not all its members would necessarily be Christian in their individual dispositions.[63]

What should be the church's contribution to the transformation of the world? It certainly should keep before society the ultimate Christian goals for society. It should not get involved, however, in the details or in the methods to be used to attain those goals. It should apply the Christian spirit and ethic to the methods but not dictate the details of the methods to be used. William Temple expresses this general idea as follows: "The Church may tell the poli-

[62] L. S. Hunter, *Church Strategy in a Changing World* (London, Hodder & Stoughton, 1950), p. 61.
[63] *Op. cit.,* p. 41.

tician what ends the social order should promote; but it must leave to the politician the devising of the precise means to those ends." [64]

The church should leave to the social scientist, the business and professional man, and the practical politician the matter of methods or means. The church should hope and pray that these scientists and politicians will be Christian in spirit and will have a sense of divine mission. Organized Christian forces should humbly admit their need for the cooperation of those who have the technical skills to implement Christian ideals. It takes more than Christian love and goodwill to discover a solution for the world's ills.

A word of warning may be in order, although it is not needed by anyone who faces realistically the needs and problems of the social order. There may be some, however, who will tend to be too optimistic concerning what can be done. We should remember that the Christian ideal will never be realized fully within the framework of history unless we include the divine and eternal along with the human and temporal within history. Christian ideals "can only be realized by a victory over time, by the transition from time to eternity, by the triumphant passage from the historical to the superhistorical process." [65] This failure to realize Christian ideals in the social order is not the failure of Christianity or of God. It is due to the failure of man, and simply means "that man is destined to realize his potentialities in eternity." [66]

In speaking of the Christian's attitude toward civilization, Baillie says:

He must strive to bring it as near to the Christian ideal of life in community as is possible in a world of sinful men, but he must never give it his absolute approval or unconditional loyalty; he must place in it only such a strictly qualified hope as would, even if it were to suffer complete shipwreck, leave his ultimate hope as securely anchored as before.[67]

5. *Conclusion.* The preceding historic strategies are also contemporary strategies. They are all followed, to some degree, by some Christians and Christian groups. There are comparatively few,

[64] *Op. cit.,* p. 47.
[65] Nicolas Berdyaev, *The Meaning of History,* trans. George Reavey (London, Geoffrey Bles: Centenary Press, 1936), p. 200.
[66] *Ibid.,* p. 201.   [67] *Op. cit.,* p. 56.

however, who have followed or do follow consistently any one strategy.

One test of any proposed Christian strategy is the contribution it will make to lifting the world toward the Christian ideal. Is the strategy workable? Can it be used to carry the Christian spirit and Christian principles out into the life of the world? A strategy may sound good on paper, but if it will not work it is worse than worthless.

There is, however, another important test of any method or strategy. Does the strategy itself conform to the Christian spirit and ideal? It is possible for so-called Christian strategies to be basically unchristian. They may negate the Christian spirit and deny the validity of the basic Christian ethic. This negation of the Christian spirit and ethic is a constant temptation and danger of those who support an accommodation approach to the world and its problems. They would approve or justify methods that admittedly do not measure up to Christian standards. From their viewpoint, such methods are justified because they seem necessary in an evil, resisting world. They argue that the world will not respond to the idealistic approach of a perfectionistic Christian ethic. After all, if Christian ends are attained one cannot label as unchristian the methods used to attain those ends. Such reasoning, which is common to many Protestants, is closely akin to the Jesuit and communist view that the end justifies the means, any sort of means.

It is recognized that there is a fine line of distinction, but a very important distinction, between this position and one outlined earlier. At least there is a difference of emphasis and degree. It was previously suggested that the Christian, being evil and being in an evil world, will frequently find that his choices, in general and in regard to Christian strategies or methods in particular, will not be between an unmixed good on the one hand and an unmixed evil on the other. Choices must be made between relative goods and relative evils. There will be an element of evil and possibly of good in whatever choice he makes.

The lesser-of-two-evils approach or strategy is not particularly damaging to the Christian ethic so long as there is a frank recognition that the decision or the method falls short of the Christian

27

ideal. But when the decision, which may be a mixture of good and evil, is given the stamp of divine approval there is an undermining of the Christian ethic and the Christian ideal.

It should also be said in conclusion that the various Christian strategies are not exclusive. They do not operate in water-tight compartments. They blend into one another. For example, one may agree that the over-all strategy should be the transformation of society. That strategy is a rather sharp contrast with the withdrawal and identification strategies. Even the latter strategies, however, may be so used as to be a part of the general transformation strategy.

In addition, the various accommodation strategies may all be used to transform society. They represent, in the main, median positions between the radical strategy of withdrawal and the synthetic strategy of identification. Some are closer to one of these extremes than to the other, but all of them may be used, to varying degrees, in the over-all Christian program for the transformation of society.

II

CHRISTIANITY
AND THE INDIVIDUAL

An IMPORTANT phase of the church's message to the world is its message concerning man. Man and his worth are integral phases of all the major issues that challenge our world and are important factors in the deepening crisis that is gripping our world.

Cave, who does not believe there is a doctrine of man but rather a Christian estimate of man, says, "It is the view of man which is to-day in the centre of conflict." [1] For Berdyaev "the essential and fundamental problem is the problem of man." [2] The same general emphasis is found in the opening sentence of a book by David Cairns. He says, "There is no more fundamental debate in the world today than that about the nature of man." [3] This debate is one of the most prevalent and significant discussions not only in theological but also in contemporary political circles.

The modern debate concerning man, along with the companion debate concerning God, is the debate or the battle of our age. It is possible that its outcome will determine the destiny of our nation and of our world. Cairns, near the end of his book, sums up the

[1] Sydney Cave, *The Christian Estimate of Man* (London, Gerald Duckworth, 1944), p. 10.
[2] Nicolas Berdyaev, *The Destiny of Man*, trans. Natalie Duddington (3rd ed.; London, Geoffrey Bles, 1948), p. 11.
[3] David Cairns, *The Image of God in Man* (London, S.C.M. Press, 1953), p. 9.

29

matter as follows: "What are we to make of the rights, the dignity, the sacredness of our fellow men? Man today stands at the crossroads. Will mankind, in its future development, declare itself for or against man?" [4] The contemporary discussion concerning man is also closely related to the more immediate problems of life. It is a factor, to a considerable degree, in every problem we shall discuss in succeeding chapters. There is a sense in which man or the individual is the central issue in every issue facing our world.

The centrality of the conflict concerning the individual in the contemporary period is underscored in a statement by Brunner. He says:

The fact that binds together the most influential thinkers of recent generations, those whose thought was capable of determining the thought not only of other thinkers, but also of the masses, and through them of determining the whole course of political development—Charles Darwin, Friedrich Nietzsche and Karl Marx—was this: that each of them gained power, directly or indirectly, over a considerable section of mankind by his view of man, by his "anthropology." Whether they were aware of it or not, it was not their scientific systems or their systems of philosophy which made history, but their view of man. [5]

The Christian View of Man

We cannot possibly outline a complete doctrine of man. [6] We shall limit ourselves to a few suggestions that are closely related to the general emphases of this book. Our main concern is the high value placed on the individual by Christianity and the reasons for that value.

The Psalmist asks an abidingly searching question:

[4] *Ibid.*, p. 249.

[5] Emil Brunner, *Man in Revolt*, trans. Olive Wyon (Philadelphia, Westminster Press, 1947), p. 34. Used by permission.

[6] For a discussion of the Christian doctrine of man by several theologians with varying viewpoints see the Official Oxford Conference volume entitled *The Christian Understanding of Man* (Chicago, Willett, Clark, 1938). There are many other books that do a thorough job from differing viewpoints, such as Reinhold Niebuhr's *The Nature and Destiny of Man* (2 vols.; New York, Scribner's, 1941, 1943); Brunner's *Man in Revolt*, which carries the subtitle "A Christian Anthropology"; Berdyaev's *The Destiny of Man;* and G. Ernest Wright's *The Biblical Doctrine of Man in Society.*

> What is man that thou art mindful of him,
> and the son of man that thou dost care for him?

He deepens the mystery, while at the same time he may hint at an answer to his question, when he says:

> Yet thou hast made him little less than God,
> and dost crown him with glory and honor.
> Thou hast given him dominion over the works of thy hands;
> thou hast put all things under his feet.[7]

Possibly here is the secret to his worth and dignity: he has been created a little less than God, or to use a common scriptural term—man is made in the image of God.[8]

1. *Created in the image of God.* The Bible reveals that man was the crowning act of God's creative work. It is also evident that there was a unique element in his creation. The record says, "Then God said, 'Let us make man in our image, after our likeness;' . . . So God created man in his own image, in the image of God he created him; male and female he created them." [9]

What is meant by "the image of God"? Is a distinction to be made between the image of God and "after our likeness"? Irenaeus made a distinction between *tzelem* (Latin, *imago*) and *demuth* (Latin, *similitudo*). He claimed that the latter referred to man's original righteousness which he lost when he fell, while the former, the image of God, man continued to possess even after the Fall.[10] This interpretation persisted for centuries and is still the position of the Roman Catholic Church. It was not until Luther that "this 'two-storey' edifice was destroyed. . . . Luther, with his sure feeling for exegesis, recognized the nature of Hebrew parallelism, and saw that the distinction between the *Imago* and the *Similitudo* was untenable." [11]

Let us return to an interpretation of "the image of God" and its

[7] Psalm 8:4–6.

[8] Berdyaev (*The Destiny of Man,* p. 53) says the Christian conception of man is based upon two ideas: "(1) man is the image and likeness of God the Creator and, (2) God became man, the Son of God manifested Himself to us as the God-man."

[9] Gen. 1:26–27.　　　　　　　　　　　[10] Cairns, *op. cit.,* p. 20.

[11] Brunner, *op. cit.,* pp. 93–94.

relation to the dignity of man. Brunner suggests that "the whole Christian doctrine of man hangs upon the interpretation of this expression." [12] As we seek for the proper interpretation of the image we should remember that if the dignity and worth of man are dependent on the fact that he is made in the image of God, and they are, then there can be no basis for the dignity and worth of all men unless all men have within them the image of God. This means that the image must be and is universal. Ferré concludes, "Every man has within him God's image, however unearthed, however covered over, however twisted and contorted in relation to other leading drives." [13]

Christian groups may and do vary considerably in the meaning they attach to "the image of God," which is a common possession of all men. Those with a classical leaning give major emphasis to the rational nature of man. They claim that man is like God because he has the capacity to judge or to reason. This conception may be correct as far as it goes, but it is too narrow and restrictive. It is not man's rational nature which makes him in the image of God; rather it is what he can and does do with that rational nature. Any satisfactory interpretation of the image of God in man must give primary emphasis to man's capacity for spiritual communion.[14] His rational nature is used as an instrument in that communion.

Even Calvin's conception of the image of God as a mirror or as a reflection of the glory of God, when it is properly understood, includes the idea of communion. It involves a response to God "in such a way that God may be able to behold Himself in man as in a mirror." [15] Simply because Calvin thinks of the image as a mirror it does not follow that it is to be a static reflection of God, "but a dynamic reflection by way of active response to the Will of God and to the Word of God." [16] E. C. Rust similarly concludes that the cen-

[12] *Ibid.*, p. 92.

[13] Nels F. S. Ferré, *Christianity and Society* (New York, Harper, 1950), p. 127.

[14] There is a difference between the contemplation of God, prominent in much Christian thought but which came into the stream of the Christian movement through its contact with certain forms of Greek philosophy, and communion, which involves communication.

[15] T. F. Torrance, *Calvin's Doctrine of Man* (London, Lutterworth Press, 1949), p. 51.

[16] *Ibid.*, p. 64.

tral idea in the Genesis conception of the image of God "is the thought that man has endowments which fit him for kinship with God and therefore with a capacity to respond to His Word." [17]

While the communion may be initiated by God and may primarily be self-communication, nevertheless man has the God-given capacity to respond and must respond if there is to be any communion. Communion, either on the human or the divine level, involves at least two persons. Man not only has the capacity to respond to God, but he is also unable to escape the presence of God. He was made for fellowship with God and he has a sense of homelessness when he is separated from God. Augustine's classic statement was: "Thou madest us for Thyself, and our heart is restless, until it repose in Thee." [18] Man may drift far away from God; he may go deep into sin; but there is something within waiting for the voice of God to come to him through the gospel else the message of redemption would have no meaning. Brunner suggests that "man, in contrast from all the rest of creation, has not merely been created by God and through God, but in and for God." [19] The "in and for God" is what gives to man his infinite worth and value, which, in turn, are so centrally important to the democratic movement and to the world in general.

Man, who is a creature of nature and suffers the limitations of the things of this world, does not find the full meaning of the self either in nature or within himself. He is of nature and yet, because he is made in the image of God, he stands above nature. "He has the capacity for indeterminate transcendence over the processes and limitations of nature." [20] In a sense he even stands outside himself. He "is not a fragmentary part of the world but contains the whole riddle of the universe and the solution of it," yet he "is a profound riddle to himself." [21] The thing that makes him most distinctly man finds satisfaction only in fellowship with God, and in a lesser sense with man.

[17] E. C. Rust, *Nature and Man in Biblical Thought* (London, Lutterworth Press, 1953), p. 121.

[18] *Confessions* (Everyman's Library Ed.), p. 1.

[19] *Op. cit.*, p. 92.

[20] Reinhold Niebuhr, *The Children of Light and the Children of Darkness* (New York, Scribner's, 1944), p. 3.

[21] Berdyaev, *The Destiny of Man*, p. 45.

The individual becomes a person in fellowship with other persons. He alone, of God's created beings, has the capacity for an I-thou relation with God and man. It is at least interesting to note that two of the three Old Testament references [22] to the image of God in man are not to man alone but to male and female. They are made to adjust to the "thou" of the opposite sex. It is not good for them to be alone.[23] They are made, as the marginal reading in the American Standard Version suggests, to answer to one another. They find their fulfillment in one another. Man's spiritual nature likewise is made to answer to God, to find its fulfillment in fellowship with God. This is what is meant, in the deepest sense, by the image of God in man.

If man is made for fellowship or communion with God, if there is something within him with which he can respond to the message of redemption, then he is a morally and spiritually responsible being. This is one thing that distinguishes him from the animal creation and gives him a dignity and worth that other created beings do not possess. One Old Testament passage that clearly relates the image to the value God places on man is the statement of the law of retaliation as found in Genesis 9:6: "Whoever sheds the blood of man, by man shall his blood be shed; for God made man in his own image."

2. *Sin and the image of God.* But what has the entrance of sin done to the image of God? It is sin that breaks the fellowship of man with God. Man is a creature of sin,[24] and sin is not something attached to a restricted segment of his life. It lies at the very center of his personality—in his will—and involves his total personality. The crux of the problem is that man has made of himself a god. "He pretends to be more than he is." [25] His will is made supreme rather than the will of God. His sin is basically inner and spiritual rather than outer and casual.

This view concerning the moral nature of man has tremendous implications economically and politically as well as spiritually. Many of the basic weaknesses and ills of modern society are traceable to either a too optimistic or a too pessimistic view concerning

[22] Gen. 1:26–27; 5:1–3; 9:5–6. [23] *Ibid.*, 2:18.
[24] Isa. 53:6; Rom. 3:10, 23.
[25] Niebuhr, *The Nature and Destiny of Man*, I, 16.

man and the power of sin in his life. Some have lacked a proper
sense of the innate sinfulness of man, of the strength of his inordi-
nate love of self, of the depth of the inner conflict between self-
interest and social or community well-being, of man's own inner
conflict between what Niebuhr calls the will-to-power and the will-
to-live-truly. On the other hand, a too pessimistic view concerning
the moral nature of man, which is very prevalent today, leads man
to lose faith in himself, and contributes to the rise of the absolutist
state or collective. 966626

Regardless of the position one may hold concerning the seriousness of sin in the life of the individual, what did the entrance of
sin do to the image of God in man? If the image was totally destroyed, then there would not remain a valid basis for a universal
respect for human beings. The only ones with real worth and
dignity would be those who had had the image restored by the
grace of God through the new birth. Most of those who have contended that the image has been totally destroyed have thought of
the image as referring to moral righteousness. God made man in
his image; he made him morally righteous. This righteousness, so
it is said, man lost in the fall.

But what if we think of that image as primarily a capacity for
communion with God—has man lost completely that capacity? The
fellowship has been broken through sin, but has man lost the capacity for the fellowship? Is there still enough of the image left
that man not only has the inner equipment with which he can
respond to the appeal of God, but is he actually restless and hungry
until the fellowship is restored? While man is basically egocentric,
which is the sin not only of our age, as Davies suggests, but also of
every age, yet man longs for "his fuller destiny." "Though his actual
nature is weighted toward self, his essential self is satisfied by nothing less than God's will for him," [26] or possibly better "than God's
fellowship with him." To use Kierkegaard's expression, "man is
the synthesis of time and eternity." But as Kierkegaard also suggests, "it is a perpetually shifting synthesis at one moment inclin-
ing towards eternity and at another falling under the sway of
time." [27]

Biblical scholars, past and present, may use different terms to

[26] Ferré, *op. cit.*, p. 148.
[27] Quoted by Berdyaev, *The Destiny of Man*, p. 75.

express the idea, but there has been and is almost universal agreement that the image of God was not totally destroyed when man sinned. Athanasius said the image was effaced and had to be repainted by the Artist. Augustine suggested that the image had been wounded and needed to be healed by the love of Christ. Calvin speaks of the relic of the image which sinful man retains, while Brunner suggests that man retains the formal image of God but that he has lost the original content of the image.[28] Berdyaev says that "man is a sick creature longing to be healed." [29] Regardless of the particular expression used, they all agree that there is a point of contact within man for God.

What is the conclusion concerning the image of God in man? Sin did not totally destroy the image. It could not because the image was of God's creation. Sin did not change God's basic purposes for man. Even sinful man retains, to a degree, the image of God. He retains it fully in the sense that God's purposes do not change fundamentally for him. He retains it only to a limited degree in his present state, if we are thinking of his immediate ability to have communion with God. He is made, however, to respond to God and is responsible to him. This is true of all men—saint and sinner. It is this fact that gives dignity and worth to all men. "Even in his fallen state he retains the mark of his high origin and remains capable of a higher life." [30]

The major emphasis in the New Testament doctrine of the image is the restoration of the image, marred by sin, through faith in Christ. Cairns, for example, suggests that the central emphasis in the New Testament teachings concerning the image is its use "to describe the likeness of God into which believers enter through faith in Christ." [31] It is God's purpose that the believer should be conformed to the image of his Son, who in turn is the express image, the exact reproduction, of the glory of God, the Father. God gave his Son, and the Son gave himself to restore the image of God in man that had been marred by sin. The fact that Christ died to redeem man, along with the universal image of God that is, to some degree, in all men, is the basis for the value, the worth, the dignity of man as man. "In plain fact, Calvary has done what philosophy

---

[28] Cairns, *op. cit.*, pp. 184–85.
[30] *Ibid.*, p. 11.

[29] *The Destiny of Man*, p. 75.
[31] *Op. cit.*, p. 32.

could never do in bringing into the world a new attitude not only to God, who so loved men, but to men, who were so loved by God." [32]

The point of contact within man for the experience that makes the believer a child of God is the image of God within, admittedly marred. The experience itself achieves God's purposes in the image. One thing it does is to restore within man the content of the original image. Man, through the new birth, is brought into communion with God in a meaningful way; the fellowship which he retained in his fallen state, as a potentiality, now becomes a reality in his life through a vital, life-changing union with Christ. He is brought into the family of God.

It is his relation to God as his Father and his dependence on God that give to man the proper sense of his own value. The more he is aware that he is a child of God, "the more he realizes that his life has a value" and that the lives of other men have value. It is because of man's relation to God that "Christianity from the outset has asserted the sovereign worth of man." [33] It was Jesus who said, "For what will it profit a man, if he gains the whole world and forfeits his life? Or what shall a man give in return for his life?" [34]

Separate man from this consciousness of being an actual or a potential child of God, and he becomes no more than an animal. Berdyaev pointedly says, "*Where there is no God there is no man.*" [35] In the contemporary period we are seeing the results of the separation of man from God and from a sense of fellowship with and dependence upon God. This divorcement of man from God, with the attendant dehumanizing of man, explains, to a large degree, man's extreme inhumanity to man so characteristic of recent years.

3. *Equal yet unequal.* There is a sense in which every phase of the Christian doctrine of man is an outgrowth of and, to a considerable degree, merely a different way of looking at its doctrine of the image of God. This is certainly true of the Christian doctrine

[32] F. J. Sheed, *Society and Sanity* (London, Sheed and Ward, 1953), p. 29.
[33] Ernest F. Scott, *Man and Society in the New Testament* (New York, Scribner's, 1946), p. 5.
[34] Matt. 16:26.
[35] *The End of Our Time,* trans. Donald Attwater (New York, Sheed and Ward, 1933), p. 80.

or conviction concerning the equality of all men. This doctrine of equality is of considerable importance, if one is to understand the contemporary age and to evaluate correctly some of the major trends of our day.

Christianity has persistently, although not always too consistently, proclaimed a message of human equality. Its message has been that God is no respecter of persons; that he shows no partiality; [36] that all men are created equal, in the sense that they are equally men and are to be treated with equal dignity; and that certain fundamental rights are theirs simply because they are human beings. Why is all this true? It is true because all men have been created in the image of God. They have been made for fellowship with him; they are by creation children of his and may become by re-creation members of his spiritual family.

This emphasis on the equality of all men has been a major factor in the rise and spread of democracy in political and economic life. Some of the problems of our day stem from the fact that the masses of men have taken this basic Christian and democratic principle seriously. Some problems have arisen and do arise because of a misunderstanding of the meaning of equality and of the companion truth that men are also unequal. "There is not a single quality in which all men are equal. . . . All men are equal only in the sense that all men are equally men. . . . men are equal to one another in all that is involved in being a man." [37]

Possibly we should remember, however, that "in the Christian view, being a man is itself so vast a thing, that the natural inequalities from one man to the next are a trifle by comparison." [38]

The idea of the inequality of men is just as definitely grounded in the New Testament as the companion and complementary doctrine that all men are equal. It is just as truly a part of the Christian view of man. On one hand, there is equality of personal dignity and, on the other hand, inequality of function and responsibility. Paul compares the church to a body; each member of the church, as is true of various parts of the body, has a distinctive function to perform.[39]

---

[36] Acts 10:34; cf. Rom. 2:11; Gal. 3:27–29; Eph. 6:9; Col. 3:25; 1 Peter 1:17; and James 2:1, 9.

[37] Sheed, *op. cit.*, p. 7.   [38] *Ibid.*, p. 33.   [39] 1 Cor. 12:14–30.

The family is a good illustration of this doctrine of inequality in equality. Each member of the family is to be treated with equal respect and dignity. Each is to remember that the other is a human being, created in the image of God. But on the other hand, the members of the family are unequal in functions. It is the proper recognition of this inequality in the midst of equality that gives to the family its inner strength and stability.

The failure to retain these two scriptural emphases—equality and inequality of men—in proper balance is one of the factors in the present world crisis and in many of the issues facing the world. A too exclusive emphasis on equality leads to a one-sided individualism that magnifies the rights rather than the responsibilities of the individual. On the other hand an unbalanced emphasis on the inequality of men leads to a one-sided, extreme collectivism which magnifies the rights and privileges of the collective or of a "superior" segment of society.

4. *The Christian versus the classical view of man.* There is not only a Christian view (or views) concerning man; there is also a classical conception of man which differs fundamentally from the Christian view.[40] The former comes from the Bible; the latter from the Greco-Roman world. "All modern views of human nature are adaptations, transformations and varying compounds" of these two views. Modern culture has been a battleground for the opposing views.[41]

The classical view is that man is to be understood primarily from something within himself—his rational nature; while the Christian view is that man must be understood and evaluated by something outside himself—by his relation to God. The classical view also involves a dualism that is incompatible with the Christian view. Ac-

---

[40] Berdyaev (*The Destiny of Man*, p. 47) says M. Scheler established four types of anthropological theory: "(1) The Jewish-Christian—the creation of man by God and the Fall; (2) the ancient Greek conception of man as the bearer of reason; (3) the natural science view of man as the product of the evolution in the animal world; (4) the decadence theory which regards the birth of consciousness, reason and spirit as biological retrogression, a weakening of life." Berdyaev adds a fifth theory which he claims is the most prevalent in modern Europe. It is that man as a social being is a product of society. It is "social life [that] turns the animal into man" (p. 49). This view is represented by Durkheim and Marx.

[41] Niebuhr, *The Nature and Destiny of Man*, I, 5.

cording to the classical view, based largely on Platonic, Aristotelian, and Neoplatonic conceptions of human nature, evil is identified with the body and goodness with the mind or the spirit. In contrast "the Bible knows nothing of a good mind and an evil body." [42]

Some have interpreted the classical view as being optimistic concerning man, while the pessimistic view is identified with Christianity, particularly with conservative Christianity. But such an identification is not entirely correct. The classical view may, on the surface, seem to be optimistic because the point of reference is man, but it should be remembered that it is the rational nature of man that is the point of reference. And the classicists did not believe that the rank and file of men were capable of the rational life on the highest level; this was reserved for a few wise or virtuous souls. Such a view, which really represents a deep-seated pessimism in regard to human nature in general, explains the very limited or restricted view of democracy in Greek and Roman thought.

A more thoroughgoing optimism is characteristic of much recent philosophical and theological thought. This optimism, which has no secure foundation in divine revelation or in human history, has been one of the weaknesses of a great deal of Christian liberalism. The disappointment and disillusionment, resulting from recent world events, concerning the innate goodness of man and man's ability, in his own strength and through his own resources, to correct the evils of the society he has constructed is one of the chief factors in the uncomfortable position of theological liberalism in recent years and in the rise of the Neo-orthodox or Neo-Protestant movement. The latter movement was a more or less natural reaction to the unrealistic optimism of liberalism.

The Christian view, based on the Bible, is not as pessimistic as it first appears. By placing God at the center of life, as the point of reference for life, it can be and is more realistically optimistic than any view can be that places its faith in human nature.

The Rights and Responsibilities of the Individual

It has been suggested that the contemporary debate or battle concerning man is the debate of the age. On its outcome hangs the

[42] *Ibid.*, p. 7.

destiny not only of man but of his civilization. The battle represents the climax of competing trends that have been more or less prevalent through the centuries. Recognizing that both the individual and the community have rights and responsibilities, it has been extremely difficult to maintain these two—the individual and the community, whether as state or church—in proper balance. One or the other has tended to be dominant, has tended to use the other for its own purposes, and to demand its rights without accepting its full responsibilities.

1. *The rights of the individual.* We shall not consider here the legal rights of man. We shall restrict our discussion to rights that are more fundamental than the legal or constitutional ones, and shall touch on the latter only as they are related to man's natural rights. These fundamental rights in contrast to legal rights are variously called human, natural, or divine rights. "They belong to man because he is man, and are valid even against society." [43] These rights are rooted in the nature of man. They belong to man because he was created in the image of God.

Legal or constitutional provisions for the rights of the individual, in the main, result from or are justified by the so-called inherent or natural rights. Locke defines natural rights as "the view that each man has certain unalienable rights, which other men (and therefore the State) must respect and cannot assail." He further adds that the state has the "positive duty of preserving these rights." [44] They belong to man whether or not his government legally provides for them.

The influence of this conception of natural or inherent rights is seen in the American Declaration of Independence and in the provisions of our national Constitution. For example, the second paragraph of the Declaration, which provides, in a sense, the theoretical or philosophical foundation for the specific allegations and proposed actions to follow, includes the following:

We hold these truths to be self-evident, that all men are created equal, that they are endowed by their Creator with certain unalienable Rights,

---

[43] Sheed, *op. cit.*, p. 7.
[44] J. D. Mabbott, *The State and the Citizen* (London, Hutchinson's Univ. Lib., 1948), p. 57.

that among these are Life, Liberty and the pursuit of Happiness, That to secure these rights, Governments are instituted among Men, deriving their just powers from the consent of the governed.

There is no human right more important or significant for the democratic way of life than the right of worship or of conscience. There is no clearer statement of this right and the obligation of constituted authority to provide for it than the one by Roger Williams. He said:

All civil states with their officers of justice, in their respective constitutions and administrations, are proved essentially civil, and therefore not judges, governors, or defenders of the spiritual, or Christian, state and worship. It is the will and command of God that, since the coming of his Son the Lord Jesus, a permission of the most paganish, Jewish, Turkish, or Antichristian consciences and worships be granted to all men in all nations and countries; and they are only to be fought against with that sword which is only, in soul matters, able to conquer, to wit, the sword of God's Spirit, the word of God.[45]

This right of individual conscience has tremendous implications. It is really a very radical doctrine and is dangerous if it is not properly balanced by a deep sense of social and religious responsibility.

Natural rights belong to all men. This fact correctly implies that men have the right to be treated with equal dignity or worth. There is to be no hierarchy of respect. Men, all men, are to be treated as actual or potential children of God. This dignity of the human person is as central as any concept which has created and shaped Western civilization.

2. *Limitations of the rights of the individual.* For healthy individuals and for a healthy society there must not only be a provision for the rights of individuals but there must also be a limitation of those rights. Some of the most serious problems of the contemporary period are related, in one way or another, to the extreme emphasis on the rights of the individual.

"Man, as created by God, was God-centered. Man, as re-created by himself, is self-centered," and it is "from this revolt of man against

[45] "The Bloody Tenet of Persecution" in A. S. P. Woodhouse, *Puritanism and Liberty* (London, J. M. Dent, 1938), p. 266.

God that the whole tragedy and evil of history arise." [46] Berdyaev similarly says that modern man has broken with "the depths of his own soul," [47] and that when he broke away "from the spiritual moorings of his life . . . he went to the surface and he has become more and more superficial." [48] This "self-centered" man over-emphasizes his rights without a corresponding emphasis on the limitation of those rights for the sake of others and the world.

Much of the chaos and confusion of the contemporary period stems from the unchristian, unbalanced individualism that has plagued the West. Niebuhr correctly suggests that modern culture seeks to raise the idea of individuality beyond the limits set for it in the Christian faith.[49] Man needs to remember that he not only has a center within himself but also a center beyond himself. It is the latter—the center outside himself or his capacity for self-transcendence—that is the only true and abiding basis for freedom, and it is this that distinguishes him more than anything else from animal existence.[50] On the other hand, "When man becomes a god: he becomes a monster," [51] and we have had some monsters walking in our midst in recent years.

Lovers of the democratic philosophy of life need to rethink the whole concept of the individual which has been so central in Western thought. It should not be hard to see that no adequate provision can be made *for* the rights of all without at the same time having some limitation *of* the rights of all. For example, the state cannot, as J. D. Mabbott suggests, protect rights without at the same time infringing on those rights. "If I am to have my right to free speech politically protected, the speech of those who would shout me down must have its freedom checked by the State." [52] There is no real freedom without some surrender of freedom.

What about the natural rights of man that have not been incorporated into the law of the land: can they and should they be limited? If they are to be limited or restricted, who is to do it? The state certainly cannot prescribe or limit such natural rights. Society through social pressure can limit them to some degree, but any

[46] D. R. Davies, *The Sin of Our Age* (New York, Macmillan, 1947), p. 138.
[47] *The End of Our Time*, p. 22.   [48] *Ibid.*, p. 17.
[49] *The Nature and Destiny of Man*, I, 57.   [50] *Ibid.*, p. 55.
[51] Davies, *op. cit.*, pp. 122–23.   [52] Mabbott, *op. cit.*, p. 57.

effective limitation of the individual's natural rights, that have not been incorporated into law, must be by his own self-discipline and personal restraint.

Such a voluntary renunciation of personal rights and liberties is a part of New Testament individualism. It is plainly revealed in the gospels and in the writings of Paul. The latter sums up the general principle as follows: "For you were called to freedom, brethren; only do not use your freedom as an opportunity for the flesh, but through love be servants of one another."[53] This represents a surrender of one's liberty for the sake of others. It is a self-limitation. It is thinking primarily of the rights of others rather than of one's own personal rights. Paul's famous passages concerning the eating of meat offered to idols clearly illustrate the principle of the self-surrender of one's rights for the sake of others.[54]

This whole approach, which is so characteristic of the New Testament message, represents the ethic of the cross, which is the central, distinctive unifying element in the ethical teachings of Jesus and Paul. Jesus invited his followers to deny self, to take up a cross, and to follow him. His invitation was not to self-realization but to self-sacrifice. But the glorious truth, as central as anything in the teachings of Jesus, is that one who loses his life in unselfish devotion to God and to man will find it.[55] He will discover life on its higher levels.

The fact that man will find life by losing it implies that there is something in the nature of man that demands, to some degree, a voluntary limitation of his rights. He finds his fulfillment in communion with others and in service to others. He cannot find fulfillment for his capacities apart from fellowship with other human beings. Man cannot successfully secede from the community. It is no mere accident that Robinson Crusoe was a fictitious character, and even he had his man Friday.

There is no communion without some give-and-take, and there is no effective give-and-take in human relations without some restriction of rights or liberties. Thus, man's nature not only demands certain basic rights, but it also demands some limitation of those

[53] Gal. 5:13.   [54] Rom. 14 and 1 Cor. 8.
[55] See Matt. 10:39; 16:25; John 12:25.

rights. This must be true if he is to be most fully human, if he is to discover life at its highest and best.

What is true on the purely human level is even more true on the human-divine level. Man finds his most complete fulfillment in communion or fellowship with God. However, for man to have communion with God he must accept God's way and will for his life. The depth of the communion will be determined by the degree of his cooperation with the will of God. This means that he must surrender his will to the divine will. But how glorious it is that when man accepts God's will he finds that the Father's will is always best for him as well as for the kingdom of God! In surrender he finds real liberty. In limiting his rights on one level, he discovers on another level rights and liberties of which he had never dreamed. These are paradoxes, but the gospel and the Christian experience are filled with glorious paradoxes.

3. *The responsibilities of the individual.* The rights of individuals may be so strongly and exclusively stressed as to lead to moral and social anarchy. This is certainly true of the autonomous individualism created by the Renaissance, and which has continued to be very prevalent in humanism and political liberalism. These movements have "cultivated a pernicious separation of individual rights from individual duties" [56] and have trained "people to receive," and only hope "that they will give." [57] Even Christian individualism "may become the source of anarchy" if divorced from a sense of responsibility to God and of genuine humility before God.[58] The right kind of Christian individualism stresses both the rights of the individual, particularly the rights of other individuals, and the responsibilities of the individual to others, to the Christian community, and to the world in general.

It should be remembered that there is no right or privilege without a corresponding responsibility. One of the quickest and surest ways to lose the rights we now possess is to fail to accept the responsibilities those rights entail. This is true whether we are think-

[56] William E. Hocking, *The Lasting Elements of Individualism* (New Haven, Yale University Press, 1937), p. 40.
[57] *Ibid.*, p. 6.
[58] Niebuhr, *The Nature and Destiny of Man*, I, 59.

ing of our rights as citizens of our nation or of our more basic rights as men created in the image of God. There is a sense in which everyone has the right, a natural right, to have some worthy responsibility for the work of the world. This he must have if he is to develop into a morally and spiritually mature personality.

Each political right has a corresponding or closely related responsibility. For example, the citizen in a democracy has the right to vote, but this also is a responsibility and is a part of his citizenship and Christian stewardship. Every citizen, but particularly the Christian citizen, has a responsibility to be a good citizen: he should obey the laws of the land, should pay his taxes, and should support the government, except when such would violate his Christian conscience.

Man, as suggested previously, has the right of conscience. He and he alone has the right to decide what is right or wrong for him to do. What a glorious privilege; how thankful man should be for it! On the other hand, what a tremendous responsibility! One cannot have the right without accepting the responsibility—now and for eternity. This, which may sound as if it is applicable to the Christian alone, is fully applicable to all men. The universal message of the Christian religion is: "The soul that sins shall die." [59] There may be a shared responsibility by the family, the school, the community, and even the church; but the ultimate responsibility rests squarely upon the shoulders of the individual.

The Individual and the Community

In this section we shall use the terms "group," "community," and "collective" without making any clear distinction. Berdyaev has suggested that there is a deeper sense in which the "collective" and the "community" are drastically different. He suggests that a collective does not know the meaning of "neighbor" from the Christian viewpoint, that it is antipersonal, and is the union of strangers. On the other hand, a "community" is personalistic, representing the communion of personalities. He further adds that collectivism "means not only the socialization and collectivization of economic and political life, but of conscience, thought, creativity; there is an

[59] Ezek. 18:4.

exteriorization of conscience, i.e. its removal from the depth of man's being, of man as a spiritual entity, and its transfer to the collective, which possesses the organs of authority." [60]

In our usage "collective" could be equated with "group." In other words, it is a collection or a group of individuals. In addition, the term "community" will not necessarily and exclusively refer to a group that has attained true community of spirit. It likewise is used to refer to a collection or group of individuals. To achieve variety these three words will be used, to some degree, interchangeably.

1. *The individual versus the community.* There has been a continuing conflict between the individual and the community throughout the stream of human history. Seldom, if ever, has a proper balance been maintained. There is no easy solution for the abiding tension between the individual and the community. Berdyaev goes so far as to say that "history never solves the conflict between personality and society," [61] and that never before has the conflict been so strongly or sharply drawn. In the contemporary period, "man is being betrayed. He has ceased to be the supreme value." [62] The tragedy is made even darker by the fact that many men in many areas accept this self-destruction by the historic processes as inevitable, and even welcome it. The latter is particularly true if the group or collective promises to them relative economic security. This represents what Reinhold Niebuhr calls the "remarkable self-destruction of individuality in modern culture." [63]

As we shall see later, the above does not mean that the group or community is inevitably an enemy of the individual. It simply means that at the present time the balance or pendulum has swung in the direction of the group. The individual finds the currents of contemporary life strongly against him. The pressure is terrific for him to subordinate himself to the group. Practically all the movements that make the modern period one of such confusion, chaos, and crisis are related, to a lesser or to a greater degree, to this struggle between the individual and the group or community.

[60] Nicolas Berdyaev, *The Realm of Spirit and the Realm of Caesar,* trans. Donald A. Lowrie (New York, Harper, 1952), p. 121.
[61] *The Fate of Man in the Modern World,* p. 2.
[62] *Ibid.,* p. 53.   [63] *The Nature and Destiny of Man,* I, 57.

As suggested previously, the struggle is not new. Similar intensity, however, has been found only in periods of major transition and change. It may be that out of the contemporary crisis will come a better balanced synthesis.

2. *The individual and his fulfillment in the community.* It should not be concluded from the preceding that the individual and the community are inevitably opposed to each other. They "are not opposing concepts but are involved in one another. Behind every individual is a community because it is man's nature to communicate himself to others." [64] "In one sense there is no such thing as an individual man." [65] Contacts with others are absolutely essential if he is to be lifted to the level of human personality. He cannot find fulfillment for his capacities apart from fellowship with other human beings. In a very real sense "man is more than an individual. He is a society." [66] He was created for fellowship. "Personality from its very nature presupposes another. . . . A person cannot exist as a self-contained and self-sufficient Absolute." [67] The institutions of society are written into man's nature, or as Brunner expresses it, "They [communities] are innate in the God-created individual with his capacity and need for completion." [68] On the highest plane the personality of God and man presuppose each other.

Community life, which conforms to the nature of man but is not created by him, greatly influences the individual. This influence is so noticeable that, to a degree, we can correctly consider the individual as a product of the groups or communities to which he has or does belong—the home, the play group, the school, the church, the neighborhood, the state, the nation, the race.

While the individual as a person demands the community for fulfillment, yet he "always tends to go beyond it." [69] In other words, he is both dependent upon and independent of the group or com-

---

[64] Wright, *op. cit.*, p. 51.
[65] Scott, *Man and Society in the New Testament*, p. 7.
[66] Lynn Hough, *Evangelical Humanism* (New York, Abingdon Press, 1925), p. 153.
[67] Berdyaev, *The Destiny of Man*, p. 57.
[68] *Justice and the Social Order* (London, Lutterworth Press, 1945), p. 78.
[69] Jacques Maritain, *The Person and the Common Good* (New York, Scribner's, 1947), p. 69.

munity. This is due to the divine-human or transcendental-earthly nature of man. Belonging to the earth he is dependent on the community; but there is a transcendental point of reference in his nature that makes him independent of the community.

The individual's human-earthly functions cannot find fulfillment apart from his relations with others and with the community. For example, man and woman find the fulfillment of their physical natures in their relations as husbands and wives and in cooperation with God in the creative act. On the other hand, they find their higher spiritual fulfillment in communion with God and with him alone.

It may seem strange but it is true that communities likewise find their fulfillment in and through the individuals they serve. They serve their own best interests, in the long run, when they recognize that the individual is not only dependent on the group but that he is likewise independent of the group. The freedom of the individual from dominance and control by the community and from full containment within the historic process gives to the community its best assurance of new insights and higher reaches of justice and freedom. This is one reason that it is so basically important for the world and for the Christian movement to preserve the rights of the prophetic souls who blaze new trails.

3. *The rights and responsibilities of the community.* The group or the community, as well as the individual, has both rights and responsibilities. This is true of the family, the school, the church, the labor union, the civic club, the fraternal order, the neighborhood, the state, the nation, the world. The problem is, as suggested earlier, to maintain the rights and the responsibilities of the individual and the community in proper balance.

The rights that the community or group has are not derived entirely from the individuals who compose the group. The basic, God-ordained social institutions have certain inherent rights. The social contract or compact theory did not properly recognize this fact. That is one reason for its unfortunate effects on marriage and the family. A contract that is entered into can be dissolved. But the family has some rights as an institution that are not dependent upon the rights of the man and woman who formed the family by joining together as husband and wife. The same can be said for the state or any other social group.

On the other hand, the social group or community, as well as the individual, is responsible to God, who is the author of the laws determining the proper relation of the individual and the community. A correct sense of responsibility to a sovereign, transcendent God will save the world from individual anarchy and from community despotism. This is one reason that some believe that Europe and the world in general would not be in such a serious crisis if Protestantism had followed more faithfully the Calvinistic tradition with its emphasis on the sovereignty of God.

The social group, as well as the individual, should recognize that its rights are limited. This is particularly true in its relation to the individual. While every basic social institution is derived from God and is ultimately responsible to God, it also derives a portion of its authority from the consent of the people and hence is responsible to the people. God has seen fit to mediate a portion of his authority for the family, the church, and the state through the people who are the members or citizens of those institutions.

Furthermore, God has reserved for himself the final word with the individual, whether he is a member of the family or the church, or a citizen of the state. The abiding question of the Christian conscience, when faced with a choice between the will of God and the dictates of the home, church, or state, has been: "Whether it is right in the sight of God to listen to you rather than to God, you must judge." [70] A plain answer is found in Acts 5:29: "But Peter and the apostles answered, 'We must obey God rather than men.'"

There is another phase of our subject that should be mentioned. These basic social institutions not only have some inherent rights in relation to individuals, but also in relation to one another. These rights are inherent within the democratic tradition; and in the case of the home, and to a less degree of the state, they are clearly revealed in the purposes of God. A permanently sound social order is one where these and other institutions are rightly related to one another and where they keep in proper perspective their respective rights, but particularly their responsibilities to one another and to the individual.

[70] Acts 4:19.

Happy is the country that has strong healthy families, schools, churches, and other social groups and human institutions, with all of them properly related to one another and with all of them holding in proper balance their rights and their responsibilities to one another, to the entire social order, to the individual, and ultimately to God himself.

Happy also is the individual who keeps in proper balance in his life his rights and his responsibilities; who thinks primarily in terms of the rights of others instead of his own rights; and who accepts and fulfills, as best he can, his responsibilities to the family, the church, the state, and all other human groups to which he belongs; and above and beyond all of these he recognizes that his ultimate responsibility is to God, who created him in his own image and who desires that that image be fully restored by his faith in and fellowship with God's Son and our Lord and Savior, Jesus Christ.

4. *The individual and the community within historic Christianity.*
Just as is true of history in general, so within Christian history there have been a continuing interplay and struggle between the individual and the community. An interesting approach to church history would be to trace the varying emphases of the Christian movement regarding the relative value of the individual and the community—both secular and ecclesiastical.

In original Christianity, as represented by the life and teachings of Christ, there was found a twofold emphasis on the individual and on the Christian community. The primary emphasis of Jesus, however, was on the individual. He always thought of men as individuals. He never lost them in the mass. With the streets lined with people, he saw Zacchaeus up a sycamore tree. This incident was typical of him. He "discovered the individual. He was the first to recognize that every man has a worth of his own." [71]

In his social teachings, Jesus placed the emphasis on service to individual men and women. Individuals, however, were not to give primary consideration to their own rights. They were not to think about themselves. Jesus taught repeatedly that men find life by losing it, that his followers are to deny self, to take up a cross and

[71] Scott, *Man and Society in the New Testament*, p. 77.

follow him. The emphasis is on the individual but primarily on the value of and service to other individuals.

An emphasis on the community is found, to some degree, in the teachings of Jesus, but particularly in the ministry and epistles of Paul. Paul, the organizer and builder of churches, gave to those churches very specific instructions concerning the internal life of the Christian community and concerning the relation of the Christian community to and its responsibility for the individual members of the churches. Through the messages to the churches he also passed on to the individual disciples instructions concerning their responsibilities to the social order and to the institutions of society such as the family and the state.

In the early days of the Christian movement, there developed tendencies toward the stratification of a developing ecclesiasticism, the exaltation of Christian institutions, and the recognition of an authoritarian church. This church gradually claimed authority over the individual and his conscience, and even over the secular order. In other words, the Christian community became the primary value rather than the individual.

After several centuries of the rise, the development, and the increasing dominance of all of life by the church, a swing back to an emphasis on the individual was natural and inevitable. The movement was made more inevitable by the fact that the church by external restraint and force sought to maintain its authority over all of life long after the inner unification of the civilization it had so largely built had been lost.

A general movement arose which broke the restraining bands of a decadent church and freed tremendous creative vitalities that ushered in one of the most constructive periods in the history of the world. One phase of that movement was the Renaissance, which created what Reinhold Niebuhr calls a "very unchristian concept and reality; the autonomous individual." [72] Many of the problems of the contemporary period result from this autonomous individualism, which goes beyond the limits of a wise, constructive, Christian conception of the individual.

The Reformation, which may properly be considered a phase of the same general movement as the Renaissance, contributed a

[72] *The Nature and Destiny of Man,* I, 61.

great deal to the rediscovery of the individual. The general theological position of the Reformers, and particularly their emphasis on justification by faith and the companion doctrine of the priesthood of all believers, created or revived the conception of a responsible Christian individualism. However, the emphasis of the Reformers, particularly Calvin, on the sovereignty of God saved the Reformation from the extremes of the Renaissance which created what has been called "the Renaissance man."

Parenthetically it should be said that this rediscovery of the individual and the emphasis on his worth as contrasted to the former emphasis on the church or the Christian community affected as deeply economic, political, and social life in general as it did religious life and institutions. Lynn Hough says:

> The sixteenth century stands in the sharpest antithesis to the thirteenth. The age of solidarity has been succeeded by the age of individuality. The old unity is gone. It has broken into a thousand fragments. The individual nation has a new self-conscious life. . . . The individual man is learning to stand in stark and lonely self-assertion ready to defy the world. Luther at Worms is the very embodiment of the new sense of the awful integrity of the individual life.[73]

Roughly, with varying emphases, one continuing distinction between the Roman Catholic Church and Protestantism has been that the former has given primary emphasis to the church or the Christian community, while the latter has emphasized primarily the individual. There have been widely divergent emphases among Protestant groups. The closer akin they are to Roman Catholicism, the more they magnify the church and its authority over the individual. The more democratic church and sectarian groups generally follow more closely the individualistic traditions of the Reformation.

Contemporary Threats to the Individual

There are many trends and movements, in the contemporary period, which threaten man and his civilization. That threat is particularly acute within Western civilization and most immediately acute in Western Europe, which has been the creative center of Western civilization.

[73] *Op. cit.*, p. 17.

Western civilization was and is a product, in the main, of Grecian culture, Roman law and organizational genius, and the social and moral ideals of the Judaeo-Christian tradition. Possibly the most important and distinctive contribution of the Christian movement to the West has been its conception of the worth of the individual, its respect for human personality as such. Any philosophy or movement which challenges this basic Christian concept not only threatens the individual but also Western civilization.

There are modern movements that would strip man of much if not all of his dignity and worth. The most significant phase of these movements, from the viewpoint of this study, is not their economic or political program but their basic philosophy or ideology. Particularly important for the individual and the Christian cause are their theology and anthropology, and every modern "ism" that threatens the individual has both a theology and an anthropology.

1. *The threat from humanism.* No one of these movements has a longer, and in many ways a more honorable history, than humanism. The movement, which goes back to the Greek philosophers, was revived in the days of the Renaissance. In the early days of its revival it was theocentric. It acknowledged its heavy indebtedness to the Christian movement and joined hands with the reformers in breaking the dominance and control of the Roman Catholic Church. Protestantism and humanism have had so much in common that one astute scholar refers to the past four hundred years as the "Protestant-humanist" era.[74]

Humanism, which contributed so much to the central values of Western civilization, drifted away from its earlier theistic base. It became largely anthropocentric, and the Western world "with single-minded intensity . . . has concentrated" upon the humanistic notion of the individual, "upon man the individual, upon his value, his worth, his rights, and his freedom, with the result that the sense of the meaning and purpose of community has been evaporating."[75] Most of the movements that have plagued the modern world have arisen as a more or less natural reaction to this extreme individual-

[74] Paul Tillich, *The Protestant Era* (Chicago, University of Chicago Press, 1948), p. 274.
[75] Wright, *op. cit.*, p. 20.

ism, to this atomization of society. "Man's lostness," in the contemporary period, "results in part from his loss of community." [76] He is tending to turn to the collective to recapture his lost sense of community.

Humanism, which was revived in the days of the Renaissance, not only tended to separate man from the community of men, but it also tended to exalt man apart from God, to enthrone man in the place of God, and to relieve man of any sense of dependence on God. But when man is separated from God he becomes no more than an animal. If he fails to recognize the image of God in his fellow man, he will treat the latter as an animal. There has been plenty of evidence in recent years of the ultimate results of such an appraisal of or attitude toward man. The world has been traveling, to a distressing degree, "the path towards inhumanity." [77] Only those with a basically Christian perspective will, to use an expression of Immanuel Kant, "act so as to use humanity, whether in our own person or in the person of another, always as an end, never as merely a means."

The humanists have emphasized, in the main, the dignity of man and have equated that dignity with his moral goodness. They claim that man innately has or can attain, in his own strength, that goodness. He is not in need of salvation from sin and its enslavement. His dignity is not dependent on his relation to God. To make him dependent on God, so it is claimed, would reduce, if it did not destroy, his dignity and worth.

For the sake of emphasis the preceding may be slightly overdrawn, but it represents the general direction of humanism. It has tended to humanize God, if there is any place for God at all, and to deify man. It has contributed to what Davies calls *The Sin of Our Age*, which he identifies as the exaltation of man to the place that belongs to God.

The humanistic conception of man, at least in its final results, contains within itself a deep-seated contradiction. While freeing man it ultimately enslaves him; while releasing his creative energies, it also, by separating him from God, assures the exhaustion of his

[76] *Ibid.*
[77] Albert Schweitzer, *The Decay and the Restoration of Civilization* (London, A. and C. Black, 1923), p. 24.

creative powers. It claims to exalt man but it really ultimately debases him by ceasing to regard him as a being made in the image of God. We are reaping some of the ultimate, inevitable consequences of the application of the humanistic-Renaissance anthropology. "Having put aside God in order to become self-sufficient, man loses his soul." [78]

What Hough says about humanism could be said concerning most Western thought, including some supposedly Christian thought: "Entirely honest humanism has an empty throne room in its heart waiting for a worthy Deity to take possession." [79] There is a vacuum at the heart of the West and at the center of the value system of Western man. That vacuum or throne room will not remain empty. If it is not occupied by a "worthy Deity" it will be occupied by unworthy deities. This is one explanation for the rise and spread of fascism, communism, and other modern ideologies.

It may seem strange, but when man is separated from God and made central there also is created within him a curious conflict or complex. He fluctuates between considering himself everything and nothing. "By turns, he swaggers with self-importance and shivers with fright." He alternates between a sense of "despair and megalomania." [80]

While the individual is threatened with self-destruction, as Niebuhr, Davies, and others have suggested, he also is threatened by forces and movements outside himself. While humanism is a major factor in man's threatened suicide, it as a movement is also an external threat to man. Communism is the ultimate expression of an anthropocentric humanism, but we should remember that the anthropocentric tendency seems to be an inevitable feature of humanism, even the humanism that has permeated or infiltrated certain theological circles.

2. *The threat of materialism.* Without any attempt to be exact, we can agree in general with Maritain that communism, capitalism or "bourgeois individualism," and "totalitarian or dictatorial anti-

---

[78] Jacques Maritain, *The Twilight of Civilization* (New York, Sheed and Ward, 1943), p. 6.

[79] *Op. cit.,* p. 142.

[80] Walter M. Horton in the Official Oxford Conference book *The Christian Understanding of Man,* pp. 222–23.

communism and anti-individualism," all "disregard the human *person* in one way or another, and, in its place, consider, willingly or not, the *material individual* alone." [81] Whether such materialism is communistic or capitalistic, it is a real enemy of the individual, actually threatening his dignity and worth as a human person:

Materialism can provide no principle of personal value. . . . Born of matter for no special reason, held briefly above the surface of inanimate matter for no special reason, merged again into the great mass of unliving matter, man is no more than a material accident. No mind conceived him or endowed him with a purpose. To see man thus is to see him as nothing. All men are equal, and all are equal to nothing.[82]

Man is nothing. He belongs to society and society can do with him as it wills. Sheed further suggests, "The great difficulty about Materialism is that it fails to provide any fundamental difference between men and animals; and its tendency, now everywhere visible, to judge men and animals by the same rules, is all the more dangerous because of the half-truth in it." [83]

Marxism, which has made a religion of its dialectical materialism, portrays man as "inevitably bound up with society; creating it, and at the same time created by it . . . not possessing a private individuality. . . . Marxism misses the essential character of the I-Thou relation altogether. One might almost say that man is regarded not as a person, standing in a personal relation with his fellow, but as a thing, the effect of a cause." [84]

The blindness of Marxism as to the dignity of persons, as Cairns suggests, "is due to its blindness to the I-God relationship." He then concludes, "It is here, in the sphere of the treatment of persons, that the true conflict between the Marxist ethic and the Christian ethic arises today." [85] The communist ethic is anti-individualistic. Instead of finding and creating community, the communist creates a substitute for community—collectivity. "Communism forms society, like briquettes of pulverised individuals, by outward pressure." [86]

[81] *The Person and the Common Good*, p. 81.
[82] F. J. Sheed, *Communism and Man* (New York, Sheed and Ward, 1938), p. 137.
[83] *Ibid.*, pp. 137–38.   [84] Cairns, *op. cit.*, p. 213.   [85] *Ibid.*, p. 216.
[86] Emil Brunner, *The Church in the New Social Order* (London, S.C.M. Press, 1952), p. 26.

Davies suggests that "man as spirit, as personality, as moral agent—has declined as never before" in our completely secular civilization.[87] This secular faith is about to reach full maturity, and the world is reaping some of the results. Man in this materialistic, mechanized, secularized society has become materialistic in his thinking. "He has been conditioned to accept the tin whistle as a satisfactory substitute for the silver trumpet." [88]

Man has also been conditioned to accept the claims and the control of dictatorial, totalitarian régimes. Separated from God, and having lost his sense of being made in the image of God, man has lost, to a distressing degree, his sense of personal worth and dignity. He is seeking to recapture, in the contemporary period, his sense of significance. He is turning in many portions of the world to the collective man, hoping to discover in the collective the sense of personal importance and worth he so largely has lost.

Furthermore, in a period when the material values have been accepted as supreme by so many people, it is more or less natural that millions of men and women have been willing to surrender their basic rights and liberties, the very things that have contributed most to their dignity and worth, for economic security and well-being. The latter cannot be described as "a mess of pottage"; but as important as economic well-being may be, it does not compare at all with the importance of the fundamental freedoms of life.

3. *Conclusions.* It now seems that man must discover some means or course that will enable him to recapture his sense of worth and dignity. In a search for that source or means it seems that he will turn to a political, economic, or ecclesiastical totalitarianism, which will be a false hope, or to a vital type of Christian experience. The latter is his only real hope. It will provide for him a center for the reorientation of his life. If it is to serve this purpose, his religious experience must be so vital and dynamic that it will become the total for his life, to which everything else will be subservient. As the Christian religion becomes spiritually totalitarian, it will provide for any man or for men in general a creative basis for a recapture or a renewal of a sense of dignity and worth.

Let us return, for a moment, to the central importance of the

[87] *Op. cit.*, p. 107.   [88] *Ibid.*, p. 103.

doctrine or the estimate of man for our nation and our world. Sheed suggests that the Christian message "that man, every man, was not only a being of value, but a being of eternal value," revolutionized the world.[89] He goes so far as to say that the whole nature of society depends upon the value attached to the person.

One may properly conclude that what is done about man as such, within the next few years, will determine, to a considerable degree, the destiny of organized Christianity, of our nation, Western civilization, and the world. What is done about man and to man will be determined by the generally accepted estimate of the worth and dignity of man. This estimate, in turn, will be determined by the commonly held viewpoint concerning the relation of man to God.

Men everywhere need to see man as one made a little lower than God himself; one whose feet are planted upon the good earth, but whose soul reaches up to the throne of God. He should be seen as a human person, with all the limitations and weaknesses of the fleshly carnal nature, but at the same time as one with a divinely given potential, a potential beyond the imagination of the most discerning minds and the most creative souls.

[89] *Communism and Man,* p. 135.

III

THE FAMILY
AND ITS FUTURE

N O INSTITUTION is more sensitive to basic social changes than the family. The modern crisis in family life stems, to a considerable degree, from the contemporary crisis in the world. This crisis is so pervasive that it inevitably affects every phase of life, every institution of the social order, including the home. On the other hand, the crisis in family life "is one of the deep causes of world-disturbance today." [1] And while the family may have been continuously in a critical state, yet the present crisis in family life, which is "a wholly new phenomenon," [2] presents to the Christian ethic its "most serious" and "most difficult problem." [3]

The Importance of the Home

The family "has been basic throughout the long history of man," and "remains the most fundamental unit of modern culture." [4] When its importance is considered, surprisingly little attention has been given to the study of the family. In the contemporary period, how-

[1] Nicolas Berdyaev, *The End of Our Time*, p. 118.
[2] Emil Brunner, *The Divine Imperative*, trans. Olive Wyon (Philadelphia, Westminster Press, 1943), p. 340.
[3] *Ibid.*, p. 341.
[4] Arnold Gesell and Frances L. Ilg, *Infant and Child in the Culture of Today* (New York, Harper, 1943), p. 9.

ever, there is an awakening interest in the family and a deepening awareness of its contributions to every phase of the corporate life. Some of this interest may be and is rather negative and even morbid, but most of it is wholesome and encouraging. There is a growing understanding of the importance of the home, of its contributions to and interrelatedness with the problems of our day, and also a deepening realization that society and the other institutions of society cannot solve the problems of the social order without the cooperation of the home. These institutions, with society itself, are largely dependent on the home. As goes the home so will go the school, the church, the nation, and even civilization.

1. *As a source for children.* God has ordained and human experience has proved that children should come into the world through properly established, socially approved homes.[5] The child needs the love and care that his parents alone can provide. The children from the homes of the people provide the pupils for the school, the members for the church, and the citizens for the state. These institutions could not exist without the human product of the home.

2. *As a molder of character.* "The family provides most of the intimate and influential relationships between persons,"[6] and is "the most influential factor in the social processes which determine the individual's personality."[7] Lofthouse goes so far as to say, "Personality, in its proper sense, can only grow up in the family."[8] The home is important as a developer of personality because, as L. Foster Wood says, "The home is a place where the roots of life are nourished."[9] The home has the advantage over other institutions because it has the child during the early, the most formative months and years of his life. Gesell suggests: "The developmental transformations which occur in the first year of life far exceed those of

---

[5] Arnold Gesell *et al.* in *The First Five Years of Life* (New York, Harper, 1940), p. 4, said that there were, when they wrote, 250,000 neglected and dependent children cared for in 1,500 institutions and 350 child-placing agencies, and that a conservative estimate was that one in thirty-five of the population was born out of wedlock.

[6] M. C. Elmer, *The Sociology of the Family* (Boston, Ginn, 1945), p. 3.

[7] *Ibid.*, p. 437.

[8] *The Family and the State* (London, Epworth Press, 1944), p. 14.

[9] Ray V. Sowers and John W. Mullen (eds.), *Understanding Marriage and the Family* (Chicago, Eugene Hugh Publishers, 1946), p. 53.

any other period excepting only the period of gestation. . . . [The child's] personality and his diversified abilities at one year of age are the product of an extremely swift season of growth." [10]

The home, more than any other institution, provides, and in turn shapes, the factors that go into the making of character and personality. The home will largely decide whether the individual will have a body that will be an asset or a liability to him, whether he will be balanced or unstable emotionally, and whether he will have healthy or unhealthy attitudes toward others and toward life in general. In the home he will receive, in the main, his systems of values, his conception of success, and the driving motives and purposes of his life.

One of the distinct advantages of the home as a developer of human personality is the fact that in the home there is carried on a continuous educational process. It is continuous not only in the sense that it goes on hour after hour and day after day, but it also continues through life—from birth to the grave! "It is as much an educational organization for the adult members of the group as for the children." [11] This process of education is made more meaningful and formative because it is carried on within the framework of the most intimate, face-to-face, primary relationships.

It is through contacts with the members of the family and by means of the atmosphere and teaching—both formal and informal—in the home that the personality patterns of most individuals are shaped more than by any other combination of forces. It is the early experiences of life, so largely limited to the home, that "build up mental sets that condition all later learning." [12] "As the twig is bent so is the tree inclined." These early childhood patterns of personality may be changed, but they strongly resist change and survive to a considerable degree.

From the home the child receives, to a large degree, the inheritance of the past; and through the influence of the home he is led to conform, in the main, to the mores and traditions of society. If the home fails to perform these functions for the child, he frequently will mature into a maladjusted individual.

---

[10] Gesell *et al.*, *op. cit.*, p. 16.   [11] Elmer, *op. cit.*, p. 405.
[12] Meyer F. Nimkoff, *Marriage and the Family* (New York, Houghton Mifflin, 1947), p. 340.

The homes that make the most constructive contribution to the advancement of society are those in which the children are led to make an intelligently discriminating response to the patterns and demands of society. A universal conformity to the customary would eliminate all hope for new insights and advance. The home has a responsibility to help the maturing individual to know when and how to disagree and protest. He should be led to understand that nonconformity as such should never be considered a virtue. One sign of moral and spiritual maturity is the ability to discriminate between the essential and the non-essential, the important and the unimportant. And in regard to non-essentials, the slogan may be followed that when one is in Rome he should do as Romans do. There should always be a real and an important reason for one's refusal to accommodate himself to the generally accepted pattern. And when one must refuse to conform he should do so in the spirit of love and humility, asking the Lord to save him from the self-righteous spirit, which seems to be the besetting sin of nonconformists.

If the maturing child cannot be led to discriminate wisely and disagree agreeably, he may develop personality problems, if not conflicts. He may become "a problem child" and later "a problem adult"—a problem to himself, his loved ones, friends, neighbors, and society. Another evidence of intellectual, social, moral, and spiritual maturity is one's ability to live in reasonable harmony with those with whom he may disagree and to adjust himself, at least to a workable degree, to a society against which he may be in constant revolt. The individuals, who succeed in reaching such a stage of emotional balance and general maturity, will be, in the main, those who have grown up in a home atmosphere where the adult members had made a satisfactory adjustment to one another and had maintained a wholesome tension with and yet a healthy attitude toward the world and life in general.

3. *As a pattern for the social order.* The family is a little social order, "a concentrated nucleus of a larger society maintaining and carrying on the procedures and processes of the larger group in a miniature and intensified form." [13] The family is an embryonic

[13] Elmer, *op. cit.*, p. 3.

school; a more important educational institution than the school. It is an embryonic state; a more important institution for law and order than the state. It is also an embryonic church; a more basically determinative religious institution than the church.

Moreover, the home provides the goal or the pattern for these institutions and for the social order. In the home the mature and the strong serve the young and the weak. The home should be and usually is a shared fellowship of love and devotion. Every institution of society and society itself should seek, and down deep they do seek, to capture something of the family spirit. The family becomes a pattern for them, the goal of their striving. This should be particularly true of the church.

Jesus spoke no greater parable nor told no more appealing story than the parable of the prodigal son, which could just as appropriately be called the parable of the forgiving father.[14] God, for Jesus, was his Father and the Father of his disciples. He taught them to pray, "Our Father." They were and we as Christians are in the family of God. We are children of God and are brothers and sisters in Christ. If children, then we are heirs, "heirs of God and fellow heirs with Christ." [15] We are brethren of all, from every nation and race, who know Christ as Savior and acknowledge him as Lord. The ultimate goal and hope is that men everywhere will be brought into the family of God, and that the world which has become one neighborhood may become one brotherhood. The only hope for such a brotherhood is in the acceptance of a common Father by the peoples of the world.

4. *As a symptom of the condition of society.* No institution of society reflects more accurately the conditions of that society than the home. A study of the history of nations and civilizations—their rise, growth, decline, decay, and ultimate collapse and destruction—reveals that the family is a remarkably accurate barometer of the health or sickness of a nation or a civilization. "No house can be built with mouldering stones; no sound body can grow out of diseased cells. If the social basis, marriage, is rotten, the whole community is rotten." [16] Osborn similarly suggests: "The question of

---

[14] Luke 15:11–32. [15] Rom. 8:17.
[16] Emil Brunner, *Justice and the Social Order,* p. 129.

the right relationship between man and woman lies at the very heart of civilization. If the ties of marriage and the family are broken, there can be little hope for a stable society." [17]

While it is correct to say that as goes the home so will go everything else, yet some have gone to the extreme and tended to make the home the scapegoat for all the ills of our society. This is not fair to the home. While the home may be more responsible than any other agency or institution for the disturbing problems of our world; yet the school, the church, the state, and the business community must share in that responsibility. It should also be remembered that the home is influenced by these other institutions and by its general environment. If the modern home is decadent, what has made it so? Conditions in the home may be "an effect" as well as "a cause." Society and the institutions of society must share some responsibility for the home and conditions in the home—good or bad. Nevertheless, if one wants to understand the situation in a nation or a civilization he should study the home, which is a more or less true barometer of the conditions in the social order. There will be, of course, many homes that will be striking exceptions to the norm. They will rise above the average. They will surmount their environment, and will stand as a standard for and a judge of all that surrounds them.

The Church's Message Concerning the Family

The church has a big stake in the home, just as the home has a big stake in the church. They are laborers together in the promotion of the cause of Christ among men. It is not surprising that the family has been one of the major interests of the Christian church through the centuries. The church has expressed its interest in the family with a considerable degree of consistency, and has given some guidance for every phase of family living. In the main the church's contributions to the home have been constructive.

1. *Concerning the home in general.* One of the distinctive and significant contributions of original Christianity to the family was

[17] Andrew Osborn, *Christian Ethics* (London, Oxford University Press, 1940), p. 179.

what it did to purify family relations and to lift the level of family living. It made these contributions, to some extent, by the use it made and has continued to make of family terms to illustrate and to enrich the spiritual life. "Jesus drew upon it for symbols of the highest attributes of God . . . indeed, the idea of the family may be regarded as one of the most fundamental features of His feeling for human life." [18] Similarly Paul used the relation of the husband and wife as a symbol of the relation of Christ to his church. [19]

Jesus, in relation to his own family, demonstrated the proper relation of a child to his parents. When twelve years of age he went back home from Jerusalem with his mother and Joseph and was subject or obedient to them. [20] He evidently worked with Joseph in the latter's carpenter shop; [21] and later, after the death of Joseph, following the Jewish custom, he, as the eldest son, accepted the responsibility of the headship of the family. He also demonstrated the limits of family loyalty. In response to a deepening sense of his messianic mission he left his family. From henceforth family relations were made subservient to spiritual relations. [22] That he continued to love his mother, however, is evidenced by his solicitude for her while he was dying on the cross. [23]

Jesus also had some specific things to say concerning the family. He taught that marriage was a part of God's original plan for men and women, that he made them male and female, and that when they were joined together in physical union they became one flesh. [24] He then concludes, "What therefore God has joined together, let no man put asunder."

Jesus closely related the proper provision for the material needs of one's parents with the Old Testament command: "Honor thy

[18] Troeltsch, *The Social Teaching of the Christian Churches,* I, 61.
[19] Eph. 5:22–33.   [20] Luke 2:51.   [21] *Ibid.,* 4:22; Matt. 13:55.
[22] Matt. 12:48–50.   [23] John 19:26–27.
[24] Matt. 19:3–6. The Revised Standard Version omits the word "flesh" here, as it does in Ephesians 5:31 and 1 Corinthians 6:16. In Matthew and 1 Corinthians a footnote says "Greek *one flesh.*" The Greek word *sarx* is found in all three places. While in these places and in Genesis 2:24 more than a fleshly union may be involved, yet the union is basically physical. Certainly that would have to be the case of a man's union with a prostitute as referred to in 1 Corinthians 6:16. For a book dealing, to a considerable extent, with this whole matter, see Derrick Sherwin Bailey, *The Mystery of Love and Marriage* (London, S.C.M. Press, 1952).

father and thy mother." He accused the Pharisees of circumventing that commandment by a tradition of theirs.[25] Nevertheless, he placed loyalty to God above loyalty to one's family and demanded supreme love and devotion from his disciples.[26] To put the kingdom first might mean for some the living of the celibate life, the giving up of the privilege of a home.[27] He assured them, however, that they would be amply rewarded.[28] He also plainly said that marriage relations will not carry over into the next life.[29]

Paul also had a number of things to say concerning marriage and the home. In 1 Corinthians 7, he seems to consider virginity superior to or at least more advantageous than marriage.[30] He implies, however, that the celibate life was to be lived only by those who had a special divine gift.[31] Even in this chapter, which cannot be interpreted correctly without some imaginary reconstruction of the letter from the church at Corinth, Paul evidently suggested marriage as the more normal and the safer course for most men and women.[32]

That Paul had a deep appreciation for the family is proved by his figurative use of family terminology to describe his relations to his converts,[33] God's relation to his children,[34] and Christ's relation to his church.[35] In contrast to what may be the correct interpretation, at least on the surface, of 1 Corinthians 7, Ramsay says that the beautiful comparison in Ephesians 5 implies that

in Paul's judgment marriage is in the highest sense the divine life and the perfect harmony of human nature. The church is the body to which Christ is the soul. . . . Each is the necessary complement of the other. The church is the inheritance of Christ and the completion of the purpose of God. So also marriage is the perfection of the life of mankind. The one member of the pair is not complete alone. The two form a unit. Marriage is a part of the purpose of God.[36]

Since the days of Christ and Paul there has been a continuous emphasis by the Christian movement, with varying degrees of consistency, on the home as a divine institution and marriage as a

[25] Matt. 15:1–9; Mark 7:1–13.   [26] Matt. 10:34–39; Luke 14:26.
[27] Matt. 19:10–12.   [28] Mark 10:28–31.   [29] Matt. 22:23–30.
[30] See verses 1, 7, 8, 28, 32, 33, 38.   [31] V. 7.
[32] Vv. 2, 9.   [33] 1 Thess. 2:11.
[34] Rom. 8:15–17; Gal. 3:26; 4:6–7.   [35] 2 Cor. 11:2; Eph. 5:22–33.
[36] William M. Ramsay, *The Teaching of Paul in Terms of the Present Day* (London, Hodder and Stoughton, 1913), p. 264.

sacred union. Claiming the authority of Augustine, and going back to the Douay translation of Ephesians 5:32,[37] the Roman Catholic Church considers marriage one of the sacraments.[38] One Catholic writer sums up the significance for the Roman Catholic Church of the sacramental conception of marriage as follows: "It may be justly said that this doctrine is the basis of the Church's attitude towards matrimony. . . . This is the explanation of her claim that jurisdiction over marriage belongs to her and not to the State." [39]

The reformers considered marriage sacred but not sacramental. Although sacred, it belonged to temporal things and was to be governed by the state and not the church. Luther's advice was that ministers should not interfere in matrimonial questions, that they were obligated to marry those who came to them, but that a religious ceremony was not necessary for it to be a valid marriage. Nevertheless, Luther retained considerable religious content in his suggested marriage procedure and ceremony—in the publication of the banns, the ceremony proper, and the benediction.[40] Under Calvinism marriage belonged to the civil order but the latter was subject to the law of God. "Ministers of the Word were to teach that law, magistrates were to learn and administer it. . . . the courts of the State undertook the control of marriage, but they were themselves under the control of the theologians." [41]

2. *Concerning the nature of marriage.* The church has consistently taught that marriage and the home are written into the nature of men, women, and children. God created us "male and female," he created woman to answer to man,[42] to supplement him or to supply what he lacked. Men and women "answer to each other" both biologically and psychologically. Neither is complete without the other. Just as the bow is made for the violin and the

[37] The reading of this verse in the Douay version is as follows: "This is a great sacrament; but I speak in Christ and in the church."

[38] A sacrament, from the Catholic Church's viewpoint, is "an outward symbol to which Christ has attached a gift of inward grace."

[39] George Hayward Joyce, *Christian Marriage* (2nd ed.; London, Sheed and Ward, 1948), p. 147. See Chapter IV, "The Sacrament of Matrimony."

[40] See "A Marriage Booklet for Simple Pastors" in *Works of Martin Luther,* VI, 225–30.

[41] T. A. Lacey, *Marriage in Church and State* (rev. ed.; London, S.P.C.K., 1947), p. 148.

[42] Gen. 2:18 (ASV—marginal).

violin for the bow and both are necessary if the artist is to produce beautiful harmony; likewise, men and women are made to find their fulfillment in each other. "Marriage is not an artificial regulation of human life, but a natural necessity"; [43] so natural that, to use Voltaire's expression, if we did not have the family "it would have to be invented." [44] It is an integral part of the natural order. And "natural" means "That state of things . . . in which man finds the fullest and most satisfactory development of his nature." [45]

The preceding view of marriage, based on the biblical record of the founding of the home, implies that marriage and the home are not distinctly Christian ordinances or institutions. There are certain fundamental God-ordained natural laws that govern all marriages—Christian and nonchristian. This means that Christian marriage is not a particular kind of marriage, although it should have a unique quality. This view that marriage belongs to the natural order is quite important if one is to interpret correctly the statement by Jesus: "What therefore God has joined together, let no man put asunder." [46]

The church's message, also based on the Bible, is that marriage is not only a natural union but that it should be an exclusive union. The word of the Bible is: "Therefore a man leaves his father and his mother and cleaves to his wife." [47] Marriage is the entire union or, as Lacey expresses it, "an entire conjunction of two lives, to be lived as one." [48] It involves physical union, which is essential to the consummation of marriage, but it involves more. It is the union of two personalities. This means that marriage is much more than a mere contract. There are some minimum requirements that are essential before marriage can be entered into validly, but

the contract is only the instrument by which the state of marriage is brought about. It is not a continuing contract, subject to revision, or capable of being rescinded with due regard for law by agreement of the parties interested. It is completed by consummation. Thenceforward the relations of the parties are determined, not by contract, but by law, divine and human; they are bound to the fulfilment of their mutual duties, not by their own consent, but by a natural obligation.[49]

[43] Lacey, *op. cit.*, p. 2. [44] Lofthouse, *op. cit.*, p. 13.
[45] Lacey, *op. cit.*, p. 1. [46] Matt. 19:6. [47] Gen. 2:24.
[48] Lacey, *op. cit.*, p. 9. [49] *Ibid.*, p. 29.

It seems evident that not only is the union itself but also the exclusive nature of that union written into the nature of men and women. God's command, "Thou shalt not commit adultery," and the statement of Jesus, "What God hath joined together let not man put asunder," are not the arbitrary fiats of an Oriental despot. They are written into the nature of man and into the nature of the home which God himself instituted. In other words, it is only in an exclusive union that men and women find the fullest and most satisfactory development of their natures. Anything less than such an exclusive union is destructive of the best interests not only of the home and society but also of individual men and women.

God not only wrote the home into our natures "from the beginning," but he also has written its basic purposes into our natures. To the first couple God said, "Be fruitful and multiply." This, the propagation of the race, is a continuing purpose of the home. Any husband and wife who can and should have children and who deliberately and permanently thwart this basic purpose of marriage are violating a fundamental law of marriage and will have to pay a penalty for their violation.

There are other natural functions or purposes of the home. By many the home is considered a channel or means for the legitimate expression of the sex urge. Some think of this as a rather low conception or purpose of marriage. We may be convinced, however, that such is not necessarily true if we will consider properly the strength of the sex urge, the lift and enrichment that it can and does bring to human personalities when expressed within proper limits, with proper motives, and in the right spirit; and its terribly degrading effects when expressed wrongly or on a low level. However, for a proper evaluation of sex expression as a purpose of marriage we must place this purpose in its proper setting, surrounded by more positive functions.

Another original purpose of marriage is at least implied in the creation story. God said, "It is not good that the man should be alone." [50] The home supplies or should supply for men and women what their natures, their total personalities, demand. The home should provide a place of abiding love and understanding sympathy. It should be a place of renewal of faith and courage. It should inspire and put purpose and drive into life.

[50] Gen. 2:18.

There is at least one distinctively Christian purpose for the home. Once this purpose becomes a living reality in the home, it will flavor every phase of family life. This purpose, which is the promotion of the kingdom of God among men, is strongly implied, although it is never directly stated, by Jesus. The Christian home is not an end; it is a means to a broader and a more significant end. If the Christian husband and wife will let this conception of the home grip their lives, it will tend to purify and glorify every relation within the home and will deepen and make more meaningful every natural purpose of the home. It will give an added quality to every phase of their lives together. They will recognize themselves as co-laborers with God in his work in the world.

3. *Concerning celibacy.* In the church of the early Christian centuries there were two paradoxical trends, trends that are still prevalent to a considerable degree. There was a rather high regard for marriage and the home attended by high standards of sexual morality—before and after marriage. On the other hand, there was a strong ascetic emphasis with a glorification of celibacy and a rather low conception of sex and its place in life—within as well as outside marriage.[51]

The tendency to glorify celibacy, which was manifested so early in the Christian movement in general but among the heretical groups in particular, was not derived from the Jewish heritage of Christianity. Marriage was considered by the Jews "a duty to be performed for the sake of the Law, and . . . for the sake of preserving the nation."[52] Why, then, was this ascetic trend, with its exaltation of celibacy, accepted into the stream of the Christian movement? The following are some possible explanations: (1) the immoral conditions within the Roman Empire, (2) the identification of sex with the worldly or carnal life which the Christian was supposed to renounce, (3) the sharp division, in so much Christian thinking of the times, between the flesh, which was considered evil, and the spirit, which was considered good—a distinction which came primarily from certain phases of Greek philosophy, (4) the

[51] Troeltsch, *op. cit.*, I, 129-32.
[52] Armin H. Koller, *The Foundations of Jewish Ethics* (New York, Macmillan, 1929), p. 211; cf. *Jewish Encyclopedia* (New York, Funk & Wagnall's, 1904), VIII, 335-49.

influence or at least the utilization of certain of Paul's writings such as Romans 8, 1 Corinthians 7, and Galatians 5, and (5) the expected early return of the Lord.

Among the early church fathers were some extremists who considered marriage little better than adultery. Tertullian said that marriage "consists of that which is the essence of fornication," one is legal, the other illegal; there is a "diversity of illicitness." [53] Jerome said that whatever praise marriage had was had because it furnished virgins.[54] Other church leaders, such as Chrysostom [55] and Augustine,[56] in a sense and to a degree, defended marriage. Cadoux sums up the general position of the early church as follows: "Marriage . . . was regarded as a very good and providentially ordained second-best." [57]

It was more or less natural that clerical celibacy should become a fixed pattern.[58] "By the middle of the fifth century the law of clerical celibacy had obtained general recognition in the West." [59] The Eastern Church, however, was not so strict. The reformers, who did not object to voluntary celibacy, were united in their opposition to compulsory clerical celibacy. Zwingli and his associates were the first to make a concerted attack on it,[60] followed later by Luther and Calvin. It was Luther who, in his rather crude way, said: "The pope has as little power to command this, [celibacy] as he has to forbid

[53] "On Exhortation to Chastity," IX, in Alexander Roberts and James Donaldson (eds.), *Ante-Nicene Fathers* (New York, Christian Literature Co., 1885), IV, 55.

[54] "The Letters of St. Jerome," XXII, 20, in Philip Schaff and Henry Wace (eds.), *Nicene and Post-Nicene Fathers* (2nd series; New York, Christian Literature Co., 1893), VI, 30.

[55] "Homilies on Hebrews," VII, in Philip Schaff (ed.), *Nicene and Post-Nicene Fathers* (1st series; New York, Christian Literature Co., 1889), XIV, 402.

[56] See "On the Good of Marriage" and "Of Holy Virginity," *ibid.*, III, 397–438.

[57] Cadoux, *The Early Church and the World*, p. 444.

[58] For a study of clerical celibacy see Henry C. Lea, *History of Sacerdotal Celibacy in the Christian Church* (4th ed., rev.; London, Watts and Co., 1932); and Herbert B. Workman, *The Evolution of the Monastic Ideal* (London, Epworth Press, 1927).

[59] H. A. Ayrinhac, *General Legislation in the New Code of Canon Law* (New York, Longmans, Green, 1923), p. 274.

[60] See S. M. Jackson, *Huldreich Zwingli* (2nd ed. rev.; New York, Putnam's, 1900), pp. 25–39.

eating, drinking, the natural movement of the bowels or growing fat." [61]

Through the centuries the general Protestant position has remained about the same. Celibacy has been approved if voluntary, but it has not been especially honored. Many women and a few men have given up marriage and a home for the sake of the kingdom. It has been believed, however, that anyone who should be a celibate will be given the grace or the gift to live a life of "undisquieted continency." Marriage has been honored and considered the normal life for most people. Sex expression within marriage has been defended as a natural and potentially an enriching experience. Any expression of sex outside marriage has been strongly condemned.

4. *Concerning women.* One of the major contributions of Christianity to the family has been what it has done for women. Here again the picture has not always been entirely clear. The tendency in the main, however, has been toward an improvement of the status of women which, in turn, has contributed to a more democratic and generally a higher type of family life.

Jesus lifted the level of womanhood, just as he did for every other oppressed, underprivileged group. He associated with them more freely than was the custom in his day. Some of his followers and closest associates were women. They proved their appreciation for him and their devotion to him by being the last at his cross and the first at his tomb. He demonstrated his confidence in them by revealing himself for the first time after his resurrection to one of them, Mary Magdalene, and by sending her to his disciples with the message that he had risen from the dead. [62]

While Paul counseled women to conform to the customs of their day, restricted considerably their participation in church life, advised subordination to their husbands in the home and in the church, and seemed to fear that they might abuse their new-found liberty, yet his fundamental principle was: "There is neither male nor female; for you are all one in Christ Jesus." [63] The husband was to be the head of the wife; "nevertheless the subjection of the body to the head is of another order than that of a slave to a master. The dif-

---

[61] Luther, *op. cit.*, II, 122.   [62] John 20:4–18.   [63] Gal. 3:28.

ference is one of function, not of standing or essence. The head and the body are complements of each other." [64]

What seemed, on the surface, to be an inner conflict in Paul, became a clear paradox in the early Christian movement. Because celibacy was generally accepted as superior to marriage, there was a more or less inevitable tendency to condemn, or at least to deprecate sex expression of any kind. Women as the means or instrument, from man's viewpoint, for such expression were looked down on or condemned. One church council [65] decreed that women, because of their impurity, could no longer receive the sacrament with naked hands. Tertullian, whom Cadoux calls the woman hater,[66] went so far as to say: "The sentence of God on this sex of yours lives in this age: . . . *You* are the devil's gateway: . . . *you* are the first deserter of the divine law: *you* are she who persuaded him whom the devil was not valiant enough to attack. . . . On account of *your* desert—that is, death—even the Son of God had to die." [67]

But the tendency to glorify celibacy also contributed to an exaltation of women and enlarged their place in the life and work of the churches. Orders of virgins and widows arose, dedicated to service in and through the churches. Not only those who were members of these orders but women in general came to fill "an important and recognized place in the life of the Christian community." [68]

The double tendency to honor woman and to place her on a spiritual equality with man, but at the same time to make her inferior to or at least subservient in certain areas to man, has been the continuing position of the Christian movement. The relative emphasis has differed at various times and among different groups, but these two elements have been constant phases of the picture. For example, Thomas Aquinas says, "The image of God in its principle signification—namely, the intellectual nature—is found both in man

[64] Osborn, *op. cit.*, p. 183.

[65] Una B. Sait, *New Horizons for the Family* (New York, Macmillan, 1938), p. 153.

[66] *Op. cit.*, p. 443.

[67] "On the Apparel of Women," Book I, Ch. 1, in Roberts and Donaldson (eds.), *The Ante-Nicene Fathers*, IV, 4.

[68] Cadoux, *op. cit.*, p. 597.

and in woman. . . . But in a secondary sense the image of God is found in man and not in women: for man is the beginning and end of woman, as God is the beginning and end of every creature." [69]

Lecky [70] contends that Christianity glorified the feminine qualities or virtues of gentleness, humility, and love, and that this fact tended to give women a conspicuous place in the early work of the Christian movement. He makes the rather interesting observation that in the "great religious convulsions of the sixteenth century the feminine type followed Catholicism, while Protestantism inclined more to the masculine type." [71]

The main thing of significance is to remember that the general tendency of Christianity has been to give women a new dignity and an improved status within and outside the home. This, in turn, has made a distinct contribution to the shaping of the home, in areas touched and influenced by the Christian movement.

5. *Concerning divorce.* In the days when Christianity was born, divorce was prevalent among the Jews and the Greeks, but particularly prevalent among the Romans. The latter considered marriage a civil contract and permitted divorce at the will of either party. Divorce became so general that "the stability of married life was very seriously impaired." [72] By the time of the Augustan Age divorce was so common that "it had become a public scandal." [73]

It was natural that Jesus and Paul would both have to face the matter of divorce, although it should be remembered that they never attempted to discuss it systematically. Most of what they said concerning it grew out of particular questions that were directed to them. In the case of Paul's teachings in 1 Corinthians 7 we would know better how to interpret what he said if we were acquainted with the exact nature of the problems that had arisen in the Corinthian group and knew the questions the church had asked Paul in the letter sent to him.

[69] Bede Jarrett, *Social Theories of the Middle Ages, 1200–1500* (London, Ernest Benn, 1926), p. 70.

[70] Lecky, *History of European Morals*, II, 363 ff.

[71] *Ibid.*, p. 368.   [72] *Ibid.*, II, 307.

[73] Willystine Goodsell, *A History of Marriage and the Family* (rev. ed.; New York, Macmillan, 1934), p. 145.

The difference, at least on the surface, in Matthew's and Mark's
record of what Jesus said in response to the question of the Pharisees,[74] and between Matthew's record of the teachings of Jesus and
Paul's instructions to the Corinthians, where he claims the authority
of the Lord,[75] have led more or less naturally to varied viewpoints
concerning the message of the New Testament concerning divorce.[76]
Some Christian groups, including one major group—Roman Catholics, have contended that there is no justifiable grounds for divorce
in the New Testament. Those who have taken this position have
followed, in the main, Paul's teachings. When they refer to the
teachings of Jesus concerning divorce they have used, in the main,
Mark's account rather than Matthew's. They have explained away
the latter by saying that the exception—"for fornication"—that Matthew credits to Jesus [77] is either an interpolation, or that it does not
give the right of remarriage even to the innocent party.[78]

There are other Christian groups and leaders who have justified
and do justify divorce, with the right of remarriage for the innocent
party, in the case of adultery. Some few others believe the New
Testament would justify divorce and remarriage not only on the
grounds of adultery but also for desertion. The latter is based on
what is generally called the Pauline privilege.[79]

Some Christians take a more liberal position than any of the
above. They consider divorce or annulment justifiable on several
grounds. This was true of most of the Reformers. One reason for
their liberality was the fact that they considered the Old Testament
equally authoritative with the New Testament. In addition, their
position grew, to a degree, out of their viewpoint concerning the purpose of marriage, which in turn was, to a considerable degree, a re-

[74] Matt. 19:3-12; Mark 10:2-12.   [75] 1 Cor. 7:10-11.
[76] A study of standard commentaries on the passages from Matthew, Mark,
and 1 Corinthians would reveal widely divergent viewpoints. The same diver-
gence would be seen in a study of books on the teachings of Jesus.
[77] Matt. 5:32; 19:9.
[78] The Scriptures referring directly and by strong implication to divorce are:
Deut. 22:13-19, 28-29; 24:1-4; Lev. 21:7, 14; Ezek. 44:22; Mal. 2:15-16;
Matt. 5:31-32; 19:3-12; Mark 10:2-12; Luke 16:18; Rom. 7:2-3; 1 Cor.
7:10-11.
[79] 1 Cor. 7:12-16. For a study of the Pauline privilege from the Roman
Catholic viewpoint, see Francis J. Winslow, *The Pauline Privilege and the
Constitutions of Canon 1125* (New York, Field Afar Press, 1948).

sult of the day in which they lived. For them a chief purpose of marriage was to serve as a channel for the legitimate expression of the sex urge. Anything that prevented a marriage from fulfilling this, or other of its fundamental functions, was a justifiable grounds for divorce or annulment, and it is difficult at times to know which of the latter they meant.

There also have been rather sharp differences of opinion concerning the applicability, within the framework of an evil world, of the New Testament ethic in general, including its family ethic. The Christian conception of marriage and of divorce was "a novelty in the world into which Christianity" was born.[80] It ran counter to the whole tenor and spirit of the age. The conflict or tension between what the church taught and what the people, even many Christians, practiced became so great that it seemed that an adjustment of the ideal was practically forced upon the Christian movement. By the fourth century "the yoke of Christian marriage was proving too heavy for the half converted masses who were beginning to invade the Church." [81] The Reformers were conscious of this problem. Lacey says that they denounced as not only untrue but immoral the Catholic doctrine of the indissolubility of marriage; they contended that human nature was too corrupt for the doctrine "and therefore divorce without remarriage was a direct encouragement of sin." [82]

There were two paths followed by Christian groups in the adjustment of the ideal to an evil world. One was annulment or nullity and the other was divorce.[83] The Eastern or the Greek church, followed in the main by Protestants, took the divorce route, while the Western or Roman Catholic Church took largely the route of annulment.[84] There is always a real danger, when an adjustment of the Christian standard is considered necessary, that the adjustment will be defended as the ideal and hence the vision of the ideal will

[80] Kenneth E. Kirk, *Marriage and Divorce* (2nd ed.; London, Hodder and Stoughton, 1948), p. 33.

[81] *Ibid.*, p. 43.   [82] Lacey, *op. cit.*, p. 151.

[83] For a definition of nullity and the distinction from divorce, see Arthur Tarleton Macmillan, *What Is Christian Marriage?* (London, Macmillan, 1944), pp. 80 ff., and Kirk, *op. cit.*, p. 41.

[84] It is the contention of Roman Catholic writers that "in the West the principle of indissolubility was upheld. The Roman See never wavered" (Joyce, *op. cit.*, p. 331). Three of the thirteen chapters in Joyce's book are on the indissolubility of marriage.

77

be lost. This has happened at times in regard to marriage and divorce.

One of the chief factors determining the viewpoint of various Christian groups in regard to divorce has been their relation to and theory concerning the state and its functions. This helps to explain the difference in the Eastern and Western churches. The Eastern or Greek church was under greater pressure from the state, and "tolerated divorce in accordance with the civil legislation." [85] Similarly, Luther contended that the law of Christ was for the conscience of the individual and was not necessarily to be the standard of secular law.[86] He considered marriage a civil matter, and hence the state had the right to legislate in regard to marriage and divorce. Calvinism, likewise, made marriage a civil matter, but the civil authority was under the command of God and judges were to learn from theologians. The basis for divorce under Calvinism differed rather fundamentally from the general position of Lutheranism. According to the latter, whatever the state decreed was to be approved. According to Calvinism the state was to recognize as grounds for divorce only what the church considered to be approved by the revelation of God.

The Western or Roman Catholic Church has persistently contended that she, and she alone, has authority in regard to marriage. Whenever the state legislates concerning marriage and divorce it is an intruder. "Marriage is . . . by its very nature above human law." [87] Marriage of the baptized is considered a sacrament, and where a sacrament is involved the civil courts have "no competence." "Matrimonial causes must belong to the ecclesiastical forum." [88]

5. *Conclusion.* Christianity by "placing the child in the midst," by lifting the level of women, by making marriage a sacred union, and in many other ways has contributed to the stability of the home. It has tended to keep before the people the Christian ideal for the home. It must be admitted that the church's message is always more Christian than its practice, but the church has never lost entirely

[85] *Ibid.,* p. 331.   [86] Macmillan, *op. cit.,* p. 94.
[87] *The Catholic Encyclopedia* (New York, Appleton, 1910), IX, 699.
[88] Joyce, *op. cit.,* p. vii.

the vision of the Christian ideal for the home. The pull has been toward a higher, a more Christian type of family life. The Christian ethic has been a major factor in shaping and reshaping family life wherever the Christian movement has spread.

The Contemporary Family

Let us turn now from the biblical and the historical to a consideration of the contemporary family, giving particular emphasis to the American home, with some attention to its historic roots.[89]

1. *Characteristics of the contemporary home.* There have been and are so many different American family types and patterns that one may question if we can correctly speak of a "traditional American family." We have the rural family and the urban family, the Negro family and the Mexican family, and the families of many other racial and national groups. [90] However, in spite of wide variations there has been and is a more or less generally accepted ideal or dream for the American family. Although the various types of families have certain distinctive characteristics, yet the pull is toward conformity to the American ideal. The variants in turn shape, to a degree, the American dream for the family.

The above correctly implies that the traditional American family,

[89] Examples of books that discuss family life in different cultures are the following: Arthur Phillips (ed.), *Survey of African Marriage and Family Life* (London, Oxford University Press, 1953)—a comprehensive, scholarly work; A. R. Radcliffe-Brown and Daryll Forde (eds.), *African Systems of Kinship and Marriage* (London, Oxford University Press, 1950)—a publication of the International African Institute, as is true of the one edited by Phillips; Marion J. Levy, Jr., *The Family Revolution in Modern China* (Cambridge, Harvard University Press, 1949); Irma Highbaugh, *Family Life in West China* (New York, Agricultural Missions, 1948)—more popular in style than any of the preceding; Lin Yueh-Hwa, *The Golden Wing* (New York, Oxford University Press, 1947)—subtitle: "A Sociological Study of Chinese Familism," presented somewhat in a dramatic, novel approach. A standard work for many years on primitive marriage has been the two-volume work *The Mystic Rose* by Ernest Crawley, revised by Theodore Besterman (2nd ed.; London, Methuen and Co., 1927). A recent publication—Stuart A. Queen and John B. Adams, *The Family in Various Cultures* (Philadelphia, Lippincott, 1952)—is a survey of eleven family systems; while the journal *Marriage and Family Living* for November, 1954, under the guest editorship of William F. Ogburn, presents articles on the family in sixteen countries or regions.

[90] See Nimkoff, *op. cit.*, Chaps. 5, 7, and 8.

as is true of the family in any area of the world, has its roots deep in the past. In other words, the family at any particular point in history has a long ancestry.[91] Those who have come to our shores from other parts of the world have made their distinctive contributions to the American family pattern. We should acknowledge our indebtedness to those of every nation who have made us "a nation of nations," the melting pot of the world.

Space will not permit a thorough discussion of the many factors, some ancestral and others environmental, that shaped the early American family. Among the most important of those factors were the democratic ideals of the founders of our nation and the Christian principles so closely related to that democratic dream. Respect for human personality as such and the attendant emphasis on the rights of the individual were conducive to a democratic type of family life. The application of this democratic spirit to family life, however, has only been made in recent years, and even then quite imperfectly and incompletely in some areas.

The fact that the United States has been predominantly Protestant helps to explain the dominant conception of marriage and the home. The authority of the state over marriage and divorce has been rather generally recognized. The church, with the exception of the Roman Catholic, has relinquished most of its controls in the area.[92]

A major characteristic of the modern family, in the United States and elsewhere, is that it is a changing family. Baber suggests that no social institution, including the family, "can make a *final* adjustment to society if it wishes to survive." [93] However, the contemporary period is one of extraordinary transition and change for civilization in general and for the home in particular.

In America the home is changing in type—from a patriarchal to a democratic type of home; in size—from an average family unit of 4.7 in 1900 to 3.8 in 1940, with some increase since 1940; in functions—from a home where most of the interests of the members of the family centered, to one reduced to one or two of the more important functions of life; in stability—from a home relatively stable to a home that is badly disorganized.

[91] Goodsell, *op. cit.*, gives several chapters to the American home.

[92] Nimkoff, *op. cit.*, p. 277.

[93] Ray E. Baber, *Marriage and the Family* (New York, McGraw-Hill, 1939), p. 4.

Goodsell concludes that "perhaps the characteristic of the twentieth-century family that most sharply challenges the attention of the student of family history is its instability." [94] Nimkoff rather conservatively suggests, "The family today seems to be in considerable distress." [95] The prevalence of divorce is one indication or symbol of this instability. During a recent year there were approximately one-third as many divorces as marriages in the United States, with a continuing rate of about one-fourth.

There are two extreme views concerning the results of the changes in contemporary family life. There are some people who predict doom and destruction for the home and for the world. There are others who as strongly contend that the family is merely adjusting itself to changing conditions, and that out of the contemporary changes will come a higher type of family life. There seems to be some truth to both contentions. Some of the changes in family life must be viewed with concern and even alarm. This is certainly true of the increasing instability of the home. On the other hand, there are some changes that are necessary if the family is to survive, and still others that seemingly may eventuate in a higher type of family life. For example, the tendency toward a democratic type of family living seems to be a natural and necessary trend in the contemporary period. The democratic home, in turn, has contributed to the instability of the modern family, but it may eventually mean a higher quality of family experience.

2. *Factors shaping the contemporary home.* It has been suggested that the contemporary family is a changing family and that this must be true, to some extent, if it is to adjust itself to a changing culture. The changing nature of the family has created problems for it because of the rapidity of the changes, "the changeableness of change," and the attendant necessity to adjust itself "to the condition of continuous change." [96]

The loss, to a considerable degree, of some functions and the shifting emphases in regard to others has created for the contemporary family many of its problems. "The historic family was . . . a multifunctional institution, with affectional, biological, economic,

---

[94] Goodsell, *op. cit.*, p. 481.   [95] *Op. cit.*, p. 87.
[96] Ernest R. Groves, *The Family and Its Social Functions* (Chicago, Lippincott, 1940), p. 453.

protective, educational, recreational, religious, and status-giving functions." [97] Several of these functions have been lost or reduced considerably in importance in the home. The few functions that are left, such as the biological, the affectional, and what Truxal and Merrill call "the socializing," have not only been retained but "have increased relatively in importance with the diminutions suffered in the others." [98] The loss or change of functions for the family are somewhat in proportion to the integration of the family into the culture surrounding it. Isolated families, those largely untouched by the main stream of cultural diffusion, remain relatively unchanged. This loss or reduction in the importance of certain functions is both an indication of and a reason for the changing nature of the modern family. There are many factors that have contributed to the changing emphasis on and significance of the functions of the family. Among the more important or more generally recognized of these factors are: the changing status of women, the industrialization and urbanization of life, and science.

There are other important factors affecting the family, not so generally recognized, that are largely psychological. Among these are what Folsom calls an "elaboration of wants," [99] "the liberation of love," [100] and "individuation and democracy," [101] all of which are contributing factors to the changing nature of the family, the latter two contributing particularly to its instability.

There can be no doubt about the important contribution of Christianity to the early American family. What about its impact on the modern American home? It may be that Christianity is less dominant in the average American home than formerly, but there is plenty of evidence that religion is a major factor in determining the happiness and the stability of the home. Burgess and Cottrell in their careful study came to the following conclusion: "Whatever data were examined to test the relation to marital adjustment of religious sentiments, interests, and activities—Sunday-school or church attendance, place of marriage, or official performing the ceremony —all agree in showing a positive association." [102] Truxal and Merrill

[97] Andrew G. Truxal and Francis E. Merrill, *The Family in American Culture* (New York, Prentice-Hall, 1947), p. 326.

[98] *Ibid.*, p. 350.   [99] Sowers and Mullen, *op. cit.*, p. 6.

[100] *Ibid.*, p. 13.   [101] *Ibid.*, p. 21.

[102] Ernest W. Burgess and Leonard S. Cottrell, Jr., *Predicting Success or Failure in Marriage* (New York, Prentice-Hall, 1939), p. 126.

conclude: "Although the close reciprocal relationship between church and family has been considerably modified by the secular changes taking place in our society, the teachings and precepts of historical Christianity are still fundamental to the family." [103]

3. *Increased interest in the home.* One of the most encouraging signs in the contemporary period is the awakening concern about, interest in, and provision for the family and its problems. For many years there have been family service agencies, which have majored, in the main, on provision for the material needs of families in trouble. In more recent years the emphasis has been more on counseling service for the family. In a study of thirty-five agencies providing marriage counseling service, Emily Hartshorne Mudd discovered that the two oldest of these services were opened in 1928. In contrast, thirteen of the services were opened in one five-year period—1945–1950.[104] There are now several national agencies working in the field, with some of them having branch organizations on the state and local community levels.[105] Mrs. Mudd lists [106] the following as the best known and most active agencies on the national level: Family Service Association of America, with 238 member agencies; the National Council on Family Relations, with twenty-five state and five regional councils; the National Catholic Welfare Conference; the Central Conference of American Rabbis; the National Council of the Churches of Christ in America; and the American Association of Marriage Counselors. The last, which was organized in 1943, is composed of those who work professionally in the field.

There have been and are a number of conferences on the family; among these have been the National Conference on Family Life in Washington and the Mid-Century White House Conference on Children and Youth at Washington in 1950. Typical of an annual conference is the Groves Conference on Conservation of Marriage and the Family, which has met annually for the past fifteen years or more at Chapel Hill, North Carolina.

[103] *Op. cit.*, p. 52.
[104] *The Practice of Marriage Counseling* (New York, Association Press, 1951), p. 63.
[105] For a list of agencies, see Mudd, *op. cit.*, pp. 251–56, and for a brief statement of the history, purpose, and program of a number of the better known agencies, see pp. 257–325.
[106] *Ibid.*, p. 11.

There are a number of localized agencies that provide much more than a counseling service to a local constituency. Some of these provide a very broad service to the community, and the influence of some reach out far beyond the borders of the local community. A good example of such an agency is the American Institute of Family Relations of Los Angeles. It is one of the oldest agencies, having been organized in 1930. The staff consists "of nearly 50 marriage counselors," and they "give about 15,000 consultations a year," in addition to a widespread educational program.[107] The Institute has available pamphlets for distribution, provides extension courses for groups and for home study, and publishes a monthly news bulletin entitled *Family Life*. The Association for Family Living of Chicago is another agency that provides a service beyond the confines of its own city. It has made available for several years a well organized listing of recent pamphlet publications on the child, sex, courtship and marriage, and other related subjects.

The National Council of the Churches of Christ carries on a rather extensive program. Under the Division of Christian Education there is a Joint Department of Family Life. The work of this department is carried on through five standing committees. "They are: (1) marriage and family counseling; (2) the family and the community; (3) education for Christian family life; (4) National Family Week; and (5) literature and other resources."[108]

There has also been a noticeable increase in the interest in the family on the college level. Mudd lists thirty-five specific marriage counseling agencies: ten of these are under the auspices of a college or university. An increasing number of colleges are also offering courses on the family and with more of an emphasis on preparing college men and women for the responsibilities of married life. While courses in the family had been offered in a few colleges and theological seminaries since the turn of the century, Ernest R. Groves began his pioneering work of preparing college men and women for marriage, at the University of North Carolina, as late as 1927. Bowman in 1949 made a study of 1,370 colleges, junior and senior, and universities. Of the 1,270 that replied, 632 (49.8

[107] From a personal letter from Paul Popenoe, Nov. 18, 1954.
[108] Letter from Richard E. Lentz, Executive Director of the Joint Department of Family Life, dated Nov. 19, 1954.

per cent) had at least one course in the area of family-life education. A study of thirty senior colleges in the South revealed that all
except one had at least one course on the family. The one college
that did not have a course was in the process of changing from a
junior to a senior college. Eleven of the colleges offered two or
more courses, with one having four. Many of these courses represented, however, more of a theoretical, sociological approach than
a practical, pupil-centered approach.

The family has developed rapidly as a major field of interest and
research by sociologists and other social scientists. In some of the
larger educational centers there are now departments of family
sociology, with a number of top sociologists majoring in the area of
the family. These men, along with those representing other disciplines, have produced in recent years a tremendous body of literature.[109]

4. *The church's relation to the contemporary family.* The churches
and denominations have shared in this increased interest in the family. At least one major denomination, the Presbyterian Church of
the U.S.A., has completely rewritten its church-school materials to
make them home and church centered. It is reported that approximately three million dollars were spent on this project. Another
denomination, the Southern Baptist Convention, through the Training Union Department of its Sunday School Board has provided a
graded series of study-course books on the home. The same board
established in 1945 a Home Curriculum Department, which, among
other things, produces *Home Life*, a monthly publication which has
reached a circulation of approximately 750,000.

It is natural that churches should respond favorably to the modern
interest in the family. These two basic institutions are very closely

---

[109] Most of the major publishers of textbooks have one or more titles available.
Among them are books with varying emphases written or edited by Anshen
(Harper), Baker (McGraw-Hill), Becker and Hill (Heath), Bernard (Harper),
Bowman (McGraw-Hill), Burgess and Locke (American Book Co.), Cavan
(Crowell), Christensen (Ronald), Elmer (Ginn), Fishburn and Burgess
(Doubleday), Folsom (Wiley), Groves (Lippincott), Harper (Houghton Mif-
flin), Skidmore and Cannon (Harper), Truxal and Merrill (McGraw-Hill).
There are a number of texts, written by and presenting the viewpoint of Roman
Catholics. One of the best and most recent is John J. Kane's *Marriage and the
Family: A Catholic Approach* (New York, Dryden Press, 1952).

related—they belong together. The home, if really Christian, is in the truest sense a church: a group of called-out ones, an agency for personal evangelism, a place of worship, a school for the teaching of basic religious and moral principles, and a fellowship of kindred hearts. The church, on the other hand, is a family and should have the spirit of a family. It is composed of brothers and sisters who should love one another and share with one another in every time of need.

Although the church and home may not be as close to each other as formerly, nevertheless they are still dependent, to a large degree, on each other. At their best, both of them have common aims or goals. They "work with the same purpose and the same material. The purpose is highest human fulfillment, and the material is human life." [110] Neither can fulfill most effectively its functions without the assistance of the other. They are laborers together in the training of children, in the maturing of adults, in the promotion of the well-being of society, and in the moral and spiritual guidance and renewal of civilization. Their own future and the future of the world are dependent, to a considerable degree, upon the faithful performance by each of its distinctive functions, and at the same time their constructive cooperation with each other in the attainment of their common purposes.

The Future of the Family

Does the family have a future? There are conditions that threaten it; will they destroy it? Is it possible that society has reached the stage when it no longer needs the family? Can the functions of the family be performed by the state or by other social institutions, under the supervision of the state?

1. *The threat to the family.* It must be admitted that there are conditions within our nation, within Western civilization, and within civilization in general that threaten the family. As suggested previously, the family is inevitably influenced by its environment, as well as being a contributor to the shaping of that environment. If conditions surrounding the home are corrupt, decadent, or chang-

[110] Regina W. Wieman, *The Modern Family and the Church* (New York, Harper, 1937), p. 143.

ing they will affect the home. If the world is in a period of major transition, if a whole new world order is in the process of being born, then the home will be in the process of transition. A period of major change is always dangerous. If the transition is not made intelligently and rapidly enough, serious maladjustments may arise, so serious that they may threaten the continuance of society and its institutions.

There are one or two more tangible, if not more immediate threats, particularly to the American home. One is the high divorce rate,[111] which many believe threatens to undermine the very foundation of the American home. In 1867, when the first reliable statistics on divorce in the United States were gathered, there were 9,937 divorces, or a rate of 0.3 divorces per 1,000 population. After that, the divorce rate increased more rapidly than the marriage rate or the rate of population growth. In 1914 the annual figure of 100,000 divorces was reached for the first time, with a rate of 1.0 divorces per 1,000 population. By 1929 the number had reached 205,876, or a rate of 1.7 divorces per 1,000 population. The peak was reached in 1946 when 613,000 divorces were granted in the United States, or a rate of 4.3 divorces per 1,000 population. Since then the number of divorces and the rate have tapered off somewhat, but time alone will reveal whether or not this decrease is permanent or temporary. "A rate of one divorce for about every four new marriages seems probable . . . for the immediate years ahead." [112]

Another threat to the American home is the growing prevalence of extramarital sex relations. If Kinsey's controversial studies [113]

---

[111] There are a few publications dealing with the divorce problem in general, such as Edmund Bergler, *Divorce Won't Help* (New York, Harper, 1948), and Ernest R. Groves, *Conserving Marriage and the Family* (New York, Harper, 1944). Bergler has another book entitled *Conflict in Marriage* (New York, Harper, 1949) with the subtitle, "The Unhappy Undivorced." J. Louise Despert has a book on *Children of Divorce* (Garden City, N.Y., Doubleday, 1953).

[112] John Sirjamaki, *The American Family in the Twentieth Century* (Cambridge, Harvard University Press, 1953), p. 165. Desertion and separation, according to the census of 1940, were more than twice as common as divorce.

[113] Alfred C. Kinsey *et al.*, *Sexual Behavior in the Human Male* (Philadelphia, W. B. Saunders, 1948); and *Sexual Behavior in the Human Female* (Philadelphia, W. B. Saunders, 1953). For appraisals of the Kinsey reports, from somewhat different viewpoints, see Albert Deutsch (ed.), *Sex Habits of American Men* (New York, Prentice-Hall, 1948), a symposium on the first of the Kinsey reports; Seward Hiltner, *Sex Ethics and the Kinsey Reports* (New York, Associa-

are even relatively correct, they paint a very dark picture of the sex morals of American men and women. While there does not seem to be available any reliable comparative studies, yet irregular sexual behavior, including sex perversion of all kinds, is evidently more prevalent today than at any time in the history of our nation. Is this fact a threat to our nation and to the institutions of our society, including the home? It is certainly true that there is no surer indicator of the moral decline and the possible collapse of a nation or a civilization than for the sex morals of the people to become decadent.

The threat to the family is not so great as long as deviations from the norm are recognized as deviations. There is real danger, however, when any deviation becomes so common that it is defended as a part or a phase of the norm. There is a tendency in that direction in regard to divorce and extramarital relations. Many people defend both as the normal and natural thing under certain conditions. They are not to be condemned as wrong within themselves. If such an attitude becomes dominant, then the pattern of the American family ethic will have been changed and the whole family structure will be threatened.

2. *The permanence of the family.* We do not mean to imply by what we have said that the actual continuance of the home is endangered. It is even possible that the high divorce rate may not be an unmixed evil. It may represent a struggle toward a higher type of family solidarity: a family that will provide reasonable satisfaction to the mother and the children as well as to the husband and father.

Possibly Westermarck goes too far when, after suggesting that increasing divorce rates do not mean ruin to marriage, he says: "Far from being its enemy, divorce is rather its saviour. . . . it is . . . a means of preserving the dignity of marriage by putting an end to unions that are a disgrace to its name." [114] We can agree, however,

---

tion Press, 1953), which takes into account both of the reports and appraises them from the viewpoint of Christian ethics; and W. Norman Pittenger, *The Christian View of Sexual Behavior* (Greenwich, Conn., Seabury Press, 1954)—subtitle, "A Reaction to the Kinsey Report"—is a brief attempt at a statement of Christian sexuality, at a discussion of sex within a theological context.

[114] Edward Westermarck, *The Future of Marriage in Western Civilisation* (New York, Macmillan, 1936), p. 152.

with Sirjamaki that "the great volume of divorces and separations today . . . do not appear to be a protest against marriage itself." [115]

Those who believe that the sexual irregularities of the contemporary period will destroy the home may tend to base marriage too largely upon sex and to make the expressions of sex too exclusively physical. The fullest expression of the sex urge is as much psychological as physiological. "Marriage embraces much more than the gratification of the sexual impulse; and purely sexual relations can never serve as substitutes for those more comprehensive relations between men and women which, under the name of marriage, constitute a social institution of great importance." [116] Some of the deepest and more persistent hungers or urges of the human person can be satisfied only in a love-motivated relation of a husband and a wife. God has written the home deep into the nature of men and women. They are made to answer to one another, to find their fulfillment in one another. The home will continue as long as men are men and women are women. "It is as secure as the human race itself." [117]

The home will have to continue to make adjustments to changing conditions. It has, in the past, demonstrated a remarkable capacity for survival. Cultures and civilizations have risen and fallen but the home has continued. It has "survived every social change and has outlived the disintegration of one social system after another." [118] Westermarck comes to a similar conclusion. He says:

> So far as I can see . . . there is every reason to believe that the unity of sensual and spiritual elements in sexual love, leading to a more or less durable community of life in a common home, and the desire for the love of offspring, are factors which will remain lasting obstacles to the extinction of marriage and the collapse of the family, because they are too deeply rooted in human nature to fade away, and can find adequate satisfaction only in some form of marriage and the family founded upon it.[119]

Sirjamaki goes so far as to say that there is "nothing fundamentally wrong with marriages, but married people are, as a matter of fact,

[115] *Op. cit.*, p. 171.   [116] Westermarck, *op. cit.*, p. 155.
[117] Groves, *The Family and Its Social Functions*, p. 557.
[118] Sidney E. Goldstein in Sowers and Mullen, *op. cit.*, p. 202.
[119] *Op. cit.*, p. 170.

happier as a group than ever before and hold to higher standards than prevailed in any previous period." [120]

The preceding is not meant to be a superficially optimistic view. It merely means that the actual existence of the family is assured. On the other hand, the family can suffer additional disintegration. It can and may become a major factor in the further decadence and even the ultimate collapse of Western civilization.

3. *The family and the future of civilization.* As Groves suggests, "The future of the family . . . will be determined by the future of the civilization in which it is embedded." [121] It is also true that the future of civilization will be determined by the homes of the people. The family and civilization interact on each other.

One of the hopes for the renewal and salvation of Western civilization is an inner revival beginning within the basic institutions of the West, particularly the home and the church. Most Protestant as well as Roman Catholic students of family life would agree with Joyce's viewpoint that the Christian family is "a great formative factor of civilization." [122] The same author suggests that

the civilization of Christendom—the civilization of which we are the heirs —was founded on Christian Marriage. . . . And where the Christian ideal of marriage prevails, the family, strengthened by supernatural sanctions, will hold good through every crisis, and even in the greatest political convulsions provides the principle of eventual recovery. [123]

One of the chief hopes for civilization is that the Christian ideal for the family will not be entirely lost but will become increasingly the goal not only for the family but for the other institutions of society and for the social order itself. The Christian ideal kept alive and embodied in the home can become again the integrating center, the rallying point for a rebirth of Western civilization, or at least for a reorientation of that civilization.

[120] *Op. cit.,* p. 191. [121] *The Family and Its Social Functions,* p. 594.
[122] *Op. cit.,* p. vii. [123] *Ibid.,* p. v.

IV

RACE AND
RACIAL TENSION

ALTHOUGH THERE are many "loaded" words, yet "when it comes to arousing people's prejudices, loyalties, animosities, and fears, none is the equal of race." [1] This has not always been true. Arnold Toynbee says that modern Western race feeling dates from the last quarter of the fifteenth century.[2] Race and color prejudice and conflict were created, to a considerable degree, by the discovery of America, the establishment of trade routes to India, and were increased tremendously by the developing slave trade. The last heightened the white man's sense of superiority. In addition, the Industrial Revolution contributed enormously to the wealth and prestige of the white peoples of Europe and America. Then came Darwin's doctrine of evolution and the survival of the fittest, which "was warmly accepted by the people of European stock who saw no reason to doubt that they were the fittest of all." [3]

A distinction should be made between "race" and "racism." A racial group is a "group of men possessing in common certain physical characteristics which are determined by heredity." [4] In con-

[1] Brewton Berry, *Race Relations* (New York, Houghton Mifflin, 1951), p. 50.
[2] *A Study of History* (2nd ed.; London, Oxford University Press, 1935), I, 223.
[3] Alan Burns, *Colour Prejudice* (London, George Allen and Unwin, 1948), p. 23.
[4] Otto Klineberg, *Race Differences* (New York, Harper, 1935), p. 18.

91

trast, "racism is the dogma that one ethnic group is condemned by nature to congenital inferiority and another group is destined to congenital superiority." [5] It is racism that is a dangerous myth, [6] a myth because among scientists "there is practical unanimity of conviction that races are not inherently superior or inferior." [7] The scientists agree with the biblical conception that God is no respecter of persons. It is racism, in the main, that creates racial tensions, and is antithetical to the genius and spirit of the Christian movement.

The whole problem of race, racism, and racial tension is closely related to the present disorder in the West, in Africa, in the Orient, and around the world. To some degree, contemporary racial tensions grow out of and are factors in almost every problem discussed in preceding and succeeding chapters of this book. Racial tension is one of the major elements in the mounting crisis in our world. The existing crisis in civilization cannot be resolved unless a satisfactory solution is found for the race problem or problems with an attendant easing of racial tensions.

To cover the subject of race thoroughly, we should have to consider the racial conflicts and tensions of Asia, Africa, Europe, and the islands of the sea. However, we must restrict ourselves, and hence we shall center our attention almost exclusively upon the Negro-white problem in the United States, hoping that the suggestions that are made will be found applicable to other areas of racial tension. It is assumed that most of us are more familiar with the Negro-white problem and that it touches our lives more directly.

Another introductory statement that should be made is that the race problem is primarily a moral problem, a problem that creates inner tension. Myrdal, based on his comprehensive study, came to the following conclusion:

The American Negro problem is a problem in the heart of the American. It is there that the interracial tension has its focus. It is there that the decisive struggle goes on. . . . The "American Dilemma," referred to in the title of this book, is the ever-raging conflict between, on the one hand, the valuations preserved on the general plane which we shall call

[5] Ruth Benedict, *Race: Science and Politics* (New York, Viking, 1940), p. 153.

[6] See Ashley Montagu, *Man's Most Dangerous Myth* (2nd ed.; New York, Columbia University Press, 1945).

[7] Edmund D. Soper, *Racism: A World Issue* (New York, Abingdon-Cokesbury, 1947), p. 38.

the "American Creed," where the American thinks, talks, and acts under
the influence of high national and Christian precepts, and, on the other
hand, the valuations on specific planes of individual and group living.[8]

If Myrdal is correct in his conclusion, and it is assumed that he
is, then the moral forces of the nation should take the lead in solving the race problem and in relieving racial tension. While the
church is not the only moral agent in the community, nevertheless
the church should provide much of the inspiration and leadership
for every social and moral advance.

The Contemporary Acuteness of Racial Tension

There are abundant evidences of the seriousness of racial conflict
and the acuteness of racial tension around the world. The underprivileged masses of the world are moving uneasily and possibly
somewhat uncertainly. The stirring among the Negroes and other
colored peoples is a part of a world-changing people's revolution.
Pearl Buck concludes that "the deep patience of colored peoples
is at an end. Everywhere among them is the same resolve for freedom and equality that white Americans and British have." [9] This is
true of the masses regardless of color. They are on the march and
that march seems to be inevitable.

The situation is increasingly acute in the United States, as well
as in the world at large. There are many factors that have tended to
heighten racial tension in the contemporary period. World War II,
in which race and racial theories played an important part, and the
subsequent crisis "have tended to accentuate interest in the meaning
of democracy and equality." [10] There has arisen a greater demand
for the consistent application of basic democratic principles to

[8] Gunnar Myrdal, *An American Dilemma* (2 vols.; New York, Harper, 1944),
I, xliii. For a criticism of Myrdal's methods and conclusions see Oliver Cromwell
Cox, *Caste, Class and Race* (Garden City, N.Y., Doubleday, 1948), pp. 509–38;
Herbert Apthekar, *The Negro People in America* (New York, International Publishers, 1946); and W. T. Couch's "Publisher's Introduction" to Rayford Logan
(ed.), *What the Negro Wants* (Chapel Hill, University of North Carolina Press,
1944).

[9] Quoted by Buell G. Gallagher, *Color and Conscience* (New York, Harper,
1946), p. 66.

[10] E. Franklin Frazier, *The Negro in the United States* (New York, Macmillan, 1949), p. 699.

Negro and other minority groups. Recent court decisions, particularly the Supreme Court decision abolishing segregation in the public schools, have speeded the movement toward the achievement of first-class citizenship for the Negro; but these decisions have also, in some areas, increased considerably the tension between the races.

Some believe that the tension has become so acute that some release must be found for it, or we shall face some very serious problems. Gallagher says, "Both individually and collectively, we stand at the crisis that calls for decision." [11] Another writer contends that our nation cannot postpone a settlement of the problem of Negro-white relations "without consequences of extreme seriousness to men everywhere." [12] Nelson suggests that the world is in need of an example of the democratic way. The American creed places on Americans a peculiar responsibility to be that living example. He also believes "that time is running out on America." [13] The acuteness of the problem is deepened by the fact that another great power has arisen on the world's horizon, a power with no such creed and historic background as ours, but one that through its promises to the underprivileged of the world has "stirred the deepest hopes in the hearts of forgotten men." [14]

Deepening racial tensions have not only created serious problems for our world and for our nation but also for the Christian movement. Harry V. Richardson considers the race problem "American Christianity's test case." [15] Gallagher correctly concludes that the present crisis, of which the race problem is an important factor, will not threaten the essential genius of Christianity but that it does threaten the present organized forms of Christianity.[16] If the Christian church will not dare to be the church in the fullest possible sense, if it will not take seriously the Christian ethic, applying its principles to race and other areas of life; then it will lose its own soul. Without the Christian ethic the Christian church becomes an empty shell, a corpse that has lost its power to give life because the life principle no longer resides in it.

The Christian forces of the United States have a "rendezvous with

[11] *Op. cit.*, p. 35.
[12] William S. Nelson (ed.), *The Christian Way in Race Relations* (New York, Harper, 1948), p. 3.
[13] *Ibid.*, p. 7.   [14] *Ibid.*, p. 8.   [15] *Ibid.*, p. 113.
[16] *Op. cit.*, p. 178.

destiny." The future of the Christian cause in America and in the world may be determined, to a considerable degree, by what American Christian groups and individuals do in the immediate future about the racial tensions of our communities and our country. If we do not attempt honestly to apply the Christian spirit and Christian principles to race relations, how can we expect others to respect our Christian claims or to hear and accept the message we proclaim?

The Scope of Racial Tension

1. *A world-wide phenomenon.* A glance through Soper's *Racism: A World Issue*, Eric John Dingwall's *Racial Pride and Prejudice*,[17] or Paul A. F. Walter's *Race and Culture Relations* [18] will give one abundant evidence that racial conflict and tension know no geographic boundaries. Possibly the two most acute areas of infection are South Africa [19] and the southern part of the United States. But in the United States, the conflict is not restricted to any one section or to any one minority group.[20]

It should also be remembered that there are not only conflicts between races which create serious tensions within our nation, but as Myrdal so pointedly emphasizes there is a conflict within the soul of America. This inner tension grows out of the discrepancy between the American creed and the very imperfect application of that creed to the minorities in our midst. Myrdal concludes that "the subordinate position of Negroes is perhaps the most glaring conflict in the American conscience and the greatest unsolved task for American democracy." [21] Negroes, along with other minority and underprivileged groups, are second-rate citizens; "they are still eating the crumbs of democracy and religion." [22]

Without retracting a thing said concerning the national and

[17] (London, Watts and Co., 1946).

[18] (New York, McGraw-Hill, 1952).

[19] See Eugene P. Dvorin, *Racial Separation in South Africa* (Chicago, University of Chicago Press, 1952).

[20] For example, see the following books written by Carey McWilliams: *Prejudice; Japanese-Americans: Symbol of Racial Intolerance* (Boston, Little, Brown, 1944); *A Mask for Privilege: Anti-Semitism in America* (Boston, Little, Brown, 1947); *North from Mexico, The Spanish-Speaking People of the United States* (Philadelphia, Lippincott, 1949).

[21] *Op. cit.*, I, 21.   [22] Nelson, *op. cit.*, p. 24.

world-wide phases of the problem, we must agree that the race problem is acutely and deeply a problem of the Southern states of the United States. It might correctly be called *the* problem of the South. One author suggests that more words are spent upon it in the South than on all other social problems combined.[23] The crisis within the conscience of the South is particularly acute. The American creed and the Christian ethic are, "at least as philosophies, a vital part of the southern tradition. The problem is that there have not yet been found sufficient ways of implementing these common convictions."[24] This conflict, within the soul of the nation in general and of the South in particular, may help to explain the strength and vitriolic expressions of much racial prejudice.

2. *Within the church.* The church is a creator of tension and is involved in that tension. The message it proclaims is a factor of considerable importance in the creation of racial tension. Among the underprivileged the gospel contributes to tension by the high value it places upon the individual. Being created in the image of God, he is of greater worth than all things material. He is lifted above the animal level. Through the acceptance of Christ he comes into the family of the heavenly Fathers; "he is a child of a king." He learns that his Father is no respecter of persons; that in his presence the privileged and powerful are on the same level as the underprivileged and oppressed. This creates within the hearts of the disinherited greater self-respect and a deepened, although somewhat restrained, dissatisfaction with the inequalities of life. The consequent pressure toward the equalizing of opportunities may be eased somewhat by the "other-worldly" emphasis which is innate, to a degree, in the gospel.

The message of the gospel would restrain one from selfishly seeking through revolution improved status for himself, but it would and does inspire him to seek in Christian ways improved status for others. The gospel also creates tension, if taken seriously, within the minds and hearts of the privileged. It may be that the church is "the author of social refinement,"[25] is very conservative and some-

[23] Cox, *op. cit.*, p. 434.
[24] Charles S. Johnson and Associates, *Into the Main Stream* (Chapel Hill, N.C., University of North Carolina Press, 1947), p. v.
[25] Cox, *op. cit.*, p. 390.

times remains "among the stubborn strongholds of racialism"; [26] but the gospel it preaches and teaches is always more challenging than the one it practices. Paradoxically, the Christian church, which is usually a defender of the *status quo,* is, through the message it proclaims, the source for much if not most of the pioneering spirit that provides leadership for social and moral advance along many lines, including the racial. The church, which inspires through its message social and spiritual pioneers, frequently ostracizes and persecutes as heretics the same pioneers. In other words, many of the heretics of the Christian faith have simply been those courageous souls who took seriously the ideals and purposes mediated to them by the church. Because many of those inspired by the church no longer feel free within the church, they frequently give themselves to leadership of movements outside the church, but movements which may represent advanced Christian positions. This is one of the reasons that the church is in constant danger of losing her moral and spiritual leadership. That leadership is threatened in the area of race. This threat is one of the factors in the growing tension within the church.

The progressive steps taken by the church also contribute to heightened tension within the church. For example, the disapproval of segregation by the Roman Catholic Church and by the Federal Council of the Churches of Christ in America [27] stirred the minds and challenged the consciences of many church groups and individual Christians. The wave of pronouncements on the race question by various Christian groups is both an evidence and a creator of increasing tension. These pronouncements, at times, may come close to being hypocritical, are frequently "couched in such general terms of sweet moralizing that they mean little in the practical world," and tend to skirt "around important matters." [28] On the other hand, they may and often do represent real progress. At least they are used by the social pioneers of the church as a beachhead for additional exploration and advance.

3. *Within the individual.* The church as an institution not only faces the problem of tension within the church body but also within

[26] Johnson *et al., op. cit.,* p. 282.   [27] Now the National Council.
[28] Gallagher, *op. cit.,* p. 100.

the minds and consciences of its members. "It is as a moral issue that the problem presents itself in the daily life of ordinary people." [29] This war within the Christian conscience is between the Christian ideal and the very imperfect practice of that ideal. There is always a danger that the failure to narrow the gap between an ideal and its practice may lead one to doubt the validity of the ideal. Frustration concerning the application of the ideal to real life situations may and frequently does lead to moral cynicism. Some seek to escape the moral demands and the social implications of the Christian faith by a "high indifference." But psychology and psychiatry have taught us that one does not solve one's problems by pushing them out of the conscious mind. In the subconscious they tend to create tensions and complexes that may be very damaging to one's personality.

The conscientious Christian faces over and over again the whole matter of the best Christian strategy. Is it wisest and best for him to seek to apply fully the Christian ideal now or to move gradually toward that ideal? If he does not apply it fully now is he failing to do so because he is honestly convinced that such represents the most effective strategy, or is it because he is a moral coward, afraid to face the consequences of full application? These are questions that more or less constantly disturb the socially and morally sensitive Christian; the more sensitive he is, the more he is under constant tension. This is a type of tension which cannot be understood by those who have not had to answer those and similar questions in an environment where whatever strategy one follows would seem to involve some evil as well as good. The sensitive Christian souls, who have a constant inner struggle between the demands of the Christian ideal in their lives and in their world and the very imperfect realization of that ideal, are the very ones who are the chief hope for progress in the application of the Christian spirit and Christian principles to every phase of our common life. The preceding correctly implies that there is no easy and universally applicable answer to the question of Christian methodology or strategy.

Tensions are felt not only by individuals of the majority race but also by those of the minority group. One writer suggests that the

[29] Myrdal, *op. cit.*, I, xlvi.

Negro "feels guiltless with regard to the racial situation." [30] This may be true of most Negroes, but it does not relieve them of inner conflicts because of racial situations. The Negro, as is true of others in minority groups, has to fight against fear and hate, which are self-defeating and are contrary to the Christian spirit. He has to battle against a tendency to lose his faith in the Christian ideal and particularly in the efficacy of established Christian methods for the attainment of the Christian ideal. And "the minority man, when he abandons his ethical standards . . . is tempted to find refuge either in other-worldliness or in some brand of fanaticism." [31] There is a disturbing element of truth in Gallagher's suggestion that "for the minority man or for the Caucasian, failure to resolve the inner conflict of conscience leads through uncertainty about ethical ideals to an open doubting of them, and finally to the abandoning of ethical standards in favor of some more easily sustained position." [32]

Of course, there will not and cannot be a perfect realization of the Christian ideal in the area of race or any other realm of life. The test is not have we arrived at perfection, but are we working toward perfection. This is the test in our individual lives and also in the world. There is no progress toward the ideal without pressure toward or tension in regard to that ideal. This means that a certain amount of tension within the individual, the church, and the world is a healthy sign. It is one evidence that there is a pull or a struggle toward a higher, a better, a more ideal way of life. We should not be too worried about the prevalence of racial tension; we should be concerned about our response and the response of others to that tension.

The Sources of Racial Tension

There is no one explanation for any phenomenon as complex and pervasive as the race problem and its attendant racial tension. We have previously suggested that the message the church proclaims is one source of the mounting tension in the area of race relations. That message places a high evaluation on the individual.

[30] Hortense Powdermaker, quoted by Cox, *op. cit.*, p. 566.
[31] Gallagher, *op. cit.*, p. 31.   [32] *Ibid.*, pp. 30–31.

When understood and accepted, it gives to the individual an attitude of humility in the presence of God but a spirit of self-respect and innate dignity in the presence of his fellow men. This in turn contributes to a dissatisfaction with man-made and man-sustained inequalities of life. Pressure, unconscious as well as conscious, results in a lifting of the level of life for the underprivileged. On the other hand, the consciences of the privileged, who are morally sensitive Christians, are condemned because of the treatment of those of the minority group by the society in which they live.

The following additional sources of racial tension are all clearly interrelated, and to some degree they are both causes and effects of racial tension.

1. *Racial prejudice.* Prejudice is certainly both a cause and an effect of racial tension.[33] According to the etymology of the word, prejudice is a prejudgment, a judgment not based on knowledge or experience. That "prejudgment" may be good or bad, but "prejudice" is usually used in the bad sense. It "implies judgment on the basis of insufficient or irrelevant data."[34] Racial prejudice can be defined "as the tendency to evaluate the individual primarily on the basis of identity with a group thought of as racial."[35]

Regardless of what may be the correct definition of prejudice, it is what Pearl Buck has called "the dark shadow," a shadow not only over the Negro and other minority racial groups, but over all of us, and possibly darkest over those who feel it least.[36] It is like a "cancer in the heart of human society."[37]

[33] For an excellent small book on prejudice, written on the high-school level, see Hortense Powdermaker, *Probing Our Prejudices* (New York, Harper, 1944). Arnold Rose has a concise booklet published by UNESCO. The title is *The Roots of Prejudice* (1951). Philip Mason's *An Essay on Racial Tension* (London, Royal Institute of International Affairs, 1954) approaches the problem primarily from an English and an African viewpoint. For thorough, scholarly discussions, see George Eaton Simpson and J. Milton Yinger, *Racial and Cultural Minorities* (New York, Harper, 1953), pp. 65–260; and Gordon W. Allport, *The Nature of Prejudice* (Cambridge, Mass., Addison-Wesley Publishing Co., 1954).

[34] Naomi F. Goldstein, *The Roots of Prejudice Against the Negro in the United States* (Boston, Boston University Press, 1948), p. 28.

[35] *Ibid.*, p. 32.

[36] Dorothy W. Baruch, *Glass House of Prejudice* (New York, William Morrow, 1946), p. 11.

[37] Henry Smith Leiper, *Blind Spots* (rev. ed.; New York, Friendship Press, 1944), p. xi.

There is general agreement among scientists and scholars that racial prejudice is not instinctive,[38] although it may have some psychological foundations, as will be suggested below.

What are the main sources of racial prejudice? One source is the social heritage. Prejudice is an integral part of that heritage for most children. The child "is certain to have his mind canalised, even before he starts going to school, into habitual acceptance of the prevailing attitudes of the group within which he lives." [39] In other words, he catches his prejudices very much as he catches the measles. He lives in an environment where the contagion runs high. It would be a miracle if he did not contract the disease. This does not necessarily mean that racial prejudice is entirely irrational. In a very true sense it may be, to a degree, both rational and irrational.[40] It may be rational at least in the sense that there is some basis in fact for a certain amount of prejudice.

MacIver suggests two types of prejudices with a different source for each type. The first type is the one largely described above wherein one takes on his prejudice through "indoctrination and habituation," [41] or what Baruch calls "imitation," [42] or what Myrdal labels as the "bad apple theory"—nineteen fresh apples do not make a bad apple good, while one bad apple "rapidly turns the fresh ones rotten." [43] The second type is prejudice that owes its chief impetus "to the life history and personality problems of the individual," [44] or what Baruch calls "unfortunate association" [45] and "frustration and defeat." [46] Regardless of the source of one's prejudices, what Tenenbaum says is true of the individual and also of society. He says, "It seems that an individual first acquires a prejudice and afterwards discovers reasons to justify it." [47] Whatever the source, racial prejudice is most damaging in its effects. "Prejudice can

---

[38] See Bruno Lasker, *Race Attitudes in Children* (New York, Henry Holt, 1929), and Otto Klineberg (ed.), *Characteristics of the American Negro* (New York, Harper, 1944), pp. 158–84.

[39] Lasker, *op. cit.*, p. 370.

[40] See R. M. MacIver, *The More Perfect Union* (New York, Macmillan, 1948), pp. 77 ff.

[41] *Ibid.*, p. 196.   [42] *Op. cit.*, p. 89.   [43] *Op. cit.*, I, 79.

[44] MacIver, *op. cit.*, p. 198.   [45] *Op. cit.*, p. 90.

[46] *Ibid.*, p. 100.

[47] Samuel Tenenbaum, *Why Men Hate* (New York, Beechhurst Press, 1947), p. 138.

provide an excuse or rationalization for economic exploitation or political domination." [48]

2. *General psychological factors.* In addition to prejudice, which is largely psychological in its basic nature although not exclusively so in its operation, there are other psychological influences that are important contributors to contemporary racial tension.

Fear is certainly a major factor. Horace Cayton suggests that the Negro is caught in a fear-hate-fear complex, while the white man in turn is plagued with a guilt-hate-fear complex. [49] Such fear is detrimental both to the white man and to the Negro. It creates inner tension that must find constructive release, or permanent injury will result to the individual and to his society.

A sense of insecurity and frustration is another factor that operates in more than one way in creating racial tension. Those who are insecure and frustrated seek a scapegoat, some individual or group that they can blame for their troubles. This was the technique of Hitler and the National Socialists, who made the Jews the scapegoat. It is possible that "the scapegoat technique" of the frustrated is one of the explanations for the mounting racial tension in South Africa, the United States, and elsewhere. It helps to explain the unusually strong pressure against minority groups by those of the majority group who feel most keenly the social and economic competition stemming from the minority groups.

Another factor creating tension, but also definitely a result of racial prejudice, is what we have called racism or the supposed inherent superiority and inferiority of certain races. Benedict says that of all human questions that of superiority and inferiority "lies closest to the heart of man." [50] It does not make any difference if "there is not the slightest scientific proof that race determines mentality"; [51] as long as men act as if there is an innate superiority

[48] Rose, *The Roots of Prejudice*, p. 7. This is one of a series of booklets on "The Race Question in Modern Science" published by UNESCO. Some of the other titles are "Race and Culture," "Race and Biology," "Race and Psychology," "Race and Society," "Race and History," "Racial Myths," and "The Significance of Racial Differences."

[49] Bucklin Moon, *The High Cost of Prejudice* (New York, Julian Messner, 1947), p. 160.

[50] *Op. cit.*, p. 99.

[51] Franz Boas, *Race and Democratic Society* (New York, J. J. Augustin Publisher, 1945), p. 15.

and inferiority of races the results will be the same. It may be that man's sense of superiority is an inverted inferiority complex. And, like an individual with an inferiority complex, man in general may compensate for his sense of inferiority by bragging about his superiority, the superiority of his family, of his section of the country, of his nation, and of his race. This may help to explain the presence of such a sense of superiority even among the disinherited of a majority group. They belong to the "in-group" or the "we-group." They may consider themselves superior to those of the "out" or "you-group" who are actually far superior to them in native ability, in culture and education, in economic standing, and even in the moral and spiritual standards maintained in their lives. This "in-group" and "out-group" or "we-group" and "you-group" division, which seems to be innate, is what Franklin Giddings called "consciousness of kind." This "consciousness of kind" will not create racial tension unless it carries with it the idea of the natural inferiority of those in the "you-group." The best hope for an effective antidote is the all-inclusive "we-group" concept of Christianity at its best.

3. *Economic pressure.* Economic pressure is an important factor in the racial tension of the contemporary period. In the slave days there was little, if any, economic rivalry between the slaveholder and the slave; or even between the poorer white man and the slave, and hence comparatively little racial prejudice.[52] When the slave was freed and became an economic competitor, there developed a deepening prejudice against him and an increasing tension between him and the poorer whites. The slave tradition was used by the whites in this struggle, and it has continued to be a factor of considerable importance in "keeping the Negro in his place." [53] This tension between the poorer whites, who are under constant economic pressure themselves, and the Negroes, who are competitors with them, has continued to be a major cause of conflict between them. Myrdal concludes that "the lower class groups will, to a great extent, take care of keeping each other subdued." [54] Others suggest

[52] Frazier, *op. cit.,* p. 669.
[53] For a book that gives a great deal of emphasis to the slave tradition as a factor in racial prejudice and conflict, see Goldstein's *The Roots of Prejudice Against the Negro in the United States.*
[54] *Op. cit.,* I, 68.

that both the poorer whites and the Negroes are exploited by the privileged whites, and that prejudice among the underprivileged of both groups is encouraged by the privileged to help to maintain their dominant position in society.[55]

Whether or not the last idea is correct, there is certainly a close relation between economic conditions and racial tension. Tenenbaum has a chapter in his book entitled "Hard Times and Hate," and cites a study by two Yale psychologists showing that there was even a relation between the price of cotton and the number of lynchings.[56] Much of the pressure coming from the Negro grows out of his economic handicaps. He has made marked progress along economic lines, but he is still in great need of improved employment opportunities and better pay. The economic is a major factor in every basic problem he faces. Myrdal found that the economic had first priority in the Negro's list of wants.[57]

The economic was found to be the lowest in the rank order of discrimination by whites. This fact may explain the progress the Negro has made along economic lines. Even if this is true, it does not mean that the problem is solved for the Negro, or that the pressure is greatly relieved. Generally speaking, he is still the last to be hired and the first to be fired. There are many vocations and professions either closed entirely to him or he finds many racial restrictions within them. In industry, where he has made great strides forward in recent years, he finds his occupational opportunities limited; and in many and possibly in most individual plants, in the North as well as in the South, he is not upgraded as are white employees.

Possibly it should also be suggested that in the economic area, as in the field of health, education, and general social standards, the "principle of cumulation" or the "vicious circle" is in operation. White prejudice restricts the economic opportunities of Negroes, thus keeping their standards low along all lines. Low standards, in turn, result in increased prejudice by white people. Prejudice and economic and social standards are both cause and effect. If one of these factors changes there will follow a corresponding change in the other factors. They interact on one another.[58]

[55] See Cox, *op. cit.*, p. 525, and Nelson, *op. cit.*, Chap. 3.
[56] *Op. cit.*, p. 107.   [57] *Op. cit.*, I, 61.
[58] Myrdal, *op. cit.*, I, 75 ff.

4. *Segregation.* Segregation, like low economic and social standards, is both a cause and an effect; it is a source of racial tension and at the same time a result of racial prejudice. There is abundant evidence that the "close segregation of racial groups in expanding urban communities . . . has increased inter-group tensions and disturbances." [59] On the other hand, the "close segregation" results from racial prejudice.

Many white people profess to believe, and possibly some of them honestly do believe, that Negroes want segregation. Many Negroes may want voluntary separation, but few if any of them want segregation, whether it is by custom or by law. Particularly distasteful to them is legal segregation which, from their viewpoint, implies inferiority, and which means for them discrimination. Charles S. Johnson suggests that theoretically segregation merely means separate but equal treatment of equals, but that both in legislation and in practice there is discrimination. [60] The same author defines social discrimination as "the unequal treatment of equals, either by bestowal of favors or the imposition of burdens." [61] He suggests that while Negro leaders of the South have been willing to work for improvement of conditions within the framework of the segregation pattern, "for the Negro to accept segregation and all of its implications as an ultimate solution would be to accept for all time a definition of himself as something less than his fellow man." [62]

Many Negroes recognize that there are other racial and minority groups that are segregated and discriminated against. However, as Johnson suggests, "The Negroes as a group experience the most persistent and the most pervasive forms of segregation." [63] One of the reasons for this is the "high visibility" of the Negro. This "high visibility" is the background for the following from Channing Tobias:

> If you discriminate against me because I am dirty,
>   I can make myself clean.
> If you discriminate against me because I am bad,
>   I can reform and be good.
> If you discriminate against me because I am ignorant,
>   I can learn.

[59] MacIver, *op. cit.*, p. 41.
[60] *Patterns of Negro Segregation* (New York, Harper, 1943), pp. 318–19.
[61] *Ibid.*, p. xvii.   [62] Johnson, *Into the Main Stream*, p. vii.
[63] *Patterns of Segregation*, p. 318.

If you discriminate against me because I am ill-mannered,
    I can improve my manners.
But, if you discriminate against me because of my color,
        You discriminate against me because of some-
        thing God himself gave me and over which I
        have no control.[64]

The segregation pattern is found even, and some would say "especially," in the churches. One writer contends that Protestant
churches and their institutions conform, at least in practice, to the
status quo in white-Negro relations. He makes the charge that Protestantism, "far from helping to integrate the Negro in American
life, is actually contributing to the segregation of Negro Americans." [65] While Loescher may have been too general in his statement, and while it was more true when he wrote than it is today;
yet his statement contains too much truth, even for our day, to be
comfortable. However, the actual practice of segregation is not the
most damaging phase of the picture. The practice would not be so
bad if so many churches and church leaders did not place the stamp
of divine approval upon it. When the church identifies the Christian ideal with something less than the ideal, it loses the vision of
the ideal and its ability to challenge and lift the world toward the
ideal.

However, the segregation pattern of the Christian churches and
the theoretical defense of that practice by some is creating tension
within the conscience of the church. There is too much in the gospel
the church preaches and teaches that is opposed to such a position.
The word the Lord speaks to the churches and through them to the
people creates an uneasy conscience on the part of the churches and
the people to whom they minister.

5. *Increased mobility of people.* An element in the rise and increasing seriousness of racial conflict and tension is the more fre-
quent contacts of the different races with one another, which results
from the increased mobility of people everywhere:

[64] Tenenbaum, *op. cit.*, p. 282.
[65] Frank S. Loescher, *The Protestant Church and the Negro* (New York, Association Press, 1948), p. 15.

If societies were content to live to themselves, in isolated, self-sufficient communities, there would be no interracial conflict, no clash of cultures, no race prejudice, and no necessity for ethnic groups to adjust their differences. They would have their problems, to be sure, but *not* the so-called racial problems which afflict our heterogeneous modern nations.[66]

Berry is here speaking of what might be termed horizontal mobility. People move more and more freely. They move from country to country, from section to section of the same country, from farm to city, and from city to farm. Everywhere they are on the move. A considerable portion of that movement is by racial groups. For example, there has been the movement of the Japanese into the Western portion of the United States, the Mexican into the Southwest, and the immigrants from Europe to the large population centers of the Northern and Eastern portions of our country. There has also been a considerable movement, beginning about the time of World War I, of the Negroes from the farms of the South to the urban centers of both the South and the North but particularly the latter. We cannot determine how much of a contribution all of this movement has made to the racial tension of the contemporary period, but it has certainly been and is one cause of that tension. Then, too, the fact that Negro young men, in the armed forces in recent world conflicts, have traveled around the world in defense of a democracy that has not been applied fully to them and to their people has deepened their demand for first-rate citizenship.

Another type of mobility, sometimes classified as vertical, has also contributed to modern racial tension. By vertical mobility is meant the movement from one class to another, usually although not necessarily from a lower to a higher class. As we have implied previously, Negroes have been moving upward. There is a growing middle class among them and even, to a limited degree, an expanding upper class. Much of the pressure, at least the vocal kind, for improved status has come from these classes.

6. *The changed status of the minority*. The vertical mobility just mentioned is a part of that changed status. There is a growing racial consciousness on the part of Negroes and of color consciousness around the world. The Negroes are developing a racial pride,

[66] Berry, *op. cit.*, p. 22.

which is based, to a degree, on the knowledge of the accomplishments of many of their people and of the contributions of the Negro to American life.[67]

The Negro's improved educational status is another important contribution to his growing racial pride and consciousness and hence to the increase of tension between the races. For example, the number enrolled in Negro colleges and universities had increased from 2,624 in 1900 to 74,526 in 1950, or 28.4 times as many as in 1900, as compared to 10.7 times as many in all such institutions. There were 156 bachelor's degrees conferred by Negro institutions in 1900 as compared to 13,108 in 1950, representing 84 times as many as fifty years earlier. This compares to 16 times as many for all colleges and universities.[68]

The status of the Negro has improved noticeably along practically all lines in recent years. An important element in that improvement has been the victories he has won in the courts.[69] These victories have not only been a result of a more volatile and militant attitude, but they in turn have contributed to an increasing militancy which is a decided factor in mounting racial tension.

Organizations, some all-Negro and others biracial, such as the National Association for the Advancement of Colored People, the National Urban League, the National Negro Congress, and the National Council of Negro Women have been important contributors to "the new racial situation." At least they have provided much of the leadership for the increasingly vocal and militant protest against what they have considered the second-rate citizenship of the Negro. The Southern Regional Council, a biracial Southern group, which considers racial issues as a part of the total regional situation, has contributed considerably to the movement for an improved status for Negroes.

Pressure or tension tends to be cumulative. This is definitely true

[67] For a compact statement of some of those achievements and contributions, see Gallagher, *op. cit.*, pp. 122 ff.

[68] Jessie Parkhurst Guzman (ed.), *1952 Negro Year Book* (New York, Wm. H. Wise & Co., 1952), p. 218.

[69] See Morroe Berger, *Equality by Statute* (New York, Columbia University Press, 1950), for a discussion of court decisions, particularly the actions of the Supreme Court from 1937 through 1950. The same author has a briefer treatment entitled *Racial Equality and the Law* (UNESCO, 1954).

of racial tension. Every improvement in the status of the minority group increases its dissatisfaction with existing inequalities. This tends to heighten the tension not only within the minority group but also between the minority group and the majority, unless the latter moves ahead as rapidly as the minority group. In other words, the majority must release restraints or the pressure is increased with every advance made by the minority.

The Release of Racial Tension

Racial tension arises because of the pressure for improved status by the disinherited or the limited minority; because of the pressure of restraint by the controlling majority or dominant group, which seeks to hold in check the minority; and also results from the inner pressure common to the minority and the majority but particularly prevalent among the latter owing to the disparity between the ideals theoretically adhered to and the very imperfect expression of those ideals. These areas of tension can be correctly considered types of tension. The tension in each of the areas is rather distinctive. All three contribute to and, in a way, constitute "racial tensions" in the general sense. Any remedy for or release from racial tension will have to be related to one or more of these pressure areas, and any adequate remedy or remedies must release the tension in all three areas. In addition, an adequate remedy must be related to the sources of tension considered in the preceding section.

Because racial tension is so complex and complicated, not only in its source but also in its social, economic, political, and religious consequences, the remedy for that tension is likewise complex and complicated. All we can do is to suggest briefly a few of the approaches that give promise of making some contribution to the release of tension at some points.

1. *Acknowledge the existence of tension.* The first step in the curing of any disease is a recognition that the patient is ill. This is followed by a study of the symptoms and a diagnosis of the basic causes for the illness. The first step toward solving the race problem is to recognize that our society is sick at that point. We may hide our heads in the sand, as some do, and say: "The Negro is

perfectly satisfied. The trouble is a few radical whites and Negroes who stir things up. There is nothing fundamentally wrong with the *status quo.*" Such an attitude will merely deepen racial tension and make more explosive the whole issue. The tension will be increased not only because of the increased pressure from beneath against an increased restraining pressure from above, but it will make more serious the tension within the soul of all who have accepted, at least theoretically, basic Christian and democratic principles.

To relieve the pressure and to release the tension we also need to recognize that it is urgent that we do something immediately. The situation is acute for the church, for our nation, and for our world. For the Christian church and for American democracy our racial situation is one of our most vulnerable points. If our way of life is lost it will not be lost primarily because of competing forces and ideologies from without but because of inner weaknesses and inconsistencies. And one of our weakest spots is our failure to apply our basic principles and concepts to a great group of our people.

Some contribution to the release of tension can be made simply by a recognition that tension is a natural and necessary part of life, that it usually is an indication of growth or progress. Tension will also be released, to a degree, by recognizing that much of the pressure for improved status by the underprivileged is justified.

2. *Relieve the pressure areas.* There are two general ways that pressure may be relieved. The individual or the group may become convinced that the existing situation is more or less inevitable, and adjust to it or accept it. The other method is to attempt to remove, as far as possible, the occasions for the pressure. In the case of race relations, the latter method may be utilized by the minority or by the majority group. When it is a part of the strategy of the minority it is hard to keep it from increasing tension, at least for the time being, rather than decreasing it.

This method for the release of tension, if used by those of the majority group, would operate somewhat as follows: Let them examine the areas where those of the minority group are exerting the greatest pressure, and see if anything can be done to relieve the pressure in such areas. For example, if the main problem is segregation and particularly legal segregation, could the segregation laws be repealed? To answer the question wisely one would have to consider the effect of such repeal on the majority and on the entire racial situation. It is possible that the elimination of all "racial laws" would not change noticeably the relation of the races. The main thing, however, is that an honest effort to do something about any source of tension is a necessary step in its release. This is just as true of a group as it is of the individual. There must be a clear conscience, if such is ever entirely possible. At least there must be an honest effort to do something constructive.

3. *Education and release.* Education in a number of ways and in several areas can contribute considerably to the release of racial tension. The lifting of the general educational level of both the majority and the minority groups, at least in the long run, will help. It may tend to increase the pressure by the minority for improved status; but even this increased pressure may be an element in the solution of the problem, and ultimately it may reduce the tension.

There is also needed a specialized program of racial education. This is particularly important for the majority. An intelligent approach to the racial issue will help to reduce the restraining pressure of the majority, and hence it will reduce some of the existing tension. It will enable the majority to keep in step, to a greater degree, with the pressure exercised by the better educated of the minority, and this will reduce the friction between the two groups. Among the important purposes of an effective "racial education program" are the following: to help people to get away from their prejudices and to change their habit of stereotyping races and individuals; to lead them to think of people as human beings rather than as members of a race or a class; and "to substitute new indoctrinations for old." [70]

If the educational program is to be adequate it must utilize many different educational agencies, instruments, and procedures. It must include more than the public school. The education received at the public school "is only a small part of that larger education which men receive from direct contact with the world." [71] It is even possible, as Montagu suggests, that men do not really believe what

[70] MacIver, *op. cit.*, p. 21.   [71] Montagu, *op. cit.*, p. 246.

they are taught in school, and they act only on that which they believe. An effective racial educational program must include not only the more or less formal educational institutions such as the home, the school, and the church; but it must include also the tremendously important informal and more or less incidental educational agencies such as the daily newspaper, magazines, the motion picture, the radio, and the television.

All of these agencies, if they are to make an effective contribution to the releasing of racial tensions, must give some attention to techniques, to strategies, to programs of action, as well as to the dissemination of information and the formulation of basic principles. This emphasis is particularly needed by the church. The church seems to have a weakness, although it is not peculiar to the church, to think that it solves a problem when it makes a pronouncement concerning it, or sets out in a very general way moral and spiritual principles applicable to the problem. The latter is tremendously important and should not be belittled, but the church must go beyond such generalizations if it is to be a constructive educational agency in the field of race relations. This does not mean that the church should identify itself with any organization or program of change. It does mean that it should do something specific within the framework of its own organization and program.

As a part of its educational approach to the race problem the church can and should utilize every educational agency that it has. The programs of these agencies should be used not only to inform the people but also to challenge the prejudices of the people. The agencies also can maintain mutually helpful contacts with those of other racial groups, entering into cooperative services with them. In addition, church members should be led to understand and to cooperate discriminatingly with agencies working for better race relations in the community.

In the whole program of education for better race relations, the Christian college maintains a difficult but strategic role.[72] Logically the Christian college should blaze new trails in social strategy; it

[72] See William Lloyd Imes, "The Role of the Christian College" in Nelson, *op. cit.*, pp. 128 ff. Also see Loescher (*op. cit.*, pp. 96–97), who reports the number of Negroes enrolled in denominational junior and senior colleges and in theological seminaries.

should provide much of the leadership for social and moral advance. It seems on the surface that Christian colleges should be the first to open their doors to all qualified young people regardless of their race. Under the pressure of legal action the tax-supported colleges and universities have been forced to receive as students those of the minority group. The problem of the church-related college is not so much with its faculty or its students as with its board of trustees and its constituency in general. The more directly these schools are controlled by the denomination owning them, the more difficult it seems to be for them to break with traditional patterns. This should be understood by those who tend to be unduly critical of the social conservatism of so many church-related colleges.

There is a possibility, however, that the opening of its doors to Negro students will not be the main contribution of the Christian college to the releasing of racial tension. The Christian college should pass on to its students a Christian philosophy of life, a Christian interpretation of all of life. It should seek to build into their lives basic Christian principles and send them out into the world with a genuine Christian spirit and a driving passion to dedicate themselves to God and his will and way among men. If the Christian college can do that, those young people will make a definite and distinctive contribution to the righting of the wrongs of our society, and hence they will be factors in the releasing of the tensions of society. Such, conceivably, might increase considerably the tension between such Christian-motivated young people and their friends and elders. This is the price frequently paid by social and moral pioneers. But the glorious thing is that this fact will not increase inner tension if one is conscious of working within the will of God and can hear his "Well done."

4. *Religion and release.* The church is both a creator and a reliever of tension. It is the church's responsibility to create tension in any area of life that does not conform to the Christian ideal. The religion which the church proclaims also possesses the most effective resources for the release of conflicts and tensions. It contains a message of sin and judgment, but also of repentance and forgiveness. It should be remembered, however, that true repentance is accompanied by an honest effort to overcome sin, to correct any

wrong spirit or attitude, to make things right with those sinned against. In other words, repentance will not relieve tension in any area unless we attempt to do something about the conditions that have created our inner dissatisfaction and tension.

Unfortunately, however, the sincere Christian is frequently caught in a frustrating dilemma. For example, he may be convinced that if he goes too far right now in applying consistently the Christian ethic to race relations, or to other pressing social problems, he may lose all opportunity to serve. In other words, the tension may become too great between him, his friends, his neighbors, his community, and even his church. This posits a threat for him, but even worse for his family. He may find himself frustrated on every side. He wants to go all the way right now in applying the Christian ethic, yet he feels that he must compromise, to a degree, or be crucified; and he is not ready to be crucified. And what is more significant, he is not sure whether his crucifixion would serve the kingdom of God better than for him to relax the pressure a little, but to see that the tension is maintained in the right direction.

The Christian religion has a message that will give some relief to such frustrated individuals. It seems that they must maintain, in a sense, a constant interplay of action and repentance. They can be assured that God will graciously forgive and will give the sustaining grace and wisdom that is needed for the next advance. All of us can hope and believe that God will judge us not so much by our attainment as by the direction of our lives and by the rate of our progress to his ideal for us and our world.

Some may contend that the above represents a compromise, and that it is not true to original Christianity. Those who make such suggestions, in the main, have failed to read discriminatingly their New Testament, particularly its teachings concerning slavery. Furthermore, in the main, they are not involved personally in the most crucial phases of social conflicts such as the race problem. It is comparatively easy for a person to work out a theoretical solution for the most complex problems of life, so long as he does not have to apply his theory to actual situations. An understanding of some of the problems faced and some of the inner struggles of soul by many sincere Christians, particularly in the South, would mean more Christian charity by those who are not so directly involved in the conflict.

The church not only needs to deliver a message that will relieve the tension within the minds and hearts of its members, it also needs to do something to relieve the tension within the church as an institution. Churches have attempted to satisfy their consciences by making pronouncements, some quite liberal, on race relations. While pronouncements can and do make some contributions to the release of racial tension, yet they have inevitable limitations. The church cannot permanently pacify its conscience by beautiful generalities. The church as an institution, just as is true of its individual members, must undertake a consistent, constructive program to implement the ideals expressed in its pronouncements. "The profound hunger of our time is not for brotherly words, but for brotherly deeds, not for the publishing of brave resolutions, but for the launching of brave experiments." [73] Such a program of action will create, at least in many churches, friction and tension. But the only hope for permanent relief is through such a program.[74] The church should remember that any effective program of action involves more than moralizing, which Gallagher [75] suggests is only the beginning of strategy. An effective program involves social engineering, and social engineering will require the cooperation of the church with those who have the social skills required to cope with racial pressure and problems.

A constructive program of action must also include the disinherited masses. The message of the church contains a vital word for the underprivileged and the dispossessed or, as Thurman expresses it, those "who stand with their backs against the wall." [76] Jesus had a message for these; he was particularly interested in them. "Wherever his spirit appears, the oppressed gather fresh courage; for he announced the good news that fear, hypocrisy, and hatred, the three hounds of hell that track the trail of the disinherited, need have no dominion over them." [77]

[73] Fred D. Wentzel, *Epistle to White Christians* (Philadelphia, Christian Education Press, 1948), p. 91.
[74] For specific suggestions see Nelson, *op. cit.*, chapter 6 on "What Can the Church Do?" and Gallagher, *op. cit.*, chapter xi on "Deeds." Some of their suggestions represent ultimate goals, but others can be immediately attained while pressure is maintained toward the more distant ideals.
[75] *Ibid.*, p. 101.
[76] Howard Thurman, *Jesus and the Disinherited* (New York, Abingdon-Cokesbury, 1949), p. 7.
[77] *Ibid.*, p. 29.

The Christian religion can give to the oppressed and disinherited inner peace and victory. They can be assured that if they will, God can and will be their heavenly Father; that he looks on the heart and not on the outer conditions and circumstances. If God is a living reality within them, his presence will give them release from the inner tensions that are so destructive of all that is highest and best. It will prevent them from contending for the right in the wrong spirit. It will enable them to recognize the inequalities of life without hate. It will save them from frustration, because they can have a deep conviction that their heavenly Father will be on their side, will keep them from frustration, if their goals are within his will and their spirit is right. They can be assured that ultimately love and truth will triumph because God is truth; he is love; he is sovereign.

5. *The individual's responsibility.* The church, through the gospel it proclaims, may offer release to whites and Negroes who are under tension; but they, if they are to have release, must appropriate the message delivered. Even the Lord himself cannot help an individual or a group that does not want to be helped.

This message of individual responsibility is in accord with the basic nature of the Christian gospel. Its word is addressed primarily to individuals; men as individuals are judged and redeemed. Furthermore, as individuals, men and women are held accountable by God, and if accountable unto God, then man "is not a slave to his environment." [78] The Christian, as a citizen of two worlds, must not only answer to the mores but also to the Master.

It is the conflict between his environment, which would restrain and limit him, and the Christian message, which would lift and challenge him, that creates for the socially and spiritually sensitive soul his keenest and most distressing inner conflict. The main hope of progress, however, is in this tension, and the most reliable assurance of an easing of the tension is a movement toward the Christian ideal coupled with a genuine sense of humility and a continuing spirit of repentance and renewal of fellowship with God, who has "made from one every nation of men to live on all the face of the earth." [79]

[78] Benjamin J. Mays in Nelson, *op. cit.*, p. 224.　　　　[79] Acts 17:26.

V

ECONOMIC
LIFE AND RELATIONS

A DISCUSSION OF world issues would not be complete without some consideration of economic life. "Economic activity is an important part of human experience. It fills most of our waking hours, and to it we devote much energy and talent. . . . It involves us in many of our most rewarding (and most difficult) human relationships. . . . It places heavy responsibilities on us." [1] Economic values for many people have become the chief values of life. The past century has been appropriately called "The Century of Economic Man." Most of the problems of the modern period are economic, to some degree, and some of the most perplexing of them are primarily economic. The conditions that threaten and the movements that challenge our generally accepted way of life are largely

---

[1] John C. Bennett *et al.*, *Christian Values and Economic Life* (New York, Harper, 1954), p. 183. This book is one in a series on "Ethics and Economic Life" produced by a Study Committee, authorized by the Federal Council (now National Council) of the Churches of Christ in America in 1949. The other volumes, all published by Harper, are the following: Kenneth E. Boulding, *The Organizational Revolution* (1953); Howard R. Bowen, *Social Responsibilities of the Businessman* (1953); Elizabeth E. Hoyt *et al.*, *American Income and Its Use* (1954); A. Dudley Ward, Stanley Leavy, and Lawrence Fieldman, *The American Economy—Attitudes and Opinions* (1955). Drawing on the insights of economists as well as Christian theologians, the series is the most ambitious attempt that has been made to relate the Christian religion and the Christian ethic to economic life.

economic, although when properly understood they are basically spiritual. The same conditions and movements, to a considerable degree, are shaping the present and determining our future.

Christianity and Economic Life

Admitting that the economic is of major importance in our lives and in our world, does it necessarily follow that the Christian movement should be concerned about economic matters? Or should Christianity limit its concern to the individual and his inner life? Is religion exclusively "the art and theory of the internal life of man," or "what the individual does with his own solitariness"? [2]

The latter expressions reflect one aspect of the Christian life. Central and basic in the Christian religion is the individual's relation to and fellowship with God. This experience, however, does not have to be entirely solitary. It may be, and it seems that it must be to a degree, communal. At least it is not most significantly meaningful unless it is shared with others. Worship, which is usually what we are referring to when we speak of religion as what the individual does with his solitariness, is only one phase, although a very important phase of the Christian religion, and even it may be deepened when it is a group experience. Furthermore, worship is not the end of the Christian life. It is essential, but it is, in the truest sense, instrumental. The end or purpose of life for the Christian is the glory of God through service for him and one's fellow man. A true worship experience, when a man is made conscious of the God revealed by Jesus Christ, impels him to go out into the world to make the dream he has received from God a reality among men. What does all of this have to do with economic life?

1. *Theoretical.* The individuals to whom our churches minister do not live in solitary confinement. Unless we are going to segment the human person into many water-tight compartments, a thing that cannot be done, then what he is in one area will inevitably influence him in every other realm of his life. That means that his economic life and relations will shape, to some degree, his moral

[2] Alfred N. Whitehead, *Religion in the Making* (New York, Macmillan, 1926; reissued, 1956), p. 16.

ideals and his spiritual life. The reverse, of course, is also true. What he is morally and spiritually and what he interprets to be his ethical and religious responsibility will affect his economic practices and determine, to a degree, his appraisal of economic values.

A leading economist relates the economic and religious as follows: "Man's character has been moulded by his every-day work, and the material resources which he thereby procures, more than by any other influence unless it be that of his religious ideals; and the two great forming agencies of the world's history have been the religious and the economic." [3] If the Christian forces are interested in influencing the lives of people, they must be concerned with the economic relations and evaluations of those people and with the application of Christian moral ideals to the economic environment in which those people live. This all means that "economic life in all its ramifications is of profound ethical significance" [4] not only for the individual but also for the church and the world. On the other hand, the great moral principles of the Christian faith are germane to economic life and are of profound economic significance when properly understood and applied.

The National Study Conference on the Church and Economic Life, meeting in Detroit in 1950, outlined the church's function in the economic realm as follows:

The Church, as the custodian of "the sacred and imperishable message of eternal salvation," is charged with a fourfold duty, as Christians in fellowship confront the economic life. It must be the teacher of the principles of conduct; a voice of judgment; a guardian of moral and spiritual values already won; and the herald of a better day. [5]

The message the church proclaims, which contains the great ethical principles that are germane to economic life, has as its central core its doctrine of God and his relation to the world. God, the sovereign ruler of the universe, is interested and active in every area of life. He is the author of the basic laws of the universe. His will is the final determinant of right and wrong in every realm of life. "Both man and economics must finally be studied in the light of God." [6] This means that God and his will are the ultimate

---

[3] Alfred Marshall as quoted by Bennett *et al., op. cit.,* p. 184.
[4] *Ibid.,* p. 191.   [5] *Ibid.,* p. 14.
[6] Nels F. S. Ferré, *Christianity and Society,* p. 212.

point of reference for the society of men as well as for individual men. And "only when men seek to do His Will can the economic order be expected to function effectively." [7]

God climaxed his creative work by creating man in his image. It is this fact that sets man apart from the rest of creation and gives him his worth and dignity. The test of any economic practice, program, or system is what it does for and to men, women, and little children. The human person is worth more than all things material.

The guiding principle in every area of human relations is love: a love that partakes of the divine quality, a love for our neighbor which is our response to God's love for us and our neighbors, a love that reaches up to the level of *agape,* and finds its highest expression in the Cross. That kind or quality of love expresses itself through intelligent, redemptive self-sacrifice. God so loved the world that he gave his only Son; [8] Christ so loved the church that he gave his life for her.[9] His followers, as individuals and groups, will be redemptive influences in the world to the degree that they love enough to take up a cross, on which they crucify self and selfish purposes and ambitions for the sake of others. Notice it is "for the sake of others." It is not the sacrifice of self just for the sake of sacrificing self. Really the one who loves in the deepest sense will not be calculating about his sacrifice of self. He will simply forget self as he serves God and his fellow man.

2. *Practical.* There are many who agree that the Christian religion has a message that is theoretically germane to economic life, but who insist that it cannot be applied at the present time. It may serve as a basis for the judgment of the present level of life, but they contend that it cannot give the laboring man or the businessman any direct guidance as he faces the day-by-day problems and decisions of his life.

Some go so far as to suggest that religion and economics operate in two entirely different realms. While this viewpoint is not as prevalent as it was formerly, it still persists. We should frankly admit that there are phases of economic life that merely involve techniques and are amoral. But economic matters do touch and influence

[7] John F. Sleeman, *Basic Economic Problems* (London, S.C.M. Press, 1953), p. 15.

[8] John 3:16.   [9] Eph. 5:25.

the lives of individuals, families, communities, and nations. When the human person and human values enter the picture the Christian movement is immediately and correctly concerned. It is also concerned with motives, purposes, and Christian insights. "The most fundamental issues of economic life are basically ethical." If we probe deeply enough we shall find that each economic question involves some ethical and spiritual values.

The viewpoint that the Christian love ethic cannot be applied in a sinful world is very prevalent. Reinhold Niebuhr, typical of his general position, says that "the love commandment is always partly contradicted in actual life by the immense force of self-love, particularly the self-love of groups and collectives," but he adds that the love commandment "remains nevertheless the law of life." [10] At least it is to serve as the basis for the judgment of the present level of life. The fact that men actually do not live by the law of love does not abrogate the law.

There are some timid souls who say that the Christian church should not deal with economic issues because they are so controversial and hence divisive. If the church avoids issues simply because they are controversial, it will not make a very constructive contribution to the lives of the individuals to whom it ministers or to the shaping of the world. It will become a mere appendage to the body politic. It may be a refuge for disturbed souls, but it will not be a disturber of men's souls, which is a major function of prophetic religion. Muelder speaks of a prophetic tension, a tension caused by the prophetic element in the Christian movement. He also speaks of "a dialectical unity of accommodation and dissent." [11] He explains further by saying: "At one pole we have the conservative or static function. At the other pole we have the dynamic and the prophetic function." [12] The church, of necessity, must perform both of these functions. It is the effort to keep the two in proper balance that creates inner tension within the church. The prophetic element in the message of the church will not let the church settle down to be a mere conservator of the *status quo*.

[10] A. Dudley Ward (ed.), *Goals of Economic Life* (New York, Harper, 1953), pp. 449–50.
[11] Walter George Muelder, *Religion and Economic Responsibility* (New York, Scribner's, 1953), p. xiv.
[12] *Ibid.*, p. 18.

One other thing should be said concerning the application of the Christian spirit and message to economic life. The Christian religion does not have and should not claim to have a blueprint for the economic order. Through its message it does, however, "bring to the study of economic life a religious perspective, a sensitive concern for the human consequences of all economic behavior, a spirit of dedication and self-criticism." [13] This concern, dedication, and self-criticism cannot be applied effectively unless the ordinary men and women in the pew are gripped with a deep sense of divine vocation. They must recognize their responsibility to God to live as he would have them live in their daily work, and the opportunity they have of being living witnesses to those they touch in the shop and store, in the office and on the street, in the field and in the home.

3. *Biblical.* Throughout the stream of the Christian movement there has been a constant interplay of the conservative or static and the prophetic elements inherent in that movement. In original Christianity the prophetic was more prevalent, as has been true in its great periods of renewal. The impact of Christianity on society has been measured, to a considerable degree, by which of the two elements—the conservative or the dynamic and prophetic—has been most dominant at the time.

Original Christianity drew heavily on the prophetic spirit of the Old Testament. John the Baptist was a second Elijah, pronouncing the judgment of God. Jesus proclaimed a message of release for the poor and the disinherited of society. It was the common people who heard him gladly. While he did not come as a social reformer, he enunciated principles and revealed attitudes that were revolutionary in their implications. The simplicity of his approach to the problems of life and his indifference, in many ways, to things material were and are a radical departure from the generally accepted. Most of what he said specifically concerning material possessions was to point out their danger to the child of God. Except for the grace of God, according to Jesus, it would be impossible for a rich man to enter the kingdom.[14] Riches tend to give one a false sense of security.[15] A man should beware of covetousness, "for a man's life does not consist in the abundance of his possessions." [16]

<hr/>

13 Bennett *et al.*, *op. cit.*, p. xiv.   14 Mark 10:23–27.
15 Luke 12:16–21.   16 *Ibid.*, 12:15.

The child of God should be possessed by a singleness of purpose. He should not treasure the things of this life. Such things are insecure and uncertain, and will tend to become the center of one's affections. One cannot serve God and money. It is psychologically and spiritually impossible. His disciples should simply trust the heavenly Father, putting his kingdom first in their lives, with an abiding confidence that God will provide the necessities of life.[17] It is true that this mammon of unrighteousness can be used to make friends that will receive us into an eternal habitation,[18] but it is the mammon of unrighteousness. Without specifically saying so, property rights are made subservient to human rights. The one who cares for his fellow man cares for the Lord himself.[19] The parable of the Good Samaritan is one graphic illustration of the proper use of material goods.[20]

After the death and the resurrection of Jesus there arose a religious community which attempted to give practical expression to his ethic of self-sacrificing love. This spirit found expression in one way that has created some problems for subsequent interpreters. The record says: "And all who believed were together and had all things in common; and they sold their possessions and goods and distributed them to all, as any had need." [21] Again it says:

And they were all filled with the Holy Spirit and spoke the word of God with boldness. . . . and no one said that any of the things which he possessed was his own, but they had everything in common. . . . There was not a needy person among them, for as many as were possessors of lands or houses sold them, and brought the proceeds of what was sold and laid it at the apostles' feet; and distribution was made to each as any had need.[22]

Here in the Jerusalem fellowship there was some community of property. However, if this was communism it was a communism of love. The background for it was the fact that they "were of one heart and soul." It was spiritually based. It was limited to property and was voluntary. Ananias was condemned for lying and not for withholding some of his property. Peter's word to him was: "While it remained unsold, did it not remain your own? And after it was

---

[17] Matt. 6:19–33. [18] Luke 16:9. [19] Matt. 25:40, 45.
[20] Luke 10:25–37. [21] Acts 2:44–45. [22] *Ibid.*, 4:31–32, 34–35.

sold, was it not at your disposal?" [23] We also know that the practice did not become the accepted pattern for the churches.

There is a spirit revealed in it, however, that is eternally valid: Christians should share voluntarily with one another in any time of economic need. This should be done even if one has to sell what he has. We are members of the body of Christ, of the family of God; we should rejoice, suffer, and share with one another. This spirit of sharing was quite prominent in the ministry and writings of Paul. He took a collection for the saints at Jerusalem and admonished those to whom he wrote to give systematically, willingly, and cheerfully. [24] Paul also had a special warning for the rich. They should guard against the temptations that beset them, remembering that the love of money is the root of all evils. They should remember that they brought nothing into the world and will take nothing out of the world, which may imply that all of us should be content with the simple necessities of life. At least the rich should not set their hope on their riches but on God, and should take heed that they are rich in good deeds. [25]

While admonishing the Colossians to seek the things that are above, [26] Paul also exhorted the Thessalonians to work with their own hands so they might command the respect of outsiders, and be dependent on nobody. [27] In his second epistle to the Thessalonians he exhorted them to avoid the shirker, and reminded them of his former instruction that "if anyone will not work, let him not eat." [28] One reason for the Christian's working is that he may have the material means to share with those in need.

4. *Historical.* [29] The early Christian movement spread most rapidly among the common, laboring people. This helps to explain the general tendency of the early church to deprecate, and at times even to condemn, not only wealth but also active participation in many

[23] *Ibid.*, 5:4.   [24] 1 Cor. 16:1–2; 2 Cor. 9:7.
[25] 1 Tim. 6:6–19.   [26] Col. 3:1–3.   [27] 1 Thess. 4:11–12.
[28] 2 Thess. 3:10.

[29] For a study of certain aspects of the relation of Christianity to economic life see C. J. Cadoux, *The Early Church and the World,* which covers the economic along with several other areas for the first three centuries of the Christian era; Ernst Troeltsch, *The Social Teaching of the Christian Churches,* which gives some attention to the economic; R. H. Tawney, *Religion and the Rise of Capitalism,* and Max Weber, *The Protestant Ethic and the Spirit of Capitalism,*

phases of economic life. Clement of Alexandria, who died about 220 A.D., took a more liberal view than most of the early church leaders concerning wealth and the wealthy. This is seen particularly in his "Who Is the Rich Man That Can Be Saved?" After some introductory statements, he gives the incident when the rich young ruler came to Jesus and the comments of Jesus about how hard it was for a rich man to be saved. Clement suggests that Jesus did not and does not require the rich man to throw away his riches. The Master stresses the right inner attitude toward possessions. If rich people make the proper use of and maintain the right attitude toward their riches, the possession of riches need not and will not interfere with their salvation.[30]

The viewpoint of Clement reflected a more or less inevitable change from the stricter view of the earlier church leaders. The change was inevitable, to some degree, because increasing numbers of the people of the well-to-do upper classes were identifying themselves with the Christian movement. There began a readjustment of the church's attitude toward wealth and the wealthy. There was a partial reevaluation of the processes by which wealth was accumulated. The emphasis was shifted to the proper use of wealth. Almsgiving was magnified, and gradually the emphasis was on giving to the church. The church became the dispenser of alms; in many cases churches became wealthy, and suffered the temptations of the wealthy.

The change of perspective concerning wealth and economic matters was a phase of the shifting strategy of the church regarding the world. As a part of its long-term strategy the church worked out rather strict regulations concerning such matters as the just price [31]

---

both of whom concentrate on the Reformation and more particularly Calvinism, with Weber giving his main attention to the idea of callings in Calvinism, especially as expressed in Puritanism; Joseph F. Fletcher (ed.), *Christianity and Property*, which begins with the Old Testament and includes chapters on the New Testament, the early church, the Middle Ages, the Reformation, and a special emphasis on "Anglican Thought on Property"; and Kathleen Walker MacArthur, *The Economic Ethics of John Wesley*.

[30] Alexander Roberts and James Donaldson (eds.), *The Ante-Nicene Fathers*, II, 591–604.

[31] See Rudolf Kaulla, *Theory of the Just Price*, trans. Robert D. Hogg (London, George Allen and Unwin, 1940). A general discussion rather than strictly historical.

and usury; [32] both of which have continued to be of some concern to economists and theologians. The Roman Catholic Church, which has persistently disapproved usury, changed during the Middle Ages its conception of what constituted usury; [33] while Calvinism placed the stamp of divine approval on interest. The latter, along with the Calvinistic idea of callings, made a distinct contribution to capitalism, the new economic order that was arising.[34]

Following the days of the Reformation, the economic area increasingly asserted its independence of its moral and spiritual foundation. It claimed to have its own laws and should not be controlled or judged by laws or regulations external to the economic. It lost its sense of divine reference. This fact, along with a developing anthropocentric humanism which tended to assert man's independence of God, contributed to the rise of modern sensate culture—to use Sorokin's term—which has dominated Western civilization but which has exhausted itself and is in the process of collapse. This collapse is one explanation for the crisis in our world.

There has been a growing uneasiness on the part of the Christian movement concerning economic life and the relation of Christianity to the economic. With varying emphases, different branches of organized Christianity have continued to point out some of the evils and needs of the economic order. Pope Leo XIII, May 15, 1891, released a famous encyclical, "Rerum Novarum" ("The Condition of the Workingmen"), which touched on such subjects as labor, private ownership, socialism, employer and employee relations, the right use of money, the church and the poor, the state and poverty, hours of labor, and just wages. Forty years later, Pope Pius XI released "Quadragesimo Anno" ("Reconstructing the Social Order"), in which he gave considerable attention to a reinterpretation and contemporary application of the earlier encyclical by Leo XIII.[35]

[32] See Bernard W. Dempsey, *Interest and Usury* (Washington, American Council on Public Affairs, 1943), but particularly Benjamin N. Nelson, *The Idea of Usury* (Princeton, Princeton University Press, 1949), which is more systematically historical.

[33] Bede Jarrett, *Social Theories of the Middle Ages*, pp. 167–73.

[34] See Tawney, *op. cit.*, and Weber, *op. cit.*; cf. J. Milton Yinger, *Religion in the Struggle for Power* (Durham, N.C., Duke University Press, 1946), Chap. IV.

[35] Joseph Husslein's *Social Wellsprings* (Milwaukee, Bruce Publishing Co., 1940) gives an English translation with explanatory notes of fourteen documents

There has also been a renewed emphasis on the application of the Christian message to economic life by Protestant groups. This has been true of local congregations of some of the major denominations and of the ecumenical movement. The Oxford Conference of 1937 was particularly vocal on economic life,[36] while the World Council of Churches in its meeting in Amsterdam in 1948 aroused a great deal of interest and considerable criticism by its statement concerning communism and capitalism. One sentence that somewhat summarized the statement was: "The Christian churches should reject the ideologies of both Communism and *laissez-faire* capitalism, and should seek to draw men away from the false assumption that these extremes are the only alternatives." [37]

Christian Ethics and Economic Values

The Christian religion not only provides a point of reference for life; it also gives some specific guidance for many areas of life. This guidance comes from its ethic which represents "the implications of Christian faith for the moral life." [38] Really the ethical demands of the Christian religion are more than implications: they are inherent in the faith itself. To be a real Christian means, among other things, that one is a moral person applying more or less consistently the ethical principles of his religion to the economic and every other area of his life.

1. *Property and wealth.* Property may be private or public; it may be held for use or for power. It may be considered an institution rather than a thing, and "if we removed the institution of prop-

---

by Leo XIII. It includes a special index to "Rerum Novarum." The Benziger Brothers, "Printers to the Holy Apostolic See," released in 1943 both the earlier encyclical by Leo XIII and the reinterpretation by Pius XI. The two encyclicals are given in Latin text with an English translation. A cheap paper edition of *Five Great Encyclicals,* including "Rerum Novarum" and "Quadragesimo Anno," was put out by the Paulist Press in 1939.

[36] See J. H. Oldham (ed.), *The Official Report of the Oxford Conference* (Chicago, Willett, Clark, 1937), pp. 75–112.

[37] W. A. Visser 't Hooft (ed.), *The First Assembly of the World Council of Churches* (London, S.C.M. Press, 1949), p. 80.

[38] Bennett *et al., op. cit.,* p. 202.

erty, modern civilization would fall to pieces." [39] In this section we shall consider primarily "private" property or personal wealth.

The general Christian conception is that property as such is from God and hence it is good. This idea is particularly prevalent in the Old Testament. The New Testament emphasis is more on the dangers of property and wealth, although property as such is not considered evil. The right of ownership of private property is assumed in the Bible and has been defended, in the main, by the Christian movement as a God-given right of man. However, property does not belong to man unconditionally.

The Christian view is that all belongs to God. "The earth is the Lord's and the fulness thereof." [40] Every beast of the forest and "the cattle on a thousand hills" are his.[41] The silver and the gold belong to God.[42] Man and all that he has belong to God. Man is a steward, a trustee, an administrator for God. F. Ernest Johnson claims that "the Christian doctrine of stewardship is the most radical of all doctrines concerning property." [43]

The proper sense of God's ownership, if deeply ingrained into the soul of man, will at least save him from "that hard sense of ownership that so easily becomes an obstacle to any ethical sensitivity in relation to property." [44] This will be true only if the Christian conception of stewardship includes more than tithing or the giving of a tenth. The Christian is responsible unto God for giving a tithe, but he is also responsible for what he does with the nine-tenths and for the methods he uses to accumulate his wealth. Wesley's famous summary concerning wealth was: "Gain all you can. Save all you can. Give all you can." [45] Muelder says this means "give all you have" and labels it radical giving and says that it is "the only way of extracting the poison from riches." [46]

There is also a sense in which man is not only a steward of God but also a steward of the people. There is "no such thing as unrestricted and irresponsible ownership. The owner is a trustee account-

---

[39] Muelder, *op. cit.*, p. 138.   [40] Ps. 24:1.
[41] *Ibid.*, 50:10.   [42] Hag. 2:8.
[43] Howard R. Bowen, *Social Responsibilities of the Businessman* (New York, Harper, 1953), p. 244.
[44] Bennett *et al.*, *op. cit.*, p. 254.
[45] For the complete sermon on "The Use of Money" see *Wesley's Works* (New York, B. Waugh & T. Mason, 1831), I, 440–48.
[46] *Op. cit.*, p. 8.

able to God and society." [47] To a degree, man derives what he has not only from God but also "from the people and he holds it in trust for the people." [48] All property is acquired, to some degree, "under conditions which the acquirer has not himself created." [49] For this reason Brunner suggests that the community or the state has the right to what the individual has acquired. The generally accepted Christian view is that the community or state has such a right only if it is needed and will be used for the common good, and that if it is confiscated by the state the original owners should be adequately compensated. The state also has the obligation to protect the rights of private property as well as to define the limits of those rights. The selfish accumulation and use of property by the state would be as bad and possibly worse than such control by the individual. "Christian ethics is fundamentally opposed to all selfish use of wealth, whether privately or collectively owned." [50]

The Christian position is that property should always be subservient to human needs and welfare. "Property is not only *from* God, but *for* man." [51] Rauschenbusch pointedly said: "It is the function of religion to teach society to value human life more than property, and to value property only in so far as it forms the material basis for the higher development of human life." [52] Whatever property the Christian may have, little or much, should be used for God's glory and the common good.

It seems that some property, at least the ownership of a homestead, is good for man. Some would say that a certain amount of property is necessary; that it contributes to the individual's sense of dignity and to a feeling of security for himself and his family. Brunner says, "Without private property no true freedom of action is possible." [53]

2. *Work and wages.* The church should be concerned with work and wages. It must be if it "is to show its relevance to life." For most church members their work is as central in their interest as

---

[47] Bowen, *op. cit.*, p. 33.

[48] Walter Rauschenbusch, *Christianity and the Social Crisis* (New York, Macmillan, 1907), p. 388.

[49] Emil Brunner, *Justice and the Social Order*, p. 134.

[50] Alban G. Widgery, *Christian Ethics in History and Modern Life* (New York, Round Table Press, 1940), p. 266.

[51] Ferré, *op. cit.*, p. 219.   [52] *Op. cit.*, p. 372.

[53] *Justice and the Social Order*, p. 59.

their home. In addition, "work is . . . a great formative influence on a man's character." [54] Garbett also says that "a church concerned only with its own organization and worship is neglecting its duty towards the millions to whom it should minister." [55] Those millions toil daily in the shops, the factories, the offices, and on the farms.

It is the church's business to help them to understand that work for man is not the result of the temptation and fall. It was a part of God's original plan for man.[56] "Man is born to work as the bird is born to fly." [57] The National Study Conference on the Church and Economic Life at Pittsburgh in 1947 stated: "Each person under God has a right and a duty to take his share in the world's work." Notice that it says, "a right and a duty." Man needs some useful work; it is best for him; it is his right. For this reason, "unemployment in the sight of the Christian must always be an evil." [58] It is also his duty. It is doubtful if any one has the right to live entirely on the work of others, except those who are too young, too old, or unable to work. "It is by work that man is called upon to earn his living, and work is intended to be a co-operation with God in His creative work." [59]

Another important plank in the Christian conception of work is that any honest and socially useful occupation is honorable. From the Christian viewpoint, there is no hierarchy of the white shirt or of any particular vocation or profession. Cameron Hall expresses this general idea as follows: "All useful daily work becomes of equal worth before God. Because men at work are co-workers with God the Creator, their daily work is 'co-worthy' before God." [60] The church should guard against losing the proper sense of the dignity of work as such. The thing that makes it possible for even the most menial and monotonous work to be clothed with a sense of dignity and worth is the fact that it is done for the glory of God and in the service of man. We should never forget that both Jesus and Paul

[54] Cyril Garbett, *In an Age of Revolution* (New York, Oxford University Press, 1952), p. 270.

[55] *Ibid.*, p. 271.   [56] Gen. 2:15.

[57] Charles P. Bruehl, *The Pope's Plan for Social Reconstruction* (New York, Devin-Adair, 1939), p. 310.

[58] Garbett, *op. cit.*, p. 276.   [59] Sleeman, *op. cit.*, p. 19.

[60] J. Richard Spann (ed.), *The Church and Social Responsibility* (New York, Abingdon-Cokesbury, 1953), p. 94.

toiled with their hands. They would be at home among the manual laborers of our day or any day.

The preceding is closely related to the Christian conception of divine vocation or calling. There may be and are some callings that are uniquely holy just as there is one day each week that is uniquely holy; but just as every day for the Christian should be a holy day, so every honest, honorable vocation can and should be sacred or holy for the Christian. Various vocations perform distinctive functions, but in the eyes of the Lord there are no degrees of honor.[61] The main thing is to be working within the will of God with a resultant conviction that through our vocation we are co-laborers with him in accomplishing his purposes in the world.

Bowen suggests "that one of the great needs of modern life is to restore the sense of vocation so that one's job in which one spends most of his life is regarded as more than a mere means to a weekly pay check and more than a necessary evil to which one devotes as little of his talent and energy as possible." [62] Any work for the Christian "is unworthy unless it has a religious reference." [63] He can and should have a sense of divine partnership and stewardship as he works at his vocation. He can and should recognize that he has a unique opportunity to serve his God and his fellow man in and through his vocation. Overarching and permeating his vocation should be a general sense of divine vocation common to all children of God. That universal vocation is the call of God to all his children to dedicate their lives, including their vocations, to the service of man and to the promotion of the kingdom or rule of God among men. All are to minister or serve; some through one vocation or channel, others by other means and methods. One's vocation should be considered instrumental. This should be true of paid vocational religious workers as well as those in so-called secular vocations.

The Christian view also is that the individual should give to his vocation an honest day's work. For this honest day's work he should

---

[61] Cf. Paul's symbol of the church as a body with the members of the church as parts of the body, each with his distinctive function to perform—1 Corinthians 12:12–31.

[62] *Op. cit.*, pp. 36–37.

[63] William G. Peck, *A Christian Economy* (London, SPCK, 1954), p. 3.

receive a "just wage," and a "just wage" is not necessarily the same as the legal wage or the wage agreed on by the employer and the employee. A "just wage" must be an adequate wage, adequate to meet the needs of the worker and his family; and those needs are not to be interpreted as the bare necessities of life. An adequate wage would provide for health, comfort, and security of the worker and those for whom he is responsible. This adequate or living wage "should be the first charge on the profits of any industry." [64]

Some interpret "just wage" in terms of a just proportion of what the worker produces. Rauschenbusch, for example, contended that the justice of the economic system could be proved only if it could be demonstrated that the wealth, comfort, and security of the average workingman, in the day in which he wrote, had kept pace with the wealth of mankind in general.[65] This would mean that a just wage in the United States in the twentieth century would not be the same as a just wage in the United States in the nineteenth century; neither would it be the same as a just wage in China or any other part of the world.

3. *Motives and incentives.* This section is concerned with why men *do* and *should* work. It will apply to labor, to management, and, to a degree, to the investors or stockholders. All three of these groups are involved in large-scale industrial production. Some portions of the discussion will apply more directly and specifically to the owners and managers than to the laborers.

There are many incentives that may impel men to work. Some of those incentives may be primarily economic, while others are more psychological, and some even moral and spiritual. They may be driven by the desire for approval or acceptance, for power and prestige, for self-expression and for security. They may have a genuine desire to do a good job or they may simply enjoy the competitive game. Some of these desires require money for their fulfillment; while others do not. This means that the economic incentive, which should be distinguished from the profit motive, is not the only drive motivating the laboring man, the businessman, or the executive of a giant concern.

The profit motive as such has frequently been brought under

[64] Garbett, *op. cit.*, p. 278.   [65] *Op. cit.*, pp. 232–33.

the scrutiny of the Christian ethic. Before examining the profit motive, possibly a definition of profit should be given.

It may be defined as the surplus remaining after all the costs of running a business, including the wages of management and labor, allowances for depreciation, interest on capital borrowed, etc., have been met. . . . It is the effort to secure a part or all of this surplus, aside from compensation for work done, that constitutes the pursuit of profit, in the strict sense of that term.[66]

The rather general view in contemporary Christian circles is that profit and hence the profit motive are not necessarily wrong within themselves. "The question of the profit motive is less regarded today as a question of morality than as a question of priority." [67] It is correct, however, that the profit motive, as is true in the main of economic incentives, is self-centered. When such self-centered motives or incentives are considered in relation to other motives and in their impact on human life and relations, they properly become a concern of Christian ethics.

There are some who still contend that there can be no conflict between the profit motive and service to mankind. This faith is one phase of the traditional theory of *laissez faire* capitalism. Although it is no longer generally accepted, yet it may be so interpreted as to have a considerable element of truth in it. While it is not necessarily true of individual businesses and businessmen, it may be true of the entire business community. Howard Bowen has something of this in mind when he says:

We are entering an era when private business will be judged solely in terms of its demonstrable contribution to the general welfare. Leading thinkers among businessmen understand this clearly. For them, therefore, the acceptance of obligations to workers, consumers, and the general public is a condition for survival of the free-enterprise system.[68]

The whole matter of incentives and motives should be brought to the light of the Christian ethic of love. The chief, the dominant, motive for the Christian in every area of his life should be love—

[66] Cameron P. Hall, *Economic Life: A Christian Responsibility* (New York, The Federal Council of the Churches of Christ in America, 1947), p. 42. A booklet.

[67] Bennett *et al., op. cit.,* p. 25.   [68] *Ibid.,* p. 244.

love for God and man. What Toyohiko Kagawa calls "Cross-embracing love" [69] John Bennett speaks of as the "radical ethic of sacrificial love," and frankly admits that it is not easy to move from this radical ethic to principles and attitudes that seem relevant to present-day economic life.[70] But those more relevant principles and purposes should be kept under the constant judgment of the radical ethic of love. Every incentive and motive should be judged by love, kept subservient to Christian love, and, at least to some degree, infused by love. It is love that will enable one to give primacy to the service motive—to one's fellow man, to the community, the nation, the world—and to keep economic incentives under proper control.

4. *Human values and economic life.* One thing that Christian love would dictate is a proper appraisal of and care for the dignity and welfare of people as such. From the perspective of the Christian ethic, incentives and motives, work and wages, property and wealth are to be evaluated in the light of what they do to people. The test of the economic institution or system is not the quantity of goods but the quality of life it produces.

One of the main charges against the competing economic systems of the contemporary period is that they stimulate the materialistic spirit to such a degree that material values overshadow human values. Machines are frequently treated as of more value than the men who operate those machines. Paul G. Hoffman, in "A Critique of American Capitalism," sums the matter up as follows: "I found out . . . that an economic system should not be judged by statistics alone. The only valid basis for judgment is how it affects people. What does it do *for* them, and what does it do *to* them?" [71]

Contemporary Problems and Trends

There are additional problems, some of which represent definite trends, that should be the concern of Christian leaders and churches.

[69] *Brotherhood Economics* (New York, Harper, 1936), p. 34.
[70] Bennett *et al., op. cit.,* p. 206.
[71] William Scarlett (ed.), *The Christian Demand for Social Justice* (New York, New American Library, 1949), p. 61.

1. *Labor and labor unions.*[72] The labor movement has become a powerful force in American life, and in other industrialized nations. The total membership in the American Federation of Labor, the Congress of Industrial Organizations, and in the Railroad brotherhoods and other independent and unaffiliated unions, is estimated to be 15,000,000 to 20,000,000. This represents from a fourth to a third of the gainfully employed in the United States. The importance of organized labor, however, cannot be measured by its numbers alone. Its strength is concentrated in the big industries, the ones which so largely control, from the economic viewpoint, our whole way of life. Furthermore, organized labor has been a major factor in social legislation and in political life in general in recent years.

The labor movement is reaching maturity. It has now attained status under law. Its right to organize and to bargain collectively was guaranteed by the National Labor Relations Act passed by Congress in July, 1935, and declared constitutional by the Supreme Court in April, 1937. This means that the old *laissez faire* concept of labor is a relic of the past. Labor is no longer a commodity that can be purchased on the open market, with the supply and demand determining the wage to be paid. Labor has become independent and at times very vocally independent and self-assertive. It has become one of the power groups in our economy. This fact tends to give the church greater independence in its approach to economic conflicts. It should not feel under compulsion to be either on the side of management because of its power or of labor because of its weakness. The church should be free to see equally the good and the evil in the demands of both management and labor.

The church should seek to help its members, union and nonunion, to understand labor—its organization, achievements, program, and grievances.[78] They should understand that labor not only wants a

[72] Of the many books on labor the following are a few of the better and yet more readable ones: Aleine Austin, *The Labor Story* (New York, Coward-McCann, 1949)—a compact, popular history of the American labor movement; Bernard H. Fitzpatrick, *Understanding Labor* (New York, McGraw-Hill, 1945); P. Sargant Florence, *Labour* (London, Hutchinson's Univ. Lib., 1949)—a study of labor and labor problems in Great Britain; Liston Pope (ed.), *Labor's Relation to Church and Community* (New York, Harper, 1947); and Frank Tannenbaum, *A Philosophy of Labor* (New York, Knopf, 1951).

[78] For a compact but thorough discussion of labor see James Myers, *Do You Know Labor?* (rev. ed.; New York, John Day, 1943).

living wage, but that it also wants what it considers to be a fair share of what it produces and some voice in determining policies and distributing profits. Labor wants full employment, with a guaranteed annual wage. Their leaders argue: "Why should management be paid an annual salary; while labor is paid by the hour? They both live by the year." They also suggest that the matter of a guaranteed annual wage is not only economic justice for the workers but also an economic necessity for our society. It would help to maintain full employment, full production, and full distribution.[74]

While organized Christianity should not identify itself with labor or with any other class, yet it should be sympathetic with the laboring people. It should recognize that the labor union fills just as necessary and should fill just as respected a place in our society as the Chamber of Commerce. It should encourage Christians who are members of labor unions to be active in those unions, and to use their influence in their unions for Christian purposes. When labor, through its unions, does something that violates the Christian spirit and principles, the church should just as readily, but no more readily, remind it of its error as it would remind management.

2. *Freedom and justice.* Freedom and justice are both values or goals highly prized by man, particularly by Western man. The idea of justice, as applied to economic life, has been quite prominent in recent years. The term "justice" when applied to economic matters usually means distributive justice, or what Tillich would possibly call proportional justice.[75] The big question is whether or not man can have full distributive or proportional justice and at the same time preserve his freedom.[76] Bishop Oxnam suggests that "if free-

[74] See Jack Chernick and George C. Hellickson, *Guaranteed Annual Wages* (Minneapolis, University of Minnesota Press, 1945), for a general discussion, with special attention being given to the big three of annual wage plans—Hormel, meat-packers of Austin, Minnesota; Nunn-Bush, shoe manufacturers of St. Louis; and Proctor and Gamble, soap manufacturers of Cincinnati.

[75] Paul Tillich, *Love, Power, and Justice* (New York, Oxford University Press, 1954), p. 63.

[76] Frank H. Knight has a chapter in Ward's *Goals of Economic Life* entitled "Conflict of Values: Freedom and Justice." Albert Lauterbach's *Economic Security and Individual Freedom* (Ithaca, N.Y., Cornell University Press, 1948) has a question appended to the title: "Can we have both?"

dom is to be maintained, justice must be established." [77] It may be that man can have justice and still preserve his freedom if "freedom" is properly understood; but there remains the question: "Can justice in the fullest sense be guaranteed in the contemporary order without some restriction of freedom?" Professor Knight says, "It is alike indefensible to set up either freedom or justice as an absolute principle; so taken, the one means anarchy, the other despotism." [78] It seems that the problem is the maintenance of a proper balance between the two, without any expectation of the complete or absolute attainment of either.

One phase of the struggle for justice, very prevalent in the contemporary period, is the matter of social and economic security. With the high premium that is placed on economic or material values, it now seems that millions of people are willing to give up, if need be, their freedom or liberty to gain economic security. This is one of the reasons for the rise and the constant threat of modern dictators and totalitarian régimes. It seems that in a highly industrialized age a certain amount of governmental provision for social security is necessary, but its dangers should also be realized. How far can the government go in providing for the material needs of its citizens without developing in them an overdependence on the state? How can they be kept from losing individual initiative and incentive? Can a government provide extensive social security service for its people without the state's developing a strong, centralized, paternalistic, bureaucratic government? Does such a government inevitably limit, to a degree, the liberties of its citizens? These questions, which should concern every Christian citizen, have not been answered satisfactorily.

3. *Planning and economic freedom.* The whole matter of economic planning is one of the major problems of the contemporary period. [79] Karl Mannheim, German-born British sociologist and economist, considers it *the* major problem of the modern world. He summarizes the present situation as follows:

We are living in an age of transition from laissez-faire to a planned society. The planned society that will come may take one or two shapes: it will

[77] Bennett *et al., op. cit.,* p. 33.   [78] Ward (ed.), *op. cit.,* p. 229.
[79] Sleeman (*op. cit.*) devotes two chapters of his brief book to planning.

be ruled either by a minority in terms of a dictatorship or by a new form of government which, in spite of its increased power, will still be democratically controlled.[80]

The general thesis of Mannheim's approach is that there is no necessary conflict between planning and freedom, that freedom should be included in the planning. He believes that the Christian movement has a distinctive contribution to make to the effective transfer from a *laissez faire* to a planned economy.[81]

There are many who would disagree with Mannheim about the inevitability and the desirability of planning. John Chamberlain speaks of "planning," along with "full employment," "freedom from want," and "social security," as among the shibboleths of our times. For him "they are the fool's-gold words," and express things that cannot "be had when they are made conscious objects of government policy." [82]

What should we conclude concerning planning? Is it compatible with democracy, or will it destroy democracy? It depends on what is meant by planning, the degree of it, and the methods that are used to achieve it. The National Study Conference, meeting in Detroit in 1950, representing all phases of the business community, adopted among other things the following statement: "The Christian must face up to the issues that are involved both in free enterprise and in adequate planning for the common good. There is a planning that does mean serfdom. There is a planning that does

[80] *Diagnosis of Our Time* (New York, Oxford University Press, 1943), p. 3. Other books by the same author and with a similar emphasis on a planned economy are: *Man and Society in an Age of Reconstruction,* trans. Edward Shils (New York, Harcourt, Brace, 1940), and *Freedom, Power, and Democratic Planning* (New York, Oxford University Press, 1950).

[81] See particularly *Diagnosis of Our Time,* pp. 109 ff.

[82] In Foreword to Friedrich A. Hayek, *The Road to Serfdom* (Chicago, University of Chicago Press, 1944). This book is a rather devastating attack on planning by one who has lived in England since 1931 but who is a native of Austria. With a more definitely British orientation, John Jewkes, a professor of political economy at the University of Manchester, has written another careful but unfavorable appraisal of planning. The title is *Ordeal by Planning* (New York, Macmillan, 1948). And still another book written from an English background, and in a sense an answer to Hayek, is Barbara Wooton, *Freedom Under Planning* (Chapel Hill, University of North Carolina Press, 1945). Still another interesting book, this one by an American economist, which does not deal so directly with planning is John M. Clark's *Alternative to Serfdom* (New York, Knopf, 1948).

contribute to freedom." [83] Attention was directed to existing areas of governmental planning, generally taken for granted by most people, such as education, health, conservation of national resources, foreign policy, national defense, and control of monopolies. In other words, we now have planning. The choice is a matter of degree. Either absolute freedom or absolute control is unhealthy. "The wisest communities have mixed the two creeds in varying proportions." [84]

John M. Clark suggests that thoroughgoing *laissez faire* and complete collectivism are equally unthinkable in the United States. He suggests that "absolute laissez-faire or free enterprise is a myth, the nearest approach to it involves a good deal of control." He offers as one definition of "free enterprise" the following: "A system of controls mainly negative, telling people what they must not do, and leaving them free to choose within the limits thus set. Such a system has elastic limits, which may change with time." [85]

What we have in the United States, and everywhere else, is a mixed economy—some freedom, some planning and control. The only difference is a matter of degree. No country has a purely free-enterprise system. [86] Likewise, there is no country, not even the Soviet Union, in which all of the economy is completely planned and controlled.

The experience of the nations of the world seems to prove that a certain degree of centralized planning, even by the state, will not mean the loss of democracy if that planning is not tied in with a highly emotionally charged ideology that becomes a fanatical faith. In other words, planning, in a way and to a degree, may threaten democracy, but it will not necessarily destroy it. It is possible, in the long run, that the most effective planning will be within the framework of political and economic democracy. It is also possible

[83] Bennett *et al.*, *op. cit.*, pp. 18–19.
[84] Reinhold Niebuhr in Ward (ed.), *op. cit.*, p. 437.
[85] Scarlett (ed.), *op. cit.*, p. 49.
[86] Charles W. Lowry in *Communism and Christ* (New York, Morehouse-Gorham, 1952) suggests that there are five factors in our American mixed economy or personalistic society. They are: (1) free enterprise, (2) state controls—taxation, credit-management, outlawing of monopoly, (3) organized labor, (4) cooperative ventures, and (5) limited governmental agencies for strengthening the business economy, such as social security (p. 133).

that in the midst of the complexities of the contemporary period political democracy cannot be preserved without some economic planning and control. The choice may be between the control of the economic by the political or the state, or the control of the state by a particular economic group, who will use the power of the state for their own privilege and benefit rather than for the good of the people in general.

4. Distribution: National and International. Walter P. Reuther, president of the International Union of United Automobile, Aircraft and Agricultural Workers of America and president of the C.I.O. Division of the A.F. of L.–C.I.O., speaking at a luncheon meeting on the opening day of the National Study Conference on the Church and Economic Life, at Detroit, discerningly said:

We know how to split the atom but we don't know how to feed hungry people when there is too much to eat in the world.[87] We have achieved the technique of working with materials but we have not learned how to work with men. That's the thing we face today as we think about Christianity and the practical application of Christianity to the problems of the world.[88]

Feeding hungry people at home and abroad is primarily a matter of distribution. That there is inequality of distribution of wealth and income is evident on every hand. "An adequate supply of the necessities and comforts of life has been denied to all but a minority." [89]

This does not necessarily mean that we can or should have absolute equality. It is true, however, that "justice in distribution must always be under the criticism of the principle of equality." [90] Equality may and should serve as a corrective principle but not as an attainable goal. To attain absolute equality, at least at the present time, would involve so much regimentation that more would be lost than gained in the process. There is, however, one type of equality that should be an immediate and a continuing goal—equal-

[87] It is doubtful if there is too much to eat in the world. There may actually be inadequate production for all the peoples of the world, although the most immediately pressing problem is distribution.

[88] *National Leaders Speak on Economic Issues* (New York, Federal Council of the Churches of Christ in America, 1950), p. 14, a pamphlet.

[89] Sleeman, *op. cit.*, p. 24.

[90] John Bennett in Ward, *op. cit.*, p. 422.

ity of opportunity. This means an equal opportunity for health, for education, for an opportunity to develop and to utilize one's native abilities.

This matter of a more equitable distribution, rather than an equal distribution, has world-wide implications. The world-wide aspects of the problem have a particularly pressing relevance to the United States and more especially to the Christian citizens of the United States. Our country, with only about 6 per cent of the population of the world, produces about 50 per cent of the world's manufactured goods. Our per capita income is the highest in the world, being many times as much as some of the more backward but also more populous countries of the world. For example, the per capita income of Indonesia was recently reported to be $22 annually as compared to $554 in the United States.[91] The "enormous differences in wealth and standards of living between developed and undeveloped countries have [or should have] long troubled the conscience of men of good will." [92]

Frank Laubach, who possibly knows the illiterate masses of the world as no other man, says that four-fifths of the people of the world are hungry,[93] and that "out of the 2200 million people in the world, 1700 million, usually in debt all of their lives, are in want, more or less oppressed and exploited, and increasingly unhappy and determined to be free from want." [94] It was the Detroit study conference that said, "The hunger of any man anywhere becomes the concern of Christian men everywhere." Christian love would impel the child of God to respond to every human need.

Once one has the Christian concern, or the desire to share, there remains the major problem of methodology. This is not only a problem for the individual Christian, but also for the nation. The privileged individual should be constantly disturbed by an uneasy, sensitive conscience. He should be willing to share with those less fortunate, but he should also keep in mind their moral and spiritual welfare as well as their economic well-being. He may discover

[91] Elizabeth E. Hoyt *et al., American Income and Its Use* (New York, Harper, 1954), p. 86.
[92] Bennett *et al., op. cit.,* p. 165.
[93] *Wake Up or Blow Up* (Westwood, N.J., Revell, 1951), p. 9.
[94] *Ibid.,* p. 30.

that his best service to others will be to attempt to help them to help themselves.

The nation can do some constructive things to distribute more equitable wealth and income, both within the nation and on the international level. A graduated income tax is one approach within the nation. A better distribution can also be accomplished, to a degree, by a minimum wage law, social security benefits, and other provisions made by the government for its citizens. A more equitable distribution of wealth and income is not only just but also wise. Increasing the purchasing power of the lower-income groups would contribute to a more prosperous and healthy economic order.

The same thing would be true, in the long run, on a world scale. The improvement of living standards in the backward, undeveloped areas of the world might entail some sacrifice by the United States and other more prosperous countries, but in the long run it would contribute to the increased prosperity of all nations.[95] Even if it would mean that we, as citizens of the United States, would have to lower, more or less permanently, our own standards of living, should we not be willing to do that for the sake of the hungry world? At least our nation, with proper regard for the independence and well-being of other peoples, should be willing to share with others something of our techniques, our industrial and agricultural know-how.[96] Such an approach, after all, would be much more constructive and permanently beneficial than direct relief or aid.

Conclusion

1. *Concerning the economic system.* Can the problems of the contemporary period be solved within the framework of the existing economic system? When applied to the American economy this question receives sharply different answers. Some suggest that contemporary problems can be solved only if we retain and strengthen the "free enterprise system." Others just as strongly say that the

[95] See Eugene Staley's *The Future of Underdeveloped Countries* (New York, Harper, 1954) for a thorough comparison of the communist and democratic approaches to the problems of the undeveloped areas of the world.

[96] This is the program of Point 4. See Willard R. Espy, *Bold New Program* (New York, Harper, 1950).

system must be so drastically changed that even if the old name is retained the system will be unrecognizable.

From the Christian viewpoint, we are not very much concerned about the name of the system. Names differ tremendously in their meaning and content from era to era. And, after all, there is no Christian economic system. There is no system that can justifiably receive the stamp of divine approval. Bowen summarizes the matter as follows: "Protestant thinkers emphatically deny that *any* particular form of social organization is ordained by God's will or has any claim to support on religious grounds." [97] The Christian movement is concerned with the values preserved and promoted by the system rather than the name of the system. It is interested in what the system does *for* people and *to* people. It is not interested in labels but in achievements.

2. *Concerning economic classes.* One charge against capitalism is that it has contributed to the development of a class and caste structure in our society. Communism, on the other hand, claims that the elimination of economic classes would usher in the socialist utopia. To attain this classless society it, if need be, would liquidate all except the proletariat.

As long as men are unequal in their abilities and have different functions to perform, classes are inevitable. The Christian ideal is the elimination of all class consciousness within the Christian fellowship. In Christ there are no class divisions, and within the church there should be no consciousness of class. Is it possible that if Paul were writing to a modern American church he would change Galatians 5:28 to read as follows: "In Christ there is neither rich nor poor, employer nor employee, bourgeoise nor proletariat, white nor Negro"? Certainly as children of God we are all in his family, brothers and sisters in Christ. Our Father is no respecter of persons, which means that we should not be. Within the Christian fellowship we should not give honor or preferential treatment to any man because of what he has or the type of work he performs.

This raises some question about our class churches. We definitely have them. They tend to invoke religious sanctions for the peculiar

[97] *Op. cit.*, p. 32.

virtues of the group or class which is predominant in the church. These class churches are found in every city and town that is large enough to have more than one church. For example, in mill districts there are distinctly mill churches, in which the vast majority of the members are workers in the mills. In the same community there may be one or more churches whose membership, in the main, will be composed of the millowners, along with business and professional men and their families.[98] Pope shows that there are not only class distinctions among local churches, but also between denominations.[99]

Why this paradox of a profession of a classless fellowship and yet the maintenance of class churches? Have the churches failed to measure up to the ideals they proclaim? The latter implication is correct, but it is not a full explanation for class churches. The church, whether as a general or as a local institution, is both divine and human. In its organized forms it expresses itself in a particular environment and at a particular point in history. It inevitably is influenced by that history and environment. This it seems must be true if its ministry is to be relevant.

Furthermore, the people to whom the church ministers come from differing cultural backgrounds; they represent varying educational levels and vocational interests. Their outlook on life may differ widely. These things determine largely their choice of associates and their relations with others. This carries over to their church. Even different types of religious services appeal to people with varying backgrounds. For example, the socially and economically underprivileged express their religion more in emotional terms than those of the middle and upper classes. Most of them would not feel at home in a beautifully ornate church building, nor in a more or less formal type of worship service. They affiliate, to borrow a term used by H. Richard Niebuhr, with "the churches of the disinherited." They find there a religion that satisfies. Other classes and groups tend to join churches that satisfy their tastes.

Whether we like it or not, it seems that we shall continue to have class churches. This is not particularly bad if there is retained

[98] See Liston Pope, *Millhands and Preachers,* for a study of the mill communities of Gaston County, N.C.
[99] Cf. H. Richard Niebuhr's *The Social Sources of Denominationalism.*

a spirit of Christian fellowship between the churches of different classes. It will be most unfortunate, however, if there arises a hierarchy of class among the churches; if denominational leaders and agencies give special recognition or preferment to the churches of any particular class or to the pastors and leaders of those churches. There is always this danger when class churches exist. It is a temptation for the larger churches and the better established and more respected denominations to cater, in the main, to the middle and upper classes. So much that they desire in their programs is dependent on money. Henson is at least partially correct when he says, "The financial obsessions of the Christian churches must take rank as among the major hindrances to their spiritual influence." He also speaks of the "paradox of ecclesiastical pomp linked with moral failure." [100]

Most major religious bodies will need to exercise particular care that they do not neglect the great mass of common people, those who toil with their hands. The masses are on the march around the world. They are moving up. They represent one of the dynamic forces back of the contemporary crisis that threatens our civilization. They will determine, to a considerable degree, the shape of the future. If the Christian churches want an effective voice in shaping the days ahead, they must keep close to the masses, they must instill the Christian spirit and the Christian hope in those masses, and provide for them the leadership that they need. If this is not done it is possible that the masses will turn, as they already have in some sections of the world, to some worldly "ism" that will give to them the challenging program that they need and the promise of a better tomorrow.

3. *Concerning the functions of the church in the economic realm.* Among the major contributions that the church can and should make in the economic area are the following: (1) "To improve the moral and spiritual climate in which economic institutions function." (2) "As the community of worshipping people from all social groups [it] can help in the overcoming of the most stubborn economic conflicts"—not only of classes but of ideas, ideals, motives,

[100] Herbert H. Henson, *Christian Morality* (Oxford, Clarendon Press, 1936), p. 281.

and purposes. (3) It "can give guidance concerning the ends of economic life and concerning the temptations against which Christians must continually guard themselves." (4) "The most concrete activity of the church in the economic order will be the daily decisions of its members as citizens and in their various occupations." [101]

All of this means that the church to fulfill its functions in society in general and in the economic order in particular (1) must maintain its independence, refusing to identify itself with any particular class, economic system or program; (2) must be satisfied to set out major goals and not get involved in any authoritative statement of techniques or methods to attain those goals; (3) must create within those touched by its message a holy discontent with things as they are, a burning desire to do something constructive to make the purposes of God more of a reality in the workaday world, and enough insight into desirable goals to give direction to them in their efforts; and (4) must give to the people a consciousness of the presence of the living God and the conviction of the possibility of working with him to achieve his will in the realm of economic life.

[101] John Bennett in Ward (ed.), *op. cit.*, p. 428. Reprinted by permission.

VI

COMMUNISM:
ITS SOURCES AND ITS PROGRAM

"A SPECTRE IS haunting Europe—the spectre of Communism." These are the opening words of the Manifesto of the Communist Party, which was written by Karl Marx and Friedrich Engels in 1848. A century later communism is not only haunting Europe but the whole world. A leading American magazine, in recognizing the centennial of the Manifesto, referred to Marx as the "Man of the Century." [1] He has been compared to Jesus as a disruptive influence in the accustomed ways of men. Both "were attacked for destroying religion, and yet both founded new religions, Christianity and Communism. . . . Today these two religious systems face each other in the world. No other force can rival them." [2]

Communism is aggressively seeking to win the world. It is challenging the old ways in the area of economics, politics, philosophy, and religion. It may be "the great unknown of our time," [3] but it is "The Greatest Revolution in Modern History." [4] It is, "without doubt, the most powerful challenge to the Christian religion to-

[1] *Time*, LI (Feb. 23, 1948), 30.
[2] William Hordern, *Christianity, Communism and History* (New York, Abingdon Press, 1954), p. 11.
[3] Martin Ebon, *World Communism Today* (New York, McGraw-Hill, 1948), p. v.
[4] Title of the first chapter in Matthew Spinka's *Christianity Confronts Communism* (New York, Harper, 1936).

day,"[5] and possibly the most formidable foe that Christianity has ever faced. The struggle between the two is for the souls of men. This struggle is an integral part and an extreme expression of the general challenge of modern life to the Christian movement. Communism merely represents the ultimate and seemingly inevitable climax of secularist-humanist trends that are evident everywhere.

The rise and the spread of modern communism[6] is a result of, a factor in, and an evidence of the world crisis that is challenging and threatening civilization in general[7] and Western civilization in particular. Sorokin considers the Russian revolution and the rise of communism as clear manifestations of the disintegration of Western sensate culture.[8] Whether or not Sorokin is entirely correct in his diagnosis, certainly communism is a major factor in the present world crisis.

The Sources of Communism

Any movement of the proportions of communism has its roots deep in the past and is indebted to many men and movements of the past.[9]

[5] D. M. Mackinnon (ed.), *Christian Faith and Communist Faith* (London, Macmillan, 1953), p. x.

[6] "Communism" as used today is "an umbrella word" meaning many different things to different people. Throughout this and the following chapter, however, unless otherwise defined or limited, "communism" will refer to the contemporary forms of the movement as formulated and developed by Marx, Engels, Lenin, and Stalin.

[7] The following are just a few of the publications on some of the world-wide aspects of communism: Conrad Brandt, Benjamin Schwartz, and John K. Fairbank, *A Documentary History of Chinese Communism* (Cambridge, Harvard University Press, 1952)—a reference work of high quality; Olaf Caroe, *Soviet Empire* (London, Macmillan, 1953)—a study of the Turks and Stalinism; Carsun Chang, *The Third Force in China* (New York, Bookman Associates, 1952)—background and history, including American foreign policy; W. P. and Zelda K. Coates, *Soviets in Central Asia* (London, Lawrence and Wishart, 1951) —report of a journey through the Central Asian Republics of the U.S.S.R.; Robert Payne, *Red Storm over Asia* (New York, Macmillan, 1951)—covers most of Asia; Rodger Swearingen and Paul Langer, *Red Flag in Japan* (Cambridge, Harvard University Press, 1952)—systematic study of 1919–1951; O. O. Trullinger, *Red Banners over Asia* (Boston, Beacon Press, 1951)—same coverage in the main as Payne.

[8] Pitirim A. Sorokin, *Leaves from a Russian Diary, and Thirty Years After* (enlarged ed.; Boston, Beacon Press, 1950), p. viii.

[9] Edward Rogers in *A Commentary on Communism* (London, Epworth Press, 1951) goes back to Plato and Aristotle, while Charles W. Lowry in *Communism*

148

1. *Marxism.* Modern communism is based on the work of Karl Marx and is frequently simply equated with Marxism. Socialists of various schools also recognize their indebtedness to Marx and frequently claim the authority of Marx. Most of them admit that original Marxism was revolutionary and they are not. Some claim, however, that otherwise they are closer to Marx than the communists. The latter, on the other hand, may acknowledge that they have made some additions to original Marxist doctrine, but they claim that those additions merely represent developments and are in harmony with the spirit of the writings of Marx and Engels.

This much must be acknowledged: communism is a child of Marxism, and it is the most robust and mature of her children. There was communism of a kind before Marx, but it "was a vague sort of concept, a hazy mingling of social idealism . . . diffused benevolence, and a yearning for a better way of life." [10] Marx's relation to communism was somewhat comparable to the relation of Walter Rauschenbusch to the Social Gospel Movement. The latter gave the Social Gospel Movement a theology and general respectability. Marx gave communism a theoretical foundation or a philosophy. He gave direction, drive, and a vision to the movement.

No doctrine was more central to original Marxism and is more central in contemporary communism than the doctrine of dialectical materialism. Other materialistic philosophies, in the main, have been satisfied to describe the world. Marx was determined to change it. Engels, in a speech at the graveside of Marx, said, "Before all else, Marx was a great revolutionist." [11] He believed that there was a law of change or of dialectic at the heart of the universe. Nature was in constant change. In harmony with the dialectical emphasis, Marx contended that the future always belonged to the new forces that were arising.

Marx borrowed the conception of the dialectic from Hegel. He rejected, however, the latter's idealism and substituted a thoroughgoing materialism. Hegel's system was an attempt to prove that a rational pattern governs reality. For him reality was not static but

and Christ would also include Rousseau in the background for socialism and communism.

[10] Rogers, *A Commentary on Communism*, p. 67.

[11] R. N. Carew Hunt, *Marxism: Past and Present* (New York, Macmillan, 1955), p. 2. Chapter I of this book defines "dialectic," and Chapter II defines "materialism."

dynamic. It was constantly in movement, in the process of becoming. In the process contradictions inevitably arose. These contradictions involved what he termed a thesis and an antithesis. The conflict between the thesis and the antithesis is reconciled in a synthesis, which represents a uniting of the best elements in both the thesis and the antithesis. This synthesis becomes a new thesis and the process starts over again. This process of conflict and of reconciliation is both the cause and the explanation of change and development. The dialectical approach may be defined roughly as the theory of the union of opposites, or "as a kind of opposition in which the opposites interpenetrate and modify one another." [12]

Marx, as thoroughly as Hegel, used the law of dialectic to explain historical development. "At the same time, he condemned Hegel for identifying the Idea with reality." [13] Alexander Miller suggests that Marx "stood Hegel's philosophy on its head and claimed that only then was it right way up." [14] Marx himself claimed that the dialectic in its original form was a dialectic of nature; that Hegel turned it upside down when he gave it an idealistic form. [15]

The development within history, which was explained by the dialectical process, is never identified by Marx and Engels with evolution. Such an identification might seem to be a more or less natural conclusion. However, they condemned all evolutionary theories as inadequate. They "were looking for a principle which would uphold a doctrine of revolution rather than of evolution, and it was because the dialectic appeared to do this that they incorporated it into their system." [16]

The dialectic of Marx was materialistic, his dialectical materialism being the basis of all of his mature thinking, "and the key to the understanding of his work." [17] For Marxism there can be only two opposing philosophical systems—idealism and materialism. For idealism, mind is primary; and the material, if it exists at all, is secondary. For materialism, matter or the material is primary. For Marxism the material is not only primary; it is the source of every-

[12] Mackinnon, *op. cit.*, p. 8.   [13] Hunt, *op. cit.*, p. 11.
[14] *The Christian Significance of Karl Marx* (New York, Macmillan, 1946), p. 7.
[15] Mackinnon, *op. cit.*, p. 11.   [16] Hunt, *op. cit.*, p. 13.
[17] Mackinnon, *op. cit.*, p. 6.

thing else. Engels quoted Feuerbach, a left-wing Hegelian who greatly influenced Marx but who was also criticized by him, as follows:

The material, sensuously perceptible world to which we ourselves belong is the only reality; and . . . our own consciousness and thinking, however suprasensuous they may seem, are the product of a material, bodily organ, the brain. Matter is not a product of mind, but mind itself is merely the highest product of matter.[18]

It was Engels himself who said that "materialism regards the concepts in our heads as images . . . of real things, instead of regarding the real things as images of this or that state of development of an absolute concept." [19] Lenin declared that "there is nothing in the world except matter and its motion." [20] For him "the material world exists objectively and independently of the perceiving mind." [21] From the thoroughgoing Marxist viewpoint dialectical materialism is the only scientific explanation for reality. Idealism is considered nonscientific and is usually associated with religion.[22]

When dialectical materialsm, or as Lowry prefers to call it dialectic-and-matter,[23] is applied to the world and to human relations the result is historical materialism and economic determinism. All of history is interpreted in materialistic terms. The determining factors, so it is claimed, in any culture or civilization are the material elements which provide the foundation on which every other phase of the culture is built. The ultimately decisive factor in past history, in contemporary society, and in the life of the individual is the economic or the material. The Marxist also believes that there are certain economic laws that are inevitably leading or compelling the world to move in the direction of socialism or communism. This is a part of his economic determinism. It is claimed that the dialectic itself guarantees the ultimate triumph of communism in society. This is true because communism is the logical outcome and

[18] Spinka, *op. cit.*, pp. 173–74.   [19] Hunt, *op. cit.*, p. 20.
[20] *Ibid.*, p. 22.   [21] *Ibid.*, p. 23.
[22] Nicolas Berdyaev claims that the materialism of Marx is very dubious; that there is a struggle between humanist and antihumanist elements in Marxism; and that the Marxists really become idealists by attributing reason, freedom, and creative power, all of which are spiritual faculties, to matter and economic ideas. See *Towards a New Epoch* (London, Geoffrey Bles, 1949), pp. 20, 102.
[23] *Op. cit.*, pp. 14–15.

the final answer to the contradictions in all other economic systems. The dialectic for the party member is comparable to what Providence is for the Christian.[24] Observing the development of history along dialectical lines, the Marxist concludes that there is a definite pattern in history. Once that pattern is discovered, one can not only interpret correctly the past but also predict the future.[25]

2. *The Russian influence.* The opening sentences of Nicolas Berdyaev's book that deals most directly and exclusively with communism are as follows:

> Russian Communism is difficult to understand on account of its twofold nature. On the one hand it is international and a world phenomenon; on the other hand it is national and Russian. It is particularly important for Western minds to understand the national roots of Russian Communism and the fact that it was Russian history which determined its limits and shaped its character.[26]

Marx was a German, and original Marxism was a product of the West. It is possible that if the influence of Marxism had been confined to the West, it would "have done much good and little harm." [27] But it was not confined to the West. It became a Western heresy. It "went to Russia and was there transformed." It became a distorted form of Marxism which was adapted to a backward society, which had been exposed to the impact of the West.[28] Marxism "was adopted to Russian conventions and was Russified. The messianic idea of Marxism which was connected with the mission of the proletariat, was combined and identified with the Russian messianic idea," [29] although the communists may have distorted the latter.[30] According to Berdyaev and others the Russian people have a deep sense of destiny. Messianism has been almost as strong among them as it ever was among the Jews.[31] Berdyaev himself has

[24] Hunt, *op. cit.*, p. 17.   [25] *Ibid.*, p. 14.
[26] *The Origin of Russian Communism* (New York, Scribner's, 1937), p. 1.
[27] John Plamenatz, *German Marxism and Russian Communism* (London, Longmans, Green, 1954), p. 317.
[28] *Ibid.*, p. 318.
[29] Nicolas Berdyaev, *The Russian Idea* (New York, Macmillan, 1947), p. 249.
[30] *Ibid.*, p. 250.
[31] *Ibid.*, p. 34. Toynbee (*Civilization on Trial* [New York, Oxford University Press, 1948], p. 172) says that the Russian sense of orthodoxy and of destiny was taken over from the Byzantine Greeks and characterized earlier governments in Russia as well as the existing communist régime.

been very definitely affected by this unique sense of mission of his people. It is this sense of a unique messianic mission that helps to explain the powerful dynamic and drive of Russian communism.

Closely related to the Russian messianic concept has been the vigorous apocalyptic and prophetic elements in Russian thought and literature. The influence of these elements can be seen in contemporary communism. The communist approach to life and history is apocalyptic. This fact helps to explain its fierce intolerance.

The preceding are only a few of the elements in the Russian soul which provided fallow ground for communism. Harold J. Laski suggests that there is "an irrepressible anarchism in the Russian mind." [32] Charles Malik says that the Russian soul, "maturing into self-consciousness amidst terrific social dislocation and estrangement . . . developed a revolutionary vision of equality and social justice." [33] While suggesting that the atheistic materialism of communism was foreign to the deepest and highest in Russian literature, he does say that there "is a genuine spiritual ground in the Russian soul which enabled atheistic communism to foist itself on it."

These apocalyptic, revolutionary, anarchistic trends in Russian life help to explain such great creative writers as Tolstoi, Dostoevski, and others. On the other hand, these men in turn provided some of the Russian background favorable to communism. They were revolutionaries, although they may be considered revolutionaries of the spirit. There are even anarchistic tendencies in some of their writings. At least they prepared the way, along with other forces and factors, for the overthrow of the old régime and the establishment of communism.

The Russian contribution to communism is seen not only in the influences that provided the seedbed for Russian communism and helped to predetermine the shape it would take. A distinctive contribution has been made by Lenin and others who have interpreted Marxism for the Russian people and have applied the Marxist theories to Russian life and struggles. Marx may have been the only "truly original and great thinker" among the four fathers of

[32] *The Dilemma of Our Times* (London, George Allen & Unwin, 1952), p. 59.

[33] *War and Peace* (New York, National Committee for a Free Europe), p. 27. This booklet, which is a concise analysis, was a statement made before the Political Committee of the General Assembly of the United Nations, Nov. 23, 1949, by the Minister of Lebanon to the United States and Chairman of the Delegation of Lebanon to the Fourth Session of the General Assembly.

communism,[34] but at least the work of Marx had to be interpreted and applied. The most creative of these interpreters was Lenin, called by Lowry "the eldest son" of Marx and "the Messiah of Communism." [35] It was Lenin who "streamlined the ponderous Marxist doctrine into a fast-moving revolutionary chariot." [36]

At least one student of Marxism does not consider Lenin a thinker of any importance. He labels him as a practical politician and a revolutionary leader who "left Marxism poorer than he found it." [37] The same author claims that Lenin added nothing to Marxism

that was really his own except some reflections about the peculiar character of the class struggle and the proper organization of a revolutionary Marxist party in a backward country like Russia, together with a variety of precepts about the tactics that party should adopt in order to get power sooner than Marxism, as most people then understood it, would lead one to suppose was possible.[38]

The contributions of Lenin to Marxism may not have been very important in the area of theory or philosophy, but the additions he made to the Marxist strategy or techniques were of major significance. Hunt sets out what he considers to be Lenin's main contributions to Marxism. In brief these were his theories concerning the following: (1) the strategy and tactics of revolution; (2) the dictatorship of the proletariat; (3) the Party as "the vanguard of the proletariat" [39] which guides the masses before and after the revolution; (4) the strategy and tactics to be adopted by communist parties in the world revolution; (5) capitalist imperialism, which he considered "the final stage of Capitalism"; and (6) his restatement of the philosophy of dialectical materialism. Space will not permit even a brief elaboration of these six contributions.[40] They are given merely to suggest that Russian communism is Marxism

---

[34] Plamenatz, *op. cit.,* p. 5. The four fathers, according to Plamenatz, were Marx, Engels, Lenin, and Stalin. It seems since the death of Stalin that most communist leaders would reject him as one of the fathers.

[35] *Op. cit.,* p. 24.   [36] Rogers, *A Commentary on Communism,* p. 183.

[37] Plamenatz, *op. cit.,* p. xxi.   [38] *Ibid.,* p. xxii.

[39] Munby and Mackinnon, in Mackinnon, *op. cit.,* p. 34, speak of the Leninist conception of the party as "the disciplined *élite.*"

[40] R. N. Carew Hunt in *The Theory and Practice of Communism* (rev. ed.; New York, Macmillan, 1952) discusses them (pp. 136–68). He also has a brief statement concerning "Stalin's contribution to Marxist-Lenin Theory" (pp. 169–71).

interpreted and applied by Lenin. The Lenin interpretation of Marxism is presently the orthodox line, accepted by the communists of the world.

Hunt goes so far as to say that Lenin was anxious "to provide a Marxist justification for a revolution undertaken in defiance of Marxist principles and requiring thereafter to be sustained by absolutist methods." He suggests that Stalin grafted Marxism "on to the Asiatic-Byzantine tradition, with a consequent return to autocracy— the only form of government the Russians have ever known." [41] Toynbee similarly says that the Russians, for a thousand years, have been members of the Byzantine rather than Western civilization. They have strongly resisted the threat of being overwhelmed by the Western world. In order to meet successfully the challenge of the West, the Russians have repeatedly adopted Western technology and turned it against the West.[42] The communists of the contemporary period are keeping up that resistance to the West. In a more recent publication Toynbee suggests that Russian communists are not only using Western technology to meet the challenge of the West; but for the first time they are using a Western ideology, a Western heresy (Marxism) to resist the West. This Western heresy, which is a criticism of the West, has been turned against the West.[43]

Thus we see that although Marxism was a creation of the West— Marx was a German and the Communist Manifesto was adopted at a meeting of socialists in London—it was adapted by the Russians, who belong both to the West and to the East.

3. *Christianity*. It may sound strange to say, but it is true, that one source of atheistic communism is Christianity. We have previously implied that one possible source for the strong eschatological, prophetic, messianic elements in Russian thought was the Hebrew-Christian tradition. The communist idea of a golden age of the past which will be realized again in the future is somewhat similar to the Christian conception of the fall of man from a state of innocency and the hope for the victory of God in the future. The latter has been particularly strong among the sectarians.[44] This element

---

[41] *Ibid.*, pp. 169–70.   [42] Toynbee, *Civilization on Trial*, p. 166.
[43] Arnold J. Toynbee, *The World and the West* (New York, Oxford University Press, 1953).
[44] Hordern, *op. cit.*, pp. 57 ff.

of hope is one of many similarities between communism and sectarian Christianity to which Hordern calls attention. He does suggest, however, that there is a marked difference in the content of and the basis for the hope.[45]

There also has been some historical relationship between certain forms of communism and some Christian groups through the centuries. Community of property was practiced, at least to some degree, by Jesus and his disciples [46] and by the Church at Jerusalem.[47] This might imply that voluntary communism would be the ultimate expression of the Christian spirit in the economic area. Whether or not such a conclusion is correct, it is true that community of goods has been practiced by some Christian groups throughout the centuries. A type of Christian communism was practiced by the monks in the monasteries who, although separated from the world, continued within the main stream of the Christian movement. The trend toward some type of communism was particularly prevalent among the sectarians of the Middle Ages, who were outside the main stream of the Christian movement and who were persecuted by the church.[48] A similar emphasis on community of goods was found among the Levellers in England in the days of Cromwell.[49]

We do not mean by the preceding that there is any necessary historic relation between contemporary communism and the Christian communism of the past. The community of goods practiced in the Jerusalem Christian fellowship, and to some degree by Christian groups through the centuries, was drastically different from Russian communism of the contemporary period. The former was a practical expression of Christian love by a minority group who were under pressure, real or imagined, by an unfriendly world. It was

---

[45] *Ibid.,* p. 87.   [46] John 12:5.   [47] Acts 2:44–45; 4:32–37.

[48] Hordern (*op. cit.*) gives particular emphasis to the sects. Also see Karl Kautsky, *Communism in Central Europe in the Time of the Reformation,* trans. J. L. and E. G. Mulliken (London, T. Fisher Unwin, 1897), and M. Beer, *Social Struggles in the Middle Ages* (London, George Allen and Unwin, 1924). For a study of a group that has maintained rather consistently community of goods for over four centuries, see John Horsch, *The Hutterian Brethren* (Goshen, Ind., Mennonite Historical Society, 1931). Arthur E. Bestor's *Backwoods Utopias* (Philadelphia, University of Pennsylvania Press, 1950) is a study of communitarian experiments in the United States such as the New Harmony Colony.

[49] See Eduard Bernstein, trans. H. J. Stenning, *Cromwell and Communism* (London, George Allen & Unwin, 1930), especially Chapters VIII and IX.

not based on a carefully formulated social theory or philosophy, and was entirely voluntary. In spite of all this, there is a considerable possibility that the roots of modern communism go back, at least indirectly, to some forms of Christian communism.

Whether the latter is correct or not "there is . . . in Communism a deposit of Christian influence of great importance," and "Communism could only have been developed on soil prepared by Christianity." [50] Toynbee suggests that while Marx would have described himself as a disciple of Hegel, yet

the elements that have made Communism an explosive force are not of Hegel's creation; they bear on their face their certificate of origin from the ancestral religious faith of the West . . . Christianity. . . . And such elements as cannot be traced to Christianity can be traced to Judaism.[51]

Communism has also been spoken of as "a Christian heresy." It was the Lambeth Conference of 1948 which said: "Marxism, by an ironic paradox, is at some points nearer to the Christian doctrine than any other philosophy, and this makes its rivalry all the more formidable." [52] Many would agree with Hordern that "Communism is 'Christian' only in the sense that it shares certain ideals of the Christian culture in which it grew. It is heretical in the sense that these ideals take on a perverted form within the Communist context." [53]

Alasdair C. MacIntyre on the title page of his book on Marxism [54] quotes O. Spengler as follows: "Christianity is the grandmother of Bolshevism." There is also included a quotation from R. H. Tawney as follows: "The true descendant of the doctrines of Aquinas is the labour theory of value. The last of the Schoolmen was Karl Marx." MacIntyre himself concludes that Marxism is "a secularism and an atheism such as only a Christian culture can produce." [55] As suggested previously, and as we shall see again later, there are marked

[50] John C. Bennett, *Christianity and Communism* (New York, Association Press, 1948), p. 46.
[51] *A Study of History* (Somervell's abridgment; New York, Oxford University Press, 1946), pp. 399–400.
[52] Quoted by Rogers, *A Commentary on Communism*, p. 115.
[53] *Op. cit.*, p. 57.
[54] *Marxism: An Interpretation* (London, S.C.M. Press, 1953).
[55] *Ibid.*, p. 14.

contrasts between Christianity and communism. There can be no abiding peace between the two as long as each remains as it is. And we might add that there can be no peace between the two as long as Christianity remains as it should.

John Macmurray in his rather sympathetic and friendly interpretation of communism claims that

Christianity is the source of Communism, and Communism has moved into dialectical opposition to Christianity through the process by which Christianity in its conscious form has been divorced from material realities. A Christianity which withdrew its beliefs from association with the temporal realties of earthly life must inevitably produce out of itself a temporal theory which divorces itself from the eternal and spiritual reality.

He further claims rather optimistically that

the clear separation of these not merely as opposing theories but as antagonistic forces in the field of social development is the necessary prelude to their synthesis in a Christianity which has become real at the full height of its mature development.[56]

Macmurray possibly goes too far in claiming such a direct relation of Christianity and communism and in predicting so positively a synthesis of the two. There can be no doubt, however, that the withdrawal of Christianity, to such a large degree, "from association with the temporal reality of life," has been a factor in the contemporary rise and spread of communism. There has been a strong tendency in Christian groups to make too sharp a distinction between the secular and the sacred, restricting God's interest and activity to the latter. Communism is the fullest expression, in the contemporary period, of this division of the sacred and the secular and the resulting tendency toward the secularization of all of life.

At the same time, communism seems to represent, in a sense and to a degree, a struggle toward a new unification of life. At least the appeal of communism is based, to a considerable degree, upon the need of mankind for a unifying force in life. This need, in turn, has arisen largely because modern Christianity has accepted its compartmental status to such a marked degree that it no longer provides

[56] John Macmurray, *Creative Society: A Study of the Relation of Christianity to Communism* (New York, Association Press, 1936), p. 126.

a basis for the unification of all of life. This is true, in the main, of individual Christians. Few of them consider their love for God and their devotion to his kingdom the unifying center of their lives. Their religion is not the total to which every other phase of their lives is subservient and instrumental. What is true of individual Christians is certainly true of society. Christianity is generally considered merely one compartment of life. But the individual and society need and demand some center of centers, some dominant value around which all of life can be built and unified. By failing to be such a center of centers, by failing to be totalitarian enough, Christianity has contributed at least negatively to the rise and the spread of communism. Communism "covers certain ground that was once occupied by the Church, but which during recent centuries has been largely abandoned by the Church." [57]

Nicolas Berdyaev emphasizes constantly this negative contribution of Christianity to communism. In one place he says:

Christians, who condemn the communists for their godlessness and anti-religious persecutions, cannot lay the whole blame solely upon these godless communists; they must assign part of the blame to themselves, and that a considerable part. They must be not only accusers and judges; they must also be penitents. Have Christians done very much for the realization of Christian justice in social life? Have they striven to realize the brotherhood of man without that hatred and violence of which they accuse the communists? The sins of Christians, the sins of the historical churches, have been very great, and these sins bring with them their just punishment. [58]

The lack of vitality and virility in many Christian groups has tended to create a spiritual vacuum at the heart of many nations, and one is almost persuaded to say at the heart of Western civilization. Communism, with a dynamic world program and a challenge to vicarious living, has attempted, and succeeded to a degree, to move into that vacuum. In other words, the spread of communism is, in various ways and to a considerable degree, an indictment against the Christian churches.

[57] Peck, *A Christian Economy*, p. 94.
[58] *The Origin of Russian Communism*, pp. 207-8.

The Program of Communism

The communist program challenges the free-enterprise economic system, the democratic political concept, the general philosophical and value system of the West, and the Christian religion. It offers a different way of life.

1. *Program for economic life.*[59] The over-all economic goal of communism can be briefly summarized as the public ownership and control of the basic means of production, distribution, and credit. The major phases of economic life would be centrally planned and directed. Decisions about prices, investments, wages, and hours would not be determined by the employees nor by the employers but by a planning group or board, which, at least theoretically, would represent all the people. Really there would be no employer in the ordinary sense of the word.

Under communism there would be a planned rather than a free economy. In fairness it should be said that there is no completely free economy today. Even in the so-called capitalistic countries there are increasing degrees of planning and control. The movement toward a planned rather than a strictly free economy may have resulted, to a degree, from the influence of communism but possibly even more from the general economic conditions in the world. Those conditions, in turn, have been created, at least to a degree, by the capitalistic system. The general economic situation in the world has been a factor in creating an atmosphere somewhat favorable to the rise and spread of communism.

As a part of its economic program, communism would eliminate the capitalist and the landlord class. The program to liquidate the capitalist and to overthrow the capitalistic system is based theoretically, at least to a considerable degree, on Marx's theory of value and surplus value. For him labor alone creates value. Profits are derived from unpaid labor time. This unpaid labor time pro-

[59] Among the better books that deal largely or exclusively with the economic phases of the communist program are: Alexander Baykov, *The Development of the Soviet Economic System* (New York, Macmillan, 1947), which is "An Essay on the Experience of Planning in the U.S.S.R."; and Maurice Dobb, *Soviet Economic Development Since 1917* (London, Routledge and Kegan Paul, 1948).

vides the surplus value that is in the product sold. When the investor or capitalist takes this surplus for his own profit, it is robbery from the communist viewpoint. The surplus, according to the communists, rightfully belongs to the one who produced it.

It should be admitted that the Soviet Union has been able to make considerable economic progress under the communist program. Dobb suggests that there are at least two reasons why the economic development of the U.S.S.R. should hold a special interest for us: (1) "It provides the first case in history of a working-class form of State . . . carrying out the expropriation of the former propertied class and establishing a socialist form of economy." [60] (2) "It affords a unique example of the transformation of a formerly backward country to a country of extensive industrialisation and modern technique at an unprecedented *tempo*." [61] After the strength demonstrated by the Soviet Union during World War II, there can be no doubt about its industrial progress under communism. The progress itself posits a question: Can contemporary communism make appreciable progress in any country that is not backward? If it *cannot,* and so far it has not proved that it can, then that fact would contradict or nullify a basic claim of Marxism. The latter considers communism as the next step in economic development after capitalism. The latter is supposed inevitably to collapse and make room for communism. But communism so far has not made much progress in the more highly industrialized countries. This fact is potentially serious enough that it may properly raise some question about the whole theoretical base of the economic program and of the political philosophy of the movement.

2. *Program for the political order.* While Marx considered the political of secondary importance, giving primary emphasis to the social and economic, his contemporary followers have an "almost neurotic obsession . . . with politics." [62] In this study of the political, as in the case of the economic, we shall restrict ourselves to basic theories and general principles. We shall not discuss the political machinery of the Soviet Union [63] or the infiltration of com-

[60] *Ibid.,* p. 1.   [61] *Ibid.,* p. 2.
[62] Mackinnon, *op. cit.,* p. 36.
[63] That has been done adequately in books such as Barrington Moore, Jr., *Soviet Politics—The Dilemma of Power* (Cambridge, Harvard University Press,

munism into American political life.[64] More basic, after all, than political machinery is the philosophy or theory back of that machinery.

The logical beginning place for a discussion of the political philosophy of the communists is their theory concerning the origin and nature of the state. Marx possessed a deep distrust of the state. He considered the state an evil [65] that would "disappear in the eventual classless society." He seemed to have held two theories of the state. One, "that it is an instrument of class oppression." The other, "that it is sometimes a parasite superior to all classes." [66] According to Engels, the state was created by society, but once created it tended to become a law unto itself.[67] Its power was and is used to maintain class distinctions. According to the Communist Manifesto, "Political power, in the exact sense of the words, is organized force of one class to repress another." Lenin similarly says that "the state is a machine to sustain the domination of one class over another." [68] According to Stalin the state "arose in order to keep in restraint the exploited majority in the interests of the exploiting minority." [69] The bourgeois state was considered "the executive committee of the bourgeoisie." The democracy of the bourgeois state, while it is not true democracy, was to act, however, "as the foster-mother of the proletariat during the state of pre-emancipation." [70] Even in the period when the bourgeois state is smashed

---

1950), and Frederick L. Schuman, *Soviet Politics at Home and Abroad* (New York, Knopf, 1946).

[64] See Morris Ernst and David Loth, *Report on the American Communist* (New York, Henry Holt, 1952), and Jacob Spolansky, *The Communist Trail in America* (New York, Macmillan, 1951). Spolansky, Russian born, was for many years a Federal Bureau of Investigation agent.

[65] There have been many Christians through the centuries who have likewise considered the state a necessary evil—necessary because of the sinful nature of man. Others have defended the state as a good, coming directly from God and provided for man's good. Leaders of the Enlightenment considered the state as contrary to nature, and hence evil.

[66] Plamenatz, *op. cit.*, p. 151.

[67] Hunt, *Marxism: Past and Present*, pp. 106, 110.

[68] Andrei Y. Vyshinsky (ed.), *The Law of the Soviet State* (New York, Macmillan, 1948), p. 11.

[69] Hunt, *Marxism: Past and Present*, p. 108.

[70] Hunt, *The Theory and Practice of Communism*, p. 69.

and the proletariat takes over, it was considered advisable and necessary to have the support of left-wing bourgeois elements.

Although the communist theory is that the state originated out of class conflicts and contradictions, yet communists recognize the need for the state in the transition period while society moves from capitalism to communism. During this transition there will be what Marx calls "the revolutionary dictatorship of the proletariat." The state will be an instrument of this proletariat dictatorship. The state under the control of the proletariat will be, as it always is, an instrument of repression and not freedom. Lenin quotes Engels as follows: "So long as the proletariat still *needs* the state, it needs it not in the interest of freedom, but in the interest of the repression of its opponents, and when it becomes possible to speak of freedom, the state as such ceases to exist." [71] However, it is claimed that there is a sharp difference between the bourgeois controlled state and the proletariat dictatorship. The power of the former is used by the minority to coerce or enslave the majority; the power of the latter is used by or at least in the interest of the majority to coerce the minority, who were formerly the oppressors. The state to be used effectively by the proletariat dictatorship must be strong and ruthless.

In spite of its ruthlessness, the communists claim that the proletariat-controlled state is truly democratic. For them there can be no real democracy in a bourgeois state, which is controlled by the economically privileged. On the other hand, proletarian democracy is equated by Lenin with the dictatorship of the proletariat.[72] Vyshinsky claims that the proletariat state "represents the highest form of democracy possible in a class society," [73] and says that Leninism "correctly affirms that Soviet democracy and the Soviet state are a million times more democratic than the most democratic bourgeois republic." [74]

If we are to understand and to evaluate properly the preceding, we must understand that

[71] Edward H. Carr, *The Bolshevik Revolution, 1917–1923* (New York, Macmillan, 1950), I, 242. Pages 233–49 are a concise statement of "Lenin's Theory of the State."

[72] Vyshinsky, *op. cit.*, p. 48. [73] *Ibid.*, p. 41. [74] *Ibid.*, p. 43.

for Russians, and for Marxists generally, a country is democratic in proportion as the land and means of production belong to the people, who
are regarded in this connection not as individuals but as classes, these
being ultimately reducible to the single class of workers and peasants.[75]

In other words, the communist conception of democracy places
the emphasis primarily and at least theoretically upon "for the
people," whereas the American emphasis has been more largely
upon "of and by the people."

There is at least one other basic Marxist concept, previously referred to, concerning the state which is of major importance in the
communist theory of the state. It is the idea of the "withering" or
"disappearing" state. The state, as suggested previously, is an instrument to be used by the proletariat during the transition from a
capitalistic, class-conscious society to classless communism. As progress is made toward the ultimate goal of a completely communistic
society, the state will wither away; and finally, when communism
fully comes, there will no longer be a need for the state. Marx and
Lenin both agreed that "the proletarian state will begin to die away
immediately after its victory, since in a society without class contradictions, the state is unnecessary and impossible."[76] Stalin similarly says: "The state is primarily a weapon of one class against
another class. Thus it follows quite clearly that as soon as there are
no classes there will also be no state."[77]

Carr, after saying that Lenin's theory of the state reflected the
dichotomy in Marxist thought "which combined a highly realist and
relativist analysis of the historical process with an uncompromising
absolute vision of the ultimate goal," then succinctly summarizes
"the essence of what Marx and Lenin believed." He says that they
believed in "transformation of reality into Utopia, of the relative
into the absolute, of incessant class conflict into the classless society,
and of the ruthless use of state power into the stateless society."[78]

What has happened to this original Marxist doctrine? It seems
that it is still considered the ultimate goal of communism, but its
attainment is now postponed to the indefinite future. Hunt goes so

[75] Hunt, *The Theory and Practice of Communism,* p. 67.
[76] Carr, *op. cit.,* I, 241.
[77] Hunt, *Marxism: Past and Present,* pp. 108–9.
[78] Carr, *op. cit.,* I, 249.

far as to say that there is no doctrine that has caused more embarrassment to present-day Marxists, and that they have come near to repudiating it altogether.[79] In fairness we should admit that Lenin, while speaking of "the inevitable withering away of the state," added the following:

We must emphasize the protracted nature of this process and its dependence upon the rapidity of development of the *higher phase* of communism; and we leave the question of length of time, or the concrete forms of the withering away, quite open, because *no material is available* to enable us to answer these questions.[80]

It is true, however, that Lenin in 1918 had put the transition period at "ten years or perhaps more"; in 1919 he predicted that "a majority of those present who have not passed the age of 30 or 35 will see the dawn of communism, from which we are still far"; still later he wrote that "ten or twenty years sooner or later make no difference when measured by the scale of world history." [81]

At times Lenin comes close to admitting that once the state becomes proletarian, the ordinary objections to it are no longer valid.[82] Stalin in 1930 first specifically modified the doctrine of the withering away of the state. He recognized that the strengthening of the dictatorship of the proletariat was inconsistent with the doctrine of the withering state. He said, however, that "this contradiction is a living thing, and completely reflects Marxist dialectics." [83]

Really, instead of the state withering away, the power of the state under Russian communism has been increased tremendously. In a sense communism has become an instrument used by the Russian state. Berdyaev, who certainly interprets sympathetically the Russian people and is quite objective in his appraisal of communism, says,

Communism in the form in which it has appeared in Russia is extreme *étatism;* it is the appearing of the monster Leviathan which has laid its paws upon everything. The Soviet Government . . . is the one totalitarian state in the world which is carried to its logical consistent end.[84]

[79] *The Theory and Practice of Communism,* p. 65.
[80] Quoted by Lowry, *op. cit.,* pp. 26–27.
[81] Carr, *op. cit.,* I, 241.
[82] Hunt, *Marxism: Past and Present,* p. 115.
[83] *Ibid.,* p. 117.
[84] *The Origin of Russian Communism,* p. 227.

It has really turned the state into a church. According to Dallin, the Soviet press no longer belittles the state but speaks of "our great state," and he suggests that "Soviet Empire" could well be adopted.[85] "In Russia . . . whatever is felt to be to the advantage of the State is justice."[86] There is no law above the state. It is a law unto itself.

Do the communists justify this shift of position in regard to the state? Yes, they do. For example, Vyshinsky says that the state will wither away only under "complete communism" and "with the triumph of communism in all advanced capitalist countries."[87] The former idea is in Marx but the latter definitely is not. The present communist viewpoint is that the state will not and cannot wither away so long as the capitalist encirclement continues. Stalin says "that the withering away of the state will come not through a weakening of the state authority but through its maximum intensification, which is necessary to finish off the remnants of the dying classes and to organize defense against capitalist encirclement."[88] Thus the communist leaders justify their totalitarian state and their departure, at least to some degree, from the original Marxist doctrine concerning the state.

3. *Program for the arts and sciences.* As one would expect under a totalitarian régime, every phase of life is controlled under the communist system. "Communism needs the technician, the skilled worker and the popular artist, but it trusts none of them."[89] It "cannot afford to offer concessions to risky thoughts." Vyshinsky expresses the general position as follows:

In our state, naturally, there is and can be no place for freedom of speech, press, and so on for the foes of socialism. . . .

Freedom of speech, of the press, of assembly, of meetings, of street parades, and of demonstrations are the property of all the citizens in the USSR, fully guaranteed by the state upon the single condition that they be utilized in accord with the interests of the toilers and to the end of strengthening the socialist social order.[90]

[85] David J. Dallin, *The Real Soviet Russia,* trans. Joseph Shaplen (New Haven, Yale University Press, 1944), p. 29.
[86] Peck, *op. cit.,* p. 111.   [87] *Op. cit.,* p. 60.   [88] *Ibid.,* p. 62.
[89] Harry Hodgkinson, *Challenge to the Kremlin* (New York, Frederick A. Praeger, 1952), p. 17. A study of communism from a background of the struggle between Tito and Stalin.
[90] *Op. cit.,* p. 617.

The "and so on" in the above quotation covers every conceivable area of life. Every phase of the arts, the sciences, and related fields are subject to party control and must serve the Revolution. They are a part of the total educational program of the Soviet Union. The educational system, including the schools and every possible informal instrument for educational purposes, constitute "the most gigantic and comprehensive marshalling of forces to shape the human mind in the whole history of mankind." [91]

There is a rather strange paradox, on the surface, in regard to science within the Soviet Union. The communists have practically substituted science for religion. They are reported to have organized a vast network of research laboratories and scientific institutes, and to have poured great sums of money into the development of science. But, on the other hand, science is treated as a handmaid of politics. It is an instrument or a weapon of the Party. The final test of the soundness of any scientific theory is not: Is it in accord with the facts of life? Can it be scientifically proved as correct? For the communist the test is: Is it in accord with socialist theory and will it contribute to the communist program? This means that Party leaders, particularly the members of the Central Committee, finally determine the truthfulness of any scientific position or theory. There is an orthodox line for scientists as well as for the leaders of the Party.

In every field of art and science there can be freedom to differ so long as the Party has not officially spoken; but, just as is true in regard to political policy, there is no freedom to differ once the official position has been stated. Anyone who digresses from the accepted line in art, literature, science, or any other area of human thought or creative activity must either recant and repent or suffer the consequences. If he recants he usually will be demoted and placed on probation. If he does not recant he may be imprisoned, exiled, or liquidated.

4. *Program for religion and the religious life.* Many people formerly thought that the Soviet Union's position concerning religion,

[91] George S. Counts and Nucia Lodge, *The Country of the Blind* (Boston, Houghton Mifflin, 1949), p. 245. The subtitle of the book is "The Soviet System of Mind Control," and among other titles it includes chapters on "Literature as a Weapon," "Drama as a Weapon," "Music as a Weapon," "Science as a Weapon," and "Education as a Weapon." These are weapons of the Revolution.

particularly the organized forms of religion, resulted largely if not exclusively from the fact that the Russian Orthodox Church was considered a part of the czarist régime. The communist attitude toward and program concerning religion, however, is an integral phase of the consistent application of its basic theories. Furthermore, the communist position concerning the church is in harmony with the traditional Russian pattern of the relation of state and church. The historic Russian position concerning the relation of these two basic institutions is a part of its Byzantine inheritance. In the East, somewhat in contrast to the Western tradition, the church through the centuries has been subservient to the state. The Russians "worked out for themselves a Russian version of the Byzantine totalitarian state." In such a totalitarian régime, "the church may be Christian or Marxian so long as it submits to being the secular government's tool." [92]

An important phase of the communist interpretation of religion is the function it assigns to religion. Marx as early as 1843 coined an expression that is still prominently used by the communists. He claimed that religion was "the people's opium." [93] This expression in its popular form—"religion is the opiate of the people"—has been interpreted in two ways. One viewpoint has been that Marx meant that religion lulls the masses into a state of insensibility; that because of the influence of religion they accept without protest conditions that should be considered intolerable. Religion lulls them into insensibility by promising them in the next life an equalizing of the inequalities of this life. It is what the communists call the "pie in the sky" idea or technique. Casey claims that when the original statement by Marx is studied in its context, one sees that the preceding is not the correct interpretation of the expression. He suggests that to Marx "religion is a pipe dream to exploited and exploiter alike. . . . The drug consists of those unwholesome elements in the social ferment which compel him [man—the exploited and the exploiter] to seek consolation and emotional color in illusion." [94] There is not a great deal of difference in the two interpretations except that in the latter the exploiters as well as the exploited are duped or drugged.

[92] Toynbee, *Civilization on Trial*, p. 182.
[93] Robert P. Casey, *Religion in Russia* (New York, Harper, 1946), p. 68.
[94] *Ibid.*, p. 69.

The theory of the communists concerning the functions religion performs in society is closely related to their idea concerning the origin of religion. Lenin in *Socialism and Religion* says:

> The impotence of the exploited classes in struggle with the exploiters inevitably gives birth to faith in a better life beyond the grave, just as the impotence of primitive people in struggle with nature gives birth to gods, devils, miracles, etc. To him who all his life works and suffers need, religion teaches humility and patience in earthly life, comforting him with the hope of heavenly reward. And to those who live by the toil of others, religion teaches philanthropy in earthly life, offering them very cheap justification for all their exploiting existence, and selling at low price tickets to heavenly bliss. Religion is opium for the people.[95]

This theory that religion arises out of economic needs and that it is maintained by the self-interest of the exploiters and the timidity and weakness of the exploited is in harmony with the historic materialism of Marxism.

Since, from the communist viewpoint, modern religion is economically based, Lenin believed that once the tap root was cut, which was the sense of economic insecurity and of dependence upon capitalism, then inevitably religion would die.[96] When the conditions that gave birth to religion are eliminated, religion will disappear. This sets the pattern of the communist party for the elimination of religion. The negative phase of the program is to limit and to handicap the Christian movement in every way possible. The churches are limited, almost exclusively, to worship services. They do not have the right to serve in any way the material needs of their members. Individual Christians are also limited in many ways. It is a real handicap, from a worldly viewpoint, for one to be a Christian in a communist-dominated country. Members of the communist party must be professed atheists,[97] which is to be expected because "communism is the profession of a definite faith, a faith which is opposed to Christianity." [98]

The communists also have a positive strategy for the elimination of religion. This strategy, in the main, is merely the other side of

[95] Quoted by Paul B. Anderson, *People, Church and State in Modern Russia* (New York, Macmillan, 1944), p. 58.
[96] Spinka, *op. cit.*, p. 157.
[97] Berdyaev, *The Origin of Russian Communism,* p. 200.
[98] *Ibid.*, p. 201.

the negative approach. A phase of this positive strategy is for the communists to provide for the social and economic needs of the people. The real remedy, so it is claimed, for religion as an opiate is a vigorous program to improve the economic conditions of the people. Remove the sense of economic need and insecurity and religion will die. "Let the proletariat arise and vigorously transform the social order. . . . Then the haunting dream of religion would be forgotten in the excitement and bustle of the new revolutionary era." [99] Section 13 of the Communist Party program is as follows: "The all-union communist party is guided by the conviction that only the effectuation of planned development and awareness in all the social-economic activity of the masses will bring to pass the complete withering away of religious prejudices." Vyshinsky claims that this statement "lies at the foundation of all the legislation of the Soviet state on the matter of religion." [100] It is his contention that the struggle with religion in the U.S.S.R. is carried on, "not by administrative repressions, but by the socialist refashioning of the entire national economy which eradicates religion, by socialist reeducation of the toiling masses, by antireligious propaganda, by implanting scientific knowledge, and by expanding education." [101]

There may properly be some doubt about the validity of the statement that there is no administrative repression. There has certainly been some repression in the past. For example, one writer says that 28 bishops and 1,215 priests were shot during the years 1918–1919, and that of 1,026 monasteries 637 were eliminated or closed before 1921,[102] while there were only 37 in existence in 1941.[103] Persecution and repression were not only directed against the Russian Orthodox Church [104] but also against the Roman Catholic Church and the evangelical movement. It has been said that there were 810 Roman Catholic priests in Russia in 1917, but that there were only 73 by 1935 with 14 of these in convict settlements and 13 others under arrest. The 230 evangelical pastors in 1914 had dwindled to 83 in

[99] Casey, *op. cit.*, p. 71.   [100] Vyshinsky, *op. cit.*, p. 607.
[101] *Ibid.*, pp. 609–10.
[102] Serge Bolshakoff, *The Christian Church and the Soviet State* (London, S.P.C.K., 1942), p. 35.
[103] *Ibid.*, p. 59.
[104] See John Shelton Curtiss, *The Russian Church and the Soviet State* (Boston, Little, Brown, 1953), which deals exclusively with the Orthodox Church and the Soviet Union from 1917 to 1950.

1937, with 40 of those in concentration camps in Siberia or elsewhere.[105]

In an attempt to stop the evangelicals who had increased rapidly among the workers, the Constitution of the U.S.S.R. was amended on April 8, 1929. The amendment, while permitting godless propaganda,

made religious propaganda illegal, as it is still. Article 17 of the Amendment prohibited the religious associations from forming mutual-aid, cooperative and productive societies, rendering material aid to their members, organizing libraries, reading rooms, excursions, general Bible studies, literary, handiwork, industrial and other circles, special children's, youths' and women's meetings, etc.[106]

If the preceding does not represent "administrative repression," what does?

During World War II and the years following there have been evidences, at least on the surface, of a changed attitude on the part of official communism toward religion and the church. Why the seeming change in attitude and program? There are several possible reasons. One explanation is that the nation while at war needed the support of all of its people. This was particularly true when Germany invaded the Soviet Union. The government made an attempt to win the support of the churches and their leaders. It seems that war usually stirs not only feelings of patriotism but also deeper religious feelings. In addition, it seems that the communist leaders recognized that the antireligious campaign had largely failed. They admitted that in spite of propaganda and persecution about half of the total population of the U.S.S.R. still considered themselves adherents of some church as late as 1937.[107] Casey makes the interesting suggestion that "Stalin's early theological training may have convinced him that the only hope of controlling and utilizing religion is by tolerating it." [108]

Does the preceding mean a real change of heart by the government of the Soviet Union? Let a statement issued by the Communist Party in 1949 answer the question. The statement declared that the

[105] J. de Bivort de la Saudée, *Communism and Anti-Religion* (1917–1937), trans. Reginald J. Dingle (New York, P. J. Kenedy & Sons, 1937), pp. 44–45.

[106] Bolshakoff, *op. cit.*, p. 44; cf. Vyshinsky, *op. cit.*, p. 609.

[107] Dallin, *op. cit.*, pp. 61–62.   [108] *Op. cit.*, p. 175.

increased freedom of the church did "not by any means signify that the Communist Party and the Soviet Government have changed their attitude towards religious prejudices." [109] If we are to judge the future by the past, then we should not expect any basic change in the general program of communism for religion. It may periodically change its strategy, but it cannot change its ultimate goal for religion without deserting an important phase of the Marx-Lenin program.

5. *Communism as a religion.* An outline of the program and the challenge of communism would not be complete without at least a brief statement concerning communism as a religion. One might define religion in such a way as to rule out communism as a religion, but at least communism serves the purpose of a religion for the communists. "It gives them a purpose in life, claims their ultimate allegiance, and gives them hope of powers greater than themselves which are carrying them to their chosen goals." [110]

J. Middleton Murry goes too far when he says that "Communism is the one living religion in the Western world to-day." [111] Arnold Toynbee is correct, however, when he suggests that communism is "a latterday religion," "a leaf taken from the book of Christianity—a leaf torn out and misread." [112] Laski claims that the Communist Party "is essentially a Church militant," [113] and that its "profoundly religious character" is "the secret of its tremendous dynamic." [114] Kenneth Ingram similarly says, "The radical virtues or the faults of communism are essentially religious, not political." [115] Communism certainly has many of the characteristics of a religion and performs

[109] Marguerite J. Fisher, *Communist Doctrine and the Free World* (Syracuse, Syracuse University Press, 1952), p. 241. See the Church of Scotland Report, *The Church Under Communism* (London, S.C.M. Press, 1952), for a survey of recent conditions of the church under communism in the Soviet Union and in the countries behind the iron curtain, including China. An earlier report entitled *The Challenge of Communism* was issued by the Commission on Communism of the General Assembly of the Church of Scotland. Additional reports are to be issued. The two so far issued are brief statements of about seventy pages, representing a high quality of work.

[110] Hordern, *op. cit.*, p. 163.

[111] *The Necessity of Communism* (London, Jonathan Cape, 1932), p. 111.

[112] *Civilization on Trial*, p. 236.   [113] *Op. cit.*, p. 224.

[114] *Ibid.*, p. 205.

[115] *Christianity, Communism and Society* (London, Rider and Co., 1951), p. 191.

most of the functions of a religion. It is, immediately at least, the most dynamically challenging religion that faces Christianity.

The totalitarianism of Russian communism is based upon the dictatorship of a world view, a general outlook on life. It claims to be the total to which every other phase of life must be subordinated. The kingdom of Caesar is equated with the kingdom of God. The state as advocated and promoted by the party is really theocratic rather than secular. Atheism and antireligion are made into a religion. The entire movement is a superhuman collectivism.

The communists believe that the kingdom of communism is at hand. Its victory is inevitable. "The process of dialectical materialism, with which man can co-operate, is carrying man inevitably to the victory of Communism." [116] The Messiah, a group (the proletariat) rather than an individual, has come. The movement has its prophets and its heretics. It has its creed based upon its sacred writings and authorized interpretations. It is absolutist like the Roman Catholic Church. "A good communist and a good Jesuit have much in common." [117] Communism is also missionary. Its program is to preach the gospel of communism to every creature. It has a consciousness of a messianic purpose. It is to bring salvation to the oppressed masses of the world.

We must conclude that

if religion is defined as man's relationship to whatever he regards as ultimate or to whatever he trusts most for deliverance from the evils and hazards of life, then Communism is undoubtedly religious. . . . Communism occupies the place in life for the convinced Communist that religions occupy in the lives of their adherents.[118]

If we accept Paul Tillich's definition that a man is religious "when he is ultimately concerned and on the basis of this concern makes an unconditional commitment," then the true communist is religious. His concern with communism "takes precedence over all other concerns; to it he says, 'Not my will but thy will be done.'" [119]

It seems inevitable that communism as a religion will fail ultimately. It does not contain the resources to satisfy the deeper spiritual hungers of men. As a false religion it will finally disappoint

[116] Hordern, *op. cit.*, p. 15.   [117] Spinka, *op. cit.*, p. 166.
[118] Bennett, *Christianity and Communism*, pp. 33–34.
[119] Hordern, *op. cit.*, p. 15.

and disillusion its adherents. On the other hand, "A virile Faith, even though false, always exerts more influence and calls forth greater allegiance than a Faith which is true but has lost its driving power, and whose devotees are paralysed by indifference." [120] This is one reason why we may properly be concerned about the immediate results of the struggle between Christianity, which is a true religion, and communism, which is a false religion. For a period of time communism may be victorious. And in so far as the existing organized forms of Christianity have departed from the spirit and the tenets of original Christianity, the victory conceivably might be complete and final over the existing forms of Christianity but not over Christianity as such. Regardless of the outcome of its struggle with Christianity, communism, if it is false, will ultimately fail. God created man, and the deeper needs of man can be satisfied only in fellowship with him. Communism will fail and fall because God has not abdicated. No one or no group can usurp his throne. He will be triumphant in the world.

One of communism's limitations as a religion is its failure to take death seriously. Alexander Miller suggests that this failure "makes for a failure in reverence for life and so for a general failure in compassion and in consideration for individuals." [121] The failure to take death seriously also means that communism fails to give to its followers the resources to meet life's most certain and for many its most grim reality. Death is very real, and no religion can satisfy man permanently that does not have a victorious message concerning death.

Furthermore, communism as a religious philosophy carries within itself the seeds of its own defeat. For example, its goal is universal brotherhood. It attempts, however, to accomplish this goal on a purely materialistic basis. It denies God and the fatherhood of God. The fatherhood of God, on the other hand, is the only sound basis for an abidingly significant sense of human brotherhood. Brothers come from a common father. Their love and respect for their father is an important factor in their love and respect for each other.

The sense of brotherhood, from the communist viewpoint, is to be built on a spirit of hate for those of other classes, at least until

[120] Church of Scotland, *The Church Under Communism,* p. 6.
[121] *Op. cit.,* p. 59.

they are liquidated. But hatred for those outside one's group tends to undermine the sense of brotherhood within the group. Berdyaev suggests that communism's failure to conquer hate is its chief weakness. He says that hatred, which always turns to the past and is dependent on the past, cannot be concerned with the future. Only love turns a man's attention to the future, "frees him from the heavy shackles of the past, and is a means of creating a new and better life. The preponderance of hate over love is terrible among communists." [122] There can be no significant brotherhood without love. The God who is love is the source of all human love that partakes of the divine quality. Only love that partakes of the divine quality lasts and lives.

[122] *The Origin of Russian Communism,* pp. 224–25.

VII

COMMUNISM:
AN APPRAISAL AND AN ANSWER

ARE THE Christian forces going to meet successfully the challenge of communism? The answer to this question may determine for the indefinite future the destiny of Western civilization and of the entire world. If the challenge of communism is to be met effectively, there must not only be a widespread knowledge of its sources and its program; there must also be an objective appraisal of it and an adequate answer to it.

Appraisal of Communism

It is difficult to appraise objectively any conflicting way of life. Most people tend to be controlled by their prejudices. They tend to fail to see anything good in their opponents. They are inclined to develop attitudes strikingly similar to the citizens of any country in times of war. Citizens, in the main, when their nation is at war, see nothing but right and good in their own country and its cause and nothing but evil in the enemy of their country. This rather prevalent attitude helps to explain the fact that although there have been produced some excellent books on communism, nevertheless it is still relatively difficult to find sources that appraise the movement impartially. Even if the resources were available, it still would be difficult for a serious student of world affairs to be objective in his appraisal of communism. If he attempts to be, he runs the risk of being labeled as a communist sympathizer if not an actual "red" or "pink." But to fail to be fair, to fail to look for the good as well as the evil, will be shortsighted. It will not be best for our way of life. We will tend to defend the *status quo,* including its evils. Nothing could more seriously endanger our way of life. The communists would continue to have a real basis for their criticism of the ways of the West. Their position would be strengthened around the world, particularly among the underprivileged masses of the world. It is also true that the challenge of communism cannot be met with falsehoods and half-truths about communism. To meet successfully its challenge we must be honest and fair in our appraisal of it. The best friends of Western civilization are those who recognize its sources of strength but who also acknowledge its weaknesses. They also recognize the weaknesses and shortcomings of communism, but at the same time they acknowledge its sources of strength.

1. *An appraisal of the program of communism.* It was more or less inevitable that some evaluation would be given as we discussed the program of communism in the preceding chapter. It is not felt necessary, therefore, to give a great deal of space in this chapter to such an appraisal.

Christianity's main criticism of communism is not directed at its major objectives or at the social, economic, and political programs to attain those objectives. Its chief objection is at the point of the basic theory or philosophy of communism. Here is where the two come into sharp conflict. Even as conservative a politician as John Foster Dulles, in addressing the World Council of Churches, said the following concerning the economic phases of communism:

It would seem that there is no inherent incompatibility between the Christian view of the nature of man and the practice of economic communism or state socialism. Communism, in the sense of "from each according to his abilities, to each according to his needs," was early Christian practice.[1]

[1] John Foster Dulles, "The Christian Citizen in a Changing World," in *Man's Disorder and God's Design* (one-vol. ed.; New York, Harper, 1949), IV, 81. Contemporary Russian communism has departed from this original communistic ideal. The policy now is: "From each according to his ability, to each according to the work performed"—Article 12 of the Constitution of the Union of Soviet Socialist Republics (1936) (New York, International Publishers, 1937).

Christians should not make the mistake of placing communism over against capitalism—condemning *in toto* the first and defending *in toto* the latter. The results of such an attitude could be tragic for organized Christianity and even for the capitalistic system.

The Roman Catholic radio and television preacher, Fulton J. Sheen, suggests that communism and monopolistic capitalism have much in common:

They both start with the primacy of the economic, both make man an economic animal; both assume that man has no other goal in life than the economic which is either to make profits, as does monopolistic capitalism, or to socialize production, as does communism. Both take sovereignty away from God; the first by making an individual absolute owner of property, the other by making the bureaucrats of collectivism the absolute owners.[2]

There is certainly not as sharp a distinction between capitalism and communism, from the economic viewpoint, as many people think. As suggested by Sheen, both consider material values supreme. What differences there are along this particular line are differences of degree and not of kind. This is one of the reasons that there is no real hope in communism. To change from capitalism to communism would merely mean a turning to a more thorough-going and dynamic materialism. This would not lead the world to a solution of its basic problems. Those problems stem, to a considerable degree, from the materialistic spirit of modern society.

The Christian can correctly be critical of communism's economic and political program at two points. (1) It claims too much—it makes of its program a world view that becomes for its adherents the supreme value in their lives. (2) It claims to free people but it really enslaves them. They lose their identity in the group and are sacrificed, if need be, for the program and party.

In actual fact there is scarcely anywhere in the whole world where there is such misery from poverty and complete injustice as in totalitarian communism, which treats the mass of the people as slaves of the State and erects at their expense a frightful apparatus of power.[3]

[2] *Communism and the Conscience of the West* (Indianapolis, Bobbs-Merrill, 1948), p. 123. Reprinted by permission.

[3] Emil Brunner, *Communism, Capitalism and Christianity* (London, Lutterworth Press, 1949), p. 21. This is an important booklet of 43 pages. For a study

The preceding is true in spite of the fact that the communists claim that communism is more democratic than the democracies. Brunner concludes that "the total-State of communism is the Leviathan of our age, a frightful demonstration of dehumanized humanity." [4] Harold Laski, in a somewhat more friendly view, compares communism with Roman Catholicism and says that the communist, just as would be true of a Roman Catholic, does not feel that his freedom is denied "when a pronouncement from Moscow compels him to unsay on one day what he has proclaimed with ardour the day before." Laski further suggests that for millions "the will to obey makes the fusion of totalitarianism and democracy not a contradiction, as it seems to the outsider, but a fulfilment in which the believer finds an intense satisfaction." [5]

The communists dream of an ideal society among men, when all class divisions will be eliminated. The fact is "that Marxian Communism, organized under Russia, is really the greatest threat to the idealistic society of which they dream." [6] Communism worships a god, a false god, "who is the unqualified ally of one group in human society and against all others." [7]

2. *An appraisal of the philosophy of communism.* Charles Malik lists the following eight basic errors committed by the metaphysics of communism and then contrasts each error with the truth in what he classifies as "the Western positive tradition":

1. That ultimate reality is through and through matter. The truth is that besides matter and utterly irreducible to it, there is an independent and superior reality, namely mind and spirit.
2. The proper attribute of reality is change and strife. The truth is that there is a changeless and stable order of existence on which the mind can really rest.
3. There is no objective and eternal truth. The truth is that such a truth exists, and that only by humbly seeking and finding it can we achieve genuine understanding and real peace.

---

of the place of the peasant in the rise of Marxism, and the effects of Marxism on the peasants, see David Mitrany, *Marx Against the Peasant* (Chapel Hill, N.C., University of North Carolina Press, 1951).

[4] *Ibid.*, p. 31.   [5] *The Dilemma of Our Times*, p. 209.
[6] Hordern, *Christianity, Communism and History*, p. 161.
[7] Niebuhr, *Faith and History* (New York, Scribner's, 1949), p. 211.

4. Only the immanent and the temporal exist. The truth is that there is a whole dimension of transcendent norms fully accessible to the mind and heart.

5. There is no God. The truth is that there is a God Who is the loving Father of all of us, including those who deny Him, and Who is the Creator of heaven and earth and the Lord of history.

6. That, so far as the nature of things is concerned, only the tradition of Democritus, Feuerbach and Marx is right. The truth is that this materialist tradition is thoroughly absorbed by the more concrete positive tradition from Plato and Aristotle to Hegel and Whitehead.

7. Man is perfectible by his own self-sufficient efforts. The truth is that man has a certain inherent perversity of which he can only be cured by transcendent aid.

8. The human person is for the sake of society and the state. The truth is that society and the state are for the sake of the human person.[8]

Some of these errors have been discussed, in a limited way, previously. Space will permit only a brief consideration of one or two that are most significant from the Christian viewpoint. One error of communism that comes very close to the heart of Christianity's objection to communism, and which was considered in the preceding chapter, is the last one mentioned by Malik. The communist position and practice concerning man is in marked contrast to Christianity's view of man. In some ways, the relation between man and society is the fundamental problem of communism.[9] There seems to be a deep-seated paradox in Marxist teachings concerning man. Man is considered self-sufficient. He does not need any divine assistance. But this self-sufficient man for Marxism is the collective man that absorbs and subordinates the individual man. "For Marx the class was always more real than the individual."[10]

While Marx condemned capitalism because it crushed human personality, yet "in materialist communism the process of dehumanization, which Marx denounced in capitalist society, merely goes on."[11] In Marxism, in harmony with its Hegelian background, "the general, the generic, precedes the particular, the individual, and

[8] *War and Peace*, pp. 24–25.

[9] Berdyaev, *The Origin of Russian Communism*, p. 221.

[10] Hordern, *op. cit.*, p. 143.

[11] Berdyaev, "Human Personality and Marxism," in the symposium *Communism and Christians*, trans. J. F. Scanlan (Westminster, Md., Newman Press, 1949), p. 219.

determines it."[12] Man as a person is a mere instrument of society, which means that his value is determined by his relation and contribution to the group; and the group's value, as with man, is determined by its contribution to the production of material goods. Man has no independent value. He finds his fulfillment in the group. In a communist society man at best is "the most precious capital,"[13] but he is "capital" and "capital" is expendable. There is no concept in communism of the eternal value of man, which is so central in Christian thought. For communism man is merely an instrument. The liquidating of individuals or the sacrificing of millions for the sake of the communist program is entirely consistent with its whole value system. Because the communists do not recognize the existence of God, there is lacking any valid basis for a high value of man as an individual. The Christian view of man naturally evolved from its concept that man was created in the image of God. Man as such is created as an end of infinite value. In contrast, communism always considers individual man as a mere means to be used to achieve the communist end or goal.

The communist conception and treatment of man is the ultimate fruitage of an anthropocentric humanism. And, incidentally, a tendency to move from a theocentric to an anthropocentric interpretation of life seems to be more or less inherent in humanism. It is also true that in the Soviet Union and in other communist-dominated countries there has been seen in recent years the natural and more or less ultimate results of trends that are evident in every country of the world. Any movement that separates man from God, who is the source of his dignity and worth, will contribute to the dehumanizing and depersonalizing of man. Separate man from a sense of being created for fellowship with God, and sooner or later he will treat his fellow man as an animal. This has actually happened in recent years not only in communistic countries but also in other totalitarian régimes. This tendency to treat man as a means is distressingly evident within our own capitalistic society.

The high value placed on man by the Christian movement, as suggested previously, stems from the biblical revelation concerning God and man. Man's dignity and worth are based on the conviction that man is made in the image of God; that he is an actual or a

[12] *Ibid.*, p. 208.   [13] Vyshinsky, *The Law of the Soviet State*, p. 629.

potential child of God; that God loves him and Christ died for him; and that he as a spiritual being contains something within himself that transcends society. Take away the God who gives man his value, and there is no basis left for the Christian conception of man. In other words, the Christian view of man is the natural result of its general theological position. The communist conception of man, in turn, also naturally evolves from its general philosophical position.

The Marxist anthropology contends that man is made in the image of society rather than in the image of God. Man, for the communist, is a product of the social class and is dependent on society. Inevitably such a view of man ultimately will degrade him. Hence, communism which claims to lift man actually lowers him to the level of the animal. It promises to free him but it enslaves him, to exalt him but it debases him, to enrich him but it really impoverishes him.

As implied earlier, the communist view of man represents a paradox and a contradiction at the heart of communism. In harmony with humanism, it exalts man apart from God. However, the man communism exalts, in contrast to humanism, is the mass or collective man. There are, nevertheless, many things in the communist program that it seems would demand that a high value be placed on man as an individual. The communist condemnation of capitalism is based, to a considerable degree, on what the latter supposedly does to man. As a proletarian movement it seems logical that communism would honor and exalt man as man. As previously suggested, this has definitely not been true. The mass man may be exalted, but the mass or collective man is impersonal. He is an instrument of the Party. Theoretically the collective man is supposed to free and to give a new sense of dignity and worth to the individual man. Actually, the latter is made a slave of the former. He loses his meaning and significance as an individual.

Another phase of the communist metaphysic which is decidedly different from the Christian viewpoint is the materialistic conception of life. This does not mean that Christianity is not concerned with the material needs of people. William Temple once said, "Christianity . . . is the most avowedly materialist of all the great religions." [14] It is possible that the materialistic emphasis of com-

[14] *Nature, Man and God* (New York, Macmillan, 1934), p. 478.

munism is an outgrowth, to a degree, of organized Christianity's failure to be as interested as it should have been in the material needs of people. Its interest at times may have centered too exclusively in eternal and otherworldly values. At least some branches of the Christian movement have not had enough of "a feeling for humanity," and have not been as understanding as they might have been concerning the needs of the common people. Wherever this has been true it has represented a departure from the spirit of the Founder of the Christian movement. He went about doing good. The common people heard him gladly. He used his miraculous power, almost exclusively, to minister to the immediate physical and material needs of the people.

Christianity, in the main, has believed in and defended "a spiritualized materialism," a materialism which recognizes the importance of material values but which will keep those values in proper subordination to the spiritual things of life. Organized Christianity should not attach supreme importance to things material. However, things material may in a real sense become spiritual when they are related to human needs. Berdyaev makes a valid distinction between bread for one's self and for others. The former he suggests is a material question, while the latter is a spiritual and religious question. He concludes that man does not live by bread alone, but he does live by bread and there should be bread for all.[15]

The main contrast between Christianity and communism is not that one is spiritual and the other materialistic. The real difference, in this area, is the relative significance of the material. The general Christian position is that communism goes entirely too far when it claims that the material is the determinative factor in all of life. It goes too far in its concept that life is made up of two stories—"the 'real foundation' and the 'superstructure,'" and that the real foundation of society is its economic structure.[16] James labels the economic determinism of communism as "a kind of secular Calvinism." [17] For communists economic laws take the place that properly belongs to the sovereign God. Economic determinism is predestination with God left out.

[15] *The Origin of Russian Communism*, p. 225.
[16] Mackinnon, *Christian Faith and Communist Faith*, p. 86.
[17] H. Ingli James, *Communism and Christian Faith* (London, Carey Kingsgate Press, 1950), p. 46.

There may not be a great deal of difference between the ultimate goal or hope of the Christian and the communist for society, but they are miles apart in the source of their hope. The communist has his hope set on man—the mass man, on the operation of economic laws, and on the material resources of the world. The Christian's hope is not in himself, in other men, or in any man-made program. His hope is in God, who is the author of the basic laws of life and who will be victorious in or over the world. Whether it is "in" or "over" will be determined by one's particular theological bent, but there is no difference in the source of hope.

Another area where the communist philosophy is inadequate is its interpretation of history. Communism and Christianity both have a strong faith in history, although the basis for their faith is miles apart. "For each history is not merely process, but process penetrated with purpose." [18] For the communist this sense of purpose is based on a more or less blind faith in the redemptive purpose of economic laws and in the revolutionary function of the proletariat. For the Christian, history itself is not necessarily redemptive. The purpose that permeates the historic process is redemptive, but this redemptive element comes from without rather than from within history. The Christian's faith is centered in a sovereign God who will see that ultimately his will is done and his kingdom comes. From the Christian viewpoint, the end of history cannot be set within history itself, unless the divine and eternal are included in the total historical process. In common with its general position, Christianity's perspective within history lies beyond history. Its point of reference for the interpretation of history is not man but God. It has faith in history only as it recognizes God as an active participant in history.

Communism "presents a view of history which has an end without a consummation. It has an apocalypse without a transcendent power behind it." [19] This "end without a consummation" is not only true of history in general; it is also true of the life of man. Communism has no answer for the end of life. Certainly for the communist death is not a consummation. Death "puts a stop to man's existence without completing it." At best communism has only a negative and a very inadequate answer to one of man's most persistent questions.

[18] *Ibid.*, p. 92. [19] Hordern, *op. cit.*, p. 123.

That question is: "If man dies shall he live again?" This question cannot be indefinitely ignored. It represents a deep heart hunger of man, a hunger that evidently was placed there by his Creator. Man will not be satisfied indefinitely with a strictly negative answer to the question. This is one reason that some believe that communism, sooner or later, will inevitably fail.

It may be that when one looks deeply enough he will find that the whole communistic philosophy and program are not as realistic, materialistic, and consistent as it claims to be. Its philosophy and program are activistic. It not only maintains a doctrine of historical and economic materialism; it also proclaims a doctrine of deliverance. This is seen in its sense of messianic vocation and in its idea of a perfect society in the future. Berdyaev concludes that "Marx's materialism turns into extreme idealism" and that this "is the soul of Marxism." [20]

3. *An appraisal of the ethics of communism.* In the opening sentences of his discussion of "The Ethics of Communism," Giuseppe Peterffy explains that he will be discussing a subject that does not really exist. He suggests that the philosophy of communism lacks an anthropology "because it denies the spiritual nature of man"; and that it lacks an ethic "because without a subject of spiritual nature, and one endowed with free will in moral actions, there can be no permanent moral laws." [21] Hordern similarly says that every type of conduct that will promote the Party program becomes "moral when the essential sacredness of the individual is lost, and nothing is left as a principle but the hope of a class victory." [22] Although Peterffy says there is no such thing as a communist ethic, nevertheless he proceeds to discuss the subject because at least from the communist viewpoint communism does have an ethic.

Lenin in a speech to the Third All-Russian Congress of the Young Communist League of the Soviet Union, on October 3, 1920, asked

---

[20] *The Origin of Russian Communism,* p. 115.

[21] In a symposium composed of papers read at a series of meetings in 1949, organized by the Pontifical Academy of St. Thomas at Rome, translated and published under the title *The Philosophy of Communism* (New York, Fordham University Press, 1952), p. 225. While the emphasis in the series of messages is philosophical, almost every phase of the communist program is considered to some degree.

[22] *Op. cit.,* p. 144.

the following questions: "Is there such a thing as Communist ethics? Is there such a thing as Communist morality?" He then proceeded to answer the questions as follows:

Of course there is. It is frequently asserted that we have no ethics, and very frequently the bourgeoisie says that we Communists deny all morality. That is one of their methods of confusing the issue, of throwing dust into the eyes of the workers and peasants.

In what sense do we deny ethics, morals?

In the sense in which they are preached by the bourgeoisie, a sense which deduces these morals from God's commandments. Of course, we say that we do not believe in God. We know perfectly well that the clergy, the landlords, and the bourgeoisie all claimed to speak in the name of God, in order to protect their own interests as exploiters. . . .

We deny all morality taken from superhuman or non-class conceptions. . . .

We say that our morality is wholly subordinated to the interests of the class struggle of the proletariat. . . . a morality taken from outside of human society does not exist for us; it is a fraud. For us morality is subordinated to the interests of the proletarian class struggle.[23]

This statement by Lenin and an earlier one by Engels are usually cited as the classic formulations of Marxist ethics. Practically everything that has been said by others has been closely related to or has been a mere restatement of what is found in those two statements. The one by Engels was as follows:

We therefore reject every attempt to impose on us any moral dogma whatsoever as an eternal, ultimate and forever immutable moral law on the pretext that the moral world too has its permanent principles which transcend history and the differences between nations. We maintain on the contrary that all former moral theories are the product, in the last analysis, of the economic stage which society had reached at that particular epoch. And as society has hitherto moved in class antagonisms, morality was always a class morality; it has either justified the domination and the interests of the ruling class, or, as soon as the oppressed class has become powerful enough, it has represented the revolt against this domination and the future interests of the oppressed. That in this process there has on the whole been progress in morality, as in all other branches of human knowledge, cannot be doubted. But we have not yet passed beyond class

[23] V. I. Lenin, *Religion* (New York, International Publishers, 1932), pp. 55–56.

morality. A really human morality which transcends class antagonisms and their legacies in thought becomes possible only at a stage of society which has not only overcome class contradictions, but has even forgotten them in practical life.[24]

It would be quite interesting to analyze the statements, phrase by phrase, if space permitted. We can summarize them by saying that here we find a revolutionary, relativistic ethic that is thoroughly consistent with the dialectical materialism and economic determinism of communism. Notice that Lenin says that "morality is wholly subordinated to the interests of the class struggle of the proletariat." Harold Laski, who certainly was not particularly unfriendly to communism, says that for the communists

moral action is action which serves the revolutionary cause. And since decisions upon such action are taken by the Party leadership, it follows that a Communist acts morally when he obeys the orders of that leadership; this obedience has priority over all other obligations.[25]

Laski also says,

The communist parties outside Russia act without moral scruples, intrigue without any sense of shame, are utterly careless of truth, sacrifice, without any hesitation, the means they use to the ends they serve. . . . The only rule to which the communist gives unswerving loyalty is the rule that a success gained is a method justified.[26]

The good is defined by the communist in terms of its contribution to the proletarian revolution. "He knows no other definition of good. From this it follows that the end justifies the means, every sort of means." [27] This moral relativism is a weapon used by the communists in their struggle with the bourgeois class, who for the communists represent the powers of darkness.

The relative nature of the communists' ethic is also seen in their refusal to admit any external, absolute, universal, transcendent moral principles or laws. This position fits in with their general dialectical approach. The dialectic operates even in the area of

[24] Fisher, *Communist Doctrine and the Free World*, pp. 228–29.
[25] *Op. cit.*, p. 210.
[26] Quoted by J. H. Oldham, "A Responsible Society," in *Man's Disorder and God's Design*, III, 148.
[27] Berdyaev, *The Origin of Russian Communism*, p. 223.

morals or ethics. There is a continuing adjustment to new conditions, a constant interplay of thesis and antithesis. There is an evolutionary movement toward a new synthesis. But does each new synthesis in the area of morals represent progress? Can there be progress unless there is some basis of measurement or comparison outside the process itself? Furthermore, can there be progress unless it is progress toward something? Engels in his statement admits the idea of progress. He also suggests that there will be a morality in the future that will transcend the class struggle and class-conscious moralities. This suggests that the ethical relativism of the communists is not as consistent and thoroughgoing as it first appears.

Whether or not the communists are consistent in regard to their ethic, the Christian finds little in it to approve. He may and should admit that there is an element of truth in the communist contention that the dominant class uses the accepted ethic to support and retain its dominance. Unfortunately, even Christian groups have been and are used to defend a corrupt *status quo*. But the true Christian ethic transcends time and provides a basis for the judgment of any contemporary ethic, even a contemporary Christian ethic. The basic principles of the Christian ethic are eternal and absolute. They are based upon and derived from the nature and the will of the Eternal, who is the sovereign God of the universe. The application of the Christian ethic may be very imperfect even by Christians, but that does not abrogate or change its basic principles.

4. *An appraisal of the methods of communism.* The communist ethic, as is true of its philosophy in general, is a part of the total strategy of the communists and is used to justify their methods. Any method is approved that will contribute to the achievement of their goals. That is the basis on which they justify the use of the proletariat dictatorship, the restriction of the basic freedoms of the people, and the control of every area of life. Anything and everything must be sacrificed, if necessary, for the sake of the revolution. This helps to explain the fact that the individual has value only as an instrument. He finds his real significance as a member of the group, sacrificing himself for the group and its program.

In appraising the methods of communism we should remember

that the essential and distinctive characteristic of Marxism is its revolutionary nature. Modern communism, which is Marxism as interpreted and developed by Lenin and Stalin, "is a revolutionary movement, with totalitarian undertones, that has become the right arm of Russian imperialism." [28] Many socialists, who chose the strategy of education and political action rather than revolution, claim that present-day communism does not accurately represent historic Marxism. However, regardless of whether the communists or the socialists are right in interpreting Marx, there is no doubt about the position of contemporary communism. Lenin declares that "the replacement of the bourgeois by the proletarian state is impossible without a violent revolution," [29] while Stalin says the present communist strategy is "to consolidate the dictatorship of the proletariat in one country, using it as a base for the overthrow of imperialism in all countries." [30] The idea that "history works toward a climax in which the proletarian class must by a 'revolutionary act' intervene in the course of history and thereby change not only history but the whole human situation" is called by Niebuhr a dangerous and contradictory dogma. [31] The contradictory nature of the dogma is easily seen. If the triumph of communism is inevitable through the operation of fixed economic laws, why is the revolution necessary? Yet it is the communist view that although capitalism is predestined to collapse, nevertheless the "red terror" or force is the midwife to bring to birth the new order.

The combination of determinism or predestination with the claim that the proletarian revolution is the agent to bring to birth that which inevitably would be born contributes to the claim by the communists of omnipotence and omniscience. They not only claim the ability to discern the inner meaning of contemporary events but also to have the ability to penetrate the future and to predict events to come. "This tendency of playing God to human history is the cause for a great deal of communist malignancy." [32] This also may be one factor in the fierce self-righteousness so prevalent among the communists. For the communist "the classes which hold property are

[28] Hordern, *op. cit.*, p. 160.   [29] Malik, *op. cit.*, p. 10.
[30] *Ibid.*, p. 12.
[31] Reinhold Niebuhr, *Christian Realism and Political Problems* (New York, Scribner's, 1953), p. 39.
[32] *Ibid.*, p. 40.

naturally evil while the 'proletariat,' the industrial workers, are the Messianic class endowed with every virtue." [33]

This self-righteousness makes possible the justification of the use of any method that will further the revolution. These methods include not only lying and deceit but also enslavement, murder, and the use of force in general. John Macmurray suggests that "the substantial practical difference between Christianity and Communism lies in its estimate of the place of violence in the process of the establishment of universal community." [34] From the Christian viewpoint the use of force to some degree and under some conditions may be justified; but few Christians would justify its use to attain the Christian goal, and most would give it a subordinate place in the attainment of a just social order. The Christian believes that "the means you employ must not be inconsistent with your aim." [35]

Answer to Communism

We are not dealing in this section with the broader matter of a general Christian strategy. Furthermore, we are not discussing here, except by implication, the possible answers of capitalism or democracy to communism. It should be stated, however, that the best answer of capitalism is to admit its errors, repent of its sins, and make more available to all the people the economic benefits that have been made possible by the productive success of the system. Similarly, the democracies can best answer communism by admitting their shortcomings and by applying consistently democratic principles to all groups of their citizens and to every area of the lives of their people.

Christianity should remember, however, that an adequate answer to communism must go deeper than economic benefits, political advantages, or military strategy. "If we are going to fight communism effectively, we must do so on its own religious ground rather than by military and police methods." [36] It is in the deeper, more signifi-

[33] *Ibid.*, p. 38.
[34] *Creative Society: A Study of the Relation of Christianity and Communism,* p. 144.
[35] H. G. Wood, *Christianity and Communism* (New York, Round Table Press, 1933), p. 32.
[36] Ingram, *Christianity, Communism and Society,* p. 196.

cant, and more positive areas that Christianity must face and answer communism.

1. *Admit the validity of much of the criticism by communism.* Too frequently when any phase of our way of life is challenged we tend to defend *in toto* the *status quo*. The tendency is to condemn the challenger without any attempt to understand the reasons for the challenge. An attempt is made to answer the challenge by appealing to the prejudices of people and by the use of slogans. Such an approach will be a big mistake in the struggle with communism. Much of what the communists have said about our economic order, our political institutions, and even concerning organized Christianity has been tragically true. Kenneth Ingram wisely says, "If christianity is sufficiently vital to survive, it ought to be sufficiently sensitive to the truths of marxism to set its own house in order." [37]

Charles Malik, living on the borderline between East and West, appraises the two as follows:

There are many phases of Western life which are repulsively materialistic. . . . there is little to choose between the soulless materialism of the West and the militant materialism of the East. . . .

Quality is in eclipse. Quantity and size dominate. Not the better and truer, but the larger and physically stronger: these call forth moral approbation. [38]

Who would dare say that organized Christianity is not involved in this "soulless materialism" and, to a degree, has even become a defender of it? What about in our churches—is "quality in eclipse"? Do "quantity and size dominate"? After all, "if Communism is to be condemned, it must be on sounder and profounder principles than that it threatens our way of life." [39] This type of answer to communism will be particularly unfortunate for the Christian movement if it permits itself to be identified with democracy and capitalism as "our way of life."

One of the best ways to disarm an enemy is to admit, as far as one can honestly do so, his accusations. This should be a part of the Christian answer to communism. When the communists say that Christianity has identified itself with the privileged and has been a

[37] *Ibid.*, p. 197.   [38] *Op. cit.*, pp. 29–30.
[39] Peck, *A Christian Economy*, p. 92.

defender of the *status quo*, it should be admitted that this has been true to a discouraging degree. It should be confessed that there has been a tendency for organized Christianity to become respectable and influential, and when this has happened it has tended to identify itself with the established order. As a result there is also a trend to place the stamp of divine approval upon the existing order.

Parenthetically it should be said that some Christian groups react to the world in an opposite direction. They magnify the sinfulness of the world and attempt, as far as possible, to separate themselves from the world and to live in "an ethereal region which is widely separated from the human conflicts by which the fate of men and nations is decided." [40] Unfortunately, they take, or at least attempt to take, God with them out of the world. Groups that tend toward such an idealistic isolationism usually glorify some era of the past and place the stamp of divine approval on "something which history has made pleasant and familiar." [41] This attitude, which is restricted in the main to minority sectarian groups, is not the answer to the challenge of communism.

There are two legitimate answers to the communist charge, which admittedly is true to a considerable degree, that Christianity has identified itself with the *status quo*, has been an instrument of class control, and has placed divine approval upon a particular social structure—past or present. First, a distinction should be made between "Christianity" and "organized Christianity." The failures of Christianity are the failures of the church or the organized forms of Christianity. Any attempt at an organizational embodiment of a great ideal or of great ideals always falls short of those ideals and stands under the constant judgment of them. This is true, for example, of the democracies. They represent a political construction of the democratic philosophy. They fall far short, however, of a perfect embodiment of the democratic dream. Similarly, the church, as the organizational attempt to embody the ideals of the gospel, falls below the level of those ideals. The church cannot escape and is handicapped by its humanity. But the message which gave it birth and which it proclaims constantly challenges and even judges the church. The religion that is guilty, at least to some degree, of the charges brought by communism is a pseudo-Christianity or at

[40] Macmurray, *op. cit.*, p. 14.   [41] *Ibid.*, p. 17.

best a very imperfect Christianity. The charges do not touch original Christianity or its Founder.

There is another answer to the communist accusations against Christianity. In spite of the weaknesses of the churches, the message they proclaim has been the inspiration for and the driving power in the lives of those who have not only cared for the victims of the contemporary system, but who also have been the pioneers for a new and better order. It even seems that communism is heavily indebted to Christianity for much of its social idealism and passion. It possibly should be remembered that all Christian groups are not middle class. Many Christians and Christian groups do not have a high stake in the *status quo* and are not defenders of it. They are contenders for change and provide considerable leadership for movements of change.

2. *Evaluate communism discriminately.* Just as we should not defend *in toto* our accustomed way of life, so should we not condemn *in toto* the communist way of life. At least we should not so condemn it until we have studied it carefully and objectively. "Those persons who refuse to see anything but complete evil and darkness in modern Communism are doing no service to the anti-Communist cause." [42] It is possible that communism, to use John Bennett's appraisal, is "a compound of half-truth and positive error." [43] Some people tend to hide their eyes from the half-truth and magnify the error. On the other hand, there are some who would hide their eyes from the positive error and emphasize the truth they find in communism. Either of these positions is unfortunate. Communism, with its mixture of half-truths and error, has been able to make progress because organized Christianity has failed, to a considerable degree, in those areas of half-truth.

One area of neglect has been organized Christianity's tendency to move away from the common laboring people. Because of this tendency on the part of so many church groups, communism has been able to make progress among the masses. The neglect of the churches has opened the door to communism. This whole trend has gone further in Europe and Asia than in the United States. Christian groups should never forget that the common people rejoiced to

[42] Hordern, *op. cit.*, p. 116.   [43] *Christianity and Communism*, p. 9.

hear Jesus and that many of them responded to his invitation to follow him. It should be remembered also that the Christian movement in the beginning was largely a laboring-people's movement. Its first converts and its early strength on most mission fields are from among the common people. It moves up only gradually to the middle and upper classes. There does seem, however, to be a more or less inevitable tendency to move up. And unfortunately many times the movement upward is frequently accompanied by a trend to move away from the common, working people. Communism has called attention to this trend and has capitalized, in some areas, on the trend. At least some understanding of this tendency for some Christian groups to move away from and to neglect the common people will help one to understand the appeal of communism to the working classes of society. In some sections of the world this appeal is felt even among those from the ranks of the common people who are identified with the Christian movement.

Emil Brunner may be right when he says that a man who is both a communist and a Christian is an oddity. Some clarification of his meaning is needed, however, before we could agree entirely with him when he says: "Appeasement of and partial sympathy with this political and social monstrosity are impossible. Totalitarian atheistic communism is an indivisible entity which can only be either completely accepted or totally rejected." [44] This seems to be an appeal to prejudice rather than a challenge to approach the study of the movement objectively and discriminatingly. A distinction can properly be made between the economic program of communism, the communist philosophy, and communism as a religion. Christianity's main criticism of communism is at the point of its system of ideas or its philosophy and its religious nature. It may be true that its economic program is an integral part of its total program, but the theoretical base for that program is not the only one on which such a program could be built or promoted. Socialism is sufficient proof of this point. Many socialists are Christian rather than atheistic in their approach. Their basic philosophy is not necessarily materialistic. Their economic goal, however, differs little if any from that of the communists.

In evaluating communism a distinction should be made between

[44] Brunner, *Communism, Capitalism and Christianity*, p. 32.

its promises and its achievements. We should seek to be fair in judging both. When measured in material terms, Russia under communism has made marked progress. It will be a mistake, and possibly a tragic one, for our nation or any other nation to brush off communism as a failure. On the other hand, if communism is judged by what it has done to men and women, then the record is not so good. It has promised freedom to them; in actuality it has enslaved them. Their well-being is definitely subservient to the over-all party strategy. The illusory dreams of yesterday have turned "into the present nightmare, which disturbs the ease of millions of men in our generation." [45] Many of those millions are in lands dominated by the communists. Even if communism could and would provide adequately for their material needs, they realize deep in their souls that man's life "does not consist in the abundance of his possessions." [46] This is true whether his possessions are many or few. These millions hunger for something that will give them inner peace and poise, that will provide for them strength and stability of character, and that will give to them a sense of purpose and direction.

3. *Maintain the independence of the Christian movement.* Christians should also discriminatingly appraise the movements that oppose communism. The most vocal opponents to communism are the Roman Catholic Church and the leaders and defenders of capitalism. The former is as totalitarian as communism [47] and possibly as relativistic in its ethic. Capitalism is materialistic and, at least in indirect ways, it challenges Christianity. When opposing communism Christian groups should not permit themselves to become identified with other movements that would destroy or at least dilute and undermine the Christian movement. They may find it wise, under certain conditions, to join with these other groups in a common opposition to communism. They should make it crystal clear, however, that they do not approve all that they find in those movements. It should also be kept clearly in mind that the Christian opposition to communism is on a somewhat different basis from the other movements. From the same background and on the same basis

[45] Niebuhr, *Christian Realism and Political Problems,* p. 42.
[46] Luke 12:15.
[47] See Paul Blanshard, *Communism, Democracy, and Catholic Power* (Boston, Beacon Press, 1951).

195

Christian groups might on occasion criticize and oppose these other movements, movements that join hands with the Christian groups in opposition to communism.

As just suggested Christianity should maintain its independence and be careful about its associates in the fight against communism. Organized forms of Christianity should not permit themselves to be used as mere tools, even in meeting the challenge of communism. "Many of those who attack Communism do it solely because it threatens their own economic well-being. . . . It is very nauseating when men thus motivated attack Communism as atheism, dragging God in on the side of their self-interest." [48] As Christians we will need to be on guard, or these selfishly motivated defenders of the *status quo* will drag us in on their side. We may find it advisable to join hands with them in the struggle against communism, but even in the midst of the struggle we should maintain our independence and the independence of the Christian movement we represent.

There is another reason that the Christian movement should maintain its independence. Every human program and movement involves some evil. This is true of the *status quo,* of groups and movements that would defend the *status quo,* and also of groups and movements that would change the *status quo.* This prevalence of evil in every human movement should not be surprising, since man at his best is evil as well as good. One of the most persistent and serious evils in many human programs is the spirit of self-righteousness, the pretense at finality. The church should remember that while a man-made and man-inspired program may promote kingdom ideas and ideals among men, yet even at its best it can never fully express or fulfill those ideals. How tragic it would be for organized Christianity to accept anything less than perfection as the fulfillment and expression of the spirit and the standards of original Christianity!

4. *The Christian movement must be revitalized.* Christianity as a spiritual movement has the answer to communism, but it is becoming increasingly clear that the contemporary forms of Christianity must be renewed and revitalized before they can meet successfully the challenge of communism. The beginning place for this

[48] Sheed, *Communism and Man,* p. ix.

196

revitalization is a genuine spirit of repentance. The church needs to confess its sins. It needs to acknowledge frankly its involvement in the evils of the world. It has failed to be the true church of Christ in the fullest and deepest sense. As members of the body of Christ, most Christians have failed to be really Christian. Communism has used the weaknesses and failures of the Christian movement and of Christians in general as steppingstones to power. Where Christians have expressed the Christian spirit and practiced Christian principles, and where the church has accepted and fulfilled its divine mission in the world, communism has had little appeal. One of the most tragic mistakes that could be made by the church and by its members would be to develop a spirit of self-righteousness, disowning any responsibility for the evils of the world and for the spread of communism.

In seeking to meet the challenge of communism the repenting church must be true to the inner genius of the movement it represents and which gave it birth. A strong faith in the sovereign God of the universe will enable the church to be true to the spirit of original Christianity. Because of its faith in a victorious God the church will not stoop to the level of communist morality in its fight with communism. It will avoid many of the methods used by the communists. These methods would rob the church of its very soul. They would be self-defeating for the church. The Christian church believes that Christian ends should be attained by the use of Christian methods, methods approved by the Christian conscience. The church can and should meet faith with faith, idea with idea, sacrificial devotion with sacrificial devotion, but it must not meet lie with lie or force with force.

It is possible that the churches, as the institutional representatives of Christianity, need to reexamine the gospel they preach and teach. How much of it is the pure gospel of original Christianity and how much of it represents the excess baggage of the historic Christian movement? Are there increments in the church's message that have crept in because of the pressure of the environment in which the church has found itself?

As a phase of the renewal of organized Christianity, there is needed a clear statement of the basic concepts of the Christian faith such as the sovereignty of God, the sinfulness and yet the dignity of man, and the redemption that is in Christ and in him alone. There is likewise needed a restatement or a reinterpretation of the meaning of the Christian life. It needs to be reemphasized that while the Christian religion begins with the individual, it is as broad as life itself. "Only a religion which is a way of living in every sphere either deserves to or can hope to survive" [49] in the contemporary period. The basic emphasis in the Christian life is on one's right relation to God, but an inevitable corollary is his right relation to his fellow man. These two—the vertical and the horizontal —were together in original Christianity. They must be kept in proper relation to each other if our churches are to meet the challenge of our day.

The spirit and the teachings of Jesus should be applied to and should find expression in every area of the Christian's life, including his economic relations. The Christian movement needs a deep consciousness of its responsibility for the social order, including economic life and conditions. It needs to recognize what John Macmurray has called the "substantial material reality of our religion." [50] Ingram suggests that "if Christianity is to survive in a communal age it will have to come down to earth. It will have not merely to interpret the world but to change it." [51] It was Marx who said that "philosophers have only explained the world in various ways: the task is to change it." It is the task of Christianity not only to change the world but also to change the individuals who live in the world. Changed individuals represent the best hope for a changed world. Christianity's best answer to communism is to major on changing the lives of men and women and inspiring those men and women to change the world into the image God has for it. Christians must be challenged to outlive, outlove, and if need be outdie the communists. The Christian spirit must be carried out into every area of life. Hordern says that "no Christian has a right to condemn Communism until his own passion for social justice equals its passion and supersedes it." [52]

In seeking to bring religion to grips with the realities of life, Christian groups must guard against a separation of evangelism and Christian living, of theology and ethics, and of what Macmurray

[49] MacIntyre, *Marxism: An Interpretation*, p. 9.
[50] *Op. cit.*, p. 147.   [51] *Op. cit.*, p. 199.   [52] *Op. cit.*, p. 105.

calls the hunger and love motives in life. Communism has made the mistake of ignoring the love motives.[53] What Macmurray terms "pseudo-Christianity" has made the opposite mistake of majoring on love and ignored the hunger motives.

When love and hunger are divorced

Love becomes an ideal and hunger is left to control and to determine action. Love becomes a sentiment or a feeling. . . . The love of God becomes dissociated from the love of man, at least in its material reality, and our practical relations with our fellows tend to be governed by fear, and the hatred, which is love perverted by fear. . . .

. . . love of humanity is divorced by this idealization from its expression in action, and becomes romantic and sentimental.[54]

If Christianity is to meet the challenge of communism in the area where the latter is theoretically the strongest—the satisfaction of the hunger motives—then Christianity must maintain in proper rapport the love and hunger motives.

It is also important that the Christian movement maintain an effective ministry to the underprivileged and the disinherited, to the neglected segments of society. It is with those groups and in those areas that communism has its best opportunity for infiltration. Some religious groups have become so dignified, respectable, ambitious, and worldly that they have moved away from the masses. Such groups will not have a very vital part in meeting the challenge of communism.

Again, the application of the gospel to life must be broadened. The lives of those who profess to follow Christ must be deepened. The further the church goes in applying the gospel to life, the deeper it must lay the foundations in the lives of the people. The rather sickly, pale, anemic Christianity of the contemporary period

[53] That communism does not satisfy the deeper needs, at least of many people, is evidenced by the comparatively large number of communists who leave the party. Among the books written by former communists are: Elizabeth Bentley, *Out of Bondage* (New York, Devin-Adair Co., 1951); Louis F. Budenz, *The Cry Is Peace* (Chicago, Henry Regnery Co., 1952); Whittaker Chambers, *Witness* (New York, Random House, 1952); and Douglas Hyde, *I Believed* (New York, Putnam's, 1950). The last is by an Englishman who was a lay Methodist preacher but became a communist. He was on the staff of the *Daily Worker* at London for some time. Still later he deserted communism for the Roman Catholic Church.

[54] Macmurray, *op. cit.*, pp. 133–34.

does not have the strength to face successfully the threat of communism. There must be a recapturing of the virility and vitality of original Christianity. The people must be made more conscious of the abiding presence of God. There needs to be a constant interplay between worship or a vision of God and service for God and to our fellow man. Rogers expressed this idea poignantly when he said, "The Christian . . . has . . . to walk the razor edge between waiting on God and serving the present age." [55] The Christians who maintain such a balance in their lives represent the main hope of Christianity in its struggle with communism.

In our anxiety to apply the Christian spirit and ethic to life we must never lose the sense of the otherworldly. In times past the Christian movement may have been too exclusively concerned with the world to come. There is a real danger, however, that at least some forms of contemporary Christianity will be too exclusively this-worldly. This tendency has been particularly prevalent in liberal theological circles. Neo-Protestantism represents among other things a reaction to this excessive emphasis on the here-and-now. It also magnifies God and his transcendence in contrast to the extreme emphasis of liberalism on man and on the immanence of God.

The Neo-Protestant movement's view of history is in rather marked contrast to the rather prevalent view of a generation or two ago. Many Christians, particularly those of a liberal persuasion, rather readily accepted the predominant general view of the past century. That view was one of inevitable progress, that the processes of history were inevitably redemptive. This optimistic view of history was coupled with an unrealistic optimism concerning man and his ability, with a minimum of assistance from God, to solve the problems of the world. Such a blind fatalistic faith is closely akin to the communist trust in the operation of economic laws that will inevitably bring victory to the communist program. A Christianity that has the same weaknesses as communism is definitely not the answer to communism. This is not meant to imply that Neo-Protestantism is necessarily the answer. It simply means that when the Christian movement is considered from the liberal viewpoint, Neo-Protestantism represents an encouraging reaction. It is possible that

[55] *A Commentary on Communism*, p. 228.

traditional orthodoxy has more or less constantly maintained the sources of strength that Neo-orthodoxy seems to have rediscovered. Regardless of theological labels, many Christians are beginning to realize that the prevailing quality of religion found in most churches will not meet the challenge of contemporary communism.

Christianity will make a mistake if it does not major on its own distinctive and unique contributions. It has the resources to meet the deeper needs and hungers of men. It has the answers to the ultimate questions of life; to questions such as: "What must I do to inherit eternal life?" "What comes after death?" "What is the meaning of life?" Communism has no adequate answers for these ultimates of life. It will be tragic if organized Christianity fails to give to men such answers. It would be most unfortunate if the Christian forces should fail to magnify their areas of strength. They can make the mistake of attempting to meet communism in its areas of strength instead of directing their attacks to its areas of weakness.

One of the things that haunts Christianity as it faces communism is the widespread lack of enthusiasm among Christians. Not only has Western civilization lost its radiance, to use an expression of Cailliet, but Christianity also to an alarming degree has lost its radiance. Communism which faces Christianity may have a false radiance,[56] but it seems to believe in that radiance passionately. Can the Christian movement recapture its enthusiasm, its lost radiance? Hordern, in the closing sentence of his book, raises a similar question. He asks: "Can we, at this eleventh hour, find again the springs of motivation that have caused Christians time and time again to overturn the world?" He then adds: "If we can, Communism will have met more than its match. The time has come for Christians to cease apologizing for their gospel and to start living it. Communist fanaticism must be met by Christian enthusiasm."[57]

If the Christian movement is to recapture its radiance, it must rediscover the meaning and the centrality of the cross. The Christian answer to communism and every other competing way of life must include the cross. This cross must be interpreted not only in terms of the redemptive purposes of God in the death of his Son, but also

[56] Emile Cailliet, *The Christian Approach to Culture* (New York, Abingdon-Cokesbury, 1953), pp. 221 ff.

[57] *Op. cit.*, p. 169.

in terms of daily life and living. The ethic of the cross must become a vital reality in the lives of Christians. The principles of self-denial and self-sacrifice symbolized by the cross must be applied by the individual Christian in his personal relationships and to the society in which he lives. The cross must be accepted not only as the way for fellowship with the crucified and resurrected Lord, but also as the way of self-realization and of social reconstruction! The Christian needs to rediscover that he really finds life and gives life to others as he takes up a cross, sacrifices self, and follows Christ. This is just as true and applicable to the Christian church as it is to the Christian individual. The cross if lifted up in our lives and in the life of the church will draw men. It will answer the challenge of atheistic communism. The Christian must meet the communist's willingness to die for his program by a corresponding willingness to live and to die, if need be, for the Christian cause. This may sound like strong medicine, but it is going to take strong medicine to cure the ills of the contemporary forms of Christianity. And Christianity must be cured of at least some of its ills if it is to answer communism.

Some people claim that Christianity should transform communism, that an integration of the two is possible and is the answer to their present struggle with each other. And it may be, as Macmurray suggests, that Christianity first needs to transform itself; [58] but the transformation of Christianity would simply mean a return to its first principles, while the transformation of communism would have to be on Christian terms. Christianity may need to Christianize and spiritualize communism; [59] but Christianity does not need to be communized. Certainly the latter is correct if it would mean the adoption of the basic principles and tenets of communism. A rapprochement between Christianity and communism may be a possibility; but if such ever happens the present forms of both will have to change, and they will have to come to terms on the basis of the principles of original Christianity.

There is an additional phase of the Christian answer to atheistic communism that must be included. Christians have a strong faith that they have God on their side. They know that this is true if

[58] *Op. cit.*, p. 131.
[59] Berdyaev, *Towards a New Epoch*, p. 46.

they are operating within his will. The God they worship, seek to serve, and very imperfectly follow is the sovereign God of the universe. He is their heavenly Father but at the same time the most actively creative force in the affairs of nations and civilizations. He may seem to lose some battles; but he has never lost a war. The last word is his. Communists and others may doubt him and scoff at him, but there will come a time when every knee will bow and every tongue will confess that he is Lord.[60] He may not be in a hurry about achieving his will in the world but he is always on time. This is the Christian hope. This is the Christian's victory. This confidence gives him a song in his heart and a peace that passeth understanding in his life, regardless of how the battle may be going at the time.

[60] Phil. 2:10–11.

VIII

CHURCH AND STATE

ONE WRITER suggests that "the whole life and character of Western Christendom consists of the incessant action and counteraction of Church and State." [1] The present period is witnessing an unusually acute struggle between these two institutions, a struggle that is a world-wide phenomenon. The rise of political totalitarianism in the modern era has intensified, while sharply conflicting ideas and ideals within the Christian movement have accentuated the conflict. Differing views by Roman Catholics and Protestants concerning the church, the state, the relative significance and authority of each, and particularly concerning the meaning and content of religious freedom have brought the entire controversy into sharp focus.

The nature of the struggle between the church and the state varies in different countries, but it exists, to some extent, in every nation of the world. [2] The tension between these two institutions

---

[1] Ranke, quoted by A. Taylor Innes, *Church and State: A Historical Handbook* (2nd ed.; Edinburgh: T. & T. Clark, n.d.), p. 1.

[2] For some books dealing with the relation of church and state in a few countries, see the following: William Halperin, *Italy and the Vatican at War* (Chicago, University of Chicago Press, 1939); Lloyd Mecham, *Church and State in Latin America* (Chapel Hill, N.C., University of North Carolina Press, 1934); Paul B. Means, *Things That Are Caesar's* (New York, Round Table Press, 1935); Stewart W. Herman, *The Rebirth of the German Church* (New York, Harper, 1946); Paul B. Anderson, *People, Church and State in Modern Russia* (New York, Macmillan, 1944); and Robert Pierce Casey, *Religion in Russia* (New York, Harper, 1946).

is a factor in the crises in the various nations of the world, and its modern acuteness is both a cause and an effect of the crisis that is gripping the entire world.

Competing Conceptions

The meaning one ascribes to church and to state and his views concerning the functions of each will determine, to a considerable degree, his viewpoint regarding their relations to each other and their relative authority over the lives and consciences of men.

1. *Concerning the church.* There are several possible definitions of the word "church." It may be used to refer to a local congregation of Christians. This usage is particularly prevalent among Christian groups that practice a congregational form of church government. The word "church" is also applied to a particular denomination such as "The Methodist Church." By some it is used in the universal sense to include "the multitude collected out of all nations" (Calvin), or as Webster says, "the collective body of Christians." Stokes suggests a somewhat different definition or interpretation. While using, to some degree, all of the preceding ideas of the church, yet he suggests that the church is inclusive of "the forces of organized religion led by the Christian groups, but including also the Jews and other bodies of worshipers of God."[3] This is a broad institutional concept. The church becomes a social institution comparable to the state, the home, and the school.

Gavin's definition of the church gives a different type of emphasis. He says that the church is "a divine institution, supernaturally founded, endowed by God and governed by the Holy Spirit, the compass of whose domain extends over the whole of the human life from the cradle through the grave to the Hereafter."[4] Most people would doubtless agree that the church is divine in its origin and supernatural in its leadership and power, although it is also a human institution. There would likely be considerable disagreement, however, concerning the "domain" of the church. Does

[3] Anson Phelps Stokes, *Church and State in the United States* (New York, Harper, 1950), I, 9.
[4] Frank Gavin, *Seven Centuries of the Problem of Church and State* (Princeton, N.J., Princeton University Press, 1938), p. 2.

Gavin simply mean that the church's influence should be felt in every area of life from the cradle to the grave, or does he mean that its word should be the final authority for man in every realm of life? If he means the latter, then there would evolve from such a comprehensive conception of the church what Gavin himself calls "the omnicompetent church," a church that claims final authority in every phase of life. Such a church usually believes that it has "a mandate from the Almighty." [5]

A church that does not have a sense of a divine purpose would be unworthy of the name "church." However, when it carries to the extreme the idea of a "this-worldly domain" it becomes an authoritarian church which stands between the individual soul and God, claiming authority over the consciences and lives of men. When this view is carried to the extreme, there is a tendency to confuse the church with the kingdom or the rule of God. There is also a failure to distinguish between original Christianity and organized Christianity. The latter embodies the ideals of original Christianity, but just as is true of the institutionalization of other ideals the embodiment is very imperfect. Such imperfection is inevitable because the church cannot escape its humanity.

What should be the scope of the work of the church? Is the church to restrict itself to the vertical or strictly spiritual relations of life; or is it to be concerned with the world and the everyday problems of men and women? How can it as a divine-human institution maintain in proper balance its this-worldly and other-worldly functions? One's answers to these and similar questions will color his views concerning the proper relation of the church and the state and the relation of both of these basic institutions to men and to society in general.

The otherworldly view, which so largely dominated Christian thinking a few generations ago and which is still prevalent among conservative Christian groups, has contributed directly and indirectly to the rise and growth of the pagan totalitarian state of the contemporary period. Such a state has a tendency to become a competing church, claiming final authority in every area of life, including the religious. It attempts to make the church subservient to its demands.

[5] *Ibid.*, p. 4.

On the other hand, the extreme this-worldly emphasis, which has been so prevalent among liberal scholars, has contributed to a shifting of attention from the spiritual abiding values of life to things material and temporary. The general trend in the modern period has been for people to give their supreme devotion to the things of this life rather than to things eternal. One result has been the tendency in recent years for an increasing number of people to turn to the state as the one social institution which can most successfully satisfy their desire for things temporal. Many of these people have been willing to surrender their basic liberties and to become a virtual slave of the state, if the state will guarantee them economic security. This inversion of values is a significant factor in the present world crisis. Those who would give up their birthright of freedom for a mess of economic security need to ponder the following words of Benjamin Franklin: "There is not in any volume, the sacred writings excepted, a passage to be found better worth the veneration of freemen than this: 'Those who would give up essential liberty to purchase a little temporary safety deserve neither liberty nor safety.'" [6]

2. *Concerning the state.* There have been and are widely differing views concerning the meaning, the nature, the origin, the functions, and the source and extent of authority of the state. Some tend to identify the state with the rulers of the state and to delegate to the rulers the powers that belong to the state.[7] This is true of any absolutist rule whether it is monarchial, fascistic, or communistic. There is also a tendency on the part of some people to identify the state with the total community or social order. They would make it co-extensive with human society rather than one of several basic social institutions. The proper meaning of "the state" will be seen more clearly as we outline something of its origin, its authority, and its functions. We shall use the term primarily in the general sense, similar to the common usage of "home," "school," and "church." All of these words serve as symbols that designate certain

[6] Stokes, *op. cit.*, I, 20.
[7] Dietrich Bonhoeffer (*Ethics*, trans. Neville Horton Smith [New York, Macmillan, 1956], p. 297) makes a distinction between the terms "state" and "government." The former, he suggests, includes the ruled and the rulers, while the term "government" refers only to the rulers.

more or less clearly defined functions in society. The state stands for or symbolizes constituted authority, the authority to maintain law and order.

There have been and are different theories concerning the origin of the state. These theories might be grouped into the following major divisions: (1) theocratic theories, (2) naturalistic or natural-law theories, and (3) power theories. There are various emphases within the framework of these theories and also several combinations of them. Space will not permit a detailed discussion of the various theories. It can be stated in broad terms that the state is either from God or from Satan. If from God it came either directly from him or indirectly from him through the nature he gave to man. If the state was founded as a result of the nature of man, it was either because of his original nature or because of the nature of his needs resulting from his sin and fall. If the latter is correct, then the state represents God's will for man in a sinful world, but it is not necessarily in accord with his original plan or his ultimate purpose for man.

The Reformers, for example, placed the origin of the state in the fall of man. "It was sin that made necessary the divine institution of government." [8] It was John Calvin who said: "Had we remained in the state of natural integrity such as God first created, the order of justice would not have been necessary." [9] In contrast, Rommen says: "So deeply is the state rooted in human nature that it would have grown also in the *status naturae purae,* i.e., without the Fall. The state is not a consequence of sin." [10] He follows Aquinas in believing that man is a social and political animal, "destined more than all other animals to live in community." [11] Aquinas suggested that "even in the state of innocence, some men would have exercised control over others." [12] This Thomist conception of the state "is found in a somewhat modified form in Anglican theology" and has even "penetrated into modern Lutheranism." [13]

[8] *Ibid.,* p. 299.

[9] Quoted by William A. Mueller, *Church and State in Luther and Calvin* (Nashville, Broadman, 1954), p. 129.

[10] Heinrich A. Rommen, *The State in Catholic Thought* (London, B. Herder Book Co., 1945), p. 228.

[11] A. P. D'Entrèves (ed.), *Aquinas: Selected Political Writings,* trans. J. G. Dawson (Oxford, Basil Blackwell, 1948), p. 3.

[12] *Ibid.,* p. 105.   [13] Bonhoeffer, *op. cit.,* p. 298.

The preceding represents a combination of theocratic and naturalistic interpretations of the origin of the state. Many who hold to a naturalistic theory do not include God in their thinking. Hobbes, for example, argued that fear, which he considered the most powerful motive in man, impelled men to form states or governments. Locke contended that man had certain natural rights such as life, liberty, and property. The safeguarding of those rights was the reason for man's entering into contract or compact to form a state. According to Rousseau, man formed the state to meet the challenge of obstructive forces in nature which were too powerful for him to cope with as an individual. However, for Rousseau the surrender of the self was "to the whole community" rather than to the government. The state or government was merely an instrument of the general will.[14] Many of those who hold to a naturalistic theory of the origin of the state suggest that it results from the natural, evolutionary process. The state represents the normal development of the family, the clan, and the tribe.

The power theories, which are the least acceptable from the Christian viewpoint, have been particularly prevalent in recent years. Those who hold to a power theory concerning the origin of the state contend that the state is created by some particular group which in turn uses the power of the state to extend and to maintain its control. This is the basic concept behind modern totalitarian régimes.

One's conclusions concerning the origin of the state will determine, to a considerable degree, his personal attitude toward and relation to the state, and will color his views concerning the functions of the state in the social order. Aristotle gave the following rather general statement of the purpose or function of the state: "The State, While it *comes into being* for the sake of mere life, *exists* for the promotion of the good life." [15] Roger Williams believed that "in the development of human society, the state fulfils its ultimate purpose." [16]

Granting that the state exists for the promotion of the good life

[14] See R. Kranenburg, *Political Theory*, trans. R. Borregaard (London, Oxford University Press, 1939), pp. 10–13.

[15] *Ibid.*, p. 70.

[16] James E. Ernst, *The Political Thought of Roger Williams* (Seattle, University of Washington Press, 1929), p. 136.

or for the development of human society, what are the specific functions it should perform? For Hobbes the state's sole object is to maintain "order and peace at any price." Locke suggests that the state should protect the natural, inalienable rights of the people to life, freedom, and property; that it "is constituted only for procuring, preserving, and advancing civil interests." [17] Jefferson says that "the most sacred of all duties of government is to do equal and impartial justice to all citizens." [18] The functions of the state on the behalf of its citizens might be summarized as follows: it is to provide or to secure for them justice, liberty, and security. In some ways the most comprehensive of these and certainly the one most emphasized by leaders of democratic thought has been and is liberty.

The emphasis in recent years has been more on security, with a particular emphasis on economic security. This shift in emphasis in regard to the basic functions of the state has been a more or less inevitable result of the increasing dominance of all of life by economic and material values, accompanied with a growing tendency toward a strong centralized, paternalistic state. This latter trend has even been evident within the democracies. The famous four freedoms of Franklin D. Roosevelt and Winston Churchill revealed this shift in emphasis. "Freedom from want" was given as one of the four, and the implication was that it is as basically important as any of the other freedoms. The church should be concerned about this shifting conception of the relative importance of the functions of the state. This will be true if the church properly recognizes the possible effects of this shift of emphasis on the citizens of the state and on the relation of the state to the church.

Some people, mostly Roman Catholics, claim that the state should even provide for the "moral and spiritual security" of its citizens because such security is one of their natural rights.[19] To do this, so it is suggested, the state should favor, protect, and shield religion.[20]

---

[17] J. M. Dawson, *America's Way in Church, State, and Society* (New York, Macmillan, 1953), p. 23.

[18] James Wallace, *Fundamentals of Christian Statesmanship* (New York, Revell, 1939), p. 69.

[19] Francis J. Powers (ed.), *Papal Pronouncements on the Political Order* (Westminster, Md., Newman Press, 1950), p. 58.

[20] John A. Ryan and Francis J. Boland, *Catholic Principles of Politics* (New York, Macmillan, 1940), p. 286.

For Roman Catholics there is only one true religion, and hence the state is under obligation to protect the Roman Catholic Church. Pope Leo XIII expressed this conviction as follows:

> Justice forbids and reason itself forbids the State . . . to adopt a line of action which would end in godlessness—namely, *to treat the various religions* (*as they call them*) alike, and to bestow upon them promiscuously equal rights and privileges. Since, then, the profession of one religion is necessary in the State, that religion must be professed which alone is true, and which can be, recognized without difficulty, especially in [Roman] Catholic States, because the marks of truth are, as it were, engraven upon it. This religion, therefore, the rulers of the State must preserve and protect, if they would provide—as they should do—with prudence and usefulness for the good of the community.[21]

3. *Concerning the authority of the church and state.* Catholics and some Protestants would agree with Pope Leo XIII when he said:

> The Almighty . . . has appointed the charge of the human race between two powers, the ecclesiastical and the civil, the one being set over divine, the other over human things. Each in its kind is supreme, each has fixed limits. . . . There must . . . exist, between these two powers, a certain orderly connection, which may be compared to the union of the soul and body in man.[22]

There are, however, elements in this statement that need to be defined. For example, what is meant by "divine" and "human things"? What is the area of authority for the church and the state? Most Protestants would challenge the extent of the authority claimed by the Pope for both the state and the church. They do not believe that either is supreme, even within its own legitimate areas of operation. There is a source of authority beyond the church and the state, and whatever authority each of these possesses is delegated authority. The limitations of the authority of both the church and the state is most specific in the area of the individual conscience. The final authority for the individual is neither the state nor the church. As William the Silent put it, "Compulsion cannot touch the soul." [23]

[21] Quoted by Conrad H. Moehlman, *The Wall of Separation Between Church and State* (Boston, Beacon Press, 1951), p. 45.
[22] Ryan and Boland, *op. cit.*, pp. 289–90.
[23] Kranenburg, *op. cit.*, p. 153.

Neither the state nor the church has the right to attempt such compulsion.

One reason for the conflict between the church and the state, and for the diversity of judgment concerning the extent of the authority of each, is the differing ideas concerning the source of the authority of these institutions. Most students of the relation of church and state agree that both of these institutions were ordained by God and derive their authority from him. Granting that such is true, there remain some important questions: How much of his authority has God delegated to the state and to the church? How far can either one of these institutions be identified with the voice of God? How does God mediate his authority to the state—directly, or indirectly through the people?

A totalitarian church or state claims a direct delegation of divine authority. It does not consider itself responsible to the people. There is a tendency to identify the laws of the state or the rule of the church with the commands of God. Robert A. Calhoun wisely says: "To identify Him [God] with the human community, or His will with decrees of a government, is absurd . . . at every stage and in all its phases, a community must grow toward God as a plant grows toward the sun." [24] What Calhoun here says concerning the community in general and the state in particular can be said about the church. He himself says: "The Church is not God, to bend the State to its will. Just as the State must learn and change, so must the Church." [25]

There have been and are those who believe that the authority of the state comes directly from God. For example, Pope Leo XIII said:

Indeed, very many men of more recent times . . . claim that all power comes from the people, so that those who exercise it in the State do so, not on their own, but as delegated to them by the people, and that, in accordance with this view, it can be revoked by the very people by whom it was delegated. But from such views Catholics dissent and affirm that the right to rule is from God as from a natural and necessary principle.[26]

[24] Henry P. Van Dusen *et al., Church and State in the Modern World* (New York, Harper, 1937), p. 69.
[25] *Ibid.,* p. 79.   [26] Powers, *op. cit.,* p. 24.

Two Roman Catholic authors summarize the position of the popes as follows: "The origin of public power is to be sought for in God Himself, and not in the multitude . . . it is repugnant to reason to allow free scope for sedition." [27] The leaders of contemporary totalitarian régimes may use the term "Providence" or "Destiny" instead of God, but they seek some type of divine sanction for their authority and claim the divine right to rule.

In contrast to the preceding, Roger Williams denied the divine origin of the state, although he did agree that there were certain divine elements in it.[28] The state originated with the people and derived whatever authority it had from the people. The people have "fundamentally in themselves the *Root* and *Power*, to set up what *Government* and *Governors* they shall agree upon," and "the agents of the state 'have not the least inch of Civil power, but what is measured out to them from the free consent of the Whole.'" [29] This sounds strikingly similar to the statement in the Declaration of Independence that governments derive their just powers from the consent of the governed.

What is the proper conclusion concerning the source of authority for the church and the state? Certainly both the church and the state originated with God. Whatever authority they have comes from God. But how has God seen fit to mediate that authority? Is it mediated directly to each of them and are they responsible alone to God (Figure 1)? Or, does God mediate his authority through one of these institutions to the other (Figure 2)? Has he seen fit to vest the people with complete authority over the church and the state (Figure 3)? Or does he mediate some authority through the people and retain a portion including ultimate authority for himself (Figure 4)? If the last is correct, it would mean that the church and the state are responsible both to God and to the people. This is, generally speaking, the most acceptable and healthiest position. If generally held it would save a nation from an authoritarian, totalitarian church or state on the one hand, and from identifying the voice of the people with the voice of God on the other hand. The latter is one of the abiding dangers in a democracy.

[27] Ryan and Boland, *op. cit.*, p. 300.   [28] Ernst, *op. cit.*, p. 33.
[29] *Ibid.*, p. 44.

Diagrams

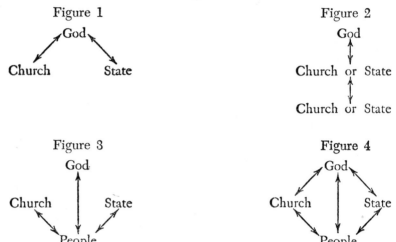

Figure 1
God
Church   State

Figure 2
God
Church or State
Church or State

Figure 3
God
Church   State
People

Figure 4
God
Church   State
People

The arrows represent the source of authority and the related direction of responsibility.

This brings us to what is the crux of the whole matter. God has not only seen fit to place limits on the authority of both the church and the state; he also places some limits on the rights of the people. They do not have the right to delegate either to the state or to the church the authority to control, or to attempt to control, the consciences of individuals. God has reserved for himself the authority to deal directly with men and women. A usurpation of this authority by church or state is most unfortunate, not only for the individual, but also and particularly for the state and the church. A healthy situation for both of these institutions depends, to a considerable extent, on a continuing ability of self-criticism, which in turn cannot be kept alive without freedom of individual opinion and freedom to express that opinion.

Possibly a brief statement should be made concerning the justifiable means that may be used by the church and the state in exercising whatever authority they may have. The right of the state to use force or "the sword" to restrain evil is practically universally accepted. On the other hand, it is almost as universally agreed that the church should restrict itself to spiritual means or methods. Jesus himself said that his kingdom was not of this world, and instructed his disciples not to defend him with the sword.

Conflicting Theories

There are a number of theories concerning the proper relation of the church and the state. Keller, comparing the church and the state to two poles that are opposite to each other, suggests that their relation to each other "varies from the closest union, as in a kind of marriage, to the bitterest enmity." But even in times "of the greatest tension or separation, the one cannot escape the other." [30]

Brown rather succinctly suggests four periods in the history of the Christian church's relation to the state.[31] During the first three centuries, "the church meets us as a minority group under an indifferent or hostile state." During the second period, beginning with Constantine and closing with the Reformation, the church and state were, at least in theory, partners, a partnership in which the church claimed "and in the main succeeded in establishing the dominant role." The ideal during the third period, which extended from the Reformation to the Enlightenment, was the unity of the church and state; but owing to the rise of national states and the consequent divisions of Christendom their unity took "the form of parallel establishments." In the fourth period, the point of departure "is neither the empire nor the nation, but the individual." Churches were considered free associations of individuals. The doctrine of the separation of church and state arose in this, the last period of the history of the church.

Moehlman suggests [32] five historic interpretations of the relation of the church and the state. They have been *Erastianism*, which assumes that the state is supreme in both civil and spiritual matters; *Hildebrandism*, which "holds that the church has the final authority in civil as well as in spiritual matters"; *coordinate jurisdiction*, which "permits church and state to be distinct in their own areas but not

[30] Adolf Keller, *Church and State on the European Continent* (London, Epworth Press, 1936), p. 151.

[31] William Adams Brown, *Church and State in Contemporary America* (New York, Scribner's, 1936), pp. 58–59.

[32] *Op. cit.*, pp. 42–43.

separated" (this was the view of Pope Leo XIII); *nominal establish-ment,* which "allows the state to furnish monetary support to the churches and their institutions"; and *voluntaryism,* or the separation of church and state.[33]

We shall attempt to discuss, to some degree, all of the theories concerning the relation of church and state under three major headings: (1) identification; (2) domination, which may be a domination of the church by the state or of the state by the church; and (3) separation, which may be a friendly or an unfriendly separation.

1. *Identification.* The identification may be partial or practically complete. Judaism in general and Old Testament religion in particular clearly reveal a tendency toward the identification of established government and the organized forms of religion. In early Jewish life there was no clear distinction between the secular and the sacred, between the political and the religious. The same individual, such as Moses, might be military chieftain, lawgiver, judge, and yet the prophet of God and a priest for his people.

There is a trend toward an identification of the church and the state in any nation where there is an established church.[34] "The original underlying idea of the State Church was the supposition that the whole nation was Christian." For example, in Sweden, which has a state church, "the Swedish people as a whole, considered from a religious angle, is the Swedish Church." [35] This conception is very prevalent in all of Europe, which is still under the dominance of Roman Catholicism or the Reformation. And the reformers—Luther and Calvin—did not depart very far from the

[33] Rommen (*op. cit.,* pp. 578–79) suggests six main eras of the relation of church and state, while Wilfrid Parsons, *The First Freedom* (New York, Declan X. McMullen Co., 1948), pp. 84 ff., discusses three great epochs in church-state relations.

[34] There is also some tendency under an establishment toward the domination of the church or the state by the other. For a discussion of some of the problems of the church under an establishment, see Cyril Garbett, *Church and State in England* (London, Hodder & Stoughton, 1950), which "is an argument for some readjustment in the existing relationship beween Church and State," and which sets out a program for more spiritual freedom without disestablishment. See also the Report of a Commission appointed by the Church Assembly in June, 1949, and published under the title *Church and State* by the Church Information Board of the Church Assembly in 1952.

[35] See Keller, *op. cit.,* pp. 168–70.

Roman Catholic position concerning the relation of the church and state. They thought in "terms of the *corpus christianum*." [36]

The theory of any Christian group concerning the relation of church and state is related to its broader view of society and of the relation of the church to the social order in general. Those who contend for a virtual identification of the church and the state usually hold to a rather optimistic view of the world order. The social order, with the state, is considered in accordance with the natural or divine law. The state is defended as divine in origin and basically Christian in its ultimate purposes.

In contrast to this rather optimistic position, sectarian Christianity tends "to condemn the whole world of nature, state, and civilization, as irremediably evil." It does this "in the interest of a sharp eschatological dualism." [37] This tendency to condemn the world and to maintain "a sharp eschatological dualism" is prevalent in the contemporary period, particularly among the Fundamentalists who major, in the main, on eschatology. Christopher Dawson, a Roman Catholic, concludes that Protestant theory concerning Christianity and politics has "always fluctuated between two extremes, sometimes identifying religion and politics, as with the old Puritans and the modern social idealists, and at other times relegating religion entirely to the inner world of the individual conscience." [38] The latter view is evident, to a degree, among many religious groups. The stronger the sectarian trend or tinge in the group, the more the tendency is manifested.

2. *Domination.* At various times in divergent ways and to different degrees, both the church and the state have sought to control the other and to dominate all of life. In recent years there has arisen again, to plague the peoples of the world, the totalitarian state. A totalitarian political régime may be unfriendly to the church and to religion in general, or it may be friendly to and even a defender of the church as long as the church will do its bidding. In other words, the domination of the church by the state may be, in a sense, physical—representing an attempt to destroy it; or it may

[36] Mueller, *op. cit.*, p. 127.
[37] Christopher Dawson, *Religion and the Modern State* (New York, Sheed and Ward, 1938), p. 129.
[38] *Ibid.*, p. 130.

be a spiritual domination—representing an attempt to control it for selfish purposes. The direct frontal attack is less damaging to the church than the more insidious effort to control the spirit and soul of the church.

Throughout the centuries there have been attempts, at times quite successful, by the church to control or to dominate the state. This has been the rather consistent pattern of the Roman Catholic Church. The Roman Church has utilized the theory of the two swords, which was originated by Gelasius in the fifth century. This theory exerts great influence even in the modern period. The two swords were and are the spiritual sword and the secular sword, both of which "are at the disposal of the Church." The spiritual sword is wielded by the priest, the secular sword by kings and knights "but *at the will of the priest and as long as he approves.*" The secular sword is subordinate to the spiritual sword. If this was not true there would be no order in the world.[39] Centuries after Gelasius, Hildebrand compared the relation of the church and state to the relation of the soul and body. The soul, which represents the church, is certainly more important than the body, which is a symbol of the state. Thomas Aquinas, who still dominates Roman Catholic theology, suggested that

the State is . . . a collaborator of the Church: it is the organization which serves to realize those temporary human ends which in the Church's judgement harmonize with man's destiny. The State ought to help to establish the *bonum commune,* as the Church sees it, on earth.[40]

One Roman Catholic writer claims that "the leading Catholic principle in regard to matters political" is "the distinct sovereignty, of the Church on the one hand and of the State on the other." He then adds: "Yet, real though this distinction between the two powers may be, it does not amount to radical separation, for it has to be reconciled with a second principle, that of the agreement and harmonization of the two for the common benefit of humanity." He suggests finally that because the church and the state are unequal there is a third principle, "that of the primacy of the spiritual power."[41] The same author says

[39] Kranenburg, *op. cit.,* p. 228.   [40] *Ibid.,* p. 231.
[41] Joseph Lecler, *The Two Sovereignties: A Study of the Relationship Between Church and State* (New York, Philosophical Library, 1952), p. viii.

Church and State do not belong to the same order, and the two orders have their fixed hierarchical places. The Church is superior to the State as the spiritual is superior to the temporal, as an institution of supernatural origin takes precedence over an earthly organization, the creature of human nature and of its social needs.[42]

Still another Catholic writer says, "Although independent of the Church in purely temporal matters, the State is nevertheless subject to the Church *directly* in spiritual affairs, and *indirectly* in temporal matters in so far as they are related to spiritual concerns." [43]

According to the Roman Catholic Church, the state should recognize true religion, and the only true religion is that held by the Catholic Church. In addressing some words to American Catholics, Pope Leo XIII, in commenting on the liberty the church enjoys in America, added these significant words: "But she would bring forth more abundant fruits if, in addition to liberty, she enjoyed the favor of the laws and the patronage of public authority." [44] Ryan and Boland clearly reveal what the recognition of the Roman Catholic Church as the established church would mean in the United States, as it has meant in other countries. After suggesting that there would be no attempt to force non-Catholics into the Catholic Church, they raise a question about freedom of worship for non-Catholics. The answer is that such freedom might be tolerated by the state if "carried on within the family, or in such inconspicuous manner as to be an occasion neither of scandal nor of perversion to the faithful." [45] Under a Catholic-controlled state there would be no freedom for the propagation of "false religion." The fact that an individual might consider his religion to be true would give him no more right to propagate it than the anarchist "to advocate his abominable political theories" or "the dealer in obscene literature . . . a right to corrupt the morals of the community. . . . Error has not the same rights as truth." [46]

The tendency for the church to dominate the state, or at least to make it subservient, has also been prevalent, to a degree, in some

[42] *Ibid.*, p. 50.

[43] Augustine J. Osgniach, *The Christian State* (Milwaukee, Bruce Publishing Co., 1943), p. 307.

[44] Ryan and Boland, *op. cit.*, p. 315.

[45] *Ibid.*, p. 317.   [46] *Ibid.*, p. 318.

Protestant circles. This has been particularly true of Calvinism. Troeltsch goes so far as to say that "Calvin's personal point of view was as undemocratic and authoritarian as possible." [47] Luther and Lutheranism differed considerably from Calvin. Whereas Calvin made the state subservient to the church, Luther made the church somewhat subordinate to the state. "Calvin's views were largely theocratic; Luther's, somewhat Erastian." [48] The relation in early Lutheranism between the church and state has been likened to a "love-match on a common Christian basis. But the Lutheran Church, in entering into such a close union with the State, soon felt its mighty grip, and gave up her liberty to a power which she not only felt to be superior, but accepted as a manifestation of the Divine Will." [49] Some contend that the Lutheran position provided much of the background for the contemporary rise of totalitarian régimes in some European countries, particularly in Germany.[50]

3. *Separation.* The United States of America is the outstanding example of a nation that provided from its beginning for the separation of church and state. Moehlman calls the separation theory "the revolutionary American ideology." [51] David Dudley Field concludes that "the greatest achievement ever made in the cause of human progress is the total and final separation of church and state." He then adds: "If we had nothing else to boast of, we could lay claim with justice that first among the nations we of this country made it an article of organic law that relations between man and his Maker were a private concern." [52]

There were several factors that contributed, directly and indirectly, to the adoption of the separation theory. There was a wide diversity of religions in the colonies, with strong minority groups in most of them. Baptists, who were comparatively strong in New England, Pennsylvania, and Virginia, and who have contended consistently on the basis of principle for separation of church and state, made a major and a distinctive contribution to the provision for separation in the Constitution. In addition, the colonies immedi-

---

[47] Ernst Troeltsch, *The Social Teaching of the Christian Churches,* II, 628.
[48] Stokes, *op. cit.,* I, 111.   [49] Keller, *op. cit.,* p. 152.
[50] See Philip S. Watson, *The State as a Servant of God* (London, S.P.C.K., 1946) for a somewhat different interpretation of Luther.
[51] *Op. cit.,* p. xi.   [52] Stokes, *op. cit.,* I, 37.

ately preceding the Revolution were tremendously influenced by the Great Awakening. This great religious movement affected every area of life, including the political. It contributed to the arousing of the democratic spirit in general and at least in important indirect ways to the separation of church and state.

One of the main reasons for the inclusion of the separation of church and state in our Constitution was the fact that the general intellectual atmosphere breathed by the colonists contained concepts of political and spiritual freedom that can be attained only through such separation. Particularly important was the influence of John Locke, whose writings had become, even for many colonial preachers, almost a second Bible. They were saturated with the religion of the prophets and with the political philosophy of Locke.[53] It was Locke who said: "The church itself is a thing absolutely separate and distinct from the commonwealth. The boundaries on both sides are fixed and immoveable."[54] While Roger Williams did not have as much influence on the colonists, even on the preachers, as John Locke; yet his *Bloudy Tenent* represents "an epoch-marking milestone in the history of the separation of Church and State and of religious freedom."[55]

Moehlman suggests that "the currents and trends moving in the direction of separation of church and state during the long colonial age became a hurricane of tremendous power during the radical transition years, 1776 to 1789, which cut the pattern of the American way of life."[56] Two men who had a great deal to do with shaping that pattern were Thomas Jefferson and James Madison. Stokes believes that "Roger Williams is the only person in our history who can dispute" Jefferson's claim to primacy in the cause of religious freedom and the separation of church and state.[57] Jefferson's famous phrase—"a wall of separation between church and state"—first appeared in a letter from Jefferson to the Baptists of Danbury in 1802.[58] Moehlman believes that this phrase or figure of speech evi-

---

[53] See Alice M. Baldwin, *The New England Clergy and the American Revolution* (Durham, N.C., Duke University Press, 1928).

[54] John Locke, *Works* (London, T. Davison, 1812), VI, 21.

[55] Stokes, *op. cit.*, I, 196. Stokes reprints in full the salient points in the *Bloudy Tenent*.

[56] Moehlman, *op. cit.*, p. 74.   [57] *Op. cit.*, I, 333.

[58] *Ibid.*, I, 27.

dently first used by Jefferson has done "more to insure the broad meaning of 'no establishment of religion' [in Article I of the Bill of Rights] than hundreds of state statutes have accomplished." [59] It was in 1878 that "the Supreme Court first stated judicially that the First Amendment was intended to erect 'a wall of separation between church and state.'" [60] That Jefferson and Madison intended for the First Amendment to the Constitution to erect such a wall of separation can be seen by a careful reading of Madison's "Memorial and Remonstrance Against Religious Assessments" drafted in 1784 [61] and Jefferson's "Bill for Establishing Religious Freedom," passed in 1786 [62] by the Assembly of Virginia. [63]

There are some writers, particularly Roman Catholics, who contend that the First Amendment to the Constitution does not mean nor necessitate the separation of church and state. Parsons [64] and others claim that the First Amendment merely forbids the establishment of a single church, with special favors to that church. According to them the Constitution does not forbid the state to aid religion in general. To this, Swancara replies: "The contention is false. The history of the First Amendment and the specific declaration of James Madison, its chief author, disprove it. The First Amendment prohibits, not only ecclesiastical monogamy, but also ecclesiastical polygamy." [65]

Some Roman Catholic writers identify separation with what is sometimes called the principle of indifferentism. [66] Rommen contends that indifferentism "denies divine revelation and the Church as the institution created by Christ for the salvation of souls." He claims that the principle of religious freedom or freedom of conscience, based upon indifferentism, "means the denial of objective truth in religion. . . . Indifferentism is thus nothing but religious and philosophical agnosticism." [67]

---

[59] *Op. cit.*, p. 76.

[60] Dawson, *America's Way in Church, State, and Society*, pp. 32–33.

[61] See Frank Swancara, *The Separation of Religion and Government* (New York, Truth Seeker Co., 1950), pp. 159–65, for a complete reproduction of the Remonstrance, and Stokes, *op. cit.*, I, 341–43, for an abridgement.

[62] Stokes, *op. cit.*, I, 334, says it was passed Dec. 17, 1785.

[63] See Swancara, *op. cit.*, pp. 166–68, for a complete reproduction.

[64] *Op. cit.*   [65] *Op. cit.*, p. iv.

[66] Rommen, *op. cit.*, p. 567.   [67] *Ibid.*, pp. 595–96.

Whatever may be one's view concerning the proper relation of the church and state most will agree with one Catholic author's statement that "Church and State cannot ignore one another without harming one another." [68] We need to examine, however, the remainder of this statement. The author adds: "This is the basic reason which has always led the Popes to reject the separation principle." This may have been the reasoning of the popes, but if so they were wrong. Separation does not necessarily mean that the church or the state ignores the other.

Separation of church and state simply means an organizational and a functional separation. C. C. Morrison defines separation as follows:

By the separation of church and state is meant the constitutional provision which forbids the making of any law, and therefore the taking of any executive action, that involves the interlocking of the official functions of the state with the official or institutional functions of any church. [69]

It is not a separation of religion and political life. Christian principles should be applied to governmental affairs, as is true of every other area of life. The state is or should be concerned about the moral and spiritual welfare of its citizens, and hence it should be interested in the well-being of all religious groups. But neither the church nor the state should seek to control the other or to use the other to promote its interests.

While most Americans believe in the validity of the separation theory, yet it should be admitted that the separation of these two basic institutions does not inevitably solve all of their problems. They both continue to exist as institutions and have to learn how to get along with each other, making constant adjustments to each other. Conflicts will and do arise, particularly in the frontier areas.

There are some scholars and writers, particularly Roman Catholics, who contend that the separation of church and state will inevitably lead to the secularization of much of life, including religion itself. For example, Osgniach says that separation will "logically lead to an atheistic and materialistic State"; [70] that it "can have no other meaning than the emancipation of civil society from God,

[68] Lecler, *op. cit.*, p. 38. [69] Quoted by Stokes, *op. cit.*, I, 28–29.
[70] *Op. cit.*, pp. 312–13.

of creature from the Creator . . . and a violent separation of man into two personalities—the citizen and the believer." [71] Some Protestants have been contending, in recent years, that the word "secular" has been abused; that it does not necessarily have a bad connotation. They suggest that "secular" simply means "not sacred or religious"; and that correctly the state and the school are secular, and that business belongs to the secular order. The secular stands in contrast to the specifically and formally religious.[72] There may be a sense in which the state and the school might be secular and yet not be a contributor to secularism, at least as the latter is ordinarily defined.

Regardless of definitions, it is wise for the defenders of separation to recognize the dangers of what is termed secularism, the danger that all of life will be organized as if God did not exist. It is a rather interesting historic fact, on the other hand, that secularism seems more likely to thrive where there is an established church than where there is a separation of church and state. The best assurance against the secularization of all of life is a vital type of religious movement, so dynamic that it will permeate all of life, so pervasive that the secular will be infused with the sense of the sacred. The disestablished, free, and frequently small minority religious groups are the ones that ordinarily best maintain such a religious vitality.

It was Mr. Justice Frankfurter, who said, "We have staked the very existence of our country on the faith that complete separation between the state and religion is best for the state and best for religion." [73]

Continuing Problems

There are some problems of major importance that are contemporary and continuing that have not been discussed. We shall consider only three of the more significant ones.

1. *The form of the state.* It may be that "in both Protestant and Catholic political theory the question of the form of the state is al-

---

[71] *Ibid.,* p. 314.
[72] Dawson, *America's Way in Church, State, and Society,* p. 22. Dawson is one author who defends and pleads for a proper understanding of "secular."
[73] Quoted by Dawson, *ibid.,* p. 46.

ways treated as a secondary problem," and it may be that "so long as government fulfils its assigned mission, the form in which it does so is of no great importance for the Church." [74] However, there does seem to be a rather close relation between certain Christian groups and the form of the state. For example, the relation between certain organizational expressions of the Christian movement and democracy has been so close that there has been a tendency to identify the two. Some people consider democracy merely the political implementation of the Christian spirit and ideal. While political democracy in the modern sense may not be prominent in the Bible, yet it is contended that "its roots are found in the conviction developed by the prophets and consummated in Jesus of Nazareth, of the worth of every individual, rich and poor, high and low, and the attempts made to base society on this conviction." [75] There can be little doubt that there are some democratic concepts that are inherent in the Christian religion. None is more central than its doctrine of man, which, to use an expression of A. E. Holt, encourages "the emergence of the man farthest down." [76] There is in Christianity a respect for man, based on the fact that he was made in the image of God, that gives to man, regardless of race, color, or cultural or educational level, infinite worth and dignity. Lowry suggests that democracy "is in fact a segment of Christian consciousness and teaching with respect to the nature and destiny of man." [77] This fact, along with the Christian "doctrine of consent," [78] provides much of the background for political democracy.

John C. Bennett mentions three elements in Christianity "which taken together have democratic implications." He suggests that no one of these taken by itself points very clearly to democracy. The three elements are "the sovereignty of God as transcending all of the authorities and powers of the world," "God's love for all persons regardless of their status in society," and "the doctrine of sin, which warns us against any political system which allows anyone to have arbitrary, unchecked power over others." [79] The latter reminds

[74] Bonhoeffer, *op. cit.*, p. 316.   [75] Stokes, *op. cit.*, III, 699.
[76] *Christian Roots of Democracy in America*, p. 40.
[77] Charles W. Lowry, *Communism and Christ*, p. 109.
[78] Holt, *op. cit.*, p. 44.
[79] John C. Bennett, "Christianity in Its Political Setting," *Religion in Life*, XXIV, No. 1 (Winter 1954–1955), p. 9.

one of Reinhold Niebuhr's often quoted statement: "Man's capacity for justice makes democracy possible; but man's inclination to injustice makes democracy necessary." [80]

There has been a particularly close relation between certain forms of Protestant Christianity and political democracy.[81] The Reformation, with its emphasis on justification by faith and the priesthood of all believers, made a very definite contribution to the spread of the democratic ideal and ultimately to the establishment of democratic governments. This is true in spite of the fact that many of the reformers and their followers failed to see the full political implications of their basic theological concepts. G. P. Gooch discriminatingly suggests "that democracy is a child of the Reformation but not of the Reformers." [82] Nichols claims that "Puritan Protestantism" has contributed most to democracy. And "Puritan Protestantism" for him represents "a fusion of Calvinism, Spiritualism, and the Baptist sect movement." [83] While the Reformation as such may not have contributed very much immediately to democracy, yet Nichols quotes Locke as saying, "The Reformation was the real starting point of democratic ideas." [84]

There can be no doubt about the contribution of Christian ministers and the Christian movement in general to the democratic trend in American life. Many ministers during the colonial period had a Bible in one hand and the works of John Locke in the other. They used both the Bible and Locke to support the movement for separation from the mother country and to guide in the establishment of a republican form of government. And, incidentally, they could,

---

[80] *The Children of Light and the Children of Darkness*, p. xi. The book carries the following subtitle, which describes the content of the book: "A Vindication of Democracy and a Critique of Its Traditional Defense."

[81] Some Roman Catholic writers, particularly American, have attempted to prove a close relation of Roman Catholicism to democracy. For an opposite view see Paul Blanshard, *American Freedom and Catholic Power* (Boston, Beacon Press, 1949). See also two or three chapters in James H. Nichols's *Democracy and the Churches* (Philadelphia, Westminster Press, 1951). Nichols concludes that the Roman Church in recent years in the United States has "showed itself a dangerously antidemocratic force in foreign affairs" (p. 266). See also the little book by Thomas Sugrue, *A Catholic Speaks His Mind* (New York, Harper, 1951, 1952).

[82] Quoted by Bennett, "Christianity in Its Political Setting," *op. cit.*, p. 8.
[83] Nichols, *Democracy and the Churches*, p. 10.   [84] *Ibid.*, p. 18.

in good conscience, hold Locke in one hand and the Bible in the other because they believed that they found in Locke much that was fully compatible with what they found in the Bible.

Does the preceding mean that Christianity in general and Protestantism in particular was and is dependent on democracy, which is a special form of the state? No, the order of dependence is in the opposite direction. While Protestant Christianity might and does find it difficult to prosper under certain forms of government, nevertheless Christianity as such can live and has lived under the most unfavorable political régimes. Some of its most creative periods have been when it was faced with an unfriendly and sometimes even a persecuting state.

In contrast, democracy is dependent on Christianity. It seems impossible to maintain a healthy political democracy without a healthy, virile, vigorous Christian movement. Holt sums up this matter of dependence as follows: "The high cost of a democratic society is the development of a generation of people whose spirits are stirred by the great truths of Christianity, and who seek a social order which will give the spirit of Christianity a chance for social expression." [85]

2. *Problems related to separation.* There are many problems that have resulted from or are related to the American doctrine of the separation of church and state. Some of these problems have inevitably arisen out of the difficulty of applying consistently such a basic political concept to the everyday problems of civil life. Other problems have arisen because of different viewpoints regarding the meaning of separation, and particularly because of the varying evaluations of the doctrine. Some do not consider the doctrine itself valid, while others do not agree with the historic American interpretation of the doctrine. For example, one author, a Roman Catholic, says the phrase "separation of church and state" "does not mean anything"; for him it is a "clumsy and phantom phrase." [86]

The same author also contends that the basic principle provided for by the United States Constitution, particularly by the First Amendment, is not separation of church and state but freedom. He contends that the separation of these two basic social institu-

[85] *Op. cit.*, p. 172.　　　　　[86] Parsons, *op. cit.*, p. 81.

tions is merely a *"policy* designed to effectuate religious freedom on the one hand and political freedom on the other." [87] The same author suggests that while the First Amendment may provide for no establishment, yet it does not deny the government the right to favor impartially all religious groups. In contrast, Stokes claims that "no establishment" had already been provided for in the Constitution; hence those who voted for the First Amendment must have had something in mind other than the matter of establishment.[88] Stokes concludes that while "neither the original Constitution nor the Bill of Rights specifically refers to Church and State separation," yet "this does not in any way invalidate the theory supported by the Supreme Court that such separation is involved, in keeping with the plan which had just been carried out in Virginia, where Madison, Jefferson, and others of the Founding Fathers had been so influential." [89]

Space is not available for a discussion of many of the problems that have evolved from the attempt to apply the separation theory. Some of the problems will be considered in an inadequate way, while others will be merely mentioned and some sources suggested for a study of them.

There is rather general agreement in the United States that the exemption from taxation of nonrevenue-producing church property does not violate the separation theory. Stokes reports that one-third of our state constitutions require such exemption, with another third authorizing it, while the remainder—"mostly constitutions adopted in the early years when exemption was taken for granted— make no specific mention of the subject." [90]

Another area where there is rather general agreement is the matter of Christian participation in political life. Except for the extreme sectarians there are few Christians who take the position that Christians and Christian groups should abstain from political life. The main problem is to know how far the church can enter into politics without violating the principle of separation of church and state and also without violating its own inner nature.

Most Protestants would agree that the church as such should enter very cautiously into political activities. It should depend pri-

[87] *Ibid.,* p. 106.   [88] *Op. cit.,* I, 527.   [89] *Ibid.,* I, 561.
[90] *Ibid.,* III, 419.

marily upon its members as individuals to carry the message and
the spirit of the Christian religion into the legislative halls and the
courts of the land. The church should participate actively in political campaigns only when moral issues are clearly involved. Its voice
should never be raised in narrow, partisan politics.[91] The church
should cultivate a respect for the authority of the state, reminding
its people that "there is no authority except from God, and those
that exist have been instituted by God." [92] Christians should be advised to pay their taxes,[93] rendering unto Caesar that which belongs to him.[94] They should also pray for those in authority.[95] The
church can and should encourage some of its most talented and
consecrated men to enter politics with a sense of divine vocation.
These men should seek to give political implementation to Christian
ideals. Through the efforts of such men, along with the legitimate
political activities of the rank and file of Christians, the church can
set loose in society "an invasion of great ideas about God, duty,
human fellowship, sin and righteousness." [96] These great ideas can
make a tremendous impact on society.

In contrast to the preceding, there are some areas of rather sharp
disagreement. We shall call attention briefly to a few of these.[97]
One area where there has been at least occasionally rather sharp
differences of opinion has been in regard to an ambassador or some
type of American representative to the Vatican. Beginning with
1797 and continuing until 1848, consular relations were maintained
with the Vatican. From 1848 to 1867 there were official diplomatic
relations with the Papal States. After the latter period there was
no serious attempt to reestablish these relations until President
Roosevelt, during World War II, appointed a "personal representative" to the Vatican. President Truman continued this policy. Many
Protestant leaders and groups strongly protested, claiming that such

[91] See Van Dusen *et al., op. cit.,* pp. 178–83, but particularly Brown, *op. cit.,*
pp. 267–70.
 [92] Romans 13:1.   [93] *Ibid.,* 13:7.   [94] Matt. 22:21.
 [95] 1 Tim. 2:1–2.   [96] Holt, *op. cit.,* p. 157.
 [97] Some of the problems that we shall not consider and that are discussed
quite adequately by Stokes in his third volume are the following: "Government Chaplaincies and Religious Services," "Required Oaths, and Blasphemy
Laws," "Sunday Observance Laws," "Government Religious Observance of Special Days and Occasions," "Civil Courts and Church Disputes," and "The Incorporation and Tenure of Church Property."

an appointment was a clear violation of the Constitution of the United States.[98]

Many of the most acute problems in recent years in the United States regarding the relation of the church and state have been related to public and parochial schools. There are some citizens, mostly Roman Catholics, who contend that tax money should be made available to parochial schools. The argument has been that these schools serve all the people, that they save the state or the nation great sums of money, that those supporting the religious institutions pay their taxes, which places a double burden upon them, and that support of such institutions from tax funds would not violate the United States Constitution.

Admittedly there are marginal areas where it is difficult to determine whether or not the constitutional provision for separation of church and state would be violated. Some people have contended, and evidently sincerely so, that welfare services such as free transportation, books, lunches, and so forth, could properly be provided by the government for those attending parochial or other private schools. Their view is that such services would be for the pupils rather than for the institutions they attend. For example, when the free textbook case from Louisiana came before the United States Supreme Court, Chief Justice Hughes delivered the opinion of the court which affirmed the decision of the state court approving free schoolbooks for the pupils in private or sectarian as well as public schools. The Chief Justice declared that the books were not granted to the school but to and for the use of children, and that there was no violation of the Constitution when the books were the same ones provided for the public schools and were not religious or sectarian.[99]

There has been some difference even of legal opinion concerning the constitutionality of free transportation at state expense for parochial-school children.[100] By 1946 eleven cases involving free trans-

[98] See Charles Clayton Morrison, *Can Protestantism Win America?* (New York, Harper, 1948), pp. 68 ff., and J. M. Dawson, *Separate Church and State Now* (New York, Richard R. Smith, 1948), pp. 36–40, 74–82.

[99] Alvin W. Johnson and Frank H. Yost, *Separation of Church and State in the United States* (Minneapolis, University of Minnesota Press, 1948), p. 148.

[100] For an examination of court decisions, see Johnson and Yost, *ibid.*, pp. 152–64.

portation of non-public-school pupils had been decided in the courts. Seven of the decisions were against transporting parochial-school children, with four favorable.[101] J. M. Dawson said that when he wrote his book *Separate Church and State Now* (1948), there were eighteen states and Hawaii that had laws granting free bus service to private or church schools.[102] The first school-bus case to reach the Supreme Court of the United States was the Everson case from New Jersey. In a five to four decision the Court held constitutional the New Jersey law which provided for the transportation of parochial-school children at public expense.[103] Many Roman Catholics hailed the decision as a victory. But if they had looked closely they would have understood that it was a limited and a precarious victory.

In the majority opinion are found such statements as the following:

The "establishment of religion" clause of the First Amendment means at least this: Neither a state nor the Federal Government can set up a church. Neither can pass laws which aid one religion, aid all religions, or prefer one religion over another. . . . No tax in any amount, large or small, can be levied to support any religious activities or institutions. . . . In the words of Jefferson, the clause against establishment of religion by law was intended to erect "a wall of separation between Church and State."

The First Amendment has erected a wall between church and state. That wall must be kept high and impregnable. We could not approve the slightest breach. New Jersey has not breached it here.

The majority opinion suggested that the state in passing the legislation had approached "the verge" of its constitutional power.

Two dissents were filed, one by Justice Robert H. Jackson and the other by Justice Wiley Rutledge. The opinion written by the latter was concurred in by Justices Frankfurter, Jackson, and Burton. Stokes considers Mr. Justice Rutledge's dissent "the most detailed statement of the Constitutional grounds for a clear-cut, absolute, rigid separation of Church and State yet made by a justice of the

[101] *Ibid.*, p. 159.   [102] P. 51.
[103] For a discussion of the case with reactions to it see Johnson and Yost, *op. cit.*, pp. 159–63, and Stokes, *op. cit.*, II, 702–16.

Supreme Court." [104] His dissent refused to draw a distinction between direct and indirect aid to a religious school. Justice Rutledge also concluded that "two great drives are constantly in motion to abridge, in the name of education, the complete division of religion and civil authority which our forefathers made. One is to introduce religious education and observances into the public schools. The other, to obtain public funds for the aid and support of various private religious schools."

The Supreme Court soon had to pass on a case related to the first of these great drives mentioned by Mr. Justice Rutledge. It was the McCollum case from Illinois which involved religious instruction on released time during the regular school day and in public-school buildings. Early in 1948 the Court in an eight to one decision declared the Illinois procedure unconstitutional. The basis for the Court's decision was related to the Everson case. The wall-of-separation theory was repeated. The Court held that in Champaign, Illinois, tax-supported property "was used for religious instruction," and concluded that "the tax-established and tax-supported public school system" was utilized "to aid religious groups to spread their faith." This was according to the Court a violation of Amendment I of the Constitution.

In a concurring opinion Mr. Justice Frankfurter, joined by Justices Jackson, Rutledge, and Burton, left the way open for additional decisions concerning other types of weekday religious education. He repeated, however, the statement made in the Everson case that "we have staked the very existence of our country on the faith that complete separation between the state and religion is best for the state and best for religion." He then added: "If nowhere else, in the relation between Church and State, 'good fences make good neighbors.'" [105]

That the McCollum case did not close the issue of released time

---

[104] *Op. cit.*, II, 707.

[105] For the McCollum case and a good understanding of dismissed and released time for religious education, see Johnson and Yost, *op. cit.*, pp. 74–90, and Stokes, *op. cit.*, II, 488–548. Stokes also discusses on succeeding pages such related matters as "Reading the Bible and Reciting the Lord's Prayer in Public School Exercises," "Incidental References to Religion in Textbooks," "Use of Public School Buildings for Religious Purposes," the teaching of nuns in the public schools, "Compulsory Salute to the Flag in Public Schools," religion in higher education, and "Schools of Religion at State Universities."

for weekday religious education was proved by the Zorach case of New York. The Supreme Court, in 1952, by a six to three decision, declared the New York plan constitutional. The main ways the New York program differed from the plan at Champaign (McCollum case) were the following: (1) the religious training took place outside the school building, (2) the school had nothing to do with the choice or the supervision of teachers, and (3) no credit was given for religious classes.

There are plans and programs of weekday religious education that differ from and fall in between the Illinois and the New York plans. There may have to be several other cases carried to the Supreme Court before there will be a clear-cut distinction between the plans for weekday religious education that are unconstitutional and constitutional.

3. *Freedom of religion.* The struggle regarding religious freedom is a factor of considerable importance in the contemporary world crisis.[106] Some of the problems regarding religious freedom stem from differences in the definition of freedom of religion, while others result from varying attitudes toward and evaluations of freedom. The entire problem is closely related to the separation theory. Many people believe that the fullest religious freedom is impossible without the separation of church and state. Bates from his exhaustive study concluded that separation tends "in most circumstances toward a greater and more secure religious liberty than does a union of Church and State." [107]

But what is meant by "religious liberty"? The philosopher Perry suggests that "every freedom or liberty has its negative and its positive sides. There is a liberty 'from' and there is a liberty 'to' and 'for.'" [108] This is just as true of religious freedom as it is of

[106] No attempt will be made to trace historically the struggle for nor the checkered career of religious liberty through the centuries of the Christian era. M. Searle Bates does this very adequately in Part II of his *Religious Liberty: An Inquiry* (New York, Harper, 1945). Cecil Northcott's *Religious Liberty* (London, S.C.M. Press, 1948), which is a much briefer study than Bates's, has a chapter on "Religious Liberty in History." H. G. Wood has a brief book entitled *Religious Liberty To-day* (Cambridge, University Press, 1949).

[107] *Op. cit.,* p. 310.

[108] Ralph Barton Perry, *Puritanism and Democracy* (New York, Vanguard Press, 1944), p. 512.

any other basic freedom. The fullest religious freedom would include at least the following: (1) freedom of conscience, (2) freedom of worship, (3) freedom of association, (4) freedom of propaganda, (5) freedom from civil disability (the right to vote, hold office, and so on, would not be affected by religious belief or affiliation), (6) freedom from discrimination against any or all religions by the State, and the evidencing of impartial sympathy toward their work, and (7) freedom of the church, or any part of it, from control due to any financial, political or other connection with the State.[109] Some of these freedoms would be found only in a country where there is separation of church and state, while most if not all of the others would find fullest expression only where separation existed.

The preceding means that religious freedom is drastically different from toleration. There is a tendency in some circles to confuse the two. This tendency is particularly prevalent in countries with a religious establishment. For practical purposes the toleration provided by a country having an established church may be so generous that it grants the fullest religious liberty. The theoretic base, however, is quite different from separation. Such toleration is granted as a special privilege, and not as an inherent right. Rights that are provided through toleration could be withdrawn.

Toleration "generally carries with it the idea that the person, opinion, or institution tolerated is a departure from what is normally right. . . . It is the 'allowance of that which is not wholly approved.' " [110] It was Madison who said, "The right of every man is to liberty—not toleration." [111] John Leland, living in the same creative period as Madison, similarly said: "The liberty I contend for is more than toleration. The very idea of toleration is despicable; it supposes that some have a pre-eminence above the rest to grant indulgence; whereas all should be equally free, Jews, Turks, Pagans and Christians." [112]

J. M. Dawson calls "toleration" "a weasel word which must be

---

[109] Stokes, *op. cit.*, III, 723–24. For a considerably more detailed statement of complete religious freedom, see the statement by Dean Luther A. Weigle in Bates, *op. cit.*, pp. 303–6.

[110] Stokes, *op. cit.*, I, 22.   [111] *Ibid.*, I, 340.

[112] Wesley M. Gewehr, *The Great Awakening in Virginia, 1740–1790* (Durham, N.C., Duke University Press, 1930), p. 191.

looked on with suspicion." He contrasts toleration and religious liberty as follows: Toleration is negative; religious liberty is positive. Toleration is a human concession; religious liberty is the gift of God. Toleration implies grounds for censure; religious liberty recognizes the uncensurable voice of the soul. Toleration is a tribal hangover; religious liberty is the achievement of Christian enlightenment. Toleration is granted under pressure; religious liberty springs from principle. Toleration tries by ecclesiastical or state law to limit freedom in religion to worship only; religious liberty insists on freedom under constitutional guarantees for the exercise of every religious function.[113]

The people of the United States enjoy more complete religious liberty than the people of any other major nation of the world. Fortunately, full religious liberty was provided for by our original Constitution and its amendments or Bill of Rights. This liberty has been strengthened by the subsequent interpretation of the Constitution by the United States Supreme Court. There were many factors that contributed to the movement for full religious freedom in the beginnings of our nation. Some of those factors were philosophical, some religious, and others political.

Certain of the political and the religious leaders of the colonial period laid the foundation for religious freedom in our country. Men such as Washington, Jefferson, Madison, Patrick Henry, and others of lesser renown made distinctive contributions. Washington, for example, wrote to the General Committee representing the United Baptist churches in Virginia as follows:

If I could have entertained the slightest apprehension that the Constitution framed in the convention where I had the honor to preside might possibly endanger the religious rights of any ecclesiastical Society, certainly I would never have placed my signature to it; and, if I could now conceive that the general government might ever be so administered as to render the liberty of conscience insecure, I beg you will be persuaded that no one would be more zealous than myself to establish effectual barriers against the horrors of spiritual tyranny, and every species of religious persecution— For you, doubtless, remember that I have often expressed my sentiment that every man, conducting himself as a good citizen, and

---

[113] These statements are the main headings in Chapter VII, entitled "Toleration Is Not Enough," in his book *Separate Church and State Now*.

being accountable to God alone for his religious opinions, ought to be protected in worshiping the Deity according to the dictates of his own conscience.[114]

There seems to be a close relationship between religious freedom and the other basic freedoms of life. Stokes concludes from his exhaustive study that "religious freedom is necessary both to the creation and the maintenance of civil and political freedom." [115] This means that the defense of religious liberty is not optional for those who love the democratic way of life. It means that as goes religious freedom, so will go all the other basic freedoms of life. And those who defend those freedoms should inquire into the definition of freedom by those who profess to be promoters of freedom, but who at the same time restrict the religious freedom of the people they control.

The Soviet Union, for example, may claim to be more democratic than the democracies, and it may profess to provide for freedom of worship, but its conception of democracy and of freedom is drastically different from the dominant view in the United States. While the constitution of the Soviet Union theoretically provides for freedom of worship, yet it does not even claim to provide for freedom of propaganda and education. This represents a very inadequate conception of religious liberty.

In addition, the Roman Catholic Church, in contrast to the claims of some of its leaders, definitely limits religious freedom where it has the power to do so. Such restriction is in harmony with its basic theory concerning the relation of church and state and the rights of truth and error. Pope Leo XIII in the encyclical *The Christian Constitution of States* said: "That liberty is truly genuine and to be sought after, which in regard to the individual does not allow men to be slaves of error and of passion, the worst of all masters." [116] After a rather thorough study of persecution by as contrasted with the propaganda of the Roman Catholic Church, the well respected

---

[114] William Addison Blakely (ed.), *American State Papers on Freedom in Religion* (Washington, Review and Herald, 1943), p. 151. For a consideration of the contributions of a dozen additional political and religious leaders to religious freedom in the early days of our nation, see Stokes, *op. cit.*, I, 292–357. Stokes also discusses (pp. 240–44) the influence of the Great Awakening.

[115] Stokes, *op. cit.*, III, 714–15.   [116] Quoted by Bates, *op. cit.*, p. 296.

English scholar C. J. Cadoux came to the following conclusion: "When the facts are calmly viewed with eyes undimmed by any strong initial prejudice, it is impossible not to see that, by the continual growth of Catholic numbers and influence, religious liberty is threatened by a danger of the very first magnitude." [117]

A mere passing acquaintance with world conditions will convince one that religious freedom is a problem of major proportions. It is one of the big stumbling blocks to cooperation between the nations of the world and particularly to any effective movement toward a world government of any type. It is true that the United Nations Charter includes the following as a part of its formal purpose:

To achieve international cooperation in solving international problems of an economic, social, cultural, or humanitarian character, and in promoting and encouraging respect for human rights and for fundamental freedoms for all without distinction as to race, sex, language, or religion.[118]

The Charter does not define those "fundamental freedoms."

The Economic and Social Council of the United Nations appointed a Commission on Human Rights to formulate a statement of the basic human rights. The commission's "Universal Declaration of Human Rights" was adopted on December 10, 1948, by the General Assembly. The vote was 48 for, none against, with 8 members abstaining. Article 18 deals most specifically with freedom of religion. It reads as follows:

Everyone has the right to freedom of thought, conscience and religion, this right includes freedom to change his religion or belief, and freedom, either alone or in community with others and in public or private, to manifest his religion or belief in teaching, practice, worship and observance.[119]

Theoretically the statement sounds surprisingly liberal. The problem is in its implementation in the different countries of the world.

[117] C. J. Cadoux, *Roman Catholicism and Freedom* (4th ed.; London, Independent Press, 1947), p. 172.
[118] *The Charter of the United Nations*, Article 1, Section 3.
[119] For a full statement of the Universal Declaration of Human Rights, with some discussion of the background and the significance of the Declaration, see No. 76 in the Headline Series published by the Foreign Policy Association. Written by O. Frederick Nolde, it is entitled "Freedom's Charter."

IX

WAR AND PEACE

"NO ETHICAL problem . . . has so repeatedly and so deeply challenged and divided the mind of the Church as has this problem of the right Christian estimate of war."[1] Another English scholar and theologian considers the problem of war "the dominant moral and religious issue of the day,"[2] while the historian Toynbee goes so far as to say that war "is the crucial question on which the destiny of our civilization hangs."[3]

In this chapter little attention will be given directly to the causes of or the cure for war. These matters, along with other related areas, are covered adequately in a number of standard books on war.[4] We shall major on a biblical and historical approach to the problem of war. The latter part of the chapter will consider some historic and contemporary plans and programs for peace.

[1] Cecil J. Cadoux, *Christian Pacifism Re-examined* (Oxford, Basil Blackwell, 1940), p. 228.

[2] Charles E. Raven, *War and the Christian* (New York, Macmillan, 1938), p. 26.

[3] Arnold Toynbee, *War and Civilization* (New York, Oxford University Press, 1950), p. 12.

[4] See L. L. Bernard, *War and Its Causes* (New York, Henry Holt, 1944); Lynn Montross, *War Through the Ages* (New York, Harper, 1944); Willard Waller (ed.), *War in the Twentieth Century* (New York, Random House, 1940); and the most definitive of all, Quincy Wright's two volumes entitled *A Study of War* (Chicago, University of Chicago Press, 1942).

The Bible and War

It is important, from the Christian viewpoint, to know what the Bible has to say on any subject.

1. *The Old Testament and war.* In the Old Testament a twofold picture is found concerning war and God's relation to it. One is a dark, rather foreboding picture which is interpreted by many as being out of harmony with the nature and character of the God revealed by Jesus Christ. On the other hand, we get at least a glimpse into the ultimate if not the original purpose of God, which is strikingly similar to the revelation of God in the life and teachings of Jesus.

Now, for a brief look at the first picture, which many Christians would like to forget. The Old Testament records some of the cruelest, bloodiest wars of extermination that the world has known. Some of those wars entailed the unrestrained slaughter of the guilty and the innocent, of men and women, of boys and girls, of babes born and unborn. What makes the picture more disturbing is the fact that God, according to the Old Testament record, commanded his people to fight, aided them in their battles, frequently being the source of their victories,[5] and at times ordered them utterly to destroy their enemies.[6] God, through one of his prophets, reprimanded and rejected a king, who had failed, in obedience to God, to destroy all the Amalekites and their possessions.[7] What makes the picture even darker is the fact that the prophet of God had Agag, the king of the Amalekites, brought before him and the record says, "And Samuel hewed Agag in pieces before the Lord in Gilgal." [8]

This is, however, only one phase of the picture. There is revealed in the Old Testament a different conception, or at least a different perspective concerning God. There are indications even in the Old Testament that war was out of harmony with his purposes for man. David, who was a man after God's own heart, was not permitted to build the temple because he had shed much blood and had "waged great wars." [9] This fact implies that there was something wrong, in God's eyes, with war. The psalmist prays that God will "scatter the

[5] Ex. 14:24; Lev. 26:7–8.   [6] Josh. 6:17, 23, 25.
[7] 1 Sam. 15:17–31.   [8] *Ibid.*, 15:33b.   [9] 1 Chron. 22:8.

peoples who delight in war," [10] and reviewing the works of Jehovah
he says:

> He makes wars to cease to the end of the earth;
> he breaks the bow, and shatters the spear,
> he burns the chariots with fire! [11]

The prophets always pictured the ideal or golden age as a time of
peace. For example, Isaiah paints the following picture of the latter
days:

> He [the Lord] shall judge between nations,
> and shall decide for many peoples;
> and they shall beat their swords into plowshares,
> and their spears into pruning hooks;
> nation shall not lift up sword against nation,
> neither shall they learn war any more.[12]

He also saw the coming of the Messiah as a time when

> every boot of the tramping warrior in battle
> tumult
> and every garment rolled in blood
> will be burned as fuel for the fire.

He then breaks out in those familiar words:

> For to us a child is born,
> to us a son is given;
> and the government will be upon his shoulder,
> and his name will be called
> "Wonderful Counselor, Mighty God,
> Everlasting Father, Prince of Peace." [13]

2. *The New Testament and war.* What one finds in the New
Testament concerning war depends largely on what he wants to
find. The pacifist can find enough there to condemn war and the
Christian's participation in it. For example, C. J. Cadoux, a thorough
scholar, concludes that "any natural and straightforward exegesis"
of the ethical teachings of Jesus will prove that they are "obviously
and flagrantly incompatible with intentional and organized blood-

[10] Ps. 68:30. [11] *Ibid.,* 46:9. [12] Isa. 2:4; cf. Mic. 4:3.
[13] Isa. 9:5, 6.

shed, and therefore with war."[14] In a more negative vein, and yet just as positive in his conclusion, is Charles E. Raven. He says, "It is, in fact, more than doubtful whether any single utterance or action of Jesus gives any sort of sanction to war in any form."[15] In contrast, Reinhold Niebuhr says, "There is not the slightest support in Scripture for this doctrine of non-violence."[16] And by nonviolence he means the position of the pacifists. An objective reading of the New Testament will lead one to conclude that there are no specific teachings in it concerning war and the Christian's relation to it. War is not explicitly justified or forbidden. Leslie Weatherhead says that "the question of war between nations does not arise in the New Testament."[17]

Proof texts, approving and disapproving war, can be balanced against each other. Most of those on both sides can be explained away with relative ease; some few with more difficulty. The proof-text approach to the study of the teachings of the New Testament concerning war is barren of real results. However, because so much importance is attached by so many people to certain scriptures or incidents in the life of Jesus, we shall examine briefly a few of the references cited in defense of or against war.

There are some who suggest that Jesus was frequently in contact with men of the military, and the fact that he never disapproved their occupation would imply his approval of war. Based on the argument of silence one could claim that Jesus approved slavery, unjust oppression, and many other evil practices of his day. Is not "an 'argument from silence' always precarious, and never more so than when applied to the Gospels"?[18]

The cleansing of the temple by Jesus[19] is frequently cited in

[14] C. J. Cadoux, *The Early Church and the World*, p. 55. For a critical examination of the section of Cadoux on the teachings of Jesus, see Umphrey Lee, *The Historic Church and Modern Pacifism* (New York, Abingdon-Cokesbury, 1942), pp. 19–40.

[15] In Rufus M. Jones (ed.), *The Church, the Gospel, and War* (New York, Harper, 1948), p. 9.

[16] *Christianity and Power Politics* (New York, Scribner's, 1940), p. 10.

[17] *Thinking Aloud in War-Time* (New York, Abingdon, 1940), p. 25.

[18] G. H. C. Macgregor, *The New Testament Basis of Pacifism* (London, The Fellowship of Reconciliation, 1953), p. 18.

[19] John 2:13–16, Matt. 21:12–13. It is not certain whether there was one or two cleansings of the temple.

defense of war. In appraising the incident or incidents it should be remembered: (1) that John's gospel alone mentions the scourge or whip; (2) that some scholars suggest that the whip was made of litter from the floor; but granting that Jesus did make a real whip of string or rope there is no sure evidence that he used it; (3) that if he used the whip it was used, so it naturally seems, on the animals only; (4) that even if he used force, including the whip, on the money-changers, which seems far-fetched, such would not justify war. It might justify the use of force under certain conditions, but using force is one thing, and war, with the taking of human lives, is something quite different.

The statement by Jesus, "Do not think that I have come to bring peace on earth; I have not come to bring peace, but a sword," [20] is taken completely out of its context at times and given as a defense of war. The setting of the statement shows clearly that Jesus was using this word as a symbol of the division that would come within families because some accepted and followed him while others rejected him.

Still another statement by Jesus that is used to defend war is the following: "And you will hear of wars and rumors of wars." [21] This is merely a statement of fact. The most significant portion of the passage is frequently left off. Jesus says, "See that you are not alarmed; for this must take place, but the end is not yet." By no stretch of the imagination can one use this scripture as a justifiable defense of war. The master was saying to his disciples: "Do not let anyone fool you by saying every time there is a war, 'This is the end; this is the close of the age.'" And incidentally this is a warning that many need even in the contemporary period.

There are a number of other passages that are used at times to place the stamp of biblical approval on war, but there is at least one of major importance that must be examined briefly. It is the occasion when Jesus counseled the disciples, if they did not have a sword, to buy one.[22] This is a difficult passage of scripture to interpret. Without going into a lengthy discussion let us notice the following: (1) That in some way the instruction of Jesus to buy a sword was related to his approaching arrest, trial, and crucifixion. (2) That the two swords produced would have been inadequate for

[20] Matt. 10:34; cf. Lk. 12:51.   [21] Matt. 24:6.   [22] Lk. 22:36–38.

the disciples' defense of themselves and their Master, and yet he did not say anything about the purchase of additional swords. (3) That it is clear that Jesus did not expect them to use the sword in his defense or in their own defense. A short time later he commanded Peter to put up his sword and said, "For all who take the sword will perish by the sword." [23] (4) That evidently the disciples missed the whole point of his instruction. When they told him they had two swords, he said, "It is enough." It seems he meant, "That is enough of this," or "That will do." In other words, Jesus dismissed the subject. Possibly he was simply using the sword as a symbol of the difficult hours and days immediately ahead and was not referring to a physical sword at all. (5) That even if Jesus had intended that the two swords should be used in his defense this fact would not necessarily justify modern warfare.

Now for a brief consideration of a few of the teachings of Jesus that are used by those who contend that war is not Christian, and should not be approved by the Christian conscience. One of the most common arguments against war, from the Christian viewpoint, is the teaching of Jesus concerning nonresistance, nonretaliation, or the non-vindictive spirit. [24] There is rather general agreement concerning what he said but disagreement concerning its exact meaning and application. Was Jesus talking exclusively about individual relationships, or did he intend for his teachings concerning nonresistance to be applied to the broader social community? Tolstoi would say that Jesus meant the latter. Many equally sincere followers of Christ would claim that he refers entirely to individual relations. It seems that the original and primary application is to the individual. This scripture and others concerning nonresistance apply to war only in the sense that the fundamental principles of Jesus should be the ultimate goals for society and should be the standards by which the present level of living is judged.

Possibly the statement by Jesus that is cited most frequently as an argument against war is his command to Peter to put up his sword. [25] But it is doubtful if this can properly be applied to war at all. Notice the three reasons Jesus gave against taking up the sword: (1) The sword is self-defeating: they that take it up shall perish by

[23] Matt. 26:52. [24] See particularly Matt. 5:38–42.
[25] *Ibid.*, 26:51–52.

it. (This principle, by implication, might be applied to war.) (2) Jesus does not need the sword to defend him: his Father has available twelve legions of angels. (3) The sword if effective in his defense would defeat the basic purpose of God in his life. He had been sent into the world to do the will of him that sent him, which meant for him death on the cross.

There are several general emphases in the teachings of Jesus, such as love and the cross, that are used by some pacifists and others to support their position that war is not Christian. It should be admitted that the strongest arguments against war, from the viewpoint of the teachings of Jesus, are based on his general teachings and his spirit rather than on particular incidents or specific sayings.

Some attention could properly be given to Paul's epistles, but there is little if anything that is distinctive. Some people do attach considerable importance to the "powers that be" passage [26] and to such metaphorical statements as, "Put on the whole armor of God." [27] When these and other references in Paul are carefully examined, we are forced to the conclusion that Paul, as was true of Jesus, did not say anything directly approving or disapproving war in general or the Christian's participation in war. Both Jesus and Paul did set out some general principles applicable to the problem of war that may be used by the sincere Christian to give him guidance in regard to his relation to war.

3. *The Old Testament versus the New Testament.* Admitting that there are few, if any, specific New Testament scriptures that relate directly to the question of war, nevertheless there is a rather marked contrast between the kind of God revealed by Jesus and the God in the Old Testament who commanded the merciless killing of the enemies of Israel. How can one explain these differences or contrasts?

One approach to a solution of this very real problem is to seek for a satisfactory explanation for God's part in the wars of the Old Testament. There are at least four such explanations, although one or two of them do not come to real grips with the problem. First, the Old Testament reveals the current Jewish conception of God. They thought he commanded them to fight and to slaughter, they

[26] Rom. 13:1–7 ASV.   [27] Eph. 6:11.

believed that he led them into battle and gave them victories over their enemies, but they were mistaken. Second, God's part in the wars of the Old Testament discloses accurately one side or phase of his nature. He is not only a loving, heavenly Father; he is also a God of wrath and judgment. Or, possibly to state the matter more accurately, he would have to be a God of judgment to be a loving God in the deepest and most significant sense.

A third suggestion is that the wars of the Old Testament were in accord with the permissive, or to use an expression of Weatherhead's, the circumstantial will of God.[28] This would mean that war was not and is not a part of God's perfect or intentional will. He permits wars to come through the operation of basic laws that govern the relation of nations. He is responsible for war and for the results of war only in the sense and to the degree that he permits those laws to operate. Some contend that this was the extent of God's responsibility for war in the Old Testament and is the extent of his responsibility for wars today.

Another position, which is related more specifically and exclusively to the problem of Old Testament wars, is the argument that God, in the days of the Old Testament, had to adjust himself, to some degree, to the level of living of the people of that time. War was not a part of God's original, intentional will for man. Man so rebelled against God "that God had to deal with him in a different way than He had originally intended . . . if he [man] chooses to be a saint God deals with him as a saint, whereas if he chooses to be a sinner, God deals with him as a sinner." [29] This position is somewhat similar to the explanation of the differences in the Old Testament and the New Testament in regard to other social and moral questions such as divorce. It was Jesus, himself, who said that Moses [30] permitted the sending away of a wife because of the hardness of their hearts or the perversity of their lives.[31] He suggests that even in the Old Testament law there was an adjustment of God's original purpose because the people were not ready for his perfect or ultimate ideal for them. So, it is reasoned, the cruelty

[28] Leslie D. Weatherhead, *The Will of God* (New York, Abingdon-Cokesbury, 1944), p. 11.
[29] Guy F. Hershberger, *War, Peace, and Nonresistance* (Scottdale, Pa., Herald Press, 1944), p. 24.
[30] Deut. 24:1-4.   [31] Matt. 19:8.

of the wars of the Old Testament can be explained. God, even to accomplish his purposes, had to adapt his methods to a level where his chosen people and their enemies would understand.

While these, and other possible explanations for the differences in the Old and New Testaments, may not be fully satisfactory, the main thing is to remember that the full revelation of God is in his Son and our Saviour—Jesus Christ. The Old Testament is always to be interpreted and evaluated in the light of the revelation of God in Christ. We can also be assured that a full understanding would mean that there could be no conflict between the God of the Old Testament and the New Testament. He is the eternal "I am," the one who is the same yesterday, today, and forevermore. One thing that points in that direction is the fact that when one looks deeply enough in the Old Testament he will find that God's original purpose and his ultimate will as revealed there is entirely compatible with the fuller revelation recorded in the New Testament. It was Jesus himself who said, when pressed by the Pharisees concerning divorce, "From the beginning it was not so." [32] Here Jesus goes back of the law to the original purpose which expressed the ultimate will of the Creator and Lawgiver.

Christianity and War

War has continued, through the stream of the Christian centuries, to be a real problem for many Christians. We shall consider, as briefly and concisely as possible, a few of the high spots in the relation of the Christian movement to war and particularly its teachings concerning the Christian's participation in war. [33]

1. *The early Christian centuries.* [34] It seems that there were no Christians in the Roman army, in the postapostolic period, before about 165–170 A.D. Cadoux sums up the matter as follows: "The evidence for the existence of a single Christian soldier between 60

---

[32] *Ibid.,* 19:8.

[33] For the historic approach of Christianity to war, see the books by Cadoux, Heering, Lee, and Scott-Craig listed in the bibliography for this chapter on page 364.

[34] For an excellent summary see Roland H. Bainton, "The Early Church and War," in Rufus M. Jones (ed.), *op. cit.,* pp. 75–92.

and about 165 A.D. is exceedingly slight." [35] He suggests that there must have been very few Christian soldiers previous to the time of Marcus Aurelius and that those few must have been converted while in the army.[36] The earliest positive evidence that Christians had enlisted in the army after their conversion is found in the writings of Tertullian, about 200 A.D.[37]

It is also true that little attention was given by Christian writers in the early centuries to the problem of war. Moffatt concludes that previous to the time of Marcus Aurelius "military service does not seem to have presented itself as a problem at all to the conscience of the Church." [38] Why was the early church so silent in regard to war? Bainton suggests that "the reason may be either that participation was assumed or that abstention was taken for granted," and concludes that the latter was the more probable.[39] Possibly a better explanation is the fact that the problem of war was not faced seriously by most Christians of the early centuries since very few of them were confronted with the question of joining the army or of actively participating in war. Conscription was not practiced. In addition, many of the Christians, who were slaves or Jews, were ineligible for service in the army. And incidentally, for a considerable portion of the early church period, Christianity was treated as a phase of Judaism; which in turn meant that many who were not Jews were considered Jews by the Roman authorities, and hence they were not eligible for service in the army.

The relation of Christians to war seemed to have first become a serious problem when men who were in the army were converted. What should they do? Did their new-found faith necessitate that they leave the army? The answers to these and other questions varied considerably and continued to vary for some time. Some justified the Christian's continuance in the army on the basis of Paul's statement that "every one should remain in the state in which he was called." [40]

Justin Martyr (born 100–110 A.D.) was seemingly the first Christian writer to make a very clear statement concerning war. In his

[35] *The Early Church and the World*, p. 275.
[36] *Ibid.*, p. 276. [37] *Ibid.*, p. 422.
[38] "War," *Dictionary of the Apostolic Church*, II, 660.
[39] "The Early Church and War," *op. cit.*, p. 77.
[40] 1 Cor. 7:20.

"First Apology" (153 A.D.) [41] he says: "We, who once killed one another, [now] not only do not wage war against our enemies, but, in order to avoid lying or deceiving our examiners, we even meet death cheerfully, confessing Christ." [42] He also says: "And we who delighted in war, in the slaughter of one another, and in every other kind of inquity have in every part of the world converted our weapons of war into implements of peace." [43]

The fact that there were an increasing number of Christians in the army after 170 A.D. does not mean that the problem was settled. There continued to be rather sharp differences of opinion concerning the Christian's relation to war. Among those opposing military activity by Christians, the most specific, vocal, and prominent were Tertullian, Origen, and Lactantius. There were other minds, "including some of considerable depth and unquestioned sincerity," who felt that military service for the Christian was all right. [44]

Tertullian (145 to 150–200 A.D.) was antimilitary in the extreme, and disapproved of military service from the beginning of his literary career. [45] Two references from his writings will suffice to set out his view. In "De Idololatia" he has a section entitled "Concerning Military Service," in which he says, "But now inquiry is made about this point, whether a believer may turn himself unto military service, and whether the military may be admitted unto the faith." He does not directly answer his questions but he points the direction of an answer when he says that

there is no agreement between the divine and the human sacrament, [46] the standard of Christ and the standard of the devil, the camp of light and the camp of darkness. One soul cannot be due to two [lords]—God and Caesar. . . . how will [a Christian man] war, nay, how will he serve even in peace, without a sword, which the Lord has taken away? . . . the Lord . . . in disarming Peter, unbelted every soldier. [47]

[41] In most cases the dates we give will follow the chronology of Cadoux's *The Early Christian Attitude to War*, pp. xvii–xxiii.

[42] *Writings of Saint Justin Martyr* (New York, Christian Heritage, 1948), pp. 75–76.

[43] "Dialogue with Trypho," *ibid.*, p. 318.

[44] Cadoux, *The Early Church and the World*, p. 418.

[45] *Ibid.*, p. 428.

[46] "Sacrament" could refer to a military oath.

[47] "De Idololatia," XIX, Roberts and Donaldson, *Ante-Nicene Christian Library* (Edinburgh, T. & T. Clark, 1872), XI, 170–71.

Later, in 211 A.D., after he had become a Monatist, he wrote "De Corona" in defense of a Christian soldier who had refused to wear a garland or a diadem (crown) on the emperor's birthday.[48] In the eleventh section of "De Corona," Tertullian asks and answers the question whether "warfare is proper at all for Christians." He asks some questions which suggest the direction of his thinking and then makes some statements that leave no doubt about his conclusions. The following excerpts will reveal his position:

> Shall it be held lawful to make an occupation of the sword, when the Lord proclaims that he who uses the sword shall perish by the sword? And shall the son of peace take part in the battle when it does not become him even to sue at law? . . . Shall he keep guard before the temples which he has renounced? And shall he take a meal where the apostle has forbidden him? . . . Shall he carry a flag, too, hostile to Christ? . . . Then how many other offenses there are involved in the performance of camp offices, which we must hold to involve a transgression of God's law, you may see by a slight survey.

Tertullian had some special admonition for the soldier who had become a Christian after he was in the army. That made the problem somewhat different, yet there must be either an immediate abandonment of military service, which had been done by many, or all sorts of quibbling will have to be resorted to in order to avoid offending God.[49]

One of the fullest statements concerning war by an early church father is contained in Origen's "Against Celsus." [50] The latter was a reply to "A True Discourse" by Celsus, a lengthy attack on the Christian movement, written in 178 A.D. Origen replied seventy years later (248 A.D.) at the suggestion of Ambrosius, a convert, friend, and patron of Origen. It is evident from the lengthy quotations from Celsus in Origen's reply that the former had charged the Christians with refusal to serve in the army. In defending the Christian's refusal to participate in war, Origen revealed, at least by implication, the main basis for his objection to war. He reminded

---

[48] Cadoux, *The Early Christian Attitude to War,* p. 110.

[49] "De Corona," II, Roberts and Donaldson, *Ante-Nicene Christian Library,* XI, 347–48.

[50] Cadoux in *Christian Pacifism Re-examined* gives his own translation of Book VIII, chapters 68–76 of "Against Celsus" (pp. 232–40), which is being followed in quoting from Origen.

Celsus, and those who would defend the latter's criticism of Christianity, that

The priests among yourselves attached to certain statues, and the temple-wardens of the gods ye worship, keep their right hands undefiled for the sake of the sacrifices, in order that they may offer these customary sacrifices to your so-called gods with hands unstained by blood and pure from human slaughter. And not even when war has come upon you, do ye make the priests also render military service. If then this is a reasonable thing to do, how much more reasonable is it, when others are rendering military service, that these (Christians) also should render (*their*) military service as priests and servants of God, keeping their right hands pure, but striving by means of prayers to God on behalf of those who are rendering military service righteously, and on behalf of him who is reigning righteously, in order that all things opposed and hostile to those who act righteously may be put down? Moreover, in putting down by means of our prayers all the daemons who stir up wars, get oaths broken, and disturb the peace, we bring more help to those who reign than do the men who aspire to render military service.

Some contend that Origen, by saying that Christians pray for those "rendering military service righteously," is inconsistent. Cadoux answers this criticism by suggesting that this and other allusions to righteous or justifiable wars refers, either explicitly or implicitly, to wars waged by non-Christians.[51] The last sentence of Chapter 73 of "Against Celsus" should answer any question concerning Origen's personal position. It is as follows: "And we 'fight on behalf of the King' even more than others do: we do not indeed 'render military service along with him,' even 'if he press us to do so'; but we do 'render military service' on his behalf, by marshalling a private army of religion through the prayers we offer to the Divine Being."

Lactantius (250–325 A.D.), possibly the latest of the church fathers to write against war, was a man of considerable stature, being in his old age, for three or four years, the tutor for the son of Constantine.[52] He suggested that since God prohibited killing, it was not lawful for a "just man" to serve as a soldier. He concluded that

---

[51] Cadoux, *The Early Christian Attitude to War*, p. 137. For an excellent running commentary and appraisal of Origen's "Against Celsus," see pp. 131–47 of this book.

[52] Cadoux, *The Early Church and the World*, pp. 583–84.

"no exception at all ought to be made (to the rule) that it is always wrong to kill a man, whom God has wished to be (regarded as) a sacrosanct creature." [53]

How can one explain the rather general, although not universal, opposition of the early church leaders to war? The following are the reasons most frequently given or implied by the early church fathers: (1) war entailed the shedding of blood and the latter was contrary to the commandment of God and incompatible with the Christian spirit; (2) army officers had to pass sentences of death and privates were forced to carry out such orders and such sentences were in violation of the commandment "Thou shalt not kill"; (3) the soldier's oath of obedience to the emperor conflicted with his absolute obedience to God; (4) the conduct of most soldiers even in peace times was unbecoming for a Christian.[54] Heering mentions another factor, which is clearly evident in some of the writings of the early church fathers. This factor, largely negative, was of considerable importance. It was the fact that the Christians of the early centuries lacked any strong sense of adhesion or loyalty to the state. Their citizenship was in heaven. They were aliens in a foreign land. They had little voice in governmental affairs. They formed, for practical purposes, a state within the state.

What was the final situation in the early Christian centuries concerning war? By the time of Constantine, the question of the Christian and war was settled for the main stream of the Christian movement. The cross became a military emblem. In 314 A.D. the Synod of Arelate enacted a Canon

which, if it did not, as many suppose, threaten with excommunication Christian soldiers who insisted on quitting the army, at least left military service perfectly free and open to Christians. Athanasius, "the father of orthodoxy," declared that it was not only lawful, but praiseworthy, to kill enemies in war. . . . Augustinus defended the same position with detailed arguments. In 416 A.D. non-Christians were forbidden to serve in the army.[55]

Heering considers this adjustment of Christianity to war as *The Fall of Christianity*, the title of his historical study of Christianity and war.

[53] *Ibid.*, p. 583.   [54] Heering, *op. cit.*, pp. 44–45.
[55] Cadoux, *The Early Church and the World*, pp. 588–89.

The change of the church's viewpoint, to such a large degree, in regard to war, was a part of its general adjustment to the world. Its peace with the world in general and with the state in particular became practically complete with the "conversion" of Constantine in 312, the edict of Milan in 313, which made Christianity *a* legal religion of the empire, and the recognition by Theodosius some years later of Christianity as *the* legal religion.

It would be a mistake to assume that the reconcilation of the church with the state and with the war system was complete. "In many quarters the settlement was accepted only gradually and with an uneasy conscience." [56] Official Christianity "relegated to the monastic orders her old views about war and the military calling." [57] There have also been sectarian groups through the centuries, outside the main stream of the Christian movement, that have never accepted the official Christian position. War has continued, with varying degrees of intensity, to disturb the consciences of many Christians, inside and outside the main stream of the Christian movement.

2. *Augustine to Aquinas.* Augustine (354–430 A.D.) was a transition figure. In a way, he belonged to the early church period and yet he belonged to the medieval era. With his writings the church's general position concerning war was fixed for centuries. Aquinas, eight centuries later, merely polished, reproduced, and in a few minor ways elaborated on what Augustine had already said.

Augustine seemed to have had an uneasy conscience concerning war. He suggests that the wise man will wage nothing but a just war, and even that should be with deep sorrow that "other men's wickedness . . . makes his cause just . . . whether it produce war or not." [58] This attitude was held not only by Augustine, but "throughout the Middle Ages all writers were in agreement on this, that war was something foreign to the spirit of Christ." [59] The fact that the scholastics did not believe the clerics should be requested

---

[56] *Ibid.*, p. 591.

[57] Harnack, quoted by Heering, *op. cit.*, p. 57.

[58] Augustine, *The City of God*, XIX, vii (London, J. M. Dent & Sons, 1945), II, 243.

[59] Bede Jarrett, *Social Theories of the Middle Ages, 1200–1500*, p. 211.

to participate in war except "to succour, console and exhort" implies that warfare was not considered in harmony with the Christian spirit.[60]

The church's uneasy conscience concerning war may be one of the reasons for Aquinas' (1224–1274) effort to work out a philosophical-theological basis for the moral justification for war. In searching for such a basis he went back through Gratian to Augustine's conception of a just war.[61]

Aquinas, enlarging some on Augustine's three conditions of a just war, said:

> In order for a war to be just, three things are necessary. First, the authority of the sovereign by whose command the war is to be waged. For it is not the business of a private individual to declare war. . . . And as the care of the common weal is committed to those who are in authority . . . it is lawful for them to have recourse to the sword in defending that common weal against internal disturbances . . . so too, it is their business to have recourse to the sword of war in defending the common weal against external enemies.
>
> Secondly, a just cause is required, namely that those who are attacked, should be attacked because they deserve it . . .
>
> Thirdly, it is necessary that the belligerents should have a rightful intention, so that they intend the advancement of good, or the avoidance of evil.[62]

Aquinas' second article under Question 40, which is on war, considers the question "Whether it is lawful for clerics and bishops to fight?" His conclusion was that they should not fight. He says, "Warlike pursuits are altogether incompatible with the duties of a bishop and a cleric." Again he suggests that "it is altogether unlawful for clerics to fight, because war is directed to the shedding of blood."

[60] *Ibid.*, p. 201.   [61] *Ibid.*, p. 187.

[62] Thomas Aquinas, *Summa Theologica*, trans. Fathers of the English Dominican Province (printed by permission of Benziger Brothers, Inc.). Part II, Second Part, Question 40, First article. To these three conditions for a just war there was sometimes added a fourth, which was hinted at by Aquinas in his discussion of ambushes. This fourth condition was that the just war must be properly conducted. For a modern statement of the Roman Catholic position regarding war, see John Eppstein (ed.), *Code of International Ethics* (Westminster, Md., Newman Press, 1953), pp. 113–62.

3. *Luther and Calvin.* Luther's position concerning war cannot be understood without some acquaintance with his views regarding the church and state and the dualistic nature of his general ethical position. His dualistic ethic is more closely related to Aquinas, with the latter's idea of the *Corpus Christianum,* than to Augustine, with his *Civitas Terrena* and *Civitas Dei.* His dualism was, in some ways, more drastic than the Roman Catholic dualism. The Catholic dualism was and is, in one sense, an external dualism, representing two levels of morality, one for the clergy and the other for the laity. Luther's dualism was internal, creating for the individual Christian inner tension and conflict.

For Luther the Christian lives in two realms or under two domains—the spiritual or the otherworldly and the secular or the this-worldly. The morality which belongs to the spiritual order or domain is based on the Sermon on the Mount. The morality which belongs to the worldly domain is a state morality. The former is wholly Christian, the latter is only relatively so. The Christian has to conform, to a degree, to both moralities. In his personal life, in relation to God and man, he is to live by the Sermon on the Mount, by the absolute Christian ethic. As a citizen, the Christian is to live in accordance with the state morality. This is seen in what he said concerning Christians and war. His statement was: "If worldly rulers call on them to fight, then they ought to and must fight, and be obedient, not as Christians but as members of the state and obedient subjects." [63]

The most specific statement by Luther concerning war and particularly concerning the Christian's relation to war, is found in his "Whether Soldiers, Too, Can Be Saved." [64] He wrote this tract at the request of Assa Von Krasn and others, but also, it seems, because there were many who were offended by the occupation of a soldier. [65] In the tract Luther sought to answer the question if a

[63] *Works of Martin Luther,* V, 39.

[64] *Ibid.,* V, 29–74. Other tracts or letters of Luther dealing rather specifically, directly or indirectly, with war are: "Secular Authority: To What Extent It Should Be Obeyed" (*ibid.,* III), and his three letters or tracts dealing with the peasant's revolt entitled "Admonition to Peace: A Reply to the Twelve Articles of the Peasants in Swabia," "Against the Robbing and Murdering Hordes of Peasants," and "An Open Letter Concerning the Hard Book Against the Peasants" (*ibid.,* IV).

[65] *Ibid.,* V, 32.

Christian could be a soldier and "go to war and slay and stab, rob and burn." [66] His conclusion was that the work of a soldier could be right and godly.

Some of his arguments in defense of war and of the Christian's participation in war were as follows: (1) The work of a soldier may be compared to the work of a physician. What he does may seem rather drastic but it is done for the good of the body or the whole. (2) Wars may be used to promote peace and to protect the good. (3) The wielding of the sword is the work of God; it is God's hand and not man's that slays, tortures, and beheads. (4) If the use of the sword by the state to punish criminals is right, then the use of the sword in war is also right.

The central part of this treatise or tract is a rather lengthy distinction between three kinds of war. The three are wars of inferiors against superiors, of equals against equals, and of superiors against inferiors. He discusses most thoroughly the first. He concludes that inferiors should never go to war against superiors. He would apply this to princes as well as to peasants. He gives particular attention to rebellion against a tyrannical ruler which he considered rebellion against God's ordinance. Tyrannical rulers can be left in the hands of God, who has said, "Vengeance is mine, I will repay." God has many resources with which he can punish the tyrant. War with an equal is justified only when it is necessary and when fought in the fear of God. In harmony with the feudal system and with his dependence on the princes and rulers, Luther defended the right of superiors to war against inferiors. In fighting against inferiors in order to maintain peace and harmony in society, these superiors, even up to the emperor, should remember, however, that they, in turn, have superiors over them.

Luther, toward the close of the tract, seeks to answer some questions concerning the life and conduct of the soldier. Only one of these questions is of much relevance for today. In answer to the question, "Ought a soldier fight in a wrong cause?" he gives the rather surprising and interesting reply that if the soldier knew for sure that the cause was wrong then he should fear God rather than men and should not fight or serve, for he "cannot have a good conscience before God." [67]

[66] *Ibid.*, V, 34–35. [67] *Ibid.*, V, 68.

As was true of Luther, Calvin's view concerning war was closely related to his conception of the state and its functions in society. For him the civil authority was as necessary to mankind as "bread and water, light and air, while its dignity is much more excellent." [68] One of the state's functions was to see that "no blasphemy against the name of God, no calumnies against his truth, nor other offences to religion, break out and be disseminated among the people . . . that a public form of religion may exist among   Christians, and humanity among men." [69]

In considering the functions of the civil authority, inevitably one must face the relation of the use of the sword to the biblical injunction, "Thou shalt not kill." Calvin deals with the problem at some length. The main line of his argument may be summarized as follows: When the magistrate uses the sword he does not act for himself but rather as an agent of God. He administers the judgment of God on sinful men. He goes so far as to say that when Moses and David executed the vengeance committed to them by God, they by their sternness "sanctified the hands which they would have polluted by showing mercy." [70]

As the use of the sword by the magistrate to punish evildoers was justified, so war to punish offenders and to defend the magistrate's territory was likewise justified. Calvin concludes that "the Holy Spirit, in many passages of Scripture, declares [such wars] to be lawful." [71] Calvin's scriptural justification of war was largely based on the Old Testament, which for him was equally authoritative with the New Testament. He does recognize and seek to answer questions concerning the New Testament and war. He gives a threefold answer to those who suggest that the New Testament does not contain any precept or example, which would approve participation in war by a Christian. He first suggested that "the reason for waging war which existed in ancient times, is equally valid in the present age." It is assumed that by ancient times he referred primarily to Old Testament days. Secondly, he said that no express declaration concerning war should be expected in the writing of the apostles. They were not interested in organizing governments but in describing the kingdom of Christ which was spiritual. Thirdly, it

[68] *Institutes of the Christian Religion,* trans. Henry Beveridge (London, James Clarke & Co., 1949), II, 652.
[69] *Ibid.,* II, 653.   [70] *Ibid.,* II, 660.   [71] *Ibid.,* II, 661.

was implied in the New Testament writings that no change concerning war was made by the coming of Christ. He then cited the use by Augustine of the injunction by John the Baptist to the soldiers that they be content with their wages, which was certainly not a prohibition of the military life.

The preceding does not mean that Calvin would defend every war. While he does not discuss in detail the just war and lay down specific conditions for it as Augustine and the schoolmen had, nevertheless he does suggest that every possible method for settling a dispute should be attempted before "recourse to the decision of arms." He also suggests that the purpose of war should be the restoration of peace. Although Calvin does not discuss the rightness or wrongness of wars between different classes as Luther did, nevertheless Calvin would not justify open revolt against a magistrate or ruler. Citizens should submit to the government of their princes "although there is nothing they less perform than the duty of princes." [72]

It may be safely implied that Calvin, who defended war, under certain conditions, for the state or the magistrate, would justify the Christian's participation in it. He says that subjects should be obedient to their magistrates "in complying with their edicts, or in paying tribute, or in undertaking public offices and burdens, which relate to the common defence, or in executing any other orders." [73]

Plans for Peace

The Dutch theologian G. J. Heering, writing during the years between World War I and World War II, said: "World-peace is by far the greatest problem that confronts the nations to-day. It is humanity's key-problem." [74] Since that time the world has been torn by World War II, the Korean conflict, the armed truce labeled a cold war, and the constant threat of World War III with the use of the most destructive weapons the world has ever known. Peace is certainly "humanity's key-problem" in the contemporary period. "Mankind is confronted today with the alternative: either lasting peace or a serious risk of total destruction." [75]

[72] *Ibid.*, II, 670.   [73] *Ibid.*, II, 669.   [74] *Op. cit.*, p. 7.
[75] Jacques Maritain, *Man and the State* (Chicago, University of Chicago Press, 1951), p. 189.

Although the attainment of peace among the nations seems to be faced with insurmountable difficulties, yet within the minds and hearts of millions of the peoples of those nations there lives an "inextinguishable desire for peace." [76] This desire for or dream of peace "has haunted the minds of men since the eighth-century prophets." [77] Some believe that the time for the fulfillment of this dream has arrived. They would agree with Victor Hugo that "there is something greater than armies, and that is an idea when its time has come." [78] Many hope and pray and some believe that the time has come for the idea or the dream of peace to become a reality.

1. *Utopian plans for peace.* There have been dreamers through the centuries who have foreseen a world community of peace and goodwill. Some of these seers and prophets have worked out in considerable detail plans for the implementation of their dreams. Their plans, some fantastic and others more realistic, were the forerunners of the more specifically formulated political programs for peace.

One of the earliest specific plans (1305–1307) for peace was outlined by Pierre Dubois, who advocated a federation of Christian sovereign states, and was the first to suggest "an international court of arbitration." [79] Dante in his *De Monarchia* "envisioned a worldwide state with one ruler, unselfish as he was all-powerful, who would suppress all tyrannies and bring about universal peace." [80] Erasmus in *The Complaint of Peace*, written about 1517, directed his plea to kings, whom he considered the instigators of war, although he suggested that wars should not be declared except by the

[76] Isaiah Bowman, "Is an International Society Possible?" in Julia E. Johnsen (compiler), *United Nations or World Government* (New York, H. W. Wilson, 1947), p. 175.

[77] George F. Thomas, *Christian Ethics and Moral Philosophy* (New York, Scribner's, 1955), p. 358.

[78] On the flyleaf of Harrop A. Freeman, *Peace Is the Victory* (New York, Harper, 1944).

[79] Sylvester John Hemleben, *Plans for World Peace Through Six Centuries* (Chicago, University of Chicago Press, 1943), p. 3. During the tenth and eleventh centuries the Roman Catholic Church through the Truce of God and later through the Peace of God sought to promote the cause of peace. See John Alzog, *Manual of Universal Church History* (Cincinnati, Robert Clarke Co., 1902), II, 406–408.

[80] Hemleben, *op. cit.*, p. 11.

consent of all the people.[81] His emphasis on arbitration is generally considered "his greatest contribution in the interest of peace." [82] Emeric Crucé's *The New Cyneas* was "one of the most completely formulated peace plans of early modern times." [83] He suggested an assembly of the ambassadors representing various sovereigns,[84] and his plan was the first to recommend a world-wide organization "which embraced both Christian and non-Christian nations." [85] The *Grand Design*, credited to Henry IV but possibly the work of his minister Sully, sought to maintain the *status quo* and by implication to work out a balance of power.[86]

Hugo Grotius' *The Rights of War and Peace* (1625) "is still the classical work in its field," [87] and has been called "'one of those rare books that cannot die.'" [88] Although the main emphasis of Grotius was on the humanizing of war, yet he is sometimes called, although possibly falsely so, the father of international law.[89] William Penn's *An Essay Towards the Present and Future Peace of Europe*, written in 1693, did not contain anything particularly new or distinctive.[90] One of the most thoroughly worked-out schemes was the *Project for Perpetual Peace* by Saint-Pierre. It was first issued in two volumes in 1713, with an English translation in 1714. Later it was expanded. His recommended confederation was limited to Europe [91] and to kings.[92] In 1761 Saint-Pierre's project was revived by Rousseau, in what purported to be a summary of the former but in which there was "'much more of Rousseau than of Saint-Pierre.'" [93] Another famous name attached to a plan for peace was Jeremy Bentham, whose *A Plan for an Universal and Perpetual Peace* was published in 1843 after his death. His major emphasis was on the establishment of a world court.[94] There have been many other plans for the peace of the world but none of greater signifi-

[81] *Ibid.*, p. 18.   [82] *Ibid.*, p. 20.   [83] *Ibid.*, p. 21.
[84] *Ibid.*, p. 25.   [85] *Ibid.*, p. 30.   [86] *Ibid.*, p. 39.
[87] Albert C. Knudson, *Philosophy of War and Peace* (New York, Abingdon-Cokesbury, 1947), p. 120.
[88] Quoted by Hemleben, *op. cit.*, p. 42.
[89] *Ibid.*, p. 44. For a discussion of Grotius' contribution to international law, see G. N. Clark, "Grotius and International Law" in F. S. Marvin (ed.), *The Evolution of World Peace* (London, Oxford University Press, 1921), pp. 64 ff.
[90] Hemleben, *op. cit.*, p. 47.   [91] *Ibid.*, p. 58.
[92] *Ibid.*, p. 65.   [93] Quoted by Knudson, *op. cit.*, p. 139.
[94] Hemleben, *op. cit.*, pp. 82–83.

cance than Immanuel Kant's *Perpetual Peace,* published in 1795, which has become "a classic of international government," [95] and which seems to carry more weight today than in its own day.[96]

2. *The League of Nations and peace.* Any plan for the promotion of peace must be implemented if it is to become effective. If it is to be more than a dream it must be organized for action. While none of the preceding dreams eventuated in an organization, nevertheless they did help to accustom the peoples of the world to thinking in terms of peace and organizations for peace. For example, they provided some of the background for the conference at the close of the Napoleonic wars (1815). From the time of this conference "the habit of using international conferences as a means of settling disputes between States" has been steadily gaining ground.[97] It was the conference at the end of the Napoleonic wars which led to the "concert of Europe" which in turn was "a forerunner of modern international organization." [98]

More immediate forerunners of the League of Nations were The Hague Conventions of 1899 and 1907, the first of which was called by Czar Nicholas II of Russia, which established a Permanent Court of Arbitration. The second conference was also called by Czar Nicholas but at the suggestion of President Theodore Roosevelt of the United States. These peace conferences "were the first truly international assemblies meeting in time of peace for the purpose of preserving peace, not of concluding a war then in progress." [99]

The League of Nations was the more or less natural next step in the movement toward the organization of the world for peace. It was a part of the peace settlement following World War I, and was largely the product of the creative mind and the idealistic spirit of Woodrow Wilson. He was not responsible, however, for its weaknesses, which were evident to a degree from the first, but which

[95] *Ibid.,* p. 88.

[96] *Ibid.,* p. 95. Under the title of *Inevitable Peace* (Cambridge, Mass., Harvard University Press, 1948), Carl Joachim Friedrich discusses Kant's general contribution to the philosophy of peace. At the close of his book he gives his own translation of Kant's essay on peace.

[97] Norman Bentwich and Andrew Martin, *A Commentary on the Charter of the United Nations* (London, Routledge and Kegan Paul, 1950), p. ix.

[98] Daniel S. Cheever and H. Field Haviland, Jr., *Organizing for Peace* (Boston, Houghton Mifflin, 1954), p. 33.

[99] James Brown Scott as quoted by Hemleben, *op. cit.,* pp. 134–35.

became acutely evident when it was faced with the serious problems that immediately preceded World War II. It may have "realized some of the hopes of its founders" during the early years,
"although from the beginning it suffered from a fatal weakness,"
which for Bentwich and Martin, who are Britishers, was the "non-
adherence of the United States and the exclusion of the Soviet
Union." [100] There were, however, other factors contributing to the
inherent weakness of the League of Nations. Some of these factors
were equally if not more basically important that the one mentioned by Bentwich and Martin. The lack of unity among the victors at the close of World War I was a factor of considerable importance. This was not exclusively a lack of unity between the
United States and her European allies,[101] but also between some
of the European allies, particularly Great Britain and France.[102]

Mangone suggests that every peace plan from the Grand Union of
Confucius to the Dumbarton Oaks Conference, which laid much
of the groundwork for the United Nations, has been "a mirror of
the age in which it was conceived." [103] This statement would certainly apply to the League of Nations. It could not escape its environment. Herbert Hoover, an on-the-scenes observer and participant, has said that after the armistice

forces inherent in Europe began to take over the control of human fate.
. . . Destructive forces met at the Peace Table. The life and future of
26 jealous European races were on that table. The genes of a thousand
years of inbred hate and fear were in the blood of every delegation. Re-
venge for past wrongs rose every hour of the day.[104]

The statesmen "shackled by these malign forces" [105] were not free
to make peace on the basis of Woodrow Wilson's fourteen points,
which had been expanded into twenty-five.[106] Possibly the major

---

[100] Bentwich and Martin, *op. cit.*, p. ix.

[101] See Sir William Beveridge, *The Price of Peace* (New York, Norton,
1945), p. 30.

[102] *Ibid.*, p. 39.

[103] Gerard J. Mangone, *The Idea and Practice of World Government* (New
York, Columbia University Press, 1951), p. 3.

[104] Herbert Hoover, *America's First Crusade* (New York, Scribner's, 1941,
1942), p. 9.

[105] *Ibid.*, p. 10.

[106] For the original fourteen points see Beveridge, *op. cit.*, pp. 133–35, and
for the expanded group of twenty-five see Hoover, *op. cit.*, pp. 4–7.

weaknesses of the League of Nations were inevitable. It could not escape its age and environment. Whether or not the latter is correct the weaknesses were there. Its failure stemmed primarily from the fact that it was "a league of separate national states." [107] As a league of sovereign national states it had "more legal powers than it had the strength to use," which Hoover describes as "a disastrous weakness." [108]

In spite of its weaknesses the League had many accomplishments to its credit, particularly in its early days.[109] In the 1930's, however, when the League was faced with some real challenges, it failed. Japan, which was a member of the Council of the League, embarked in 1931 on a war against China, which was also a member of the League. The League did nothing effective to stop the war. The League also failed to do anything constructive concerning the economic slump, which began in 1929. It failed miserably when Italy, in 1935, marched into Ethiopia. There followed, in 1936, the German reoccupation of the Rhineland, the forceful incorporation of Austria into the German Reich in 1938, and the German occupation of Czechoslovakia in 1939. In these crisis periods the League "as an organization proved to be wholly impotent," and by the time World War II broke in 1939 "the League of Nations . . . was an empty shell." [110]

World War II did not destroy the legal existence of the League of Nations. The Covenant of the League, at least theoretically, continued in force until its formal demise by a resolution passed at the last meeting of its Assembly in April, 1946. "The nucleus, and with it the idea, of a world organization survived the catastrophe of 1939; and at no time during the war was the re-establishment of a general political organization of States seriously in doubt." [111]

3. *United Nations and world government.* A mere casual acquaintance with the League of Nations and with United Nations will reveal that they are strikingly similar in purpose, organization,

---

[107] Beveridge, *op. cit.*, p. 94.   [108] *Op. cit.*, p. 72.

[109] For a thorough, scholarly history of the League see the two volumes by F. P. Walters, *A History of the League of Nations* (London, Oxford University Press, 1952). The two volumes are divided into five parts as follows: Part I, The Making of the League; Part II, The Years of Growth; Part III, The Years of Stability; Part IV, The Years of Conflict; and Part V, The Years of Defeat.

[110] Bentwich and Martin, *op. cit.*, p. x.   [111] *Ibid.*, p. xi.

and functions.[112] The League's Assembly became the General Assembly of United Nations. The former's Council is the Security Council of the latter. The Permanent Court of International Justice was adopted by United Nations.[113] It was decided, however, by the great powers during World War II that the League should not be revived. On the other hand, they began, long before hostilities ceased, to lay the groundwork for a new international organization. The Moscow Declaration, on October 30, 1943, by the governments of the United States, the United Kingdom, the Soviet Union, and China, was the first formal statement of their purpose. Article 4 of the Declaration was as follows:

That they recognize the necessity of establishing at the earliest practical date a general international organization based on the principle of the sovereign equality of all peace-loving States, and open to membership by all such States, large and small, for the maintenance of international peace and security.[114]

The Declaration included some of the purposes and principles stated in the Atlantic Charter, which was signed by the President of the United States and the Prime Minister of the United Kingdom on August 14, 1941.[115]

The next major step in the preparation for the organization of United Nations was the meeting, in the fall of 1944, of representatives of the great powers at Dumbarton Oaks, near Washington, who formulated what were known as the Dumbarton Oaks Proposals, which provided most of the outline for the organization of United Nations. An agreement on the voting procedure in the proposed Security Council could not be reached at Dumbarton Oaks. This decision, made at Yalta, February, 1945,[116] was incorporated into the Charter of United Nations. It provided that apart from procedural matters, which were to be decided by any seven votes

[112] Cheever and Haviland, *op. cit.*, compare rather thoroughly the League of Nations and the United Nations.

[113] For a thorough study of the Court through 1942, see Manley O. Hudson's *The Permanent Court of International Justice, 1920–1942* (New York, Macmillan, 1943). The author served for many years as a judge of the Court.

[114] The complete text of the Moscow Declaration is given by Beveridge, *op. cit.*, pp. 137–38.

[115] For text of Atlantic Charter see *ibid.*, pp. 135–37.

[116] For a report of the Crimea or Yalta Conference see *ibid.*, pp. 143–51.

of the eleven members of the Council, all other decisions required the affirmative vote of seven members, including the concurring votes of the five permanent members of the Council. These five permanent members were to be and are the United States, the United Kingdom, the Soviet Union, France, and China. This was the provision for the right of veto by the major powers, which has been used and abused so frequently.

The Yalta conferees called for a "conference of United Nations" to meet at San Francisco on April 25, 1945. This conference was to prepare a Charter for a new world organization. "The Governments qualifying for invitation were those which had declared war on Germany or Japan by March 1, 1945, and had signed the Declaration by United Nations." [117] The latter was first signed in Washington on January 1, 1942, by the representatives of twenty-six belligerents and later by twenty-one additional nations before March 1, 1945.[118] The Charter of the United Nations organization was hammered out over a period of weeks and came into force on October 24, 1945, when the number of ratifications reached the minimum required by the Charter.

It may be that what was formulated at San Francisco was the best that could be done at that time and under the conditions. It may also be true that it represented some progress over the League of Nations, but it retained some of the basic weaknesses of the League and incorporated some weaknesses of its own.[119] United Nations, as

[117] Bentwich and Martin, *op. cit.*, p. xviii.   [118] *Ibid.*, p. xiii.

[119] In addition to Bentwich and Martin, cited a number of times in this chapter, the following are a few of the many books available on the United Nations: John Bauer, *Make the UN Effective for Peace* (New York, Richard R. Smith, 1952); Louis Dolivet, *The United Nations* (New York, Farrar, Straus & Co., 1946); H. V. Evatt, *The United Nations* (Cambridge, Mass., Harvard University Press, 1948); Leland M. Goodrich and Edvard Hambro, *Charter of the United Nations: Commentary and Documents* (Boston, World Peace Foundation, 1946); and a booklet entitled *From Here On!* (rev. ed.; Chicago, Rotary International, 1951). In addition the United States Department of State has available a number of pamphlets, the most relevant of which are: *Facts and Figures about the United Nations* (1950), *National Commission for UNESCO Today* (1950), and *The Universal Declaration of Human Rights* (1949). For a Bill of Rights, proposed in the formative period of United Nations, see H. Lauterpacht, *An International Bill of the Rights of Man* (New York, Columbia University Press, 1945), and for an outline of the purposes and program of UNESCO, one of the most interesting and constructive agencies of the United Nations, see Julian Huxley's *UNESCO: Its Purpose and Its Philosophy* (Washington, Public Affairs Press, 1948).

was true of the League of Nations, is an association of sovereign nations. The five great powers in that association are "above the law laid down for the others." [120] The privileges of the great powers are protected by the right of veto, which has prevented the Security Council "from serving as an effective instrument of conciliation in major disputes." [121] The veto power, however, is not the basic problem. The big problem is the division of the world into two camps, camps that are built around the two major powers of the world—the United States and the U.S.S.R. With or without the veto there can be no peace unless these two powers can get along with each other. The fact that they are so much more powerful than any of the other nations of the world makes the task of the United Nations, in some ways, more difficult than was the task of the League of Nations following World War I.

Being an association or conference of independent states and divided into two camps, the United Nations Organization has not been able to implement the provision in its Charter for a military establishment. It may be, as some have suggested, that the Articles dealing with collective security were and are "out of accord with political realities," and should be "the goal of future endeavour." [122] It may also be that "the Charter has created an illusory system of collective security." [123] Nevertheless, these very facts point up a weakness or a limitation of the United Nations. That which was established as "an instrument of world peace has proved to be a forum of world conflict," [124] and a "hotbed of frustrations." [125]

Although all of the preceding may be true, and although the United Nations Organization may be shot through "with cancerous self-contradictions," [126] yet it is the only organization for peace the world now has. It may be "a transitional organization," [127] but as such it may have an important function to perform. Hope rests in developing it, "not in abandoning it." [128] In spite of its weaknesses,

[120] William E. Rappard, "The United Nations as Viewed from Geneva," in Johnsen (compiler), *op. cit.*, p. 91.

[121] Bentwich and Martin, *op. cit.*, p. viii.

[122] *Ibid.*, p. xxviii.   [123] *Ibid.*, p. viii.   [124] *Ibid.*, p. viii.

[125] Cheever and Haviland, *op. cit.*, p. 816.

[126] Pitirim A. Sorokin, *The Reconstruction of Humanity* (Boston, Beacon Press, 1948), p. 13.

[127] Quincy Wright, "Making the United Nations Work," in Johnsen, *op. cit.*, p. 70.

[128] *Ibid.*, p. 74.

a major duty of Christians "is to do everything possible to support and strengthen" it.[129] This they should do while at the same time they recognize the need for a stronger world organization than United Nations.

Many people have advocated some type of world government, but none more consistently and persistently than Clarence Streit and those associated with him in Federal Union.[130] There are others, including some recognized scholars, who consider the hope for a world government as "a very dangerous illusion."[131] Reinhold Niebuhr has an essay in one of his books entitled "The Illusion of World Government."[132] He sums up his own arguments against the plausibility of world government in two propositions. "The first is that governments are not created by fiat. . . . The second is that governments have only limited efficacy in integrating a community."[133] This integration must come before there can be an effective organization. Niebuhr suggests that governments cannot achieve this integration or create what he calls communities "for the simple reason that the authority of government is not primarily the authority of law nor the authority of force, but the authority of the community itself."[134]

Maritain, who says that "the problem of World Government . . . is the problem of lasting peace,"[135] admits the difficulty of attaining that peace. One of the major obstacles is "the so-called absolute sovereignty of modern States."[136] He suggests that "we must get rid of the Hegelian or pseudo-Hegelian concept of the State as a person, a supra-human person," and consider it only as a part of the body politic.[137] He does not believe that the modern "trend toward supreme domination and supreme amorality" on the part of the state is inherent in the innate nature of the state.[138] For this and other

---

[129] Thomas, *op. cit.*, p. 359.

[130] See Streit's *Freedom Against Itself* (New York, Harper, 1954) for an interesting explanation for the ills of our society and for the reasons for the difficulty of attaining an effective world government. For earlier books by Streit, see *Union Now* (New York, Harper, 1940) and *Union Now wih Britain* (New York, Harper, 1941).

[131] Emil Brunner in Clara Urquhart (ed.), *Last Chance* (Boston, Beacon Press, 1948), p. 66.

[132] *Christian Realism and Political Problems*, pp. 15–31.

[133] *Ibid.*, p. 17.   [134] *Ibid.*, p. 22.   [135] *Op. cit.*, p. 189.

[136] *Ibid.*, p. 194.   [137] *Ibid.*, p. 195.   [138] *Ibid.*, p. 192.

reasons, Maritain considers the idea of world government as sound.[139] He does recognize, however, the difficulties of achieving peace and establishing an effective world organization to promote peace.

The fact that peace is hard to attain does not mean that the hope for it should be surrendered as the idle dream of visionaries. Such a surrender certainly should not characterize Christians. Every basic principle of their faith contains a demand for perfection, a command that is beyond their foreseeable attainment. It is not theirs to reason why; it is theirs to give themselves unselfishly to the promotion of every cause and to the attainment of every goal that they consider to be within the will and purpose of God. They will do this trusting the ultimate results to their all-wise heavenly Father, knowing that his will ultimately will be done among men.

[139] *Ibid.*, p. 201.

X

WAR AND THE
CHRISTIAN CONSCIENCE

W̲AR HAS been one of the most persistent and perplexing problems faced by conscientious Christians through the centuries. Scott Lidgett once said that one's relation to war is the most difficult problem "in personal philosophy which any man can set himself." [1] While the problem has been a continuing one, yet there are times, such as the contemporary period, when it becomes especially acute. For the past two or three generations there has been a growing uneasiness, on the part of many Christians, concerning war and their participation in it. That which had been accepted without question by the vast majority of Christians for centuries has now been brought under the scrutiny of the Christian spirit and ethic.

There are at least two reasons for the present-day stirring of the Christian conscience concerning war. [2] For the first time, at least in the modern era, governments are drafting men for military service. So long as governments depended entirely upon volunteers there was really no way to know how many people objected to military service. The picture was changed, however, when nations could

[1] Quoted by Weatherhead, *Thinking Aloud in War-Time*, p. 10.
[2] Lee, in *The Historic Church and Modern Pacifism*, makes a distinction between the pacifism of certain of the early church fathers and even of historic peace groups, such as the Quakers and the Mennonites, and the pacifism of the contemporary period, which he considers a product of the Social Gospel Movement (pp. 205 ff.).

no longer depend entirely on volunteers. That which previously might have been a potential problem now became a real problem for many. The matter of the Christian conscience and war not only tended to become a very real and acute issue for many individual Christians but it has also become of increasing concern to the church and the state. Another reason for the deepening awareness of the problem in the contemporary period is the indiscriminate destructiveness of modern wars. Add to this the fact that modern wars are total wars, that once started it seems impossible to stop them, and that man has now perfected instruments of destruction undreamed of a few years ago, and one can understand the growing sense of uncertainty and uneasiness concerning war.

The Christian and His Conscience

Before discussing specifically the relation of the Christian conscience to war, we shall consider briefly the meaning of conscience and the place it should have in the moral conduct of the Christian.

1. *Its nature.* There are varying definitions of or viewpoints concerning conscience. By "conscience" we do not mean a special faculty, such as sight or hearing, that God has given to man. It is not the "voice of God within" which will guide one unerringly to the right. Conscience may be man's capacity to hear the voice of God,[3] but it is not that voice.

Man does have a God-given sense of oughtness, a conviction that there is such a thing as right and wrong. "Conscience" may include more than this, but at least this is the phase of "conscience" which is innate. It is this sense of oughtness which is the "instinctive universal recognition that right is to be done, wrong is not to be done"; it is this same sense of oughtness which provides "the foundation of all morality."[4]

Such an inborn sense of oughtness is the common possession of Christians and nonchristians. It explains the uneasy conscience, which for Reinhold Niebuhr represents the "protest of man's es-

[3] Lindsay Dewar, *The Moral Conduct of a Christian* (London, A. R. Mowbray, 1951), p. 127.
[4] R. C. Mortimer, *Christian Ethics* (London, Hutchinson's Univ. Lib., 1950), p. 26.

sential nature against his present state." [5] For Brunner the conscience of the nonchristian is a "sense of unrest, a signal of alarm"; it is "like the inarticulate groaning of a prisoner in his dungeon"; man "can 'evade' the pressure of conscience, he can artificially shut down the noise of this alarm signal, but he cannot get rid of it." [6] Brunner also says that conscience separates man from God; [7] it is the fear of God, "and yet it is also the longing of the soul for God. . . . it is a kind of pain, a feeling of personal anguish, of sorrow of heart, caused by the fact that we have been wrenched away from our true home." [8] This "signal of alarm," "longing of the soul," "kind of pain," is what we mean by the universal sense of oughtness.

2. *Its content.* In the moral nature of man there is a moral constant and a moral variant. The moral constant is his innate sense of oughtness or his feeling that there is such a thing as right and wrong. The moral variant is the content of that oughtness. What one considers to be right and wrong will be determined by his total moral experience. This means that every immediate moral decision will be colored by, and to some degree determined by, the previous decisions of the individual and by the forces and factors that have touched and influenced his life in the past. The result is that the individual shares the responsibility for the content of his conscience with his parents, his teachers, his friends, his school, his church, and his community.

The fact that the content of one's conscience is a moral variant correctly implies that what we ordinarily term "conscience" may be wrong. It is not an inerrant guide. This evidently is true in regard to war, since there are such widely divergent viewpoints held by conscientious Christians concerning the Christian's participation in war. The fact that one may be honestly wrong on important moral issues should mean that any man, particularly a Christian, should be willing to examine objectively differing viewpoints and to re-examine his own position. An unwillingness to do this might be an indication that he is wrong or at least uncertain about his position on that particular issue.

[5] *The Nature and Destiny of Man,* I, 267.

[6] Emil Brunner, *The Divine Imperative* (The Westminster Press, 1947, copyright 1947 by W. L. Jenkins), p. 156.

[7] *Ibid.,* p. 157. [8] *Ibid.,* p. 158.

One result of the experience that makes one a child of God is that it tends to inform and correct his conscience. It gives to his conscience and his whole life a new orientation, a new source of authority, a new direction and dynamic. The things that were formerly considered right may now be considered wrong. The reverse may also be true.

We should not conclude, however, that simply because one has become a child of God that his conscience will be an infallible guide. Even the Christian's conscience needs to be instructed and enlightened. And while we correctly insist that the individual is obligated to educate his conscience, yet the first effect of the enlightenment of one's conscience is not to quiet it but to awaken it or to disturb it. Thus, it is not exclusively the nonchristian who has an uneasy conscience. Christians who are sensitive to moral issues are constantly disturbed by a restless conscience. The continuing struggle within the conscience of the Christian may and will be helpful if it leads to moral advance. It will be hurtful if it results in a sense of futility and frustration. The latter will not be true if the child of God will consistently move in the direction that his enlightened conscience would lead him; and if he will maintain through faith a vital fellowship with God, who is the ultimate source for the release of self-defeating tension in the Christian's life.

3. *Its authority.* While the conscience is not inerrant, it is or should be authoritative. A. E. Taylor is particularly clear in the distinction that he makes at this point. He says: "How impossible to maintain the inerrancy of a man's conscience, and yet how necessary to any serious morality to insist upon its authority, and even its absolute authority!" [9] Again he says, "The one *certain* way to miss getting a better conscience is to treat the conscience one has as less than absolutely authoritative." [10] What other source of guidance is available to man if he will not do what he considers to be right? If this is what we mean by conscience, and it is the meaning generally attached to the word, then "a man can never be acting rightly when he goes against his conscience." [11] This is true even though his conscience may be wrong and may lead him astray.

[9] *The Faith of a Moralist* (London, Macmillan, 1937), Series II, p. 237.
[10] *Ibid.*, p. 240.   [11] Mortimer, *op. cit.*, p. 26.

Some Christians say: "One's conscience cannot be trusted. It is not authoritative for the Christian. He should follow the leadership of the Holy Spirit." It is correct that conscience, for the Christian, is not the final source of authority in his life. The final authority for right or wrong for him is the will of God. It is also a glorious fact that the Christian has the promise of the leadership of the Spirit. But what inner capacities does the Christian have with which he can respond to the leading of the Spirit, with which he can know the will of God? God does not ordinarily give in some miraculous way the light that is needed for the decisions of life. He does utilize every resource we have. The innate sense of oughtness or of obligation to do the right and to avoid the evil is one such inner resource that man has. This means that one's conscience, whatever may be our definition of the term, is a means whereby he can know, at least to some degree, the will of God. The Spirit of God does not lead one contrary to his conscience. He does not ask or expect one to violate or surrender his conscience. He does ask the child of God to permit him to give additional light to his conscience.

Since one's conscience should be authoritative for him, there arise occasions when he will have to stand alone and even disobey the commands of lawful authorities. He should never do this lightly. It should be done only after much soul searching. When he finds it necessary to disobey he should do so regretfully. He should always have the greatest respect for "the group conscience," and if he is a Christian he should have particular respect for the conviction of his church. While he does not and should not consider his church the final source of authority for him, nevertheless he should value highly the judgment of his church, recognizing that it represents in a sense the combined wisdom of the centuries. He needs also to remember that the leadership of the Spirit of God is given to the church as well as to the individual Christian.

The Christian's Relation to War

There are several more or less clearly defined positions concerning the Christian's relation to war. The World Council of Churches in its Amsterdam meeting considered the question: "Can war now be an act of justice?" There were recognized three general or broad answers to the question, each held by a considerable group of people.

(1) There are those who hold that, even though entering a war may be a Christian's duty in particular circumstances, modern warfare, with its mass destruction, can never be an act of justice.

(2) In the absence of impartial supra-national institutions, there are those who hold that military action is the ultimate sanction of the rule of law, and that citizens must be distinctly taught that it is their duty to defend the law by force if necessary.

(3) Others, again, refuse military service of all kinds, convinced that an absolute witness against war and for peace is for them the will of God and they desire that the Church should speak to the same effect.[12]

Under different headings and with some difference of emphasis let us consider each of these three positions. We shall change the order of (1) and (2), which, from our viewpoint, will give a more logical arrangement.

1. *Participation in war is a citizenship responsibility.* Those who hold to this position believe that when one's nation is at war, the Christian's total responsibility is to obey. If this means to participate in active combat and to take human life, it is the Christian's obligation to do so. It is argued that there can be no maintenance of law and order in the world without the use of force, and that certainly the Christian should be willing to help maintain law and order. This position is quite prevalent, possibly more so in Europe with its state churches than in the United States with its emphasis on the value of the individual and the separation of church and state.

While it may be admitted that the use of force is contrary to the perfect Christian ethic, it is contended that nations and other social groups operate on a lower moral level than individuals, at least on a lower level than the more morally advanced who make up that group. This latter emphasis is found particularly in one of Reinhold Niebuhr's earlier books. The opening sentence of the introduction to that book is as follows:

The thesis to be elaborated in these pages is that a sharp distinction must be drawn between the moral and social behavior of individuals and

---

[12] Visser 't Hooft (ed.), *The First Assembly of the World Council of Churches,* pp. 89–90.

of social groups, national, racial, and economic; and that this distinction justifies and necessitates political policies which a purely individualistic ethic must always find embarrassing.[13]

This viewpoint forms a part of a consistent pattern in Niebuhr's later books.

What is the individual to do about the embarrassing gap between the Christian ethic and the policies of his nation? Is he to accept such an adjustment of the Christian ideal as inevitable and continuous? When commanded by the state to conform to a standard lower than his personal standard, what shall and should he do? Can he, in good conscience, shift the responsibility for the decision to his country? Such a shifting is a rather common attitude. The position is taken that whatever one does in obedience to the authority of the "powers that be" is the responsibility of the state. The individual will not be held accountable. But such an attitude would be "completely destructive of any serious loyalty to Christian standards of life," [14] and in the long run it would not be best for the nation. How could there be any lifting of the moral level of a nation if all its citizens subordinated their individual consciences to the dictates of the state? Blind obedience by all citizens would eliminate all hope for moral and social progress. While the state may not be able to conform immediately to the moral demands of the gospel, this does not excuse the Christian citizen. He should do his best to live by Christian standards in every area of his life. At the same time he should hope, pray, and work that his nation may progress as rapidly as possible toward the Christian ideal.

The Christian should also remember that although his country may not be able, at the present level of civilization, to apply fully the Sermon on the Mount and the other teachings of Jesus, this fact does not in any way nullify those teachings. They are abidingly challenging to and valid for the individual Christian and for his nation. And the application of those principles is not to be postponed by him or his nation to the so-called kingdom age. Really, much of the Sermon, as is true of the other ethical teachings of Jesus, would be entirely irrelevant in a perfect society. For example,

---

[13] *Moral Man and Immoral Society* (1932), p. xi.
[14] Cadoux, *Christian Pacifism Re-examined*, p. 151.

there would be no enemies to love or persecutors for whom to pray. And let us not forget that "nowhere in the Gospels is it suggested that disciples are to postpone obedience until such obedience can be universalized." [15]

Forsyth gives a rather unusual slant to the Christian's relation to his state and to war. In a book written during World War I he suggested that the church might resist the demands of the state, but that the individual, simply as an individual, would never be justified in resisting the commands of his nation. "The resister should be the Church, and not the individual except as a member of the Church." [16] He further states: "Loyalty to Church or State is the form in which loyalty to conscience is most safe and effective." [17] This would place the control of the individual conscience in the hands of the state or the church. The blood of the Christian martyrs and the voices of the pioneering Christian prophets through the centuries cry out against such a position.

2. *Participation in war may be the lesser of two evils.* While we are evil and live in an evil world many of our choices will not be between an unmixed good on the one hand and an unmixed evil on the other. Many decisions of life, including some very important ones, will be in the gray area. The best choice possible will be the one that involves the maximum of good and the minimum of evil. Many people contend that whether or not one participates in war will frequently if not always belong in the gray area.

Some who defend this position argue that in the kind of world in which we live war is more or less natural and even inevitable. War is considered inevitable because of the pugnacious will-to-power nature of man, the dominance of sin in human society, or the nature of the state as an instrument of power. Particularly pernicious in the contemporary period has been the dynamic theory of the state "in all its naked immoralism or amoralism." [18] This theory, advanced by Machiavelli and later advocated by such men as Hitler and Nietzsche, has been used to defend the inevitability of war. "Ac-

[15] Macgregor, *op. cit.*, p. 36.
[16] P. T. Forsyth, *The Christian Ethic of War* (London, Longmans, Green, 1916), p. 69.
[17] *Ibid.*, p. 65.
[18] Knudson, *Philosophy of War and Peace*, p. 29.

cording to this theory the state in its essential nature is might or power. It recognizes no authority, moral or otherwise, above itself. Its own might makes right. This, it is held, is true of the state both in its relation to its own subjects and to other states." [19] The only basis for the settlement of differences between states is power. This is a phase of the struggle for survival.

There are some who give the arguments for the inevitability of war a more theological base or tinge. They reason that war is the result of the operation of natural laws. Since God is the author of those laws, war is an integral part of the divinely appointed order. A complete answer to this position would require more space than we can give to it. A question or two will suggest the direction in which an answer can be found. Do wars result primarily from the operation of natural laws, or do wars arise because nations violate those laws? Would those laws if observed by the nations of the world bring peace rather than war? Is God the author of confusion, chaos, conflict, and war, or has God established certain laws of life that must be observed by the nations of the world if they are to have peace?

There are many people, including many Christians, who contend that war, at the present level of culture or civilization, cannot be eliminated. Men and nations have not arrived at the place where they will settle their disputes on a purely rational peaceful basis. At least there are some nations and people who will not settle their differences except by the use of force. For any nation to refuse to fight would simply mean it would be run over or liquidated.

The preceding correctly implies that the lesser-of-two-evils theory could be considered either a temporary or a permanent phase of the total Christian strategy. It is a theory or strategy that applies to the Christian life in general and to war in a particular way. When applied to war it is closely akin to the first of the general answers in the World Council statement, although it cannot be equated with the latter. Possibly the main difference is in regard to the last portion of the World Council statement. The suggestion is made in that statement that modern wars with their mass destruction "can never be an act of justice." Most of those who defend the lesser-of-two-evils theory would agree that neither side in any war is entirely

[19] *Ibid.,* p. 28.

just or righteous in its cause or methods. But they would contend that the Christian has a responsibility to make the decisions that will promote the maximum of justice and the minimum of evil or injustice. Justice, or at least relative justice, can be attained by the use of force or war, and hence war under certain conditions may be "an act of justice."

The position that war may be the lesser of two evils and that one's participation in war may be the choice of the lesser of two evils has been stated clearly and consistently by Reinhold Niebuhr. It is an integral part of his entire approach to the Christian religion and to the Christian ethic. For him the ethic of Jesus is "finally and ultimately normative," but it is "not immediately applicable to the task of securing justice in a sinful world." [20] The way of Christ is the way of absolute love, but absolute love cannot be applied in an evil world. The nearest approximation to absolute love is "equal justice." The latter can be achieved and should be sought by Christian men. Niebuhr also contends that because men are sinners "justice can be achieved only by a certain degree of coercion on the one hand, and by resistance to coercion and tyranny on the other hand." [21] Political controversies, and war is a political controversy, "are always conflicts between sinners and not between righteous men and sinners." [22] It seems naturally to follow that any decision concerning war would involve some evil.

Emil Brunner reveals some of the depth and possible inner tension of the lesser-of-two-evils position when he suggests that there are times when we must do evil. He says:

We never see the real meaning of "original sin," we never perceive the depth and universality of evil, or what evil really means in the depths common to us all, until we are *obliged* to do something which, in itself, is evil; that is, we do not see this clearly until we are obliged to do some-

---

[20] *Christianity and Power Politics,* p. 9. Charles Raven (*The Theological Basis of Christian Pacifism,* p. 29) charges that Niebuhr in this book rejects the pacifist plea to take Christ seriously "in favor of the warning of modern history to take human sinfulness seriously." He then concludes, "It is difficult not to feel that in this book taking sin seriously means being content to continue in it."

[21] Niebuhr, *Christianity and Power Politics,* p. 14.

[22] *Ibid.,* p. 23. For a fair statement of Niebuhr's general position and a criticism of it, see Macgregor, *op. cit.,* pp. 99–104.

thing in our official capacity—for the sake of order, and therefore for the sake of love—which, apart from our "office," would be absolutely wrong.[23]

Forsyth says that when the choice is between the lesser of two evils, for one to refuse to choose the lesser evil is to choose wrongly.[24] He even implies that God, in a sense, may at times choose the lesser evil. He suggests that God "employs sin against sin, and sides with the minor ill to bring the mightier to nought." [25] Forsyth also says that God "has His divine opportunisms and compromises," but declares that they "are not concessions for peace but strategies for a purpose." He further says that God "does not do evil that good may come; but, evil being there, He uses it to its own destruction, and He uses us in such action." He concludes that "a Christian might make his public protest against war, and then go and take his part in the Lord's controversy on the battle field as a second best." [26]

One answer of the pacifist to the lesser-of-two-evils theory is that war is the greatest possible evil. For example, H. H. Farmer says that war "cannot be the lesser of two evils for there is no greater evil, nothing more contrary to that mind of God which, so far as I can judge, is revealed in Christ." [27] Farmer further reasons that the argument from the necessity of compromise is, "in the nature of the case, an argument from the supposed evil consequences of one course of action as over against another." He then asks the searching question whether or not and how much consequences should enter into the determination of a Christian's conduct.[28] Kirby Page, in a conclusion similar to Farmer's, says that modern wars have become totalitarian and that such wars combine the worst evils that threaten the human race. His conclusion is: "*We have entered a new era of destructiveness and the old argument that war is a lesser evil is tragic delusion.*" [29] Niebuhr would not agree that war is the worst possible evil. To him tyranny is worse than war, and the only certain alternative to tyranny may sometimes be war.[30]

---

[23] *The Divine Imperative*, p. 227. Used by permission.
[24] *Op. cit.,* p. 20.   [25] *Ibid.,* p. 30.   [26] *Ibid.,* p. 28.
[27] Jones (ed.), *The Church, the Gospel, and War,* p. 65.
[28] *Ibid.,* p. 67.   [29] *Ibid.,* p. 156.
[30] *Christianity and Power Politics,* p. 42.

Many Christians fail to see that one can hold to the lesser-of-two-evils theory, at least in one sense of the word, and still refuse to participate actively in war. He may recognize that he cannot escape some involvement in the sin of the world. He may not claim that his position is totally free from evil and sin. But, on the other hand, he may consistently argue that refusal to participate in war, for him, involves less evil than participation.

3. *War is wrong and participation in war is wrong.* The third position as defined by the World Council was as follows: "Others . . . refuse military service . . . convinced that an absolute witness against war and for peace is for them the will of God." Those who take this position are usually called pacifists or conscientious objectors. There are many degrees of pacifism and many motives for conscientious objection to war. After a study of the conscientious objectors in England, from 1939 to 1949, Denis Hayes concluded that "there was no such thing as a typical Conscientious Objector." [31] Of those with a Christian motivation, there are some who refuse to have anything to do with the entire war system, while there are others who will accept limited military service.

Many of these Christian pacifists, limited and unlimited, recognize the validity of much of the argument of men like Niebuhr, but at the same time they feel to an unusual degree the tug and the demands of the absolute claims of Christ. This tends to create for them terrific inner tension. Some of them admit that they cannot escape involvement in the sin of the world, including war. They agree that they will go as far as possible in participating in war with their fellow citizens, but there is a limit beyond which they cannot go and maintain their integrity and self-respect as children of God.

The stopping place, for some, is just short of the taking of human life. They will mournfully render noncombatant service, risking their lives in the medical corps, in mechanical or clerical service; they will work in war plants, buy bonds, pay their taxes, and support the war effort in many other ways. They recognize that such service identifies them with the sin of their nation. Their contention, however, is that they cannot live without being involved in the sin

[31] *Challenge to Conscience* (London, George Allen and Unwin, 1949), p. 25.

of the world. Their attitude is one of repentance for their sin and the sin of their nation. Their limited participation in the war effort is done mournfully. In a sense such conscientious objectors are following the lesser-of-two-evils strategy.

There are some who object to certain types of war. They might defend their participation in a purely defensive war or in what they consider to be a just war. Of course, there is some question whether any war, at least in the contemporary period, can be purely defensive or entirely just. There are others who would object to the use of germs or gas in modern wars, or who believe it is immoral to use atomic or hydrogen bombs. There are some who contend that wars might have been justified in the past, but that such is not true of the terrible wars of the contemporary period, which in spite of their destructiveness achieve nothing really worth while, and can never be properly classified as an act of justice.

There have been through the centuries and are in the contemporary period a considerable number of Christians who refuse, as far as possible, to have anything to do with the entire war system. These are the "absolutists," "the unconditionalists," "the idealists," "the perfectionists." They are the ones, in the main, who are registered as conscientious objectors in the democracies in times of war, and who during recent wars have usually been placed in conscientious-objector camps. Frequently, the term "pacifist" is limited to this group of "absolutists."

Brunner charges that "pacifism of the 'absolutist' variety is practically anarchy." [32] Niebuhr, who is just as strongly opposed to pacifism as Brunner, seems to be more generous in his appraisal. He says,

We who allow ourselves to become engaged in war need this testimony of the absolutists against us, lest we accept the warfare of the world as normative, lest we become callous to the horror of war, and lest we forget the ambiguity of our own actions and motives and the risk we run of achieving no permanent good from this momentary anarchy in which we are involved. [33]

What do the pacifists have to say in their own defense? How can we summarize their main arguments? Cadoux, one of the leading

[32] *The Divine Imperative,* p. 469.
[33] *Christianity and Power Politics,* p. 31.

pacifists and a scholarly defender of Christian pacifism, states the crucial points or arguments as follows:

(1) that the activities of fighting men cannot be harmonized with any standard of conduct reasonably describable as Christian;
(2) that war inevitably tends to lead on to further war, and to worse war;
(3) that the Christian ethic definitely inculcates on its adherents the policy of overcoming evil *with good,* and of making the sacrifices incidental to any temporary failure in so doing.[34]

Cadoux believes that these arguments have never been answered. Similarly, Raven, who became a pacifist between World Wars I and II, concludes "that there is really no serious answer to the pacifist arguments." [35]

John Bennett would not agree with Cadoux and Raven. His conclusion is that *"pacifism is not the only decision open to the Christian who seeks to be sensitive and obedient."* Then he seeks to answer the main arguments of the pacifists. He suggests that "Christian love involves a double imperative"—an imperative against violence but also an imperative to restrain evil. He also says that no nation "can be expected to have the moral discipline to live according to the pacifist faith," and that the conviction that there is always open a strategy of nonviolence is not universally true. He contends that pacifists fail to face the real problem created by their position, which is the suffering of others which results from their nonviolence.[36]

Justice, Love, the Cross, and War

There is a theological background or basis, more or less clearly defined, for every social strategy. This is quite evidently true of both pacifism and nonpacifism.[37] Whatever the position may be con-

[34] *Christian Pacifism Re-examined,* p. ix. For a slightly different statement of the main convictions or arguments of the pacifists, see John Bennett, *Christian Realism* (New York, Scribner's, 1941), p. 99.

[35] *War and the Christian* (London, S.C.M. Press, 1938), p. 160.

[36] *Christian Realism,* pp. 99–108.

[37] We shall restrict ourselves, with a few exceptions, to the viewpoints of certain English pacifists such as Charles E. Raven, G. H. C. Macgregor, and C. J. Cadoux, who have set out the pacifist position clearly and scholarly; and to the criticism of pacifism by representatives of Neo-Protestantism such as Reinhold Niebuhr, Emil Brunner, and William Temple, who have given the most intelligent and damaging reply to the pacifists.

cerning war, there is involved in it some particular theory or viewpoint concerning the nature and the character of God, along with his attitude toward, relation to, and will for man and the world. One point of major controversy between the pacifists and their opponents is the meaning of the cross as related to and as a revelation of the nature of God. An integral part of that controversy is their differing viewpoints concerning the relation and the relative importance of justice and love, and the relation of both of these to the cross.

It is difficult to know at times whether pacifists and nonpacifists start with theology, or work out their theology to support their stand on war. Whichever procedure is followed, it is impossible to understand their viewpoint concerning war without some insight into their theological position.

1. *Justice and love.* One point of difference between the pacifists and the nonpacifists, as suggested previously, is the relative importance attached to justice and love, the relation of each to the other, and the possibility or impossibility of attaining either or both. For the pacifist, love is primary, justice a derivative of love. Justice may be able to check and punish evil; love alone can overcome and redeem evil. Divorce justice from love and it becomes "a soulless legalism." It is love that makes "justice tolerable." [38] The two cannot be separated "because they are united in God." [39]

Possibly we should admit that in this section, to use a distinction of Paul Tillich's, we are using "justice" in the sense of "proportional justice" rather than "creative justice." The latter, according to Tillich, is the ultimate meaning of justice, and is "the form of reuniting love," [40] while on the other hand the creative element in justice is love.[41] Tillich defines love as the drive toward unity, "the reunion of the estranged." [42] Love is considered the basic principle in justice,[43] while justice is immanent in love.[44] Since love is the basic or ultimate principle in justice, Tillich contends that "love does not do more than justice demands." [45] His viewpoint is that love has the

[38] Culbert G. Rutenber, *The Dagger and the Cross* (New York, Fellowship Publications, 1950), p. 75.
[39] G. Ernest Wright, *The Biblical Doctrine of Man in Society*, p. 168.
[40] Paul Tillich, *Love, Power, and Justice*, p. 71.   [41] *Ibid.*, p. 83.
[42] *Ibid.*, p. 25.   [43] *Ibid.*, p. 57.   [44] *Ibid.*, p. 68.   [45] *Ibid.*, p. 71.

same relation to justice that revelation has to reason. Both love and revelation "transcend the rational norm without destroying it." [46]

But let us return to the consideration of "justice" and "love" as used by the pacifists and their critics. Macgregor, in examining Niebuhr's idea of "equal justice," claims that the New Testament has little to say concerning the subject, and that justice "can hardly be said to be a New Testament category at all!" He further adds that "Jesus did not regard 'justice' as an end in itself. He taught that justice truly 'fulfilled' is nothing less than love, rather than love a by-product of justice, that if we aim at love we shall establish justice by the way." [47] The emphasis by the pacifists is on the supremacy of love. The God revealed by Jesus was a loving heavenly Father. He could be and was identified with *agape*. He so loved that he gave his only Son that we might have life.

It is not at the point of the primacy of love, however, that Niebuhr and other nonpacifists attack the pacifist position. Niebuhr certainly would not say that love is a by-product of justice. William Temple, who belongs in the same general theological tradition as Niebuhr, admits that "love transcends justice"; [48] and that "justice does not exhaust the meaning of love, and that only when love is in the heart can justice be established in the world." [49] Niebuhr himself says that love is ethically purer than justice,[50] and that love as the law of life "remains a principle of criticism over all forms of community in which elements of coercion and conflict destroy the highest type of fellowship." [51] Again Niebuhr suggests that "love is both the fulfillment and the negation of all achievements of justice in history." [52] Similarly Brunner, who says that justice is rational and belongs to the world of systems and that love is superrational and belongs to the world of persons, says that true love is always more than just. It can only do more and never less than justice requires. It is in this sense that he considers justice a precondition of love.[53]

On the other hand, Niebuhr says that a mistake is made when

[46] *Ibid.*, p. 83.   [47] *Op. cit.*, p. 100.
[48] William Temple, *Thoughts in War-Time* (London, Macmillan, 1940), p. 15.
[49] *Ibid.*, p. 29.   [50] *Moral Man and Immoral Society*, p. 57.
[51] *Christianity and Power Politics*, p. 22.
[52] *The Nature and Destiny of Man*, II, 246.
[53] *Justice and the Social Order*, pp. 114–18.

Christians attempt to apply the love ethic to society. The Christian love ethic cannot be made effective in human society. "The demand of religious moralists that nations subject themselves to 'the law of Christ' is an unrealistic demand, and the hope that they will do so is a sentimental one." [54] Niebuhr considers "the more complex political and economic relations as clearly outside of the pale of the religio-moral ideal." [55] In common with most nonpacifists, he would contend that equal justice is an attainable goal, but that absolute love in society is not. Most nonpacifists also suggest that because of sin justice cannot be attained without war or the use of force. If war will help to attain justice, then war is justified.

The pacifists, on the other hand, contend that a good end cannot be attained by using evil means, and for them war is evil. They contend that justice results from the application of the spirit of love. For them love, which is the law of life, will be victorious sooner or later. Even if love is not immediately attainable in society, the Christian has a personal responsibility to live by the law of love in every area of his life. For the pacifist this means that he cannot take human life, which for him violates the spirit of love.

2. *Love, justice, and the cross.* Practically all theological schools of thought recognize the centrality of the cross in the Christian religion. In the cross is seen God's answer to the sin problem, which is man's major problem. The cross reveals the nature of God and God's attitude toward man and his sin. It reveals that God loves the sinner while hating his sin, that he condemns man for his sin but that he also saves man from his sin. He is a God of justice and love, or possibly more accurately he is a God "of holy love." [56] "Holy love" includes the idea of justice or righteousness as well as love. This idea that the God revealed in the cross is just and holy as well as a loving Father helps to save love "from degenerating into amiability" [57] or superficial sentimentality. Raven contends, however, that justice and love do not exist side by side "as alternate modes of activity in the divine nature." [58] Love, for Raven, is supreme in the divine nature.

[54] *Moral Man and Immoral Society*, p. 75.   [55] *Ibid.*, p. 76.
[56] Walter T. Conner, *The Cross in the New Testament* (Nashville, Broadman Press, 1954), p. 174.
[57] Raven, *War and the Christian*, p. 133.   [58] Jones (ed.), *op. cit.*, p. 10.

The pacifists and nonpacifists differ in their interpretation concerning the relative importance and significance of justice and love as related to the cross. To the nonpacifist the cross reveals primarily the justice of God and God's condemnation of sin. To the pacifist the cross reveals primarily the love of God for man and God's method of overcoming sin. Raven says, "Christ by his Cross presents to us his way of overcoming the sin of the world." [59] His way is the way of demonstrated love. Evil is overcome by good, hate by love.

3. *The cross and war.* Both pacifist and nonpacifist would transfer their "strategy of the cross" to human relations and problems. War for the nonpacifist represents God's judgment against sin. He may even go so far as to think of himself and other men as God's agents or instruments in that judgment. On the other hand, the pacifist considers war a negation of the strategy of the cross, since love is the central truth of the cross. For him the love revealed in the cross is God's method for overcoming evil in the world. Evil is never overcome by evil. The cross "is Christ's witness to the weakness and folly of the sword, to the triumphant power of non-resistance, to the new way of overcoming evil with good." [60]

Most pacifists, although not all, have an abiding faith in the triumph of love. Some not only believe that the way of love is the most effective plan to overcome the evil of the world but that pacifism, with its doctrine of love, is the only workable plan to overcome evil. The triumph of love may be postponed but it is considered inevitable. Christ on the cross was the crowning demonstration of this fact. The cross for him was not defeat but triumph. It may have been a dark hour, but it was also his most glorious hour and the climax of all human history. And it should be remembered that following the crucifixion came the empty tomb. There can be no real crucifixion without a resurrection. This which was literally demonstrated in the life and death of Jesus represents a basic law of life. Life is found by losing it.

The seeming defeat of the cross was no real defeat. So it is in the lives of the followers of Christ. If the strategy of the cross is

[59] Raven, *The Theological Basis of Christian Pacifism*, p. 27.
[60] Raven, *War and the Christian*, p. 127.

followed, which is the way of self-denying love, there can be no final defeat.

Let men take every advantage of the seeming weakness of love, let them bruise and batter and seek utterly to smash it, as they did at the Cross; but let it still remain love, and in the end they will have to give up, and look upon what their hands have done, and break down in its presence.[61]

Is such faith in the efficacy and the triumph of love realistic? Most nonpacifists and even some pacifists would say no. Culbert Rutenber, a leading American pacifist, criticizes Macgregor, Farmer, and others at this point. He says that the words of Farmer, quoted above, are appealing and moving but scarcely realistic. He further suggests that there is no evidence in the ministry of Jesus or in the history of the Christian church to support the idea that love must always triumph. Rutenber's contention is that the Christian should be a pacifist simply because God wills it and not because it is necessarily and ultimately the most effective strategy.[62]

It would be wise not only for pacifists but for all Christians to consider seriously this warning concerning motivation. A Christian's decision should not be influenced very much by what he considers to be wisest under the conditions or even necessarily the most effective. His decision should be based primarily on what he considers to be the will of God. This means that the consequences of his decision will be definitely secondary. He may properly consider, to some degree, consequences to others, but he should never make his decisions on the basis of consequences to himself. To do the will of God may literally mean the cross. It may mean defeat and death. Following defeat and death may come triumph and life. The Christian, however, has not arrived at a fully Christian motivation until he does what he considers to be the will of God, regardless of the effects on himself and his future. If he calmly reasons that life will follow crucifixion, then he is not being Christian in the highest and fullest sense.

Does this necessarily mean, however, that love will not triumph, that the strategy of love will not work? Did love triumph in the cross? Yes, it triumphed then and it will triumph in the world be-

---

[61] H. H. Farmer as quoted by Macgregor, *op. cit.,* p. 70.
[62] Rutenber, *op. cit.,* pp. 50–51.

cause God is love and God will ultimately win in the world. There may be many defeats; but if we take the long look—and the Christian should always include eternity in his perspective—we can and should believe in the victory of love over hate, of good over evil. We may not be able to see the victory of the cross in our individual lives; but if our lives are tied in with the purposes of God, then in the divine perspective we can believe that the price we pay today may be a part of God's triumph tomorrow.

Conclusions

Conclusions on any subject on which Christians differ as widely and honestly as they do on war will have to be largely personal. It is believed, however, that most Christians will agree, in the main, with the following general statements. Differences may arise in regard to the interpretation and the application of the statements or propositions. The emphasis in the propositions is not so much on war as such—its rightness or wrongness—as it is on the Christian conscience and what the church, the state, and individual Christians should do about the conscientious objector. What is done about the latter may be as determinatively important for the democratic state and for the Christian church as what is done about war.

1. *That war is not Christian.* In the past many Christians and even some Christian scholars have defended war as Christian and placed the stamp of divine approval upon it. Wars were frequently defended as "holy crusades." That was true as late as World War I. For example, the well known English scholar P. T. Forsyth, during World War I identified Germany with "the Kingdom of Evil" and as an enemy of "the Kingdom of God." Germany, according to Forsyth, had repudiated national morality; it had sinned against mankind, and mankind, under God, had the responsibilty "to arrest and to judge." The war with Germany was not a mere national war; it represented "the Lord's controversy with the world." [63]

There are few Christians today, regardless of their viewpoint concerning the Christian's participation in war, who defend war as Christian or who ever label any war "a holy crusade." One reason

[63] *Op. cit.*, p. 111.

for this change in attitude is the terrible destructiveness of contemporary wars. For example, the total death toll of World War I was approximately twice the death toll of all the wars that had been fought during the preceding 125 years, beginning with the Napoleonic wars.[64] Leslie Weatherhead breaks this down and says that the average was 7,000 killed and 14,000 wounded for every day of the war.[65] World War II was much more destructive of human life, particularly of civilians, than World War I. The total dead possibly was twice as many as during World War I. Another war on a world scale promises to be much more destructive than any the world has ever known. A leading atomic scientist has suggested that as many as 40,000,000 people might be killed during one air raid on the congested population centers of the United States.[66]

Without deprecating one bit the cost of war in the destruction of property and particularly of human lives, we would suggest that the biggest price the world pays for war is what it does to moral and spiritual values. "Love, truth, beauty—these are the creative elements in life; and war destroys them all." [67] Weatherhead sums up the whole matter as follows: "Apart from the waste involved, war rouses all the worst passions contained in human personality." He then quotes F. A. Atkins as saying: "Even a righteous war can be guaranteed to send thousands down the slopes of hell. No amount of right at the beginning can save a nation from an orgy of trespass, arson, robbery, rape, adultery, lying, and murder." [68]

The terrific price of modern wars might be justified if they accomplished anything of permanent value. One student of war boldly states: "The most unfortunate thing about war is that it accomplishes nothing . . . all its sacrifices are vain . . . war does not settle anything." [69] Possibly Waller goes too far when he says that war does not settle anything, unless he intended to apply his appraisal exclusively to modern wars. It seems that war did settle some things in the days of our own Revolution, in the War Between the

---

[64] *The Encyclopedia Americana* (1950), 28, 650.

[65] *Thinking Aloud in War-Time*, p. 7.

[66] J. R. Oppenheimer as quoted by A. J. Muste, *Not by Might* (New York, Harper, 1947), p. 1.

[67] Raven, *War and the Christian*, p. 47.

[68] *Thinking Aloud in War-Time*, p. 11.

[69] Waller, *War in the Twentieth Century*, p. 31.

States, and in other wars of the past. It is true, however, that modern wars settle little if anything. The victors are also the victims. No nation really wins.

It is interesting and significant that the last chapter of Toynbee's *War and Civilization* is entitled "The Failure of the Saviour with the Sword." In this chapter and elsewhere [70] Toynbee suggests that the sword is self-defeating. It will not remain permanently sheathed. While it may be used in the hope that it may not be necessary to use it again, "this hope is an illusion; for it is only in fairyland that swords cut Gordian knots which cannot be untied by fingers." [71] There is a "chronic tendency of war to beget more war." [72]

The only possible good that war seemingly can accomplish, at least in the contemporary period, is to save a nation from enslavement by some foreign power. At best modern warfare is defensive, but even as a defense of national values and security it now seems that war will be ultimately self-defeating. The only final hope for any nation in this day of advanced weapons of destruction is to discover, in cooperation with other nations, the way of peace.

It is terrible to contemplate that Toynbee may be correct in suggesting that World War I and World War II were two in a series and furthermore that this not only represents a series but a progression. If the series continues the progression will be carried to ever higher terms "until this process of intensifying the horrors of war is one day brought to an end by the self-annihilation of the war-making society." [73]

In the light of modern developments, William Temple's classification of war as "both criminal and stupid" [74] sounds reasonable. And it should be remembered that he was not a pacifist. Latourette says that "war and Christ are poles apart" [75] and that war "works against those values for which Christ stands." [76] While some might like to delete the defining words in the following statement by Rufus M. Jones, words which make the statement sound quite extreme, yet most Christians doubtless will agree with his general posi-

[70] See *A Study of History*, pp. 534–38.
[71] *War and Civilization*, p. 142.
[72] Cadoux, *Christian Pacifism Re-examined*, p. 227.
[73] *War and Civilization*, p. 4.   [74] *Thoughts in War-Time*, p. 6.
[75] Jones (ed.), *op. cit.*, p. 93.   [76] *Ibid.*, p. 94.

tion. He says, "From my point of view war is absolutely and eternally morally wrong, and utterly and flatly incompatible with the way of life Christ has revealed and Christianity has established." [77]

The World Council of Churches meeting at Amsterdam in 1948 said: "War as a method of settling disputes is incompatible with the teaching and the example of our Lord Jesus Christ. The part which war plays in our present international life is a sin against God and a degradation of man." [78] War is not Christian and should never be defended again as being Christian. We have wars because men and nations are not Christian and do not and will not apply the Christian spirit and Christian principles to their relations with one another.

2. *That the will of God is the source of supreme authority for the Christian.* The word of conscientious Christians through the centuries has been, "We must obey God rather than men." [79] That has been true whether those Christians were speaking to the family, the community, the church, or the state. The first question of the Christian in every time of decision should be: "What is the will of God for me in this situation?" This means that "no Christian may pledge an unconditional obedience to any State or accept its orders without reference to the will of God." [80] And the will of God is not mediated to the individual by the church or the state. The individual has the right and the responsibility of determining for himself the will of God for his own life.

This position which is so central, particularly in evangelical Christianity, may create rather serious conflicts and problems for the Christian who seeks consistently to apply it to the decisions of his life. There are few, if any, areas where the problems will become more acute than in regard to war. How can a Christian accept the privileges of citizenship, including the protection and security provided by his nation, without being obligated to obey the commands of that nation and to protect her from her enemies? How can one escape his solidarity with the group? There is no easy way out of the dilemma concerning war for the serious-minded Christian. "A

[77] *Ibid.*, p. ix.
[79] Acts 5:29.

[78] Visser 't Hooft (ed.), *op. cit.*, p. 89.
[80] Raven, *War and the Christian*, p. 83.

freedom of conscience which shall escape moral anarchy, an obedience to State authority which stops short of acquiescence in evil, represent an ideal hard to define or sustain." [81] Winston King says the Christian faces a trilemma regarding war. "He is caught three ways, between his sense of responsibility for his own community, his respect for another man's community, and his loyalty to the ideal community of love." [82]

The Christian faces other difficulties when he seeks to apply the will of God to the immediate decisions and problems of his life. Should the will of God be applied fully now, or is it to be applied progressively to the everyday issues of life? Is there a relative will of God as well as an absolute will of God? Is it possible that frequently a Christian's decision will not be between an unmixed good and an unmixed evil? Might it be the will of God, under such circumstances, for one to make the best possible choice, the one that would involve the maximum of good and the minimum of evil, although such a decision would not conform to God's perfect or intentional will? Such questions reveal some of the difficulties Christians face in knowing the will of God for their lives in the everyday affairs of life. Leslie Weatherhead makes some distinctions within the will of God that it seems are valid. They can be helpful to the Christian in times of decision. He distinguishes between what he calls the intentional will of God, the circumstantial will of God, and the ultimate will of God.[83]

God's ultimate will is his big over-all will which is in line with his final purposes in the world. He moves unalterably toward that ultimate will. Men may delay the achievement of that will, but ultimately God will be triumphant. There may be circumstances or conditions under which it would be God's will for one to make a certain decision that might not conform to God's intentional or his ultimate will. This would represent his circumstantial or permissive will. If one would defend participation in war as the lesser of two evils, he might identify his decision with the circumstantial will of God but certainly not with God's intentional will. The latter stands

[81] C. E. Raven quoted by G. H. C. Macgregor, *op. cit.*, p. 80.
[82] Winston L. King, *The Holy Imperative* (New York, Harper, 1949), p. 196.
[83] *The Will of God.*

in constant judgment over against any adjustment of that will to the realities of life. A constant tension should be maintained between the intentional will of God and what the child of God considers to be God's will under the circumstances. This should mean continuous movement in the direction of God's intentional will. It also means that there will be limits beyond which the conscientious Christian will not dare to go and still claim that he is living within the will of God. That limit for him will not be identified with the intentional will of God but with his circumstantial will. This means that Christians who participate actively in war will not claim that their participation is in harmony with the intentional or perfect will of God but rather with his circumstantial or permissive will. This is as far as any Christian should go.

3. *That the right of individual conscience should be defended.* Forsyth claims that "unlimited liberty" of conscience, "even in a Christian man, is an impossible thing." He places the authority for conscience in the church or state rather than within the individual, and says that the matter of chief decision is which of these two is to be supreme.[84] Admittedly the individual should consider very seriously what his state commands and his church advises. If he differs with either he should reexamine his position; it may be that he is wrong. On the other hand, neither the state nor the church is to be a conscience for the individual. This is true regardless of how democratic either or both may be. "There is no divine right of majorities." [85] While the right of the majority to rule or make policy decisions is basic in the democratic way of life, yet the right of the minority or the individual who disagrees is just as fundamental.

To fail to respect and to defend the right of conscience for the individual violates the very genius of the democratic philosophy of government. Freedom of conscience and liberty of opinion "are founded firmly on the premise of the value of the individual." [86] This belief that the individual is the ultimate value is the central, distinctive core of the democratic concept of the state. There is

[84] *Op. cit.,* p. 65.
[85] Robert S. W. Pollard, *Conscience and Liberty* (London, George Allen and Unwin, 1940), p. 28.
[86] *Ibid.,* p. 104.

not anything that would violate this fundamental idea any more than for the state to attempt to coerce the consciences of its citizens. "Conscience must be inviolable if personality is to be sacred." [87]

What is best for individuals is also best, sooner or later, for the institutions of society. It will be destructive of the best interests of the state for it to seek to control and particularly to coerce the consciences of its citizens. Democracy to be healthy must keep its face set toward new truth and new insights. It must retain the capacity of self-criticism. This will not and cannot be true unless the right of the individual to differ from the majority is maintained.

This freedom of the individual to determine for himself what is the will of God is dangerous, but it is more dangerous not to recognize and defend it. If carried to the extreme the right of individual conscience can lead to moral and spiritual anarchy. But to fail to respect this basic concept would lead to political totalitarianism and to the stagnation of political, moral, and spiritual life.

The church, even more than the state, should defend the right of individual conscience. It may be hard for the church, as it is for the state, to determine the proper limits of individual liberty, but there should never be any hesitation about defending the principle. Both the church and the state have the right to seek to persuade the individual who differs with the majority to change his position and to conform to the majority opinion. In extreme cases the individual may have to be punished, but even then his right to differ should be respected and defended. If the church and the state are wise they will recognize that the individual or individuals who stand alone may be right and the majority may be wrong. The church, if not the state, owes a great deal to its heretics. Frequently the heretics of one generation have become the heroes of the next generation. They have on many occasions been the pioneering spirits who have blazed new trails.

If punishment for nonconformity comes to the conscientious Christian, he should accept it as a possible phase of the redemptive process. He may become a true Christian martyr, but he should guard against developing a martyr complex. If he follows the spirit

[87] Daniel A. Poling, *A Preacher Looks at War* (New York, Macmillan, 1943), p. 7.

of original Christianity, he will not lead or seek to stir up a revolution against the majority group. He may properly seek to convict them of the error of their way and convert them to his way of thinking. He will personally do what he considers to be the will of God and uncomplainingly suffer the consequences. He can have an abiding faith that if he is right his witness and his suffering will be a redemptive element, to some degree, in his church, in his nation, and in the world. Furthermore, if he is right, he can be assured that time and the Lord will be on his side.

4. *That Christians should respect those with differing opinions.* We have seen that there continue to be widely divergent opinions concerning the Christian's relation to war. This fact will not damage the Christian fellowship so long as there is a mutual respect for one another. Such a respect should be a natural and an inevitable outgrowth of the conviction that the will of God as personally interpreted is to be the final authority for the individual. One Christian may be able to go all the way, accepting without any reservation or hesitation full participation in war, including combatant service. Another concludes that he cannot, in good conscience, participate in war at all. Many others will fall in between these two positions. Regardless of what the individual's personal opinion may be, he should have the fullest respect for those who conscientiously maintain a different position.

It may help Christians to respect one another more if they will recognize that decisions concerning war for most Christians are in the "gray area." Most of them believe that some evil is involved in whatever position they take regarding their personal relation to war. Such an attitude will tend to give one a sense of uneasiness. He may feel that it is possible that others are right and that he is wrong. This tentativeness or open-mindedness will be a healthy attitude if it does not lead to constant indecision or to an unhealthy tension. It at least will tend to make one more sympathetic with those who do not agree with him. Weatherhead, in his own personal relation to war, reveals something of this tentative attitude. He changed, over a period of years, from an active participant in war to a pacifistic position and still later back to the viewpoint that it was all right for the Christian, under certain conditions, to participate actively in war. But he concludes: "Again and again I have the uneasy feeling that the pacifist may be far more right than I am." [88] This attitude revealed by Weatherhead would also be a healthy one for the pacifist.

It is not only important for individual Christians but also for religious groups to respect and to defend the right of individual conscience. This should be done regardless of how much the individual might differ from the majority. Numbers of major religious bodies have attempted to lead their constituencies to do this. A good example is the following resolution passed by the American Baptist Convention during World War II (1941):

Resolved, that we lay upon the consciences of our people the responsibility to maintain our bond of fellowship in Christ despite differences of opinion and to give moral support and protection to those who follow the voice of conscience either in personal participation or refusal to participate in war.[89]

[88] Weatherhead, *Thinking Aloud in War-Time*, p. 44.
[89] From a booklet, published by the National Service Board for Religious Objectors, entitled *Statements of Religious Bodies on the Conscientious Objector* (rev. ed., 1943), p. 8.

XI

THE WORLD IN CRISIS [1]

THE WORLD crisis is the major issue of the contemporary period. There is a sense in which all the world issues discussed in preceding chapters are related to and are expressions of the deep crisis that is gripping Western civilization and the world.

Some people contend that the world is constantly in transition. They suggest that the present period is little different from any other time in the world's history. Most students of world affairs agree, however, that the contemporary crisis is no ordinary crisis. They consider it the most serious that Western civilization has known since the days of the Renaissance and the Reformation. It seems that the way of life that was born at that time is now reaching the end of its journey. A new type of civilization, at least new in many ways, is in the process of being born.

A new way of life has not been brought forth in the past and will not be brought forth in the future without suffering and travail. The extent of that suffering will be determined by the length of the period of labor or travail. The latter in turn will be determined, to a considerable degree, by the strength of the resistance to the birth of the new. Sorokin outlines the pattern that crises follow. The first step in the process is what he calls ordeal or suffering. He suggests that this suffering is due to pressure toward change and resistance to

[1] For an expansion of this chapter into a fuller treatment of the world crisis, see the author's *A World in Travail* (Nashville, Broadman Press, 1954).

change. According to Sorokin the steps following "ordeal" are catharsis, which includes repentance and cleansing, charisma (or grace), and resurrection.[2]

Does this mean that the "resurrection" of a civilization is inevitable? A casual acquaintance with the history of civilizations proves that the answer is No. There are more dead than live civilizations. Toynbee, for example, lists twenty-six civilizations, only ten of which now survive, and two of those are in their last death throes.[3] It is possible that a new civilization may arise from the death and debris of an old one. The latter would result in what Toynbee calls an affiliated civilization.[4]

What is the situation regarding Western civilization? Spengler, one of the first to foresee the sickness of Western civilization, predicted its death. His viewpoint, which he fully developed by the close of World War I, was that civilizations go through the same life cycle as individuals.[5] They are born, then successively go through the stages of growth, full maturity, decline, senescence, and death. Spengler claimed that the processes of death had already set in for Western civilization. Many other students of world affairs agree that Western civilization is desperately sick, but they do not believe that the sickness is necessarily "unto death."

They do agree that the present crisis is not restricted to Western civilization but that it is inclusive of every major geographic area of the world. It may be and is more immediately acute within the more highly industrialized regions of the world, but there are no areas so isolated that they are not touched by it in some way and to some degree. It is not only all-inclusive geographically but also ideologically. It reaches into every area of the lives of people. The political, economic, social, and religious areas are being affected by the basic changes that are taking place. Customs, traditional modes of thought, and even systems of values are being reexamined,

[2] Pitirim A. Sorokin, *The Crisis of Our Age* (New York, Dutton, 1941), pp. 321 ff.

[3] Toynbee, *A Study of History* (one-vol. ed.), p. 244.

[4] *Ibid.*, p. 48.

[5] Spengler's manuscript was completed by 1917; the book was published in Germany in 1918, and later, under the title of *The Decline of the West,* it was published in a two-volume edition in English (1926, 1928). Still later (1932) it appeared in a one-volume English edition.

reevaluated, and may be replaced. A reorientation of all of life may be expected. It seems that a drastically different world will be the ultimate result.

Background for the Crisis

Every major crisis in the life of an individual, a nation, or a civilization has its roots in the past. Its past or background helps to explain the reasons for, the timing of, the nature of, the direction of, and the possible solutions for the crisis. Restricting ourselves to Western civilization, we shall set out, in broad outline, the road our civilization has traveled from the beginning of the Christian era. We shall call special attention to those elements in the story which are essential for an understanding of the contemporary crisis.

1. *The unification of civilization.* The three main sources of Western civilization were the Grecian, the Hebrew-Christian, and the Roman cultures or civilizations. John Macmurray says that these three old civilizations were mixed together to form our culture, and that the three have never been fully fused. Some of the major problems of European civilization, through the centuries, have grown out of the strain created by the antagonism between the three. The tension has been most acute between the Greek and Christian influences on the one hand and the Roman spirit on the other. The latter, according to Macmurray, has been the dominant influence in our civilization, seeking to keep in subserviency the other two. He suggests that crises in European development have arisen when the Greek and Hebrew-Christian elements rebelled against the Roman dominance.[6]

Although a fusion of these three elements was never completely achieved, yet there was attained during the Middle Ages a considerable degree of unity. A strong desire for unity was a part of the genius of the Roman Empire and its rulers. This desire for unity explains, to a degree, the persecution of the Christians by some of the Roman emperors. Constantine, with a similar desire for unity,

[6] *Freedom in the Modern World* (2nd ed.; London, Faber and Faber, 1935), pp. 74–83.

used a different strategy. He made the Christian religion a legal religion of the Empire and sought to control the church.

As the Roman Empire became decadent and ultimately fell, the Western or Roman Catholic Church was built on its ruins. The Catholic Church for hundreds of years dominated the state and achieved one unified civilization. This unification was most complete in the days of Charlemagne and the Holy Roman Empire. There was one dominant language—Latin; one dominant type of economic system—feudalism; one dominant world political power—Rome; and one dominant church—the Roman Catholic. The church, in the main, dominated every phase of life. There were, of course, some minor strains of the Christian movement that were not completely controlled by the church.

To win and to maintain its power the Roman Catholic Church used secular, worldly methods; became a worldly power, and hence lost its spiritual power. Walter Horton quotes Lord Acton, a Catholic, as saying that all power is corrupting and that absolute power is absolutely corrupting. Horton then adds: "The nearest thing to absolute power in the Middle Ages was the power of the Popes." [7] Hobhouse asserts that "the system of the medieval Papacy tended to secularize the Church more than it spiritualized the world." [8] The civilization that was unified, largely under the power and pressure of the church, is frequently pictured by Roman Catholic authorities as the golden age of the church and of civilization. However, this civilization fossilized and became stagnate. It was maintained by external force long after its inner unity and cohesion were gone. A collapse was inevitable.

2. *The fragmentation of civilization.* This collapse took place in the days of the Renaissance and Reformation. The Roman Church for some time had maintained an uneasy synthesis of the Greek and Christian elements in the culture. This synthesis, which had been worked out most fully by Thomas Aquinas, had been maintained largely by the power of the Roman element in that culture. With the fragmentation of civilization at the end of the Middle

---

[7] *Can Christianity Save Civilization?* (New York, Harper, 1940), p. 87.

[8] Hobhouse as quoted by Philip A. Micklem, *The Secular and the Sacred: An Enquiry into the Principles of a Christian Civilization* (London, Hodder & Stoughton, 1948), p. 117.

Ages, the Greek and the Christian elements were set free. The Renaissance represented "a re-affirmation of classical thought," while the Reformation represented "a reformulation of Christian truth." [9]

The old unification was also broken up or fragmented along other lines. Politically, the rise of independent nation states displaced the decadent Roman Empire; economically, capitalism destroyed feudalism; intellectually, humanism challenged the authority of the Roman Catholic Church; and religiously, the reformed groups broke away from the Roman Church. The dead hand of ecclesiastical control was broken. Man's creative powers were released. Science and art, business and politics became autonomous. For good or bad there was "a reorientation of the mind of man from the heavens to the earth, a rediscovery by man of the visible order and of himself in relation to it." [10]

The preceding does not mean that there were no claimants for authority over the affairs of men. From the days of the Renaissance and the Reformation there has been a continuous struggle between three such claimants, or at least between three conceptions concerning the final source of authority for man. The Roman Catholic Church continues to claim that the church is the final source of authority for men and their institutions. Protestantism, in the main, asserts that the Bible is the ultimate standard for men. Humanism, on the other hand, alleges that the eventual authority is within man. For the humanist, human reason is the final court of appeal. A history of Western civilization for the past five centuries could be written concerning the conflict and the interplay of these three competing sources of authority. There is not always, however, a sharp line of demarcation between them. This is particularly true of Protestantism and humanism, which have much in common. The close relation of the two may be one of the reasons why Tillich interchangeably speaks of the past four centuries as "the Protestant era" or as the "Protestant-humanist era." [11] Nevertheless, humanism has been classified as the most attractive alternative, for educated men and women, for Christianity.[12]

[9] N. H. G. Robinson, *Faith and Duty* (New York, Harper, 1950), p. 57.
[10] Micklem, *op. cit.,* p. 133.
[11] Tillich, *The Protestant Era,* p. 274.
[12] Garbett, *In an Age of Revolution,* p. 87.

3. *The contemporary scene.* What has happened since the days of the Renaissance and Reformation? What is the situation today?

Art, science, business, and politics which won their independence from the dominance of the church have, in the contemporary period, tended to divorce themselves too much from all moral and spiritual restraints and controls. As a result these areas of life have lost, to a large degree, the sense of the eternal and hence any sense of responsibility to any law or authority outside themselves. Except in a very limited way, they have failed to recognize that they are instruments to serve mankind. We are beginning to see, however, that art, business, politics, and particularly science, when divorced from basic moral and spiritual values, may be used to enslave and even to destroy man.

One of the reasons for the increasing self-sufficiency of the various areas of life and the accompanying secularization of life in general was the preoccupation of the churches of the Reformation with their own immediate problems and needs. Micklem suggests that they were so concerned "with the urgent task of formulating or reformulating their own institutional and dogmatic basis and of entrenching themselves within their own lines of defense, that the pressing need for a revised Christian social ethic, adequate to new social forms and forces, was largely neglected." He further says, "The field was thus left clear for the full expression of those tendencies to secular self-sufficiency latent in the Renaissance, for the assertion of a self-dependent autonomy in the realm of secular pursuits with increasing disregard for the sanctions of religion." [13] As a result, religion at best became one department of life. But when religion becomes a mere department of life it tends to be pushed to the circumference of life. The trend is to dismiss it "as an adjectival and peripheral concern, acceptance of which depends on the taste and fancy of the believer." [14]

Because modern man has divided his life and the life of the world into more or less watertight compartments, he lacks integration. He is confused and frustrated. He is pulled in several different directions at the same time. The society he has constructed also lacks a

[13] Micklem, *op. cit.*, p. 138.
[14] W. Norman Pittenger, *The Historic Faith and a Changing World* (New York, Oxford University Press, 1950), p. 83.

spiritual center around which it could find unity and integration. As a result "we are confronted with the threat of atomistic disintegration and cultural self-destruction." [15]

Lacking the perspective of the eternal, there is also lacking a world view that satisfies. There is little if any feeling of purpose or direction. But as Karl Heim reminds us, "The question about the meaning of life is the burning wound from which we all suffer and which always breaks out again." [16] The failure to have a satisfying world view, to have a definite sense of meaning or purpose, is one reason for the rise in the contemporary period of movements such as fascism, national socialism, and communism. Each of these secular movements, which possess in a sense a religious perspective, has a world view. These world views may have been and may be false, but "even a false religion can deliver man for the time from the sense of frustration and futility to which in the end the absence of a world-view leads." [17] In other words, one reason these movements have arisen in the contemporary period is that Western civilization did not present to the people a challenging world view which would give direction, purpose, and dynamic to life.

It is also true that contemporary events have rather rudely disillusioned modern man. He has failed to solve his problems. He faces the possibility of his house collapsing on his head. He has broken, in the main, with the "eternal springs" of hope and renewal. He is a confused individual, lost in a world he does not know how to control and with a gripping fear of the future. One author dedicates his book as follows:

> To Christian workers everywhere, and to those conscientious seekers after truth, men of good will and of honest mind, who have come to the candid admission that they have lost their way in the wilderness of the contemporary world. [18]

The same author suggests that contemporary man "has become a monster of uneasiness." [19] Laski claims that the prevailing mood is "one of sombre pessimism and of bitterness." [20]

[15] Matthew Spinka, "Our Secularist Age," *Religion in Life,* XXI (Summer, 1952), 386.
[16] Quoted by Cave, *The Christian Estimate of Man,* p. 206.
[17] *Ibid.,* p. 207. [18] Cailliet, *The Christian Approach to Culture.*
[19] *Ibid.,* p. 216. [20] Laski, *The Dilemma of Our Times,* p. 53.

In the geographic areas where the disintegration of Western civilization has gone the furthest, it is no wonder that men, seeking a renewal of meaning and significance in life, have turned to the superman of Nietzsche or to the superindividual collective of Marx. It seems that modern man will turn to some power outside himself in an attempt to recapture his sense of dignity, well-being, and security. There is some evidence that he is not only willing to surrender his liberty, but that he actually wants to "escape from freedom." [21] The next few years will determine whether he will turn to a totalitarian party or state, to an all-powerful ecclesiastical machine, or to a vital type of Christian experience. The latter alone will give to man a satisfying world view, will recreate within him the springs of eternal hope, and will provide for him the sense of personal responsibility that he needs.

A little more time must elapse before we can know whether or not Lowry's designation is correct that the twentieth century is "the era of the Prodigal Son coming to himself." [22] It may be that man the prodigal knows today "his alienation from the source of his true being." He may know that he has "squandered his spiritual inheritance." He may be thoroughly acquainted with "his hunger in the midst of plenty" and of "the existence which was once his in the Father's house." But there is still no clear proof that modern man is going to have the sanity and the strength of will and purpose to arise and return to the Father in the spirit of true repentance.

Reasons for the Crisis

There is no one adequate explanation for a phenomenon of the proportions of the contemporary crisis. There have been and are many factors that have contributed and are contributing to the crisis. World War I and World War II were factors of considerable importance, but they were more evidences and results of the crisis than creators of it.

Science has been a factor in creating the crisis by making us one world, by closing geographic areas, by making available to all nations instruments of production and hence increasing the competi-

[21] Tillich, *op. cit.*, p. 286.
[22] Lowry, *Communism and Christ*, p. 112.

tion for raw materials and for markets, and more recently by placing within the hands of men the means by which they can destroy themselves and their civilization. Science has also produced the modern machine age; and the machine which has been used by man to conquer nature has turned on man and conquered him. It liberates man but it also enslaves him.[23]

There are some who believe that the modern crisis is the result primarily of certain economic trends and problems,[24] of political tendencies and movements,[25] or results from the meeting of competing cultures, with a more or less inevitable conflict between those cultures.[26]

The rise of the masses is another contributor of considerable importance to the contemporary crisis. The masses are on the march around the world. They have caught a vision of better days ahead. Frank Laubach, who possibly knows the mind of the masses as well as any American, makes the following statement concerning them: "They were in despair, but now they are making up their minds that they will come up—or blow up the world. They are desperate, grim, irresistible." [27] Berdyaev speaks of "the complete occupation of the stage of history by the mobilized masses," and declares that this is "the basic factor of modern history." [28]

The scholars may not agree concerning all the factors that have created the contemporary crisis, but there is surprising unanimity of opinion concerning the nature of the basic reasons for the crisis. Practically all of them—philosophers, politicians, and social scien-

[23] Berdyaev, *The Meaning of History*, p. 152.

[24] For Karl Mannheim the central problem is economic planning. This is the main thesis in his *Man and Society in an Age of Reconstruction, Diagnosis of Our Time,* and *Freedom, Power and Democratic Planning.*

[25] Walter Lippmann, for example, in *The Public Philosophy* (Boston, Little, Brown, 1955) contends that the decline of Western society is due to two things: (1) to the dominance, in the democracies, of mass public opinion and the legislative over the executive branches of government, and (2) the failure of the democracies to defend and to maintain what he calls the public philosophy, which includes the basic concepts, principles, and precepts that gave birth to those democracies.

[26] See particularly F. S. C. Northrop, *The Meeting of East and West* (New York, Macmillan, 1946).

[27] *Wake Up or Blow Up,* p. 28.

[28] *The Fate of Man in the Modern World,* p. 62. See also José Ortega y Gasset, *The Revolt of the Masses* (New York, Norton, 1932).

tists, as well as theologians—agree that the real reasons for the crisis are spiritual.

1. *Inner decay.* In a very real sense the threatened collapse of Western civilization is due to the decadent conditions within that civilization itself. Many of the peoples of the West have drifted away from the fundamental moral and spiritual concepts that have provided the foundation for and the integrating center of their civilization. For years they have continued to give lip service to those concepts, while their lives belied their profession. This has resulted in what Trueblood aptly calls a "cut-flower civilization." [29] A cut-flower, separated from the source of its strength, may retain its beauty for a few days, but it will soon wither and die.

The integrating center of a civilization, and every civilization has an integrating center, contains the supreme value or values of that civilization. Those values represent the ends for which men live and die. They provide the point of reference for the civilization. In a very true sense that center is the religion of the civilization, although that religion may be a false one. The strength of a civilization can be largely measured by the soundness or the validity of its integrating center, the thoroughness with which all of life is related to or integrated around that center, and the inner unity or cohesion of the center itself.

Civilizations may disintegrate and ultimately fall because of competition from without or because of decay from within, particularly from within the heart of the civilization. Competition from without is not a very serious threat to a civilization so long as it accepts only the techniques, skills, or methods of a competing civilization. The threat is greatly increased, however, when any of the ends or values of a competing civilization are accepted. When the latter happens there begins a struggle in the system of values or at the center of the civilization. This struggle will tend to continue until a new center is established, until there is a reorientation of the civilization.

Usually the source of decay and ultimate destruction of stronger civilizations is from within rather than from without. This seemingly is what is happening to Western civilization. The center of

[29] *Foundations for Reconstruction* (New York, Harper, 1946), p. 37.

that civilization has become decadent. The center itself is not well integrated; hence the civilization is not well integrated. Men are confused and frustrated. The means of life are being substituted for the ends of life. Gadgets are considered of more value than God. If the West is defeated by forces from without it will be because of inner decay. Walter Horton suggests that "there seems to be only one hope left for Western civilization: to turn back to God in quest of spiritual cleansing and renewal." [30]

A symbol and a proof of the inner decay of Western civilization is the rise and spread of modern secularism. What is meant by "secularism"? It is "an evasive, often unconscious, philosophy which does not deny but ignores the presence and ethical influence of a living God." [31] "It is the ordering and conducting of life as if God did not exist." [32]

The spirit of secularism has permeated, to a distressing degree, all of life—literature and art, science and education, politics and industry, and even religion itself. "Church members are only a degree less secularized in their consciousness than the public that is completely divorced from the Church." [33]

Even the well meaning efforts of many Christians to make every area of life equally sacred has contributed, at least indirectly, to the secularization of life. Their efforts have tended to break down the distinction between the sacred and the secular. The result has been a loss, to some degree, of a sense of holiness and an indifference to things sacred. It is true that every day should be and is a holy day, but there is one day that is uniquely sacred or holy. We are to recognize that all we have belongs to God and is to be used for God-honoring purposes, but the tithe is holy unto God in

[30] *Op. cit.*, p. 3.

[31] J. Richard Spann (ed.), *The Christian Faith and Secularism* (New York, Abingdon-Cokesbury, 1948), p. 5.

[32] Georgia Harkness, *The Modern Rival of Christian Faith* (New York, Abingdon-Cokesbury, 1952), p. 16. There are some who believe that such definitions as the above represent a false viewpoint concerning secularism. They consider that the word when properly understood has no bad connotation, but that it has been confused with materialism. See particularly J. M. Dawson's *America's Way in Church, State, and Society*, pp. 61 ff. E. E. Aubrey in *Secularism a Myth* (New York, Harper, 1954) pleads for a clearer definition of secularism by Christian scholars and suggests a strategy for Christianity in relation to secular forces.

[33] Davies, *The Sin of Our Age*, p. 61.

a special way. Every house where a Christian lives and works may be and should be holy, but the church house is holy in a singular way. If we fail to recognize the uniquely holy or sacred, we shall tend to lose the sense of the sacredness or holiness of the less holy. All of life, even the uniquely holy, will tend to become secularized.

2. *Dethronement of God.* Among the chief factors that shape a culture or a civilization are what Brunner calls its "culture-trans-cendent presuppositions." [34] One of those presuppositions is the exis-tence of a holy, righteous, and sovereign God, who claims for him-self authority over the affairs of men, and whose will is the final determinant of right and wrong for men.

Following the lead of a nontheistic humanism, modern man has tended to usurp for himself the position that properly belongs to God and to God alone. Norman Pittenger suggests that someone has remarked that "while the heavens used to declare the glory of God, neon signs today proclaim the cleverness of man." He then adds: "This situation points toward the appalling loss of any sense of the ultimate meaning of things, the final 'why,' in our contemporary culture." [35]

Some students of world affairs consider the dethronement of God the major sin of our age and the chief contributor to the ills of our day.[36] Berdyaev in his particularly graphic style sets out the ulti-mate results of the exaltation of man, the dethronement of God, and hence the separation of man from God. He says:

When man follows the path of self-affirmation, ceases to respect the higher principle and asserts his self-sufficiency, he exterminates and denies his true self according to the laws of an inexorable inner dialectic. To affirm himself and preserve the source of his creative energy, man must affirm God as well. He must affirm the image of God within him. For he can have no vision of himself if he has none of the higher Divine nature . . . The affirmation of the human individuality and personality demand a tie with a higher divine principle. But when the human personality will admit no authority but itself, it disintegrates, allowing the intrusion of the lowest natural elements which consume it. When man will admit only himself, he loses consciousness of himself.[37]

[34] *Christianity and Civilisation* (New York, Scribner's, 1948), First Part, p. 11.
[35] *Op. cit.*, pp. 118–19.   [36] See particularly Davies, *op. cit.*
[37] *The Meaning of History*, pp. 154–55.

It may sound paradoxical, but when man unduly exalts himself the ultimate result is his own debasement.

Micklem expresses something of the same idea as follows:

There is more than a touch of tragic irony in the fact that a humanism which has exalted the capacity for man to provide for all his needs, and to build for himself from materials at his disposal the kingdom of his desire, and in doing so has ruled out as irrelevant any reference to the ultimate sanctions for which religion stands, has born fruit in a depersonalized humanity, and the forfeiture of that very sense of personal worth by which it sets supreme store.[38]

The primary trouble with our world is not a lack of knowledge but a lack of devotion "to the living God," [39] a God whom the world has elbowed out of the position of centrality. Having pushed God out of the center of life, the world has little place for the other-worldly. There has been a "decline of belief in the supernatural." [40] The world finds its point of reference within the time process. Its main values are in the here-and-now. The arbitrator of values is within man himself rather than in the will of a sovereign, transcendent God. What the world desperately needs is to bend back its "powers and achievements into closer contact with reality." [41]

3. *Loss of faith.* Most students of Western civilization agree that one of the major causes of the serious sickness of our civilization is its loss of faith. Western man, to a distressing degree, has lost his faith in the basic principles or assumptions upon which our civilization was built. Those assumptions, in the main, stemmed from the Christian religion. And "a civilization which has become sceptical of the religious faith on which it has been mainly founded, and has discovered no alternative faith, has begun to decline." [42] John Macmurray said some time ago that he could not think of anything that we used to believe in that we still believe in passionately and with our whole hearts. He said that our ideals have gone dead. He adds that we no longer believe in them and yet we do not disbelieve in

[38] *Op. cit.*, p. 186.
[39] Morrison, *Can Protestantism Win America?*, p. 38.
[40] Garbett, *In an Age of Revolution*, p. 61.
[41] H. D. Lewis, *Morals and the New Theology* (London, Victor Gollancz, 1947), p. 153.
[42] Ingram, *Christianity, Communism and Society*, p. 12.

them either. This he says is our dilemma. "We neither believe nor disbelieve. We are neither hot nor cold; and it paralyses our capacity to decide and to act." [43]

Western man certainly has lost his faith in science. There has come to him a rather sudden and disturbing realization that science is impartial, that it may be used to impoverish or to enrich, to bring death or to bring life, to destroy or to enrich civilization. This realization has been a rather rude shock to Western man, who had tended to consider science a savior of mankind. In desperation he has tended to turn in the last few years with a sort of grasping hope from the natural sciences to the social sciences, particularly to psychology and psychiatry. The skilled psychologist or psychiatrist, with a Christian perspective, can make a wonderful contribution to the lives of many people. But there is a tendency to make a priest of him; particularly is this true of the psychiatrist. By some he is considered a magician. The attitude of many people toward him is not rational. Some believe that he can pull strings and perform miracles. "How long this new psychological faith will endure—how long it will be tolerated, we cannot be certain." [44] This illogical faith, this grasping for a straw reveals the seriousness of the sickness of our age.

Man has also lost his faith in the inevitable progress of history. This has been the predominant view or philosophy of history [45] of

---

[43] *Freedom in the Modern World*, p. 28.   [44] Lowry, *op. cit.*, p. 68.

[45] For a study of the philosophy of history in general and of Christianity's relation to history, see the following: Nicolas Berdyaev, *The Meaning of History*—particular emphasis on humanism and the contemporary world crisis; H. Butterfield, *Christianity and History* (New York, Scribner's, 1950); Sherwood Eddy, *God in History* (New York, Association Press, 1947)—with a definite Christian orientation but with an examination of various philosophies of history; Karl Löwith, *Meaning in History* (Chicago, University of Chicago Press, 1949)—scholarly examination of theories of various men, with a closing chapter on "The Biblical View of History"; Reinhold Niebuhr, *Faith and History* —a study of the classical, the modern, and the biblical views or philosophies of history; E. C. Rust, *The Christian Understanding of History* (London, Lutterworth Press, 1947)—thorough, from the Christian perspective, central idea "salvation history"; Roger Lincoln Shinn, *Christianity and the Problem of History* (New York, Scribner's, 1953); Arnold J. Toynbee, *A Study of History* (one-vol. ed.)—while written as a history of civilizations, it really presents a philosophy of the history of civilization. If there is a desire to read on the idea of inevitable progress, which was the dominant philosophy of history in the West for a century and a half, see: John Baillie, *The Belief in Progress* (London, Oxford

modern man in contrast to what Niebuhr describes as the classical and the biblical or Christian views.[46] Emil Brunner says that the idea of an idealistic progressivism was "the bastard offspring of an optimistic anthropology and Christian eschatology." [47] Regardless of its source, the idea of inevitable progress became the working faith, "the animating controlling idea of Western civilization." [48] This idea has evoked "all the enthusiasm and faith of a genuine religion." [49]

What has happened to that faith? It is almost at the vanishing point. What was a century of hope has changed, at least for many, to a century of despair. "Since 1914 one tragic experience has followed another, as if history had been designed to refute the vain delusions of modern man." [50] Niebuhr suggests that "the tragic irony of this refutation by contemporary history of modern man's conception of history embodies the spiritual crisis of our age." [51] The contradiction between the hopes of yesterday and the realities of today has created, in some sections of the world, something like despair and "is generating a kind of desperate complacency in those parts of the world in which the crisis of the age is dimly, though not fully, sensed." [52]

As a part of his general disillusionment, man, to a considerable degree, has lost faith in himself. He is not nearly so optimistic as formerly concerning human nature; neither is he so sure that he has the ability to solve his problems and the problems of his world. He has a deepened sense of his limitations and also of the seriousness of sin in his life and in the social order. The sinister events of recent years have made clearer to him his deep need and how futile it is for him to think that he can save himself.[53]

This faith, which Western man has had and has largely lost, was his inheritance, to a considerable degree, from humanism. The latter

---

University Press, 1950), and J. B. Bury, *The Idea of Progress* (London, Macmillan, 1920). Bury is more specifically on the idea of inevitable progress, while Baillie gives more of a Christian slant to the concept of progress.

[46] *Faith and History.*   [47] *Christianity and Civilisation,* First Part, p. 55.
[48] Bury, *The Idea of Progress,* p. vii.
[49] Christopher Dawson, *Progress and Religion* (New York, Longmans, Green, 1929), p. 201.
[50] Niebuhr, *Faith and History,* pp. 6–7.   [51] *Ibid.,* p. 8.
[52] *Ibid.,* p. 13.   [53] Cave, *op. cit.,* p. 211.

had a growing faith in science and in the inevitable progress of history.[54] An integral phase of that faith was humanism's faith in man. There is a deep paradox, however, in humanism's estimate of man. It overestimates man's capacities, forming "a romantic and unrealistic picture of human nature"; while at the same time it underestimates his value, failing "to see that he is a child of God." [55]

Man's loss of faith in science, in inevitable progress, and in himself may eventually be a curse or a blessing to him and the world. It depends on what he does about his loss of faith, and what his loss of faith does to him. It will be a curse to him if it leaves him permanently in a state of despair and futility, if he turns to the collective to recapture some of his lost sense of significance and security, or if he seeks to restore his faith in himself and in the historic process simply by identifying himself and his interests with the group. The last would tend to lessen his sense of need for God. Such would be ultimately self-defeating. The collective cannot possibly satisfy the deeper needs of man. In addition, he will find when he surrenders to the group that sooner or later it will enslave, debase, and depersonalize him. He will also discover that ultimately false gods are overthrown.

On the other hand, if modern man's loss of faith leads him to recognize his need for God and will cause him to return to God, it will be a blessing to him. Such a return to God will enable him to see that any permanent progress is not only impossible but meaningless unless men progress in their understanding of God and of his way with and his will for them.

If man learns the difficult lesson of his limitations and of God's limitless powers, then the present period of defeat and despair will be a blessing to him and his world. Time alone will reveal whether or not we are going to be intelligent enough and spiritually alert enough to learn the lessons that recent events would teach us. "We have got to get back to God. Unless the world gets back to God it hasn't a chance. We ought to *hurry* back to God." [56]

---

[54] Garbett, *In an Age of Revolution*, pp. 86–87.   [55] *Ibid.*, pp. 90–91.
[56] J. A. Spender as quoted by H. D. A. Major, *Civilisation and Religious Values* (London, George Allen & Unwin, 1948), p. 9.

Remedies for the Crisis

Possibly before we consider the cure for the present crisis, we should raise the prior question: "Is there any hope for our civilization?"

Some, such as Oswald Spengler and others, would say No. They contend that the death of a civilization is just as inevitable as the death of an individual.

Others hold desperately to the theory of the inevitable progress of history. For them, there may be regression periods, but civilization inevitably marches on. They admit that the present may be a critical period for civilization, but it is merely the introductory phases of a richer and higher type of civilization.

Some of the most acute diagnosticians of the contemporary period no longer hold to the inevitable-progress theory, yet they are rather optimistic concerning the ultimate outcome. Sorokin suggests that following the decay and collapse of our sensate culture an ideational type of culture will arise to take its place.[57] Berdyaev reveals a similar faith, although he does not use the same terminology as Sorokin. He suggests that there is a rhythm in history as in nature, and he believes that the world is standing at the beginning of what he terms a new Middle Ages.[58]

Admitting that a new world is in the process of being born, it cannot be brought forth without suffering or travail. This is true although its birth may be inevitable. Every major transition period is accompanied by chaos and confusion, by struggle and wars. Or, as Berdyaev expresses it, "In the process of its re-incarnation the world must apparently go through a period of darkness." [59] It might be well, however, for us to remind ourselves that "night is not less wonderful than day, it is equally the work of God; it is lit by the splendour of the stars and it reveals to us things that the day does not know. Night is closer than day to the mystery of all beginning." [60] Civilizations as well as individuals may learn through suffering, and such learning may be "the sovereign means of progress." [61]

[57] *Op. cit.*, p. 13.　　　　　[58] *The End of Our Time*, p. 69.
[59] *Towards a New Epoch*, p. vi.
[60] Berdyaev, *The End of Our Time*, pp. 70–71.
[61] Toynbee, *Civilization on Trial*, p. 15.

Now what is the answer to the question: "Is there a remedy for the contemporary crisis?" There is no unequivocal Yes or No. There is no remedy if we are thinking in terms of the restoration of what we have had, if we are thinking of saving civilization as it is. "Western civilization does not deserve to be preserved as it is, and every effort to preserve it as it is will produce its own opposite, by a kind of moral necessity." [62]

Western civilization can be saved, but we should remember that just as its ills are not superficial so the remedy or remedies must not deal with mere symptoms. Some drastic steps must be taken to save our civilization, or at least to shorten and to relieve the suffering of the present period of transition and crisis.

1. *The economic approach.* The past century has been called the century of economic man. Economic interests have dominated the thinking of the majority of people. The materialistic spirit has permeated all of life, including the area of organized religion. "Modern man is the product of a fervid obsession with material and social progress, with a gospel of more and more things." [63] This obsession with the things of life has contributed to the tensions and problems of the contemporary period.

Man's desire for material things, stimulated by the system under which he lives—a system which has definitely an economic orientation, is not easily satisfied. This obsession or desire has been a factor in the rise of contemporary economic and political movements and programs such as communism, fascism, socialism, and even New Dealism and Fair Dealism. These movements have appealed to, and some have even taken advantage of, modern man's longing for economic security. And economic security in the modern period is not interpreted in terms of the necessities of life. "To the mass mind of to-day, the good life has become inseparable from the maximum consumption of things!" [64] Davies suggests that because the modern obsession with social security goes far beyond minimum physical needs, the problem has become primarily social and spiritual rather than strictly economic.

This high premium placed on things material and on economic

[62] Horton, *op. cit.*, p. 5.   [63] Davies, *op. cit.*, p. 59.
[64] *Ibid.*, p. 45.

security has created within man an inner conflict or dilemma. There seems to be inborn in man a desire for freedom. What is he to do when there is a conflict between freedom and economic security? "The most difficult thing is to unite bread and freedom. How can man be fed without taking from him his freedom?" [65] Can any society provide adequately for the economic needs and wants of its people and at the same time protect their liberties? It is doubtful if this can be done in an economically orientated society, where profit is the chief motive, and every means possible is used to stimulate artificially the economic wants and demands of the people. But there is no reason why it cannot be done within the democratic framework, if we can have a reorientation of our thinking concerning the values of life. We must come to the place where we see that the material values are not the supreme values of life; but that the human, the moral, the spiritual values are to have precedence.

We do not mean by the preceding that the material things of life should be deprecated. Certainly we do not mean that religion should be the opiate of the people to lull them to senseless satisfaction with conditions they should not accept. We are simply saying that the material values should fall into their proper place, into a place subservient to the spiritual. People generally—employers and employees, rich and poor—need to recognize "that in the order of God worship, not bread, is the first and foremost need of man." [66] The first words in the prayer Jesus taught his disciples were, "Our Father who art in heaven, Hallowed be thy name." Before the disciple is to pray, "Give us this day our daily bread," he is to pray, "Thy kingdom come, Thy will be done, on earth as it is in heaven." Only a society that considers things spiritual of greater importance than things material will be able to provide economic security and at the same time retain the basic freedoms.

2. *The political approach.* There are some problems that are political to a considerable degree, and these are factors in the present crisis. Among the most important are: dependent territories and colonial peoples, minorities, relation of races, the unequal distribution of the land area of the world, and the abolition of war as a

---

[65] Berdyaev, *Towards a New Epoch*, p. 77.
[66] Cailliet, *op. cit.*, p. 198.

method for the settling of international disputes. Some solution must be found for these problems.

The consistent application of democratic principles by the democracies would go a long way toward the solution of the preceding problems and would help the world to surmount the present crisis. But "the tragedy of the modern democracies is that they have not yet succeeded in realizing democracy." [67]

Democracy also needs to come back to its Christian roots.[68] Toynbee suggests that democracy is a leaf from the book of Christianity, which has been half emptied of its meaning by being divorced from its Christian context and secularized.[69] Maritain similarly says that democracy "springs in the essentials from the inspiration of the Gospel and cannot subsist without it." He then adds that during the past century the motivating forces in modern democracies repudiated "the Gospel and Christianity in the name of human liberty," while the "motivating forces in the Christian social strata were combating the democratic aspirations in the name of religion." [70] The latter has not been true of all Christian forces, but it has been true to a large degree of the dominant religious groups in most of the countries of Europe.

It is possible that more important than any of the preceding problems is the fact that it seems that an inevitable part of the new order of the future will be the political unification of the world. No one has said this more pointedly than Toynbee. His statement is as follows:

I believe it is a foregone conclusion that the world is in any event going to be unified politically in the near future. . . . I think the big and really formidable political issue to-day is, not *whether* the world is soon going to be unified politically, but in which of two alternative possible ways this rapid unification is going to come about.[71]

He gives two major reasons for the inevitability of political unification—the degree of our present interdependence and the deadliness of our present weapons of war. The two possible methods of

---

[67] Jacques Maritain, *Christianity and Democracy*, trans. Doris C. Anson (New York, Scribner's, 1944), p. 25.
[68] See Arthur E. Holt, *Christian Roots of Democracy in America.*
[69] *Civilization on Trial*, p. 237.   [70] *Christianity and Democracy*, p. 27.
[71] *Civilization on Trial*, p. 127.

unification according to Toynbee are by force or by cooperation. Wars may continue, and likely one more would be sufficient, until just one great power would survive, which would impose unification and peace upon the world by force of arms. This has been done in the past. The other method of world unification, which does not look encouraging now, is through the cooperation of the nations of the world, particularly the two great world powers—the United States and the Soviet Union.

The road ahead for the achievement of any effective world government is a difficult one. The world at the present time and for the foreseeable future is and will be dominated by the great powers. And as Reinhold Niebuhr says, "The possibility of a merger of sovereignties between the great powers into a single center of authority must certainly be regarded as very remote." [72] Typical of his dialectical mode of expression, he says that "the task of building a world community is man's final necessity and possibility, but also his final impossibility." [73] He also suggests that it will be "in actuality the perpetual problem as well as the constant fulfillment of human hopes." [74]

In a later book Niebuhr calls world government an illusion and a fallacy. He suggests that modern techniques "have established a rudimentary world community but have not integrated it organically, morally or politically. They have created a community of mutual dependence, but not one of mutual trust and respect." [75] He does say that the building of a world community, which is man's final possibility and final impossibility,

must be interpreted from the standpoint of a faith which understands the fragmentary and broken character of all historic achievements and yet has confidence in their meaning because it knows their completion to be in the hands of a Divine Power, whose resources are greater than those of men, and whose suffering love can overcome the corruptions of man's achievements, without negating the significance of our striving. [76]

A word of caution might be in order. While it may be that some type of world government is necessary and may even be inevitable

[72] *The Children of Light and the Children of Darkness,* p. 172.
[73] *Ibid.,* p. 187.   [74] *Ibid.,* p. 188.
[75] *Christian Realism and Political Problems,* pp. 15–16.
[76] *The Children of Light and the Children of Darkness,* pp. 189–90.

sooner or later, yet we should not place too much faith in such a political instrument to solve the problems of our world. Political unification may be an essential part of any adequate solution, but we should remember that the ills of the world are basically spiritual. The maladjustments and evils even of the economic and political areas stem largely from moral and spiritual decay. It is also possible that political unification would deepen the problems of the world. Resulting from world unification, particularly if that unification was achieved and maintained by force, there could arise the most completely totalitarian régime that the world has ever known. There could be a world political power allied with or even dominated by a world religious power that would seek to control even the minds and consciences of men. The world should never forget that "sinful men will pervert any form of organization." [77]

3. *The spiritual approach.* It has been suggested that the economic and political problems of the world are, in their deepest sense, moral and spiritual. This means that any adequate solution for those problems must include the spiritual approach. Just as the crisis in contemporary civilization is a crisis at the heart of that civilization, which is another way of saying that the crisis is basically spiritual, so the remedy must be primarily spiritual. Anything less than that would merely be tinkering with the machinery; it would be treating a symptom rather than getting at the root or the cause of the disease. "Better social organization is a sore need, but unless it is founded upon the spiritual and moral readjustment of society it is as empty of virtue as the sounding brass or tinkling cymbal. . . . We need not so much a new organization as a new soul." [78] This means that religion must play a major role in any real remedy for the contemporary crisis.

C. C. Morrison gives three tests for any religion that would be an adequate faith for contemporary man. The tests are: (1) it must possess in its inherent genius the resources for creating world community; (2) it must be able to live side by side with science in mutual understanding and respect; (3) it must do something radical

[77] The Archbishop of Canterbury in *Towards a Christian Order* (London, Eyre and Spottiswoode, 1942), p. 9.
[78] Ralph T. Flewelling, *The Survival of Western Culture* (New York, Harper, 1943), p. 295.

about man.[79] Tests (1) and (3) are particularly relevant for this study of the world crisis.

A religion that will pass these tests is a religion that will make men conscious of their need of God. It will lead them to return to God, to become conscious of the presence of God and their responsibility to him. What this return to God will do for the peoples of the world will depend upon the type of God to whom they return. For the most beneficial results it must be a return to the God revealed in the life and teachings of Jesus; a God who hates sin but loves the sinner, a God who is active in the affairs of nations and civilizations. Only a return to such a God will give to the world the vital and inclusive type of religion that is essential if the heart of civilization is to be renewed, and if that heart is not renewed then civilization is doomed. A return to the religion of Jesus would also assure the proper balance between a sound theology and a vigorous Christian ethic, and such a balance is necessary if the world is to recover.[80] Let us never forget that the religion revealed by Jesus "has not been tried and been found wanting; it has been found hard and therefore has not been tried." [81]

As has been emphasized previously, the crisis in civilization is a crisis within man himself. Man not only needs to return to God because of what his return will do for civilization, but also because of what it will do for him. "There is at the bottom of modern history man's break with the depths of his own soul, between life and its meaning." [82] Berdyaev says that man "must either go deep or peter-out altogether." He then rather optimistically adds: "And after the trials and shocks he has sustained a deepening seems to be indicated." [83]

Maritain suggests that man can choose only one of two roads. Those roads are "the road to Calvary" or "the road to the slaughter-house." [84] Davies likewise voices two alternatives: Christian faith or "despair—sheer, black, utter, final despair." [85] Is man going to

---

[79] *Op. cit.*, pp. 40–41.

[80] See Georgia Harkness, *The Gospel and Our World* (New York, Abingdon-Cokesbury Press, 1949), Chap. VI.

[81] Major, *op. cit.*, p. 100.   [82] Berdyaev, *The End of Our Time*, p. 22.

[83] *Ibid.*, p. 59.

[84] *The Twilight of Civilization* (New York, Sheed and Ward, 1943), p. 9.

[85] *Op. cit.*, p. 142.

have to proceed further toward the slaughterhouse before he will turn to Calvary? Has the despair become deep enough to cause him to turn to the Christian faith? How long must the present period of suffering and travail continue before men will turn for healing to the Great Physician? Why should men return to Calvary, to the Christian faith, to the simple teachings of Jesus, and to the God revealed by Jesus? What will such a turning to God do for them and through them for their world?

The first reaction of any man who becomes conscious of God's presence is a conviction of sin. Like Isaiah he will cry out, "I am a man of unclean lips." He will plead for forgiveness. Such a spirit of repentance is needed, if our way of life is to be saved. What Davies says concerning Europe could be said about all other sections of the world: "Repentance, not just intelligence, is Europe's vital need to-day. The current assumption that what the world suffers from is stupidity is utterly inadequate and shallow." [86] Again he says, "*Western civilization must repent its titanic, basic sin.*" [87] For Davies that titanic, basic sin is man's exaltation of himself to the place that properly belongs to God and to God alone.

A sense of God's presence will also give to man a keener insight into the depth and the seriousness of sin not only in his own life but also in the social order. It will enable him to recognize his limitations in the battle against sin, and will lead him to admit frankly and unashamedly his dependence on God. It will also help to keep him from identifying the kingdom of God with any social program or with any political or ecclesiastical organization. He will realize that sin is a positive factor in every human institution or social program, and that this is true both of the *status quo* and of programs of change. Thus he may be saved from many of the errors of the visionary idealists. Such a sense of the sinfulness of sin, and of its presence even in the best of programs, will also help to keep man from placing his faith in what Davies has called "prophets of the half-way house." [88] The situation is too serious for halfway measures. Drastic steps must be taken to save the patient.

Some students of world affairs have suggested that there is no solution for the problems of our world, and particularly no hope for an effective organization of the world, unless there can be a deep

[86] *Ibid.,* p. 6.   [87] *Ibid.,* p. 123.   [88] *Ibid.,* p. 124.

sense of world community or world unity. This emphasis has been made by Reinhold Niebuhr, as suggested previously, but it has also been made by Daniel J. Fleming. In one place the latter says: "Enlarging our circle of consciousness to include a world fraternity involves an unprecedented mental and spiritual change within us. . . . love of mankind is little more than an ideal which now presses for embodiment." [89]

What is our hope of attaining such a world community? There is really only one hope and that hope is in God. "Man without God cannot find unity except against another." [90] And any unity that is achieved by uniting against another ultimately brings disunity and is self-defeating. The only unity or community that will last is a unity achieved in and by the help of God. The task of world community is so tremendous "that our faith in a successful outcome might well fail us, were it not for the conviction that God wills it." [91]

Still another contribution that a return to God will make to man and to the world is a renewal of vitality, of creativeness, of dynamic to accomplish God's will in his life and in the world. Not only will man have deeper insights into the ills of society and of God's remedies for those ills, but he also will have created within him the drive and the courage to follow the leadership of the Spirit of God in doing his will in the world.

When man returns to the living God, is brought into a vital relation with him, he will see that he has no real worth, dignity, or meaning apart from God. It may sound paradoxical, but if man's loss of faith in himself causes him to turn to God, he will discover that fellowship with God will restore his faith in himself, not in himself separated from God, but in himself as a co-laborer with God.

Furthermore, when man returns to God and recognizes his need for God, he will find that his fellowship with the sovereign God will restore his faith in history and in the historic process. This does not mean a return to a superficial faith in the redemptive nature of history as such. It does not mean that man will believe that the kingdom of God can ever be fully realized within history. It does mean, however, that man will see that the kingdom of God will be ulti-

[89] Daniel J. Fleming, *Bringing Our World Together* (New York, Scribner's, 1945), p. vii. The subtitle of this volume is "A Study in World Community."
[90] Maritain, *The Twilight of Civilization*, p. 38.
[91] Fleming, *op. cit.*, p. viii.

mately triumphant within history and over history. He can have a strong abiding faith that the God he serves will be victorious in the world, and that no effort of his in cooperation with God will be lost.

When man comes to the place where he realizes that God is the only hope of the world, he will see that the Christian faith, with the Christian's God, has a unique relevance for times of darkness and despair. "Christian faith is at home . . . with human tragedy, disaster, suffering and frustration." [92] This means that Christians should not be particularly discouraged by the darkness around them. God has not vacated. He is still on his throne, although men may have pushed him off the throne of their hearts. There will come a time when the kingdom of the world will "become the kingdom of our Lord and of his Christ, and he shall reign for ever and ever." [93] Sooner or later every knee shall bow and every tongue shall "confess that Jesus Christ is Lord, to the glory of God the Father." [94] Such assurance should give to every child of God a deep calm and a peace that passeth understanding.

4. *The renewal of organized Christianity.* We have considered in general the spiritual approach to the problems of our day. Let us now turn our attention, in a specific way, to organized Christianity. It is Berdyaev who says that "in the dark and agonizing period through which we are going Christianity has a colossal responsibility." [95] He also suggests that Christianity in its organized forms "is going through a crisis and longs for some kind of renewal or renaissance." [96] The encouraging thing is that the Christian movement has within it the resources for such renewal, and has displayed through the centuries a rather remarkable ability for renewal. It has been after such times of renewal that "Christianity has arrested cultural decay and saved the essential values of civilization more than once, in the history of the West." [97] It is not Christianity as it is that will save civilization, but, to use one of Horton's expressions, it is "Christianity-as-it-potentially-is, Christianity-as-it-may-become." [98]

The implication is that present-day organized Christianity cannot

[92] Davies, *op. cit.,* p. 135.　　　　[93] Rev. 11:15.
[94] Phil. 2:10–11; cf. Rom. 14:11.
[95] Berdyaev, *Towards a New Epoch,* p. 40.　　　　[96] *Ibid.,* p. 49.
[97] Horton, *op. cit.,* p. 63.　　　　[98] *Ibid.,* p. 9.

save civilization. If this is correct, what are the sources of its weakness? Its weakness is evidently not due to a lack of numbers, or of financial support, or of educated leadership. Neither does it result from the divisions within the Christian movement, as unfortunate as some of them may be. Any weaknesses along these lines may be symptoms of ill health, but the disease goes deeper. Our churches need more members, but far more important they need better members. They need more adequate financial support, but they need far more increasing numbers of members who will recognize that they belong to God, that they are his stewards. They may need a better trained leadership, but even more they need a more consecrated and devoted leadership. Protestantism in general needs fewer divisions, but it is in more desperate need of more Christian individuals and groups who have deep convictions and a sense of divine mission. What we are bothered with is what Trueblood calls a sort of vague or mild religiosity. "We are equally shocked at hearing the faith rejected and at seeing it practiced." [99] Such a mild sort of religion cannot support a sagging civilization and "cannot long maintain even itself." [100]

Christianity to perform adequately its functions in the life of the individual and in the world cannot be one of many compartments of life. When life is so compartmentalized, Christianity and Christian principles are usually pushed to the circumference of life. But it is the nature of individuals and civilizations to seek for integration. Supreme value will be attached to something or to some things. That supreme value or those supreme values will become the religion of the individual or civilization.

Organized Christianity, in the main, has become so secularized that it has adjusted itself to the compartmental idea. It "is degenerating because it has been relegated to a corner of the human soul and has ceased to be a totalitarian attitude towards life, as, of course, it should be." [101] Notice the expression "a totalitarian attitude towards life." The world does not need an ecclesiastical totalitarianism, which would be just as bad as a political totalitarianism. What is needed is a spiritual totalitarianism. The Christian religion

[99] *Foundations for Reconstruction*, p. 38. [100] *Ibid.*, p. 39.
[101] Berdyaev, *Towards a New Epoch*, p. 106.

needs to become the total, around which every other phase of life is integrated. "If religion is only a part of life, then religion has become optional. Only a religion which is a way of living in every sphere either deserves to or can hope to survive." [102] It begins to appear that only a civilization with such a vital totalitarian religion at the center will be able to meet the challenge of communism as a competing way of life, which is thoroughly integrated around a false religious center.

What are some of the steps that organized Christianity must take, if it is to become the pulsating center of life for individuals and civilizations? The first step is genuine repentance within the Christian movement. The Christian movement itself is involved in the sin of the world. Its own inner dislocation is a major factor in the contemporary crisis. It is no time for a holier-than-thou attitude by any Christian group. We have all sinned and come short of the glory of God. There is none righteous, no, not one. With few exceptions we as individuals and groups have come to terms with the world. We have accepted the standards and values of the world. Our churches use the standards of the world to measure their success or failure. Let us frankly admit in sackcloth and ashes that "the de-Christianisation characteristic of the modern age is, to a large extent, the product of the infidelity of the Christians to their own faith." [103]

There is also needed a return to and a strengthening of institutional religion. Trueblood in several places makes this emphasis. He says that "our civilization cannot be rebuilt unless institutional religion is revived and loyally supported." [104] He further adds: "The sober fact is that the Christian churches and the Hebrew synagogues are the only organizations in our civilization whose *primary* purpose is to keep alive the moral and spiritual principles without which a decent world is impossible." [105] The renewal that the world needs is a renewal within the lives of individual Christians, but also within the existing organized forms of Christianity.

The Christian church has found renewal in the past by returning

[102] MacIntyre, *Marxism: An Interpretation*, p. 9.
[103] Brunner, *Christianity and Civilisation*, First Part, p. 105.
[104] *Foundations for Reconstruction*, p. 43.   [105] *Ibid.*, p. 50.

to the religion of Jesus, by catching again the spirit of his life, and by understanding something of the simplicity and depth of the principles that he taught.

When the Christian religion is unable to return to Jesus in order to go forward with the spirit of Jesus it will be a sure sign that Christianity has reached decrepitude and that its dissolution is imminent. To go back to the point in the road where you took the wrong turning . . . is neither reactionary nor unnecessary if you would reach your destination.[106]

If we catch again the spirit of the life and teachings of Jesus, we shall recapture our faith in God and in his purposes in the world. There will also be a renewal of Christian courage and the spirit of martyrdom that has characterized Christianity in its times of greatest triumph. Human nature seems to demand that the individual tie his life to some cause for which he is willing to die. One reason for the rise and popularity of some of the contemporary "isms" has been the loss of the spirit of martyrdom in the Christian movement and its recapture by those movements. In recent years "Christians have shown themselves to be less capable of sacrifice than revolutionaries, particularly the Russian revolutionaries of the nineteenth century." [107]

A return to the spirit and teachings of Jesus will also lead to a reinterpretation of Christian individualism. Most of the movements that challenge our way of life have arisen, to a considerable degree, as a reaction to the one-sided emphasis by our Western democracies on the value and rights of the individual. There are at least two ways in which we need to rethink our position. First, the emphasis has been too exclusively upon the rights of the individual and not enough upon his responsibilities. Second, the emphasis has been too largely upon one's own rights rather than upon the rights of others. In other words modern individualism has been too self-centered.

It was Jesus who taught that a man finds life, real life or life on a higher level, by losing his life.[108] It was Paul who said that we are free in Christ but that we are to use our liberty as an occasion to serve not the flesh, but one another.[109] The freedom the Christian has is to be voluntarily surrendered for the sake of others. This is

---

[106] Major, *op. cit.*, p. 73.
[108] Matt. 16:25.
[107] Berdyaev, *Towards a New Epoch*, p. 32.
[109] Gal. 5:13.

the spirit of self-denial and self-sacrifice symbolized by the cross.

If organized Christianity is to be an effective instrument in the saving of civilization it must maintain a proper balance between its divine and human natures. It must recognize that "the Church always stands in a double relationship to history, and it neglects either aspect of its existence at its peril." [110] As a human institution the church stands within history; as a divine institution it transcends history. In its institutional life it is largely human; in its message and mission it is divine.

Finally, let us not forget that times of crisis have frequently been times when God gave a new revelation of himself and of his power. He, who is the same yesterday, today, and forevermore, is the sovereign God of the universe. He may seem to lose some battles, but he always wins the war. He will have the last word. He is never in a hurry, but he is always on time. But let us also remember that times of crisis should challenge us as Christians to demonstrate again the courage and the spirit that have characterized the followers of Christ in the glorious, creative periods of the Christian movement.

[110] Charles D. Kean, *Christianity and the Cultural Crisis* (New York, Association Press, 1944), p. 193.

XII

CHRISTIANITY AND
WORLD TRANSFORMATION

SOME MAJOR world issues have been considered in preceding chapters. The areas covered have revealed that the world falls far short of the Christian ideal. It also has been indicated that most world issues are basically moral and spiritual. This means that if Christianity does not have an answer for the major problems of the world, they will not be answered adequately.

Christians and Christian groups, facing the conditions in the world and the challenge of the world, should search for the strategies and methods that can be used to lift that world toward the Christian ideal. There are some Christians, however, who deny that the Christian church has a mission to the world. They contend that the church should minister exclusively to individuals. For them the church is "a ship carrying . . . elect passengers to the ports of Zion." [1] This chapter and this book are not written for such Christians, unless they still retain an open mind. The conviction back of this book is that the people of God are "burdened with a God-given responsibility before and for" the peoples of the world. [2] "To be Christian is to share God's concern, through faith and grace, for the whole man and for the whole world. Thus world-transformation is

[1] Leslie Stannard Hunter, *Church Strategy in a Changing World* (London, Hodder & Stoughton, 1950), p. 68.
[2] G. Ernest Wright, *The Biblical Doctrine of Man in Society*, p. 125.

part and parcel, irremovably, of the Christian Gospel, not as a secondary or separate part of it, but intrinsically and organically." [3]

The Church's Message

An important phase of the Christian strategy for the world is the church's proclamation of the Christian message to the world. There are some important elements in that message that will not be discussed in this section. Consideration will be given exclusively to three or four phases of the church's message and mission that are most relevant to a study of world issues.

1. *Concerning the relevance of the Bible.* The message the church proclaims to the world comes primarily from the Bible. The Christians who have turned the world upside down have been men and women with a vision in their souls, the resurrected Christ in their hearts, and the Bible in their hands.

Can this Bible make any constructive contribution to the reconstruction of our world? There are many people who contend that it is an antiquated book, that its message is not and cannot be applicable to the complex social, economic, and political problems of the modern social order. They imply that the Bible is two thousand years behind the times. A careful examination of the Bible will reveal, however, that it contains principles that may be two thousand years ahead of our time. It has maintained an eternally fresh relevance to the problems of every age. It "is not merely relevant to our age, but urgently relevant." [4] The Christ of the Bible, to use the title of one of Walter Horton's books, is *Our Eternal Contemporary.* We do not mean by the preceding that the Bible is a rule book in which one can find a chapter-and-verse answer to every question or a solution for every personal problem or for every social issue. Neither do we mean that all the Bible is equally relevant. There are great sections, especially in the Old Testament, that can make no particular contribution to the solution of the problems of our day. Many of the specific instructions even in the New Testament, especially in Paul's epistles which were addressed to particular

[3] Ferré, *Christianity and Society,* p. 142.
[4] H. H. Rowley, *The Relevance of the Bible* (New York, Macmillan, 1944), p. vii.

churches with certain distinctive problems, are not relevant to the contemporary period. However, the basic principles of the New Testament, even of the least relevant sections of Paul's epistles, are just as relevant today as when they were spoken or written. The same could be said for the fundamental moral law of the Old Testament.

The relevance of these principles and of the moral law evolves from the nature and character of the God revealed in the Bible. The Bible not only reveals the nature and character of God; it also discloses his will and purpose for man. That will has not fundamentally changed. Any insight that we receive from the Bible concerning the character of God, the nature of the universe, and the demands of God upon man and his society is relevant to a study of world issues and to the resolving of the conflicts of the world.

Some people contend that the Bible is irrelevant for at least the broader social relations of life because it is too idealistic. They may agree that some of the ideals might be applied, to a limited degree, to the strictly personal relations of life; but they contend that it is "idle twaddle" to talk about applying them to the relations of races, classes, and nations.

Does the perfectionism of the basic principles of the Bible make them irrelevant for our day and our society? We certainly should recognize the perfect nature of those ideals and our inability to attain them. For us as individuals and for our world they represent what Reinhold Niebuhr calls an "impossible possibility." [5]

However, instead of the perfectionism of the principles of the Bible making them irrelevant, their perfection really adds to their relevance. The ethical ideals of the Christian religion, derived from the Bible, are "eternally transcendent." As such they stand above and beyond history, never fully realized in the historic process, but abidingly relevant to history. They constantly judge and challenge our individual lives and our social order. The transcendence of Christianity provides a perspective from which the policies of the *status quo* and the programs of change are kept under criticism. [6]

The divine-human nature of the Bible and the transcendent-immanent nature of the God revealed in the Bible also tend to make

---

[5] *An Interpretation of Christian Ethics* (New York, Harper, 1935), p. 113.
[6] Bennett, *Christian Ethics and Social Policy*, p. 60.

the Bible relevant to every age. Through the Bible the voice of the eternal God, who is the same yesterday, today, and forevermore, speaks with authority to the soul of man. The voice speaking through the Bible "finds man, searches him," and challenges him with a message that contains a moral imperative.[7] It speaks to man with an absolute claim, with a command that demands his attention. The balancing of the human and the divine in the Bible is comparable to the blending of these two elements in the life of Christ. He was the God-man, fully human while being fully divine. Just as this dual, rather paradoxical nature of Jesus made him *Our Eternal Contemporary*, so the balancing of the human and divine elements in the Bible has contributed to its abiding relevance and its continuing challenge to our world.

The men who wrote the Bible as they were led of the Lord "speak, not *of* our age but *to* it, because the Word of God is in their mouth."[8] What Scott says about the prophets could be said concerning the other spokesmen for God in the Bible. His statement is:

> The remarkable contemporaneity of these ancient spokesmen of religion and the perennial freshness of their message, spring from their power to penetrate past the maze of appearances to underlying human and religious facts stated in universal terms, but with notable concreteness.[9]

Another thing that gives the Bible its abiding relevance is the fact that human nature and hence human problems remain basically the same from age to age. If the Bible was relevant for the day in which it was written, it is relevant for our day. It contains the message needed by men of every age. It provides for them the guidance and the inner spiritual resources to meet the challenge of their world.

2. *Concerning the Christian ideal for the world.* The over-all Christian ideal for the world is that it might become fully Christian. It is recognized that this is an ideal of perfection. However, Jesus himself taught his disciples to pray

[7] W. T. Conner, *Revelation and God* (Nashville, Broadman Press, 1936), p. 95.
[8] R. B. Y. Scott, *The Relevance of the Prophets* (New York, Macmillan, 1944), p. 204.
[9] *Ibid.*, p. 205.

Thy kingdom come,
Thy will be done,
On earth as it is in heaven.[10]

If God's will were done on earth as it is in heaven we would have a perfect world. The following statement by A. D. Lindsay, concerning individual perfection, can be applied to the perfection of society: "It demands an attitude towards a perpetual quest, always something more to do and something more to find out."[11] But at least "we can set our faces in the direction of it. This is the only way in which we can fulfil the command to attain an end which is infinite."[12]

This setting of the face toward perfection is just as essential for society as it is for the individual. The supreme test, individually and socially, is not whether or not perfection has been attained, but the direction we are moving in regard to the ideals of perfection. Are we and is our society moving toward God's ideals for us and our world? It is the church's business to keep those ideals constantly before us and the world. It is not the church's business, however, to dictate the methods by which those ideals are to become a reality in society.

Without attempting to define what is meant by "socialized medicine," and the expression needs to be defined, let us use it to illustrate the extent of the church's responsibility for and its possible contributions to social change. What stand should the church take regarding socialized medicine? The position here taken is that organized Christianity not only has a right but an obligation to set out the general ideals or goals, at least as related to human and moral values, for medical science as well as every other area of life. One such goal would be that all that medical science has discovered, which will relieve human suffering and preserve and prolong human life, should in some way be available to all of the people. There is something wrong if people suffer and die simply because they do not have the financial resources to pay for the necessary medical service and skill.

[10] Matt. 6:10.
[11] A. D. Lindsay, *The Two Moralities: Our Duty to God and to Society* (London, Eyre and Spottiswoode, 1940), p. 61.
[12] *Ibid.*, p. 59.

On the other hand, it is not the church's business to prescribe or dictate the methods to be used to achieve this goal. The matter of methodology should be left to the members of the medical profession, the social scientists, and the practical politicians. The church can hope that they will be Christians, will be motivated by a genuine love for God and their fellow man, and will so cooperate with one another that they will work out a program that will approximate the Christian ideal.

The church does have the responsibility to apply the test of the Christian ethic to the methods that are used or suggested to meet the desired goal. One such test will be what the proposed method or methods will do to people. For example, in regard to medical service, it is not simply a matter of providing adequate medical care for people; there is also the important matter of the effect of the program and the methods used to achieve it upon the character of the people. For example, can and will they retain their self-respect, or will they be pauperized and develop an unhealthy dependence on the state and on society in general? Some may complain that such a testing of methods will make it impossible to attain the desired goal. Even if this is true it does not necessarily invalidate the goal or the testing of the methods. It merely emphasizes the difficulty of achieving worthy Christian goals in a non-Christian world. The attainment of such goals must be a gradual process.

To summarize: it is the church's business to maintain a consistent tension toward the Christian goal for society and a constant scrutiny of the methods used to move in the direction of the goal.

3. *Concerning the kingdom of God.* The kingdom fills an important place in the transforming message of the church to the world. It "is the unifying theme of the Bible, is still the motivating force of the living Church." [13] There is a sense in which the church is merely an instrument or a means to promote the kingdom of God. "It is as the emissary of that Kingdom that the Church makes bold to speak." [14]

[13] John Bright, *The Kingdom of God* (New York, Abingdon Press, 1953), p. 244. This is one of the most thorough recent studies of the kingdom. It traces the developing concept beginning with the Old Testament.

[14] *Ibid.*, p. 250.

The idea of the kingdom was central in the teachings of Jesus. Marshall says, "*All the ethical teaching of Jesus is simply an exposition of the ethics of the Kingdom of God, of the way in which men inevitably behave when they actually come under the rule of God.*" [15] Many problems have arisen regarding the correct interpretation of the teachings of Jesus concerning the kingdom. Most of these problems have grown out of efforts to make everything he taught fit into one particular pattern or mold. It is Marshall who concludes that Jesus "thought and spoke of the Kingdom of God in so many different ways that to harmonise them and present them systematically is out of the question." [16] That which gave unity to all Jesus taught about the kingdom was the fact that for him it was an eternal and spiritual kingdom. This should be kept central in the church's message concerning the kingdom. As an eternal and spiritual kingdom it can be identified with the reign or sovereignty of God. If we grasp this clearly, then we can understand how the kingdom can be and is, as Jesus taught, both inner and outer, a present reality and a future hope, ethical and apocalyptic, given by God and yet promoted by man.

The church's message to the world is that this eternal, spiritual kingdom can never be fully contained or expressed in any human organization or institution. This means that the kingdom should never be equated with the *status quo* or with any program to change the *status quo*. It can never be completely realized within history, unless we include eternity within history, and yet it is the most dynamic force in the historic process. In contrast to the Christian view, the Marxist believes that the kindgom or ideal order, which he identifies with the classless society, can and will be fully realized within history. While the Christian believes that the fulfillment of the kingdom "is bound to eternity and no imagination can reach the eternal," yet he also believes that "fragmentary anticipations" of the kingdom are possible in the here-and-now.[17]

At least in its "fragmentary anticipation" the kingdom of God is coming any time, anywhere—within the individual or in society— when any phase of life is being brought more fully under the rule

[15] L. H. Marshall, *The Challenge of New Testament Ethics* (London, Macmillan, 1946), p. 31.
[16] *Ibid.*, p. 25.
[17] Tillich, *Love, Power, and Justice*, p. 124.

of God. This means that it can be in constant process, without ever being fully realized. For the kingdom to come in the fullest sense in our lives or in our world would mean perfection. It would mean that God's reign or rule was complete or absolute.

As a concept of perfection the kingdom stands in constant judgment over against our lives and the world in which we live. The first message of the kingdom, as preached by John the Baptist and by Jesus, was: "Repent, for the kingdom of heaven is at hand." [18] This is the continuing message of the church. The kingdom means judgment; not exclusively judgment upon individuals who have not accepted the reign of God, but also upon nations and civilizations that have refused to acknowledge the sovereignty of God.

The kingdom the church proclaims, however, is not merely a kingdom of judgment, but also of triumph and hope. At least men can know that the kingdom will ultimately triumph. This is true because it is the kingdom of *God*. He is the sovereign God of the universe. He cannot be defeated in his ultimate purposes for the world. Ferré goes so far as to say that although men might destroy civilization, yet such would not be a real defeat for God. He then adds: "Heaven and earth may perish, but not the eternal Word of God. That stands as sure as God, and nothing can be surer." [19]

There is another sense in which the kingdom the church proclaims is a kingdom of hope. Just as was true of Israel's great prophetic souls, the church does not stop with a message of judgment. It, as was true of them, also proclaims a message of hope. That hope is in turning from sin and to God in humble repentance. God will meet the sinner, individual or nation, more than halfway. For the nation it may mean only a remnant will be saved, but that remnant may later return and rebuild the culture or civilization upon which the judgment of God has come.

The church should seek to promote the kingdom of God among men by praying for that kingdom, by cultivating true Christian fellowship within the Christian community, and by inspiring its members to practice the Christian spirit in every area of their lives. It should lead them to see that the word "Christian" should precede and define every role that the child of God plays or fulfills in his life. He may be a husband and a father, but he is a Christian hus-

[18] Matt. 3:2; 4:17.   [19] Ferré, *op. cit.*, p. 148.

band and father. He may be an employer or an employee, but he is a Christian employer or employee. He may be a member of a civic club, a fraternal order, or a labor union, but he is a Christian member. He may be a farmer, doctor, lawyer, merchant, banker, but he is first of all a Christian. He may be a white man, a yellow man, or a black man, but he is a Christian man. So it should be with every conceivable role or relation of the Christian's life. As we increasingly become Christian along these and other lines, God's reign or kingdom is being extended.

Another way of emphasizing somewhat the same thing is to say that the Christian approach to history and the world is God-centered. God is the point of reference for the Christian in every phase of his life. This is another way Christianity differs from Marxism, which is man-centered. The Christian believes that the sovereign God of the universe is active in the affairs of the nations of the world and in every realm of the life of those nations. If God is the same yesterday, today, and forevermore—and he is—then a casual reading of the Bible will reveal that he is not only active within history, "the God of History," [20] but that he is also the ultimate determiner of history.

This means that the God whose message the church proclaims is not interested merely in one little segment of life. His rule or reign cannot be restricted to one phase of life, which we might label "spiritual." He is concerned with what goes on in the laboratory, in the classroom, in the industrial plant, in the store or the bank, on the farm, in the legislative hall, in the council of nations, in the home, everywhere. Men working in cooperation with him in every one of these areas can make some contribution to the promotion of his kingdom. We can be sure, at the same time, that he is active on the side of righteousness, justice, and love; that he is doing more to give us his kingdom than all our combined efforts can do to promote that kingdom.

4. *Concerning love.* The church's message to the world is that love "is not a virtue among other virtues to which men can aspire. It is that total attitude which is brought about by exposure to the love of God as it is expressed in Christ's self-sacrifice." [21] It was John

[20] Butterfield, *Christianity and History*, p. 1.

[21] C. H. Dodd, *Gospel and Law: The Relation of Faith and Ethics in Early Christianity* (New York, Columbia University Press, 1951), p. 44.

who said: "By this we know love, that he laid down his life for us; and we ought to lay down our lives for the brethren." [22] Again he says, "We love, because he first loved us." [23] Notice it does not say "we love him" but rather love characterizes our lives. God is love, he has loved us. If he lives within us, and he does if we are children of his, then his love is within us and will find expression through us.

What kind of love is it that the church proclaims? The distinctive element or quality [24] in the love proclaimed by the church is expressed by the little Greek word *agape*. It is so different from the ordinary idea of love that some New Testament scholars do not believe it should have been translated. C. H. Dodd, for example, says it "is strictly untranslatable." He defines it as "energetic and beneficent good will which stops at nothing to secure the good of the beloved object. It is not primarily an emotion or an affection; it is primarily an active determination of the will." [25]

Such love gives itself unselfishly to the object loved. "God so loved the world that he gave his only Son . . ." [26] "Christ loved the church and gave himself up for her." [27] "Greater love has no man than this, that a man lay down his life for his friends." [28]

Love (*agape*) is the fulfillment of the law.[29] If one loved God supremely and his neighbor as himself, he would meet every requirement of the moral law. He would fill to overflowing that law. Love would lead him to fulfill the deeper law. "The law provides a framework which love fills up; is the dry bones into which love breathes life." [30]

This divine type of love or *agape* knows no limits. It reaches out and down even to one's enemies. God loved us while we were yet enemies of his. He causes his sun to shine upon the evil and the good and his rain to fall upon the just and the unjust. We prove our kinship to him by loving our enemies and praying for them that persecute us.[31]

[22] 1 John 3:16. [23] *Ibid.*, 4:19.

[24] Paul Tillich (*op. cit.*, pp. 5, 30–33) says *epithymia, eros, philia,* and *agape* do not represent different types of love but different qualities of love. *Agape* is the depth of love. "In *agape* ultimate reality manifests itself and transforms life and love. *Agape* is love cutting into love, just as revelation is reason cutting into reason and the Word of God is the Word cutting into all words" (p. 33).

[25] *Op. cit.*, p. 42. [26] John 3:16. [27] Eph. 5:25.

[28] John 15:13. [29] Matt. 22:34–40. [30] Lindsay, *op. cit.*, p. 97.

[31] Matt. 5:43–48.

The application of *agape* to social relations and problems is our best hope for a solution of those problems. There must be "energetic and beneficent good will" on the behalf of others; there must be an unselfish giving of ourselves for others if we are to relieve the tensions and distresses of our world. Only in this way can the atmosphere be created which will be favorable to a resolving of the conflicts between competing groups and classes. "Only an element of concern for the other person *for his own sake* creates community among men," [32] and there can be no solution for the basic problems of our society without such a spirit of community.

Some people consider it fantastic to believe that *agape* can and will be applied in and to the world and its problems. They contend that it is unrealistic to think that *agape* can ever be a reality in the world. The best we can hope for, so they argue, is justice or what some term relative love. What if love could not find full or perfect expression in the world: would it necessarily follow that we should not seek to apply the spirit of love to the problems of the world? We do not forsake our other ideals, some of which we frankly admit can never be fully attained in this world. At least, the divine *agape* can be used to judge the present attainments of the world and the direction in which the world is moving.

Furthermore, in an attempt to apply the spirit of love to the problems of our world, we have an inner resource in man that should give us at least some encouragement. Ferré suggests that love is at the center of human nature. God created man "in love and for love." God made man for fellowship, and Ferré says that that fellowship is drawn into being "by the lure of God's love from the depths of man's nature below and from the heights of God's revelation above." He further adds: "No life at any time, or in any stage of its being, is without this craving for love or without some capacity to give it." He then says, "In every person some Agape is found, some outgoing concern; and all such love is of God, for there is no other Source for it." [33]

A Christian can know that he is giving some expression to God's *agape*, although admittedly imperfect, when he sees his fellow man as God sees him,[34] when he has a "disinterested love for his neigh-

---

[32] Paul Ramsey, *Basic Christian Ethics* (New York, Scribner's, 1950), p. 238.
[33] *Op. cit.*, p. 127.   [34] Tillich, *op. cit.*, p. 117.

bor" (Ramsey), "an outgoing concern" for others (Ferré), or an "energetic and beneficent good will" on the behalf of others (Dodd).

5. *Concerning the cross.* This outline of the message of the church to the world would not be complete without a brief statement concerning the centrality of the cross. It was central in the life and in the teachings of Jesus. It should be central in Christian theology and in Christian ethics. It should be an integral phase of the Christian strategy for world transformation.

The world has failed to understand the meaning and the significance of the cross. The church has shrunk from it and misinterpreted it.

We enshrine it in the stained-glass window and in doctrine; we bow before it in prayer. But we want no part of it. We are possessed of the notion that the Cross is for Christ, a once-and-for-all thing of the past tense with little relation to the destiny of the militant and victorious church.[35]

The cross, however, cannot be pushed to one side. It cannot be assigned to the past. It expresses the unifying law of God's entire universe. Jesus states it as follows: "Unless a grain of wheat falls into the earth and dies, it remains alone; but if it dies, it bears much fruit." [36] The first or basic law of life is not self-preservation but self-denial or self-sacrifice. Jesus applied this law to human relations and to God's plan for the redemption of man.[37]

The cross and what it symbolizes are necessary for man and his society. "All men need suffering, some measure of suffering, to bring them to the maturity they are capable of reaching." [38] Ferré suggests "that without suffering there can be no progress in terms that have permanent meaning." [39] We do not mean, however, to identify suffering and the cross. The cross involves suffering, but suffering as such does not exhaust the meaning of the cross. Bonhoeffer says that the cross "is not suffering *per se* but suffering-and-rejection, and not rejection for any cause of conviction of our own, but rejection for the sake of Christ." [40]

[35] Bright, *op. cit.,* p. 269.   [36] John 12:24.
[37] *Ibid.,* 12:25, 32–33.   [38] Sheed, *Communism and Man,* p. 159.
[39] *Op. cit.,* p. 144.
[40] Dietrich Bonhoeffer, *The Cost of Discipleship* (New York, Macmillan, 1948), p. 72.

A cross is something on which one is crucified. But can any crucifixion be identified with the cross? No, it must involve a voluntary sacrificing of self. Could there be even a voluntary sacrificing of self that would not express the deeper meaning of the cross? Yes, it must be a voluntary crucifying or sacrificing of self for redemptive purposes. Love (*agape*) must be the motive,[41] the cross the expression of that love, and the revelation of God's love and redemptive purpose for man the ultimate result.

Does the cross have any relevance for modern world issues? Can the ethic of the cross be applied to family problems, to racial tensions, to economic and political conflicts? The answer to these questions is definitely Yes. The church's message to the world is that there is no final solution for the problems of human relations outside the ethic of the cross. The only assurance of the use of Christian methods to achieve desirable Christian ends is the application of the spirit of the cross. Really, the cross is *the* Christian method of social change.

What is meant by the statement that the cross is the Christian method of social change? Let us reexamine the meaning of the cross and then apply this meaning to world transformation. The cross is a symbol of self-denying, suffering, redemptive love. It is the language of *agape*. It means the giving of one's self in the interest or on the behalf of others. If this spirit of self-denial or of cross-bearing was applied to human relations it would mean that the strong would serve the weak, the privileged would give up, if need be, some of their privileges for the sake of the underprivileged. Furthermore, this spirit would mean that basic social changes would be initiated and promoted by those who could bring about those changes peacefully. This, which is the way of the cross in social relations, is the Christian method for the reconstruction of the social order. Furthermore, "the cross is the only power in the world which proves that suffering love can avenge and vanquish evil." [42] Thus the cross is an integral and vital phase of the church's message to the world and to every institution, group, and class of the world.

[41] 1 Cor. 13:3.   [42] Bonhoeffer, *op. cit.*, p. 125.

Christian Methods

We shall never achieve a perfect social order in this world, but we should move as far and as rapidly as possible toward the Christian ideal for the world. We shall consider in this section some of the methods that have been, are being, and may be used by Christians in their effort to lift the world toward the Christian goal or ideal.

1. *Evangelization.* The beginning place for a consideration of distinctly Christian methods of world transformation or reconstruction is evangelism. It is or should be central in the church's total program for individuals and for society. It was Walter Rauschenbusch who said that "spiritual regeneration is the most important fact in any life history." [43] While recognizing the supreme importance of the conversion experience to the individual, our primary interest in this study has been with world issues, and hence we are concerned with the social consequences of the conversion experience. It was Rauschenbusch again who said, "It has always been recognized that the creation of regenerate personalities, pledged to righteousness, is one of the most important services which the Church can render to social progress." [44]

Evangelism fills an important place in any constructive Christian world strategy. If the will of God is to be done in social, economic, and political life; and if the Christian spirit and philosophy of life are to influence these and other areas; then the inner motives, purposes, and attitudes of people must be Christianized. Such an inner transformation comes to boys and girls, men and women as they become new creations in Christ. It is the task of evangelism to bring people into this vital life-changing union with God through faith in Christ. There is no real hope for Christian relations on any level, from the smallest social unit which is the family to the largest which is the family of nations, apart from the winning of men and women to Christ and to his way and will in life. This is not a superficial experience that touches only the circumference of life. It touches and changes the deepest recesses of life. Through it men

[43] *Christianizing the Social Order* (New York, Macmillan, 1912), p. 104.
[44] *Christianity and the Social Crisis,* p. 354.

are not only saved from the final penalty of sin but also from the present enslavement of sin. Furthermore, this experience carries with it a positive purpose beyond the experience itself. We are not only saved from something but also for and to something. We are brought into fellowship with God, and in cooperation with him we are to seek to do his will and work in the world.

Oldham, after stating that the conversion of individuals is not all, and after implying that the contribution of the conversion experience to social reconstruction will be determined by the content and the quality of the new life to which the convert commits himself, sums up the matter as follows:

None the less it remains true that repentance and conversion are the starting point of the Christian life. To be a Christian is to undergo a complete change of mind. The Christian purpose in the social and political spheres can be achieved only by those who have been converted to the Christian understanding of life. While this conversion of heart and mind is only the beginning, it is the indispensable beginning. In proportion as the church is in earnest about its responsibilities in social and political life it must address itself with renewed energy to the task of evangelism. The social order can be improved only by persons whose lives have found a new orientation. To ignore this fact in thought, in policy or in practice is to evade the realities of life and to escape into a dream world of fanciful imaginations and empty hopes.[45]

The preceding is not a plea for a superficial, high-pressure type of evangelism which emphasizes immediate numerical results. The evangelistic program that is needed must "be a long-term policy which will not be served or hastened just by playing the old records with stronger needles and more amplifiers, or by tip-and-run commando raids."[46] We need an evangelism that emphasizes quality of church membership more than quantity of converts, that combines a fervent evangelistic spirit with a sound educational approach, and that challenges the new converts to accept and to apply to every area of their lives the highest Christian ethical standards. The first step in such a program of evangelism is "the inward conversion of the church itself to the gospel."[47]

[45] Visser 't Hooft and Oldham, *The Church and Its Function in Society*, p. 156.

[46] Hunter, *op. cit.*, p. 32.

[47] Hugh T. Kerr, *Positive Protestantism* (Philadelphia, Westminster Press, 1950), p. 108.

If Christian evangelism is to contribute what it should to the solution of the world's problems, all classes of society must be reached by the Christian message. This means that Christian churches must guard against social stratification within their ranks. It may be that it is inevitable that there will be class churches—churches for millhands and for millowners,[48] for the privileged and underprivileged [49] —but it will be unfortunate if any social group is neglected. The main danger is that the better established church groups will move away from the masses. The churches must reach these toiling masses if they are to meet most effectively the challenge of the issues of today's world. It is also important that the churches reach with the good news of the gospel the intelligentsia. The movements that change the face of the world come up from the masses; the intelligentsia usually provide the necessary leadership for those masses.

If the peoples of the different classes are reached with the gospel message, Christian laymen must recognize their responsibility for the evangelization of the world. "Evangelism is not an optional or voluntary occupation in which a few interested persons engage. It is a mandate for all laid down by Christ himself." [50] Ministers and missionaries alone cannot do the job. Many of those who need to be reached never come to a church. If they are won, it will have to be by someone with whom they rub elbows in the shop or store, at the club or fraternal order, on the street or bus. We cannot all go with the gospel to the uttermost parts of the world, "but we are to spread the gospel by word and act wherever we are." [51]

2. *Education.* Possibly a brief statement should be made concerning the relation of evangelism and education in the over-all Christian strategy. They belong together. The soundest evangelism is built upon an educational foundation. The quality of the conversion experience will be determined, to some degree, by the conception of the Christian life the individual had previous to his conversion experience. This conception, in turn, is largely the product of the individual's total educational experience in the home, the church, and the community.

There can be no question about the need for a persistent, constructive program of Christian education following conversion.

[48] See Pope, *Millhands and Preachers.*
[49] See H. Richard Niebuhr, *The Social Sources of Denominationalism.*
[50] Kerr, *op. cit.*, p. 117. [51] *Ibid.*, p. 125.

Some who major on the evangelistic method leave the impression that the winning of individuals to Christ will solve inevitably all of their problems and all the problems of the world. Such an attitude is most unfortunate and is contrary to human experience. "Regeneration merely creates the will to do the right; it does not define for a man what is right." [52] The definition of the right is one purpose of the educational program of the church.

The neglect of education has been one of the chief mistakes Christian forces have made in their struggle with certain social and moral problems. They have tended to depend too largely on legislation. Education may seem to be a slow and a never ending process, but it is a very necessary phase of any permanently effective Christian program of world transformation.

In the program of social and moral education the churches should welcome the cooperation of the public schools and of all other formal and informal educational agencies in the community. The building of a Christian world order is a big task, and it will require the cooperation of all men and women of good-will.

The churches in their own program of education should use every organization and technique that is available. They should seek to improve what is done in and through the established agencies such as the Sunday school, and the youth, women's, and men's groups. Church-related schools and colleges, that include or should include the Christian interpretation of life as an integral part of the total program of the school, are important factors in the church's educational program. There also are church and denominational periodicals of various kinds, radio and television programs, and many other instruments, both old and established and new and experimental, that may and should be used.

Without any attempt to give the specific details of the educational program of the churches, it should be said that the effectiveness of Christian education as a phase of the Christian strategy for the world will be determined by what it does for those it reaches. What it does for them will be determined, to a considerable degree, by the total content of the educational program. This total content includes more than curriculum materials, although those are very important. In the final analysis, the content of the program will be

[52] Rauschenbusch, *Christianity and the Social Crisis,* p. 354.

determined as much by the resourcefulness of and the methods used by teachers and leaders as by the curriculum materials. This means that it is of major importance that our churches do a better job of discovering, enlisting, and training teachers and workers.

Churches need to teach more effectively the basic doctrines and principles of the Christian way of life. These great doctrines of our faith—doctrines concerning God, Christ, the Bible, man, sin, salvation, and the world program of the Christian movement—need to become a living, pulsating reality in the lives of those reached by the church. If this happens it will give depth and balance to life. It will give strength and courage for the task of world transformation. The intelligent Christian, however, must not only be acquainted with the Bible and its theological ideas and its moral ideals; he must also be acquainted with the world and its problems. Without some knowledge of general social and moral conditions, he cannot relate effectively Christian teachings to world issues.

The impartation of knowledge, however, does not complete the Christian educational process. Those reached by that program must not only be informed, but inspired by an overpowering spiritual drive within to do what they can to carry the Christian spirit into every area of the life of the world. For education to be an effective instrument for world transformation, it must lead to action.

It is also the Christian church's responsibility to help those who have been inspired by its message to understand the methods or strategies that can be used to implement Christian ideals. This not only involves the broader social strategies, but also the more detailed methods that will help them to come to grips with the immediate problems they face in the world. It means that they must participate actively in the affairs of the community and the world, but always participate as Christians. They should have an abiding sense of Christian stewardship and of divine partnership.

Christian education in the deepest sense takes place in a God-conscious atmosphere. The principles taught represent the "Thus sayeth the Lord." To have this God-conscious atmosphere the Spirit of the Lord must be present to inform, to convict, and to inspire. If he has breathed on the teacher and the pupils, there will be a sense of alertness, aliveness, and anticipation that otherwise will be lacking.

Some may contend that this gets over into the area of worship, and hence it does not belong in the field of Christian education. But only an educational program that is permeated by a spirit of genuine worship will give the warmth and motivation that is needed if men and women are to undertake seriously the challenging task of Christianizing all their relations and the world in which they live. It is worship that gives one a vision of God, and it is that vision that impels one to go out into the world to do his best to make the revelation he has received from God a living reality among men. The deeper one goes with God, the stronger will be his urge to lead the world to conform to the vision he has received from God. On the other hand, as one participates actively in the life of the world he will have a deepened sense of need for fellowship with God. He finds that if his service to the world is to be most effective there must be a constant interplay of worship and service. Service without worship will soon sap his spiritual resources and exhaust his creative energies.

3. *Demonstration.* Another important phase of the Christian method or strategy for world transformation is a genuine demonstration by Christians of what it really means to follow Christ. H. R. L. Sheppard once said, "If doubt has slain its thousands, the unsatisfactory lives of professing Christians have slain their tens of thousands." [53] For many of them their religion is at the circumference rather than at the center of their lives. The contemporary Christian movement cannot lift the world very far toward the Christian ideal for the world until there are more Christians who take seriously their responsibility to live the Christian life in the home, on the farm, at the shop, in the office, in the legislative hall, on the streets, everywhere. Just as Jesus was the incarnate Son of God, so Christians should seek, as best they can, to be incarnations of the living Christ.

The Christian should not only seek personally to be a living demonstration of Christian truth, he also should do what he can to lead every group to which he belongs to be permeated by the Christian spirit. This should be true not only of his home, but also of the labor union or the chamber of commerce, the civic club or the fra-

[53] Quoted by Hunter, *op. cit.*, p. 84.

ternal order to which he may belong. The application of the Christian spirit should be broad enough to include his race and his nation.

An important element in the proper demonstration of the Christian life by individuals is a recovery, in so far as it has been lost, of a sense of divine vocation by Christian laymen. This sense of vocation should include the conviction that every child of God is to minister or to serve. He is to be a witness for Christ, witnessing with his life as well as by word of mouth. There has crept into Protestantism, even in the most democratic churches and denominations, too sharp a distinction between the clergy and the laity. This sharp distinction is not found in the New Testament churches. It may be that some disciples are called to be prophets, pastors, and teachers, but all are called to minister and to witness. "There are many contrasts between current Christianity and that of Christ's day, but the limitation of the ministry to a professional class of men is the most shocking of all these contrasts." [54]

Every child of God should also have a sense of being within the will of God in his vocation or profession. He should have a deep conviction of divine partnership in and stewardship for his vocation. His vocation should be recognized as a channel in and through which he can and should promote the kingdom of God among men. In other words, his ministry for God and his fellow man will not be fulfilled exclusively in what he does within his church and through its organizations and activities. An important phase of that ministry is what he does for the Lord and for mankind through his profession or daily work.

For the Christian demonstration to be most effective, it must be not only an individual but also a group demonstration. The world needs to see a living revelation of the kind of society we would have if the world were truly Christian. The churches are the institutions that should make such a demonstration. Church members, in their relations with one another, should demonstrate the spirit of justice and love that would characterize a Christian social order. What should be true within the local congregation should also be true of the churches in their relations with one another.

[54] D. Elton Trueblood, *Your Other Vocation* (New York, Harper, 1952), pp. 43–44.

Churches as they attempt to become more Christian will discover some of the limitations of their humanity. They will find out that as divine-human institutions they have many of the faults, failures, and limitations that belong to the flesh. This should mean that there will be a more or less natural and constant tendency within the church to let its divine nature judge and challenge its human nature. This, in turn, will result in an abiding tension in the church. This tension provides a basis for some hope for movement toward the divine ideal of understanding love and fellowship.

As a phase of its demonstration of the Christian spirit, the church should take the lead in pioneering movements for moral advance. More churches need to enter into contemporary social and moral frontiers. They should not leave those areas so largely to individuals and groups that are on the fringe of the Christian movement. The Christian movement through the centuries has provided much of the inspiration for social and moral pioneers, but at the same time it has frequently labeled and persecuted those same pioneers as heretics.

If the church, as the body of Christ in the world, is to demonstrate the Christian message to the world it must become the embodiment of that message. This institutional incarnation of the gospel message must include, among other things, the church's fulfillment of its mission in the world. Its purpose is to promote the kingdom or the reign of God among men. The church is a means and not an end.

Even in relation to society the church should recognize that it is in the community or the world not to be ministered unto but to minister or to serve. This attitude by our churches would enable them to recapture and to express institutionally the ethic of the cross which is the central, distinctive unifying element in the Christian religion.

4. *Legislation.* The legislative method, while it should be considered definitely secondary in the total Christian strategy, has been used nevertheless by Christian groups to attain at least limited Christian goals for society. The church should always remember, however, that its "role is not primarily that of a humanitarian busybody or social pressure group," neither is its function "that of a political bloc." [55]

[55] King, *The Holy Imperative,* p. 198.

There are two rather common mistakes that Christian forces tend to make regarding the legislative approach. First, they frequently push for premature legislation. Some Christians if they had the power to do so would make the Christian absolutes the law of the land. This is not only unwise from the viewpoint of public morals, but it also violates the inner spirit of the Christian religion. Another mistake common to many Christians is that they place too much faith in legislation. When a good law has been passed they seem to think that the problem has been solved. They should remember that the only really effective law is one that is the result of crystallized public opinion, and that favorable public opinion results from a program of continuous enlightenment and education.

The church needs to be the church in the deepest and most significant sense. It needs "to stand before the New Testament church and receive correction." [56] It needs to recognize that it "is called to be a people over whom God rules, who exhibit the righteousness of his Kingdom before the world. In other words she is to witness by her distinctively Christian conduct to the fact that she is a people set apart to God." [57] In the New Testament we have much more material emphasizing "the responsibility of the community of Christ to its Lord *before* the world than we have of an active responsibility for the salvation of the world." [58]

5. *Prayer*. Prayer has an important place in any constructive Christian method or strategy. Every method that justifiably can be used by a Christian should be bathed in prayer. Prayer many times will mean the difference between success or failure. Furthermore, when we have reached the end of our strength and resources we can call upon God "who gives to all men generously and without reproaching." [59] We can and should pray not only about our part in the struggle for a better world, but we also can and should talk to God about the broader, world-wide problems. Some of these problems are too big for us but not for our God. Some of them are beyond our reach, geographically and otherwise, but they are not and cannot be beyond our Father's reach. We can pray in confidence knowing that the God we worship is the sovereign God of the universe. He "has not seceded from history, giving it over to

[56] Bright, *op. cit.*, p. 260.
[58] Wright, *op. cit.*, p. 129.
[57] *Ibid.*, pp. 261–62.
[59] James 1:5.

other powers until such a time as he sees fit again to intervene." [60] He is the creator of the world and is actively creative in the world. Men and movements may seem to defeat him, but he is always victorious in the end. Regardless of how big the problem or the world issue, we can pray with an abiding faith because no problem is too big for our God.

In response to our prayer God will give to us the leadership of the Holy Spirit. It is the indwelling Spirit who will give us the peace that passeth understanding, who will give quietness and confidence in the face of the most discouraging circumstances. It is the recognition of the activity of the Holy Spirit in our lives and in our world which is *"the incomparably primary dimension of Christian social action."* Without "the positive, primary *agency* of God Himself *in history* . . . we are shorn Samsons." [61]

Tension and Social Change

Our age is one of tension. Many of the tensions in the lives of individuals are self-defeating and destructive. They result from and are indications of spiritual immaturity and instability. They arise primarily because of the individual's inability to accept and to adjust to the inevitabilities of life. This inability in turn stems from his failure to maintain a deep and abiding sense of the presence and fellowship of the living God.

There are some tensions, however, that may be constructive. They grow out of a serious concern with the application of Christian principles to life. These constructive tensions tend to move the individual and his world toward God's expectations for him and the world. They are felt most keenly by the spiritually mature and sensitive individuals. Such tensions are also important factors in the Christian social strategy.

1. *Reasons for tension.* There are a number of reasons for the constructive type of tension. One reason is the nature of the gospel message. That message contains a challenge to perfection. If one takes it seriously, tension will be the inevitable result. The individual Christian will realize that he and the world in which he lives fall far short of the Christian ideal.

[60] Wright, *op. cit.,* p. 136.   [61] Ferré, *op. cit.,* p. 136.

Lindsay speaks of a tension between two moralities. One he calls the morality of "my station and its duties." The other he labels "the morality of the challenge to perfection, or the morality of grace."[62] He considers the morality of one's station as imperfect, relative, reciprocal, and closed. In contrast, the morality of grace is not reciprocal; it is absolute, perfect, and an open morality. The last means that there are no limitations. For example, the morality of grace assumes that we shall do more than our duty, but it never defines how much more.[63] It is an open morality, because the perfection it proclaims is in God. This perfection is not only beyond man's reach; it is also beyond his comprehension.

There will also tend to arise tension within the church. This will be true, to some degree, because its members will not all possess the same insight into the Christian message, and they will not all agree about how seriously Christians should take the commands of perfection found in that message. While some, the prophetic souls, will have a deeper insight into the truth and will possess a stronger purpose to move toward the ideals revealed by the truth, others within the Christian fellowship will contend that such efforts represent the strivings of impractical idealists. The latter reaction will be particularly true if an honest effort is made to lift the world toward the Christian ideal.

Some tension within the church will more or less inevitably result from the nature of the church. It is a divine-human institution. These two phases of its nature are seldom kept in perfect balance. They, in turn, represent, to a degree, the this-worldly and the otherworldly elements of the church. The otherworldly element, which is inherent in the church as a divine institution, creates within it a distrust of the actual social situation and also of the programs to change that situation. On the other hand, as a human institution with a this-worldly perspective, the church cannot, in good conscience, separate itself from the world or ignore the needs of the world.

The church cannot be the church in the truest sense without creating tension for itself. "The more seriously the Church takes her task, the more deeply she is thrown into a thoroughly New Testament tension."[64] The tension is caused by a conflict between a

---

[62] Lindsay, *op. cit.*, p. 1. [63] *Ibid.*, pp. 28–52.
[64] Bright, *op. cit.*, p. 250.

victory declared in the proclamation of the kingdom, and "a victory which as a church she finds it impossible to produce." [65] If the church takes seriously her task in the world and proclaims fearlessly her message to the world, she will discover that tension is "the Church's natural habitat." [66] The more vigorously and consistently the church preaches, teaches, and practices the Christian ideal, the more tension it will create in the world and among men. A lack of tension between the church and the world would be an indication of an unhealthy condition.

The strength of the tension between the church and the world will be determined not only by the preaching and the practice of the church but also by the resistance of the world to change. Some of this resistance to change may come from within the Christian group itself. Such would mean that the tension would be increased within the group and usually decreased between the church and the world. The more thoroughly united the Christian group is, if it is on a high level, the stronger will be its tension with the world.

The church should remind the world that the Christian ideal is the ultimate goal for the world and for every area of the life of the world. God is the God of all of life. He has a will for every phase of life. The basic laws of every realm of life come from God. Men will find the basis for sound satisfactory relations in every area of life as they discover the fundamental laws of God and live in accordance with them. Those fundamental laws can be equated with the Christian ideals. The world may seem to escape or evade tension by ignoring the Christian ideals for the world, but when it does so it violates its own inner depths and will prolong and ultimately increase its own inner tension.

All tension within the Christian, within the Christian church, between the Christian, the church and the world, and within the world stems, in the final analysis, from a conflict between the will of God and the will of man. The will of God provides the inner glow that constantly challenges man. This inner glow reveals that the will of God leads by the way of the cross. Man must crucify himself. Man by nature, however, recoils from the cross. His will must be surrendered to the divine will. This is his eternal problem. Will he take up his cross and find and give life; or will he refuse

[65] *Ibid.*, p. 251.   [66] *Ibid.*, p. 253.

the cross and lose life on the higher levels and fail to be a redeeming influence in the world?

2. *Release of tension.* Is there any release for the tension the gospel message creates? Here we shall not consider the ordinary everyday worries and tensions of the average Christian. A reasonable degree of faith in God would solve most of them. We shall consider only the tensions that are greatest for the most genuine Christians, for those who are most responsive to the challenge of the will of God and most sensitive to the leadership of the divine Spirit. Are there any sources of release for such tensions?

The first step toward release, for the serious Christian, is for him to make an honest effort to apply the Christian ideal of perfection to his life and to the world. Such an effort, however, will not relieve entirely his inner tension. He may derive some personal satisfaction and some peace of mind from the progress he makes toward the ideal, but he will become deeply conscious that his best efforts fall far short of the divine purpose. The more serious he is about being really Christian, the more conscious he will be of his limitations and failures and of the insurmountable obstacles to the achievement of God's will in and for the world. In other words, the conscientious Christian cannot attain full release from tension through his own efforts.

The Christian religion, however, offers another means for the release of tension, which might be considered a second step in a program of release. That means or step is repentance. When the conscientious child of God feels the conflict within between the challenge of God and his very imperfect response to that challenge, he can cry unto God for forgiveness. He can do this in confidence knowing that he has "an advocate with the Father, Jesus Christ the righteous." [67] Our heavenly Father is not only willing and able to forgive; he is anxious to forgive.

An abiding faith in God is still another means for the release of tension. We are not referring here to a blind fatalism that will cause one to sit down and do nothing. Rather we are talking about the kind of faith that will impel one to do the will of God as best he can in every area of life. He will do this, however, with a deep

[67] 1 John 2:1.

assurance that the work is the Lord's, that he can leave the results in God's hands, and that the sovereign God of the universe ultimately will be triumphant in all the world. If we are on God's side, seeking to do his will, we are on the victorious side.

It is the sense of the presence of the sovereign God which gives the child of God an inner peace that passeth understanding. That peace provides the backdrop for the tensions of life. It is such a faith in such a God that saves the Christian from defeating fears and enables him to live "creatively, though insecurely, in the world." [68]

3. *Continuance of tension.* It is the lot of the serious Christian never to find complete release from tension. No describable pattern of life can be the last word for him. He "is a man who is always trying to be something better than he is. There is a sense in which no man is a Christian—the paradoxical sense that a man is a Christian only when he acknowledges that he is not completely one." [69]

When man repents of falling short of God's will and purpose and God forgives and restores him to fellowship, that renewed fellowship in turn gives to him a clearer and deeper insight into the will of God. He sees more clearly than before his shortcomings. He again seeks to make God's will a reality. He falls short. He repents. He is forgiven. He again receives a deepened insight into God's will for him and his world.

The preceding may seem to represent a continuingly meaningless, paradoxical round. This is not the viewpoint, however, of the understanding Christian. He recognizes that if it is "a round," that each round represents some progress toward the perfect Christian ideal, toward the ultimate will of God. The constant round is inevitable, because God is the standard of perfection. Since this is true, "there cannot be any definite, finished off, once-for-all pattern. There is no upper limit to perfection." [70]

The Christian's movement from the world to God, followed by a new movement into the world to seek to bring to reality the vision of God for the world, then the movement again back to God with a sense of failure, represent what might be termed a Christian or a

---

[68] Wright, *op. cit.*, p. 165. [69] Lindsay, *op. cit.*, p. 61.
[70] *Ibid.*, p. 60.

spiritual dialectic. This dialectic has its thesis, its antithesis, and its synthesis which becomes the new thesis. Then the round starts all over again. It represents a spiral movement toward the Christian ideal.

Tension is not only a continuing experience for the individual but also for society. "The tension between society as it is and society as it might be will always remain. If ever this tension were to cease, it would be a sign not that society had become through and through Christian, but that it had ceased to be Christian at all." [71] Lindsay suggests that the latter would be true even though perfection might have been attained, as man understands perfection, in certain areas. One source of tension in the individual, the church, and society is "discontent with our own vision of perfection."

A church that has so completely made its peace with the world that there is no tension between the church and its message and the world will not and cannot lift the world toward the Christian ideal. The tension between the church and the world will be strengthened and made more effective if it is created not only by what the church preaches or professes, but also by what it practices. An ounce of practice will be worth a pound of preaching.

In maintaining a wholesome tension between the church and the world, that tension should not become so great that the church will lose all opportunity to minister to the world. If we think of that tension as a rubber band, we may see more clearly what is meant. The speed with which the world is lifted toward the Christian ideal will be determined by the tautness of the rubber band. On the other hand, if the tension becomes too great the rubber band may break. If such happens the church has isolated itself from the world and no longer can lift that world toward God's ideal for the world. Another way of stating the same thing is to say that the individual Christian or group that ministers most effectively to the world must start where the world is and progressively lift the world toward the Christian ideal for the world. This means that the Christian ideal, for the world as for the individual, is fleeting. As we move toward it, it moves ahead of us.

It is doubtful if many churches or church leaders need the preceding warning. The greater danger to most Christians and to most

[71] *Ibid.,* p. 93.

Christian groups is that they will go entirely too far in adjusting the Christian ideal to what they consider to be the realities of life. They will tend to identify the ideal with what they consider immediately attainable. There will be a danger that the stamp of divine approval will be placed on the *status quo*. The vision of the perfect ideal will be blurred if not completely lost. This, in turn, will mean the loss of tension between the Christian message and the world, and hence the church will fail to lift the world toward God's purposes for that world. The church will tend to be conformed to the world rather than to become a transformer of the world.

BIBLIOGRAPHY

Rather than provide a lengthy bibliography, it has been decided to list a comparatively few of the more important volumes on each of the issues discussed. An attempt has been made to provide balanced lists, with authors and books representing different approaches and emphases. There are some supplementary lists on a few major topics in footnotes in the body of the book. The location of these supplementary lists will be found at the close of the references for the various chapters.

Chapt. I

THE CHURCH AND THE WORLD

Augustine. *The City of God*. Many editions. One of the great Christian classics. Concerned with the city of God and the city of this world.

Bennett, John C. *Christian Ethics and Social Policy*. New York, Charles Scribner's Sons, 1946. Chief contribution its discussion of Christian social strategies.

Butterfield, Herbert. *Christianity and History*. New York, Charles Scribner's Sons, 1950. An English professional historian. Believes "that history testifies to Christianity and Christianity interprets history."

Cadoux, C. J. *The Early Church and the World*. New York, Charles Scribner's Sons, 1925. Covers period to Constantine. Chronological and topical. Some of the topics are the state, war, family, property, and slavery.

Hobhouse, Walter. *The Church and the World in Idea and in History*. London, Macmillan and Co., Ltd., 1910. Traces relation of church and world from New Testament days to time of writing.

Latourette, Kenneth Scott (ed.). *The Gospel, the Church and the World*. New York, Harper & Brothers, 1946. One of "The Interseminary Series." Each chapter by a well known American churchman.

Niebuhr, H. Richard. *Christ and Culture*. New York, Harper & Brothers, 1951. Discusses the historic relation of Christ and culture. Various theories really represent the major Christian strategies through the centuries.

Niebuhr, H. Richard. Wilhelm Pauck, and Francis P. Miller. *The Church Against the World*. Chicago, Willett, Clark, & Co., 1935. Readable study of conflict between church and world.

Pope, Liston. *Millhands and Preachers*. New Haven, Yale University Press, 1942. A study of the mill communities of Gaston County, North Carolina. H. Richard Niebuhr's *The Social Sources of Denominationalism* (New York, Henry Holt & Co., 1929) is another study of the social stratification within Christian groups.

Scott, Ernest F. *The Gospel and Its Tributaries*. New York, Charles Scribner's Sons, 1929. One of the better books on influences shaping the early Christian movement.

Tawney, Richard H. *Religion and the Rise of Capitalism*. New York, Harcourt, Brace, & Co., 1926. Discusses the relation of the reformation, particularly Calvinism, to capitalism.

Troeltsch, Ernst. *The Social Teaching of the Christian Churches*. Translated by Olive Wyon. 2 vols. 2d impression. New York, Macmillan Co., 1949. A standard work. Covers New Testament, Roman Catholic Church, Lutheranism, Calvinism, and sectarian groups.

Additional references:

Protestantism's contribution to capitalism and democracy, footnote 32, p. 13.

Chapt. II

CHRISTIANITY AND THE INDIVIDUAL

Berdyaev, Nicolas. *The Destiny of Man*. Translated by Natalie Duddington. 3d ed. New York, Charles Scribner's Sons, 1948. Title misleading. Mostly on Christian ethics. Good section, however, on "man."

————. *The Fate of Man in the Modern World*. Translated by Donald A. Lowrie. Milwaukee, Morehouse Publishing Co., 1935. Brief statement of what is happening to man in the contemporary crisis. Author, a Russian, one of most creative minds of recent times.

Brunner, Emil. *Man in Revolt*. Translated by Olive Wyon. Philadelphia, Westminster Press, 1947. The subtitle: "A Christian Anthropology."

Cairns, David. *The Image of God in Man*. New York, Philosophical Library, 1953. Historical in emphasis. Begins with Old Testament. Chapters on Aquinas, Luther, Calvin, Brunner, and Barth. Some consideration of Marxian and Freudian conceptions of man as related to Christian view.

Cave, Sydney. *The Christian Estimate of Man*. London, Gerald Duckworth & Co., Ltd., 1944. In "The Studies in Theology Series." Historical.

Jessop, T. C., *et al. The Christian Understanding of Man.* Chicago, Willett, Clark & Co., 1938. An Oxford Conference book. Various authors with widely differing viewpoints.

Maritain, Jacques. *The Person and the Common Good.* Translated by John J. Fitzgerald. New York, Charles Scribner's Sons, 1947. French Catholic philosopher. Discusses relation of individuality to personality and the relation of the person to society. Some special attention to Thomas Aquinas.

Niebuhr, Reinhold. *The Nature and Destiny of Man.* 2 vols. New York, Charles Scribner's Sons, 1941, 1943. Vol. I on "The Nature of Man" particularly helpful.

————. *The Self and the Dramas of History.* New York, Charles Scribner's Sons, 1955. Portions common to other Niebuhr books. Ideas concerning the human self carried further than elsewhere.

Sheed, F. J. *Communism and Man.* New York, Sheed and Ward, 1938. Good analysis of Marxist doctrine of man.

Torrance, T. F. *Calvin's Doctrine of Man.* New York, British Book Center, 1949. Permits Calvin to speak. Minimum of interpretation and evaluation.

Wright, G. Ernest. *The Biblical Doctrine of Man in Society.* London, S.C.M. Press, Ltd., 1954. The work of an ecumenical committee of Chicago for the World Council of Churches.

Chapt. III

THE FAMILY AND ITS FUTURE

There are so many excellent books on the family and on family-life education that it was decided to list here a few titles that have not been referred to specifically in the footnotes of the chapter. See the footnotes for additional references.

Adams, Clifford R. *Preparing for Marriage.* New York, E. P. Dutton & Co., 1951. Practical, touching on most possible problems before and after marriage.

Anshen, Ruth Nanda (ed.). *The Family: Its Function and Destiny.* New York, Harper & Brothers, 1949. Of particular interest are chapters on the family in different countries and among different racial and religious groups.

Calhoun, Arthur W. *A Social History of the American Family.* One vol. ed. New York, Barnes and Noble, Inc., 1945.

Duvall, Evelyn Millis. *Family Living.* New York, Macmillan Co., 1950. Designed as a text for high-school use. The author has written a number of other helpful books on family relations.

Duvall, Sylvanus M. *Men, Women, and Morals.* New York, Association Press, 1952. Primarily on sexual morality.

Foster, Robert G. *Marriage and Family Relationships.* Rev. ed. New York, Macmillan Co., 1950. A comparatively simple textbook approach, majoring on potential problems.

Highbaugh, Irma. *We Grow in the Family.* New York, Agricultural Missions, 1953. An approach to family life education by one who served for many years as a missionary in the Orient.

Landis, Judson T. and Mary G. Landis. *Building a Successful Marriage.* 2d ed. New York, Prentice-Hall, Inc., 1953. One of the better college texts, with a practical approach.

Mace, David R. *Marriage: The Art of Lasting Love.* New York, Doubleday & Co., Inc., 1952. Author a native of Great Britain. Writes from rich background. Based on articles that originally appeared in *Woman's Home Companion.*

Popenoe, Paul. *Marriage Is What You Make It.* New York, Macmillan Co., 1950. Practical discussions of the problems of married couples.

Skidmore, Rex A., and Anthon S. Cannon. *Building Your Marriage.* New York, Harper & Brothers, 1951. In Harper's Social Science Series. Textbook with practical slant.

Additional references:

The family in various cultures, footnote 89, p. 79.

Textbooks on the family, footnote 109, p. 85.

Divorce, footnote 111, p. 87.

Kinsey reports and appraisals, footnote 113, p. 87.

Chapt. IV

RACE AND RACIAL TENSION

Aptheker, Herbert. *A Documentary History of the Negro People in the United States.* New York, The Citadel Press, 1951. A valuable reference work, including documents selected through painstaking research for fifteen years.

Burns, Alan. *Colour Prejudice.* London, George Allen and Unwin, Ltd., 1948. Deals particularly with white-Negro prejudice.

Bibliography

Dvorin, Eugene P. *Racial Separation in South Africa*. Chicago, University of Chicago Press, 1952. Concentrates on one of the major trouble spots in the world. Subtitle: "An Analysis of Apartheid Theory."

Frazier, E. Franklin. *The Negro in the United States*. New York, Macmillan Co., 1949. Author a prominent Negro sociologist. Comprehensive coverage of history, institutions, and problems.

Johnson, Charles S., and Associates. *Into the Main Stream*. Chapel Hill, University of North Carolina Press, 1947. Johnson, Negro sociologist, president of Fisk University. Book gives illustrations of best practices in area of race relations in the South.

Loescher, Frank S. *The Protestant Church and the Negro*. New York, Association Press, 1948. Primary attention on what churches are doing rather than saying.

McWilliams, Carey. *A Mask for Privilege: Anti-Semitism in America*. Boston, Little, Brown and Co., 1947. One of a number of books by the author covering almost every major racial conflict.

Myrdal, Gunnar. *An American Dilemma*. 2 vols. New York, Harper & Brothers, 1944. Still the definitive work on the American Negro. Arnold Rose's *The Negro in America* (Harper & Brothers, 1948) is a condensation of Myrdal.

Nelson, William S. (ed.). *The Christian Way in Race Relations*. New York, Harper & Brothers, 1948. The editor dean of the School of Religion, Howard University, which sponsors the Institute of Religion, whose members produced the papers which compose this volume.

Record, Wilson. *The Negro and the Communist Party*. Chapel Hill, University of North Carolina Press, 1951. A documented chronological record, which concludes that "red and black" are "unblending colors."

Soper, Edmund D. *Racism: A World Issue*. New York, Abingdon-Cokesbury Press, 1947. A missionary statesman writes from a world perspective.

Walter, Paul A. F. *Race and Culture Relations*. New York, McGraw-Hill Book Co., 1952. A textbook inclusive of race and cultural relations in every section of the world.

Additional references:

Criticism of Myrdal, footnote 8, p. 93.

Racial prejudice, footnote 33, p. 100.

Chapt. V

ECONOMIC LIFE AND RELATIONS

Bennett, John C., *et al. Christian Values and Economic Life*. New York, Harper & Brothers, 1954. One of a series sponsored by the National Council of the Churches of Christ in America. For all the titles in the series see footnote 1, p. 117.

Bowen, Howard R. *Social Responsibilities of the Businessman*. New York, Harper & Brothers, 1953. Another of National Council series.

Fletcher, Joseph F. (ed.). *Christianity and Property*. Philadelphia, Westminster Press, 1947. Historical in approach, in the main, beginning with Old Testament. Episcopalian in flavor with a chapter by Vida Scudder on "Anglican Thought on Property."

Lindsay, A. D. *Christianity and Economics*. London, Macmillan and Co., Ltd., 1933. Series of lectures by a recognized English scholar.

Muelder, Walter George. *Religion and Economic Responsibility*. New York, Charles Scribner's Sons, 1953. Touches on practically every phase of economic life.

Peck, William G. *A Christian Economy*. New York, Macmillan Co., 1954. An English orientation.

Root, Edward T. *The Bible Economy of Plenty*. New York, Harper & Brothers, 1939. Old but standard.

Sleeman, John F. *Basic Economic Problems*. London: S.C.M. Press, Ltd., 1953. A lecturer in social economics writes from a definitely Christian perspective.

Ward, A. Dudley (ed.). *Goals of Economic Life*. New York, Harper & Brothers, 1953. Still another of the National Council series.

Additional references:

The historic relation of Christianity and economic life, footnote 29, p. 124.

Labor and labor unions, footnote 72, p. 135.

Economic planning, footnote 82, p. 138.

Chapt. VI and VII

COMMUNISM

Almond, Gabriel A., *et al. The Appeals of Communism*. Princeton, New Jersey, Princeton University Press, 1954. An effort at a scientific study "of why people join the communist movement and why they leave it."

Bibliography

Barron, J. B., and H. M. Waddams. *Communism and the Churches.* London, S.C.M. Press, Ltd., 1950. A booklet of approximately one hundred pages. Quotes directly from official documents the position of the communist régimes of the U.S.S.R. and other European countries concerning religion. Also quotes the Vatican decree excommunicating those who affiliate with communism.

Bennett, John C. *Christianity and Communism.* New York, Association Press, 1948. Excellent brief book.

Berdyaev, Nicolas. *The Origin of Russian Communism.* New York, Charles Scribner's Sons, 1937. Major emphasis on Russian background. Closing chapter on "Communism and Christianity."

Budenz, Louis F. *The Techniques of Communism.* Chicago, Henry Regnery, 1954. Author former communist. Primarily a discussion of communism in America.

Carr, Edward Hallett. *The Bolshevik Revolution: 1917–1923.* 2 vols. New York, Macmillan Co., 1950, 1952. A very ambitious, scholarly history. Massimo Salvadori's *The Rise of Communism* (New York, Henry Holt & Co., 1952) is a much briefer (118 pages) historical sketch of the communist movement.

Curtiss, John Shelton. *The Russian Church and the Soviet State: 1917–1950.* Boston, Little, Brown and Co., 1953. There are a number of other books on the same general subject, none more thorough than this one. Restricted to Russian Orthodox Church.

Dallin, David J. *The Real Soviet Russia.* New Haven, Yale University Press, 1944. Author a leading authority on Soviet Union. Some but not much of material dated.

Fisher, Marguerite J. *Communist Doctrine and the Free World.* Syracuse, N.Y., Syracuse University Press, 1952. A study of Marx, Engels, Lenin, and Stalin, permitting them, in the main, to speak through their own words.

Hordern, William. *Christianity, Communism and History.* New York, Abingdon Press, 1954. Gives particular attention to a comparison and a contrast of Christian and communist views of history. Particular attention to the sects.

Hunt, R. N. Carew. *Marxism: Past and Present.* New York, Macmillan Co., 1954. Thorough. Based largely on primary sources.

———. *The Theory and Practice of Communism.* New York, Macmillan Co., 1951 (revised). No better general book on communism.

Kulski, W. W. *The Soviet Regime.* Syracuse, N.Y., Syracuse University Press, 1954. A ponderous book of over eight hundred pages, which majors on the program of the Soviet Union. Particularly valuable as a source of information concerning the political and economic phases of the communist program.

Lowry, Charles W. *Communism and Christ*. New York, Morehouse-Gorham Co., 1952. Brief, popularly written.

MacIntyre, Alasdair C. *Marxism: An Interpretation*. London: S.C.M. Press, Ltd., 1953. A splendid brief book, primarily emphasizing Marxist philosophy.

Mackinnon, D. M. (ed.). *Christian Faith and Communist Faith*. New York, St. Martin's Press, 1953. By a group of Anglican scholars.

Plamenatz, John. *German Marxism and Russian Communism*. London, Longmans, Green and Co., 1954. The title gives the main division of the book. More analytical and critical in approach than most books on subject.

Rogers, Edward. *A Commentary on Communism*. New York, Frederick A. Praeger, Inc., 1951. A Christian commentary on practically every phase of communism by an English Methodist.

Symposium. *The Philosophy of Communism*. New York, Fordham University Press, 1952. Many phases of communism discussed by a group of Roman Catholic clergymen and laymen.

Vyshinsky, Andrei Y. (ed.). *The Law of the Soviet State*. Translated by Hugh W. Babb. New York, Macmillan Co., 1948. The editor was for many years chief representative to the United Nations of the Soviet Union.

Additional references:

In Chapter VI
World-wide aspects of communism, footnote 7, p. 148.
Economic phases of communism, footnote 59, p. 160.
Political aspects of communism, footnote 63, p. 161.
Communism in America, footnote 64, p. 162.

In Chapter VII
Books by former communists, footnote 53, p. 199.

Chapt. VIII

CHURCH AND STATE

Bates, M. Searle. *Religious Liberty: An Inquiry*. New York, Harper & Brothers, 1945. The definitive work on religious liberty. See footnote 106, p. 233 for two briefer books on the same subject.

Dawson, Joseph Martin. *Separate Church and State Now*. New York, Richard R. Smith, 1948. Author one of the organizers and leaders of

Bibliography

Protestants and Other Americans United for the Separation of Church and State.

Ehler, Sidney Z. and John B. Morrall (translators and editors). *Church and State Through the Centuries*. Westminster, Md., The Newman Press, 1954. The subtitle: "A Collection of historical documents with commentaries." The documents are mostly Roman Catholic, some of which had not previously been available in English.

Garbett, Cyril. *Church and State in England*. New York, Macmillan Co., 1950. Historical and contemporary.

Gavin, Frank. *Seven Centuries of the Problem of Church and State*. Princeton, N.J., Princeton University Press, 1938. Scholarly but compact.

Johnson, Alvin W. and Frank H. Yost. *Separation of Church and State in the United States*. Minneapolis, University of Minnesota Press, 1948. Legal aspects of separation in the field of education.

Kranenburg, R. *Political Theory*. Translated by R. Borregaard. London, Oxford University Press, 1939. Good background on theories of government, with a chapter on "State and Church."

Nichols, James Hastings. *Democracy and the Churches*. Philadelphia, Westminster Press, 1951. With special emphasis on the contributions of Puritan Protestantism.

O'Neill, J. M. *Religion and Education Under the Constitution*. New York, Harper & Brothers, 1949. A Roman Catholic interpretation. For a book with more of a historical perspective and drastically different conclusions on the same general subject, see R. Freeman Butts, *The American Tradition in Religion and Education* (Boston, Beacon Press, 1950).

Pfeffer, Leo. *Church, State, and Freedom*. Boston, Beacon Press, 1953. Scholarly with considerable emphasis on legal aspects of church and state relations.

Rommen, Heinrich A. *The State in Catholic Thought*. St. Louis, B. Herder Book Co., 1945. Subtitle: "A Treatise in Political Philosophy." One of the four major divisions is on "Church and State."

Stokes, Anson P. *Church and State in the United States*. New York, Harper & Brothers, 1950. 3 vols. The one best source for material on church and state.

Additional references:

Church and state relations in various countries, footnote 2, p. 204.

CHAPT. IX

WAR AND PEACE

Bentwich, Norman and Martin, Andrew. *A Commentary on the Charter of the United Nations.* New York, Macmillan Co., 1950. One of the best of many good books on United Nations.

Butterfield, Herbert. *Christianity, Diplomacy, and War.* New York, Abingdon-Cokesbury Press, n.d. Related specifically to the contemporary world situation.

Cadoux, C. J. *The Early Christian Attitude to War.* London, Headley Brothers Publishers, Ltd., 1919. Historical study and explanation of nonparticipation in war by the early Christians.

Cheever, Daniel S. and Haviland, H. Field. *Organizing for Peace.* New York, Houghton Mifflin Co., 1954. A comparison, in the main, of the League of Nations and United Nations.

Heering, G. J. *The Fall of Christianity.* Translated by J. W. Thompson. London, George Allen and Unwin, Ltd., 1930. The "fall of Christianity" was when it compromised with and accepted the war system.

Hemleben, Sylvester John. *Plans for World Peace through Six Centuries.* Chicago, The University of Chicago Press, 1943. Compact volume. Includes all major plans for peace previous to League of Nations.

Knudson, Albert C. *The Philosophy of War and Peace.* New York, Abingdon-Cokesbury Press, 1947. States the apologetic for war, traces the growing sentiment for peace, and gives what he considers to be the road to world peace.

Lee, Umphrey. *The Historic Church and Modern Pacifism.* New York, Abingdon-Cokesbury Press, 1943. A comparison of the pacifism of the early Christian centuries and modern pacifism. Antipacifistic in emphasis.

Scott-Craig, T. S. K. *Christian Attitudes to War and Peace.* New York, Charles Scribner's Sons, 1938. Discusses the attitudes of Jesus, Augustine, Luther, and Grotius.

Toynbee, Arnold J. *War and Civilization.* New York, Oxford University Press, 1950. Composed of selections, chosen by Arthur V. Fowler, from the first six volumes of Toynbee's *A Study of History.*

Additional references:

War in general, footnote 4, p. 238.

United Nations, footnote 119, p. 264.

Bibliography

Chapt. X

WAR AND THE CHRISTIAN CONSCIENCE

Cadoux, C. J. *Christian Pacifism Re-examined*. Oxford, Basil Blackwell, 1940. As careful a statement as can be found in defense of pacifism.

Forsyth, P. T. *The Christian Ethic of War*. London, Longmans, Green and Co., 1916. Defends, from theological viewpoint, Christian participation in war. May be dated but some arguments still prevalent.

Jones, Rufus M. (ed.). *The Church, the Gospel, and War*. New York, Harper & Brothers, 1948. Chapters by prominent churchmen such as Raven, Farmer, Bainton, Latourette, Page, and others. Pacifism defended.

Macgregor, G. H. C. *The New Testament Basis of Pacifism*. Rev. ed. London, Fellowship of Reconciliation, 1953.

Niebuhr, Reinhold. *Christianity and Power Politics*. New York, Charles Scribner's Sons, 1940. A volume of essays, the first one entitled "Why the Christian Church is not Pacifist."

Raven, Charles E. *The Theological Basis of Christian Pacifism*. New York, Fellowship Publications, 1951. A brief statement.

————. *War and the Christian*. New York, Macmillan Co., 1938. Touches most of problems.

Rutenber, Culbert G. *The Dagger and the Cross*. New York, Fellowship Publications, 1950. Subtitle: "An Examination of Christian Pacifism." Biblical, theological, philosophical, and practical.

Temple, William. *Thoughts in War-Time*. London, Macmillan and Co., Ltd., 1940. Defends Christian participation in war, under certain conditions.

Tillich, Paul. *Love, Power, and Justice*. New York, Oxford University Press, 1954. Not directly on war, yet closely related to problems of war.

Weatherhead, Leslie D. *Thinking Aloud in War-Time*. New York, Abingdon Press, 1943. Reveals something of the author's inner struggle as he changed from active participation in war to the pacifist position and then again to a defense of a Christian's participation.

Chapt. XI

THE WORLD IN CRISIS

Berdyaev, Nicolas. *The End of Our Time.* New York, Sheed and Ward, 1933. Author one of keenest students of world crisis.

————. *Towards A New Epoch.* London, Geoffrey Bles, 1949. Somewhat summarizes thought of author on world crisis.

Davies, D. R. *The Sin of Our Age.* New York, Macmillan Co., 1947. The sin of our age interpreted as the exaltation of man to the place that belongs to God.

Laski, Harold J. *The Dilemma of Our Times.* London, George Allen & Unwin Ltd., 1952. The last of his books on world crisis by left-wing leader of British Labor Party.

Lippmann, Walter. *The Public Philosophy.* Boston, Little, Brown and Co., 1955. Deals with "the Decline and Revival of the Western Society."

Mannheim, Karl. *Freedom, Power and Democratic Planning.* New York, Oxford University Press, 1950. Author German-born English professor of economics. Main emphasis in this and other books by same author is on economic planning.

Niebuhr, Reinhold. *Christian Realism and Political Problems.* New York, Charles Scribner's Sons, 1953. Several chapters touch, directly or indirectly, on major world problems. Chapter 2 entitled "The Illusion of World Government."

Northrop, F. S. C. *The Taming of the Nations.* New York, Macmillan Co., 1952. Represents the cultural approach to world problems.

Sorokin, Pitirim A. *The Crisis of Our Age.* New York, E. B. Dutton and and Co., Inc., 1941. One of the earliest books in America to call attention to the contemporary crisis.

Spengler, Oswald. *The Decline of the West.* Translated by Charles F. Atkinson. One-vol. ed. New York, Alfred A. Knopf, Inc., 1932. Predicts death of Western civilization.

Toynbee, Arnold. *A Study of History.* One-vol. ed. New York, Oxford University Press, 1947. A study of the rise, decline, and collapse of civilization.

Trueblood, D. Elton. *The Predicament of Modern Man.* New York, Harper & Brothers, 1944. Author has since written several other books on same general subject, but none better than this one.

Additional references:

Philosophies of history, footnote 45, p. 309.

Bibliography

Chapt. XII

CHRISTIANITY AND WORLD TRANSFORMATION

Bennett, John C. *Social Salvation*. New York, Charles Scribner's Sons, 1935. Particularly Chapter III, "The Relevance of Jesus for Society," Chapter IV, "The Church as an Agent for Social Salvation," and Chapter VI, "How God Works in Society."

Brunner, Emil. *Justice and the Social Order*. Translated by Mary Hottinger. New York, Harper & Brothers, 1945. After a thorough discussion of the principles of justice, attention is then directed to its application to the family, economic life, the political order, and international relations.

Eliot, T. S. *The Idea of a Christian Society*. New York, Harcourt, Brace and Company, 1940. Concise statement. Not much more than a definition by a prominent Englishman.

Ferré, Nels F. S. *Christianity and Society*. New York, Harper & Brothers, 1950. General treatment of church and world with specific discussion of war, property, and education.

Hunter, Leslie Stannard. *Church Strategy in a Changing World*. London, Hodder and Stoughton, 1950. A good, brief book on a subject seldom discussed specifically.

Lindsay, A. D. *The Two Moralities: Our Duty to God and to Society*. London, Eyre and Spottiswoode, 1940. A study of open and closed moralities.

Mays, Benjamin E. (compiler). *A Gospel for the Social Awakening*. New York, The Association Press, 1950. Selections from the writings of Walter Rauschenbusch.

Rauschenbusch, Walter. *Christianizing the Social Order*. New York, Macmillan Co., 1912. Although old, much of the material is still applicable.

Scott, R. B. Y. *The Relevance of the Prophets*. New York, Macmillan Co., 1944. The title of the book is the title for the last chapter. While the other chapters are more general, they definitely relate to the relevance of the prophets.

Visser 't Hooft, W. A., and Oldham, J. H. *The Church and Its Functions in Society*. Chicago, Willett, Clark & Co., 1937. Portion of Oxford Conference Report.

TOPICS FOR THOUGHT AND DISCUSSION

Many students never think through to a personally satisfying and a defensible Christian position regarding many of the most common problems of life. The primary purpose of the suggested assignments based on the following subjects is to lead the student to state and to defend his position with regard to some of those problems. The papers he will prepare will not need to be more than 1,000 to 1,500 words. If the teacher desires to have three of these brief papers during the term or semester, it is suggested that the topics or subjects be divided into these groups (1–8, 9–14, 15–21), with each student selecting one subject from each group. Similar divisions could be made for two or four assignments. Some teachers may prefer to use some of these subjects for more thorough research projects.

Although no attempt has been made to relate specifically the subjects to the chapters in the book, nevertheless they are arranged in a somewhat logical order.

1. Are the teachings of Jesus relevant to our lives today? (e.g., Sermon on the Mount)

2. What has been the contribution to the world of Mennonites, Quakers, and others who tend, to varying degrees, to withdraw from the world?

3. Should a Christian minister participate in politics?

4. What is your position with regard to euthanasia?

5. What do you think about capital punishment?

6. What about artificial insemination?

7. What is your view concerning birth control?

8. Is an abortion justified to save a mother's life?

9. What does the Bible teach concerning divorce?

10. Should a minister perform the marriage ceremony for those who have been divorced?

11. What about interracial marriages?

12. Would the amalgamation of the races be good or bad?

13. Should church-related colleges admit Negro students?

14. What is your position concerning eating with those of other races—in their home, in your home, in a public eating place?

15. What is your evaluation of the cooperative movement?

16. Can a Christian consistently be a socialist?

17. How would you reply to the communist charge that the Christian religion is the opiate of the people?

Topics for Thought and Discussion

18. Is the Roman Catholic Church compatible with the American spirit?

19. What is your appraisal of a program of weekday religious education on released time?

20. What is your position concerning a Christian's personal participation in war? Should Protestants defend the conscientious objector's right to his position?

21. Is it in harmony with the Christian spirit and ethic for nations to use modern means of destruction such as nuclear weapons?

INDEX

Index

Constantine, 6, 9, 215, 251-252, 298

Constitution of the United States, 41, 220-221, 227-228, 230, 232, 235

Crisis, world, Chap. XI; 39, 60, 92, 145, 148, 205, 207

Cross, the, 120, 201, 244, 284-287, 337-338, 350

Cross, the ethic of the, 44, 202

Darwin, Charles, 30, 91

Davies, D. R., 43, 55-56, 58, 306-307, 313, 318-319, 321

Dawson, Christopher, 217, 310

Dawson, J. M., 210, 222, 224, 230-231, 234-235, 306

Declaration of Independence, 41, 213

Democracy, 38, 40, 43, 93, 95, 110, 139, 162-163, 179, 190, 210, 293, 315, 324

Democracy, Christianity's relation to, 13, 192, 225-227

Determinism, economic, 151, 183, 187

Dialectic, Hegelian, 149-150

Divorce, 75-78, 81, 87-88

Dodd, C. H., 334-335, 337

Dualism, dualistic ethic, 5, 7, 13, 21-23, 39, 217, 254

Dulles, John Foster, 177

Ecumenical movement, 11, 127

Education, 111-113, 341-344

Eliot, T. S., 20

Engels, Friedrich, 147, 149, 151, 154, 162-163, 186, 188

Erasmus, 258

Escatology, 7, 155, 217, 310

Ethic, the Christian, 24-25, 27-28, 57, 60, 94, 96, 114, 118-119, 127, 133-134, 188, 198, 200, 273-274, 277, 318, 331, 338

Ethic, the Christian relevance of, 24, 121, 274, 277, 327-329, 338

Ethics, Communist, 57, 185-188, 195

Evangelism, 339-341

Family, the, Chap. III; 39, 49-51

Farmer, H. H., 278, 286

Ferré, Nels F. S., 32, 35, 119, 129, 327, 333, 336-337, 348

First Amendment to the United States Constitution, 222, 227-228, 231-232

Forsyth, P. T., 275, 278, 287, 292

Free enterprise. *See* Capitalism

Freedom, 49, 136-139, 166, 195, 207, 210, 303, 314

Freedom, religious, 219, 233-237

Garbett, Cyril, 130, 132, 216, 300, 308, 311

Gelasian theory, 218

Gnosticism, 5, 19

God, the sovereignty of, 19, 25, 50, 53, 119, 184, 188, 197, 225, 307-308, 320, 333, 352

God, will of, 15, 32, 34, 45, 50, 119-120, 188, 208, 220, 245-246, 267, 272, 279, 286, 290-292, 339, 350-352

Great Awakening, the, 10, 221

Groves, Ernest R., 81, 84, 87, 89-90

Harkness, Georgia, 306, 318

Heering, G. J., 246, 251, 257

Hegel, 149-150, 157

Hellenism, 5

Hildebrand, 218

History, philosophy of, 184, 200, 309, 332

Hobbes, Thomas, 209-210

Hobhouse, Walter, 4, 8-9, 299

Holt, Arthur E., 13, 225, 227, 229, 315

Hoover, Herbert, 261-262

Hordern, William, 147, 155-157, 172-173, 179-180, 184-185, 189, 193, 198, 201

Horton, Walter, 56, 299, 306, 313, 321, 327

Hough, Lynn, 48, 53, 56

Humanism, 45, 54-56, 126, 300, 307-308, 310-311

Humanism, and communism, 148, 181-182

Hunt, R. N. Carew, 149, 150-152, 154-155, 162, 164-165

Hunter, L. S., 25, 326, 340, 344

Hutterian Brethren, 17

371

Index